*Misty, I hope you enjoy this and get out here one day!*

# DIVE
# PALAU

*The Shipwrecks*

## ROD MACDONALD

Whittles Publishing

Published by
**Whittles Publishing,**
Dunbeath,
Caithness KW6 6EG,
Scotland, UK

www.whittlespublishing.com

ISBN 978-184995-170-8

Also by Rod Macdonald:
*Dive Scapa Flow*
*Dive Scotland's Greatest Wrecks*
*Dive England's Greatest Wrecks*
*Into the Abyss – Diving to Adventure in the Liquid World*
*The Darkness Below*
*Great British Shipwrecks – a Personal Adventure*
*Force Z Shipwrecks of the South China Sea – HMS Prince of Wales and HMS Repulse*
*Dive Truk Lagoon*

Layout by Raspberry Creative Type, Edinburgh
Printed by Gomer Press

www.rod-macdonald.co.uk
http://www.whittlespublishing.com/Rod_Macdonald
http://www.amazon.co.uk/Rod-Macdonald

# CONTENTS

# FOREWORD FROM THE GOVERNOR OF PALAU

Palau has long held a fascination for Scuba Divers from around the world due to the beauty that lies below the waves of our small Island Nation. Most come to see the astounding marine biodiversity that is abundant throughout the waters of Palau, from Mantaso Sharks, Dolphins to Whales and of course the huge schools of reef fish that abound in our reefs and lagoon. Long have Palauans held these rich and abundant marine resources in high regard. In fact it is a way of life in Palau, and more recently these resources have achieved worldwide recognition when the Koror State Southern Lagoon was granted World Heritage Status, a significant and prestigious award that not only the residents of Koror are proud of but all Palauans.

However there is another story that lies below the waves in Palau that shares little of the limelight that the reefs and wildlife are accorded; a story that has its beginnings in 1920 when the League of Nations awarded Japan control of Palau. Over the following years Japan steadily increased her presence, both politically and militarily. Throughout Palau and the Mariana Islands this presence brought development to the local people whilst establishing Japan as a significant military force throughout the Pacific Ocean.

With the outbreak of war in the Pacific in 1941, Palau became a strategically vital base for the Imperial Japanese Navy which hosted some of its most advanced naval weaponry here. With the Japanese being forced from her captured territories throughout the Pacific as the tide of war changed Palau became a vital target for the allied forces and on the 31 March 1944, the American forces began the liberation of the Palauan lslands in what was called Operation Desecrate One. This Operation sought to render the Japanese ability to wage war from Palau obsolete with one of the key targets being the many Japanese ships that were based in Palau at the time. With wave after wave of attacks by aircraft-carrier based planes, the American Navy decimated the Japanese Naval assets in Palau sending countless ships of all sizes to the bottom of the extensive lagoon, once thought to be a stronghold for the Japanese Navy.

Over seventy years on from the commencement of Operation Desecrate One these once iconic symbols of Japanese Naval Power have been largely forgotten. Most divers rarely visit these wrecks, preferring to see the beauty on the reefs throughout Palau, and as such they are a largely underappreciated facet of Palauan diving. With the publication of this book and the detailed descriptions, history and drawings of the wrecks as they are today, this is set to change. The potential to create awareness of this small chapter in Palau's history and to educate and inform people from all around the world of the significance the Palau lslands played as a naval stronghold for the lmperial Japanese Navy is significant.

I hope you enjoy reading and learning from this book and would strongly encourage you to visit these magnificent wrecks throughout our Island Nation.

Yositaka Adachi
Governor, Koror State

# ACKNOWLEDGEMENTS

In 2013, my good friend and regular dive buddy Paul Haynes and I were asked to speak at OZTeK in Sydney – and after a crackin' weekend there we flew home via Truk for Paul's first visit there. On the long flight home I decided to write *Dive Truk Lagoon* and make my contribution to Truk's diving literature. That book was published in October 2014.

When the OZTeK 2015 organisers foolishly invited Paul and myself back again to speak in March 2015 it was natural that we should look for another diversionary adventure for the way home. The fabulous shipwrecks at Truk Lagoon have been known internationally since 1969, when Cousteau led an expedition there and started to locate and film some of the wrecks sunk by aircraft from the nine carriers of Task Force 58 in a stunning surprise attack at dawn on 17 February 1944. Some 50 ships were sent to the bottom of Truk Lagoon during the two days of Operation *Hailstone* – still filled with their cargoes of shells, trucks, tanks, artillery and ordnance, all intended to be sent ashore to reinforce the Truk Islands against the threatened US land invasion.

Just days before the US TF 58 air strike against Truk, the first reconnaissance overflight of Truk Lagoon by two US Liberator long-range aircraft had been carried out. When US strategists analysed the reconnaissance photographs they were stunned to see almost the entire Imperial Japanese Navy at anchor below, along with scores of large merchant ships. Immediate US preparations were set in motion to strike against Truk.

On Truk itself, Japanese commanders were aware of the reconnaissance overflight, and knew that Truk's secret was out and that the precious warships of the Combined Fleet were now vulnerable to air attack. Immediately, the strategically invaluable Japanese battleships, cruisers and carriers were sent west, away from the American advance. Some were sent to Japan and to Singapore, whilst others were sent to the great Japanese air and naval base of Palau, more than 1,000 nautical miles to the west and believed to be relatively safe from attack.

After the US Operation *Hailstone* air raids had neutralised Truk as a naval and air base, the Fast Carrier Striking Force, Task Force 58, broke up – the nine carriers went their individual ways to other operations.

However, less than six weeks later, Task Force 58 reformed for a raid against Palau so that Japanese naval vessels and aircraft could not threaten US forces as they embarked on a strategically important operation against the port of Hollandia in Netherlands New Guinea. America determined that Palau would be neutralised, just as Truk had been only weeks before.

The Fast Carrier raid against the Palaus was given the codename Operation *Desecrate 1*, and as with Operation *Hailstone* the raid took place over two days: on 30 and 31 March 1944. It was another stunningly successful US operation that totally destroyed any potential Japanese air threat and sent all the significant Japanese vessels found in the lagoon to the bottom.

Although much has been written about the shipwrecks of Truk Lagoon, there has been relatively little written about Palau's shipwrecks. I had first dived in Palau in 1990 and knew what to expect – but Paul hadn't visited before. I sprung my idea on him when he was expecting it least, and lubricating the idea with several pints of Guinness, I had swiftly managed to persuade him into a diversion to Palau to survey the wrecks there on the way home from OZTeK 2015. My good friend Gary Petrie (aka Garspeed), a sure and steady technical diver who dives with me in Scotland (and who had come to Truk with Paul and myself on my last trip there), also was invited, and rashly agreed. And so Team Palau 2015 was formed.

In Palau we were joined by Mike Gerken, a lovely chap and a cool diver, who is skipper of the well-known Truk liveaboard dive boat *Odyssey*. Mike has his own underwater photography company, Evolution Underwater Imaging –www.evolutionunderwater.com – and a few years ago he made the classic DVD *The Wrecks of Truk Lagoon*, which I know many of you reading this will have in your collection.

Paul, Gary and Mike were great company, each with a good technical knowledge of diving and shipwrecks. They were a great help to me, picking up on the points I'd missed. If there were things I needed specifically to check up on, I'd brief them before the dive – and between us we covered all the points I came up with. We are never happier than when we're measuring the beams of ships, engine cylinder head sizes and the like.

We spent about two hours underwater on each of the 20 wrecks we dived (or, translating for Mike's sake, 'dove') in the ten-day trip. Back ashore, after every dive we'd huddle together in a group over a coffee for a debrief so I could download as much information from their brains as I could before the memories were lost. All the dives were working dives – but working or not, the craic was as brilliant as ever on one of our Most Excellent Adventures. Paul, Gary and Mike, thanks so much for coming along, for all your help and for making the trip a blast. Where to next is the big problem – but I have an idea!

In Palau we used Sam's Tours based in Koror – just a few minutes' ride by boat from several of the Japanese wrecks. Paul Collins and Richard Barnden were the men on scene from Sam's Tours looking after us. Sam's Tours has a fantastic setup for tek divers such as us, and Paul Collins was brilliant in sorting out what we needed; he had 3-litre rebreather cylinders, banded and clipped stage cylinders, O2 and sofnolime all ready for us. The dive boats, too, were excellent – big, spacious and fast powerboats that could cover large distances effortlessly.

Paul Collins also went out of his way to show us the sort of things we needed to see, like Japanese World War II gun emplacements and burnt-out fuel dumps in caves. He also got us onto two very special wrecks – only found in the last six months or so before our arrival, and still unidentified and undived since those initial discovery dives.

Richard Barnden accompanied us on most of the dives and is getting known for his classy underwater photography – he has kindly let me use some of his shots in this book, for which I am very indebted.

Sam himself came out diving with us just for the craic. One of the original pioneers of Palau diving, he is still very interested in its shipwrecks, and took the time to make us feel very welcome. Thank you so much, Sam's Tours, Paul and Richard, for all you have done.

As with all my books, Rob Ward of Illusion Illustration has illustrated the wrecks for me, based on my survey videos, stills photos and diving notes. Rob and I must have worked on about 100 shipwrecks by now over the years, and we have got better at it. Rob will source the ship's drawings or a model and scan it into his Mac. He has software that allows him to distort the 2D image until we get the aspect we want to illustrate. We then build up superstructures and deck features in the correct places, to finally produce an image of the shipwreck on the seabed. The first draft goes through a series of tweaks and adjustments before, several hours later, we have a final image that we are satisfied with.

Rob and I made a decision long ago that as the illustrations aren't meant to be photographs but are designed to let divers see what to look for on the wrecks, we have to make certain features bigger than they actually are, so that when the illustration is reduced to fit onto the page of a book those features have a chance of being seen. Thus, for example, in a photograph of a 400-foot-long vessel seen from a bow perspective, an aft deck cargo winch would be tiny and almost unidentifiable – but by drawing the winch just a little larger Rob can ensure you see it.

Rob doesn't dive and has never seen any of the wrecks he has illustrated for me – so he does a very skilled job. Rob, thank you again for all you have done for me over the years.

The combat World War II aerial photos were sourced from the National Archives in Washington. The staff there were particularly helpful in assisting me to trace the somewhat obscure photos that so few enquire after. Peter Cundall, of the impressive and thoroughly researched www.combinedfleet.com online archive of all things about the Imperial Japanese Navy, was also greatly helpful, and I am indebted to him

Rod Macdonald
2016

The 2015 Palau shipwrecks Exped team. Left to right, Paul Haynes, Gary (Garspeed) Petrie and Rod Macdonald. (Author's collection)

# INTRODUCTION

Palau, sometimes called Belau, is a stunningly beautiful group of some 250 islands forming the western chain of the Caroline Islands in the western Pacific Ocean. Geographically, Palau is part of the larger island group of Micronesia, located to the east of the Philippines and north of Indonesia and Papua New Guinea. Palau's most populous islands are Angaur, Babelthuap, Koror and Peleliu – and the latter three lie together within the same barrier reef.

Migrants from the Philippines originally settled Palau some 3,000 years ago. Europeans first visited Palau in the 17th century, when Spain attempted to colonise the Caroline and Mariana Islands – despite the indigenous population of local inhabitants, a combination of both Polynesian and Melanesian with Malay blood influence from the Dutch East Indies. The Spanish had conferred the name 'Carolines' on the islands in 1668 in honour of their king, Charles II.

Spain however did little to develop its distant island holdings, and as the 19th century closed, Spain and the United States went to war in 1898 as a result of American intervention in the Cuban War of Independence. There had been revolts in Cuba against Spanish rule for some years – and previous war scares with their American neighbour. However, the straw that broke the camel's back was the mysterious sinking of the American battleship *Maine* in Havana Harbor; this triggered America into sending Spain an ultimatum demanding it surrender control of Cuba. The ultimatum was rejected and both sides declared war. In the short – just 10-week – war that followed, America attacked Spain's vulnerable Pacific possessions.

The war was settled by the 1898 Treaty of Paris, which gave America temporary control of Cuba and ceded indefinite colonial power over Spanish Puerto Rico, Guam and the Philippine Islands to America. Spain subsequently decided to pull out of the Pacific, and sold its remaining holdings to Germany – this at a time when Germany was beginning to gear up for war in Europe and was embarking on a naval arms race designed to challenge Great Britain's traditional naval supremacy. Germany gave Palau its present name, and no doubt coveted the rich natural resources of the region to assist in its war aims.

Now under German control, the Palau islands underwent a period of sustained economic growth. The valuable phosphate deposits of Angaur were much sought after and heavily mined. Traders from Japan, seeing the business possibilities, began to expand freight and passenger services to the Palaus and would eventually secure a virtual monopoly on import and export services.

With the outbreak of World War I, Japan saw the opportunity to further expand its power and influence in the Pacific region. Declaring that it was honouring its commitments under the 1902 Anglo-Japanese alliance, Japan declared war on Germany in 1914. In reality, Japan was moving to protect its Pacific freight and passenger shipping routes – whilst the Imperial Japanese Navy (IJN) saw the war as being an opportunity to acquire advance naval

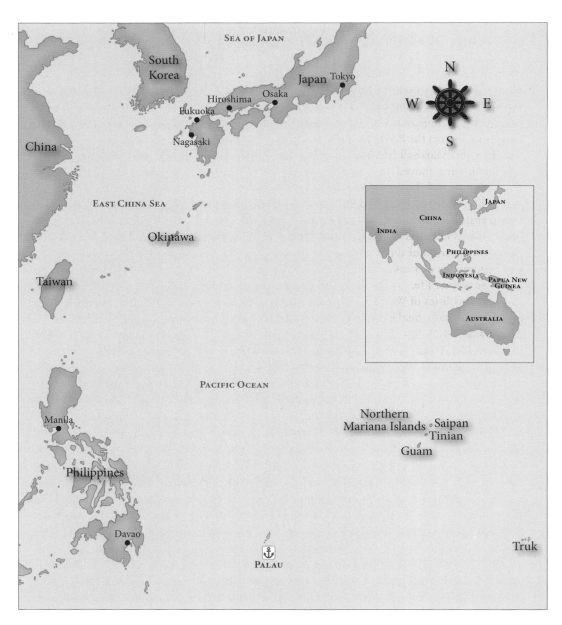

Location map of Palau

bases, such as German-held Palau, which would be strategically important in any future conflict with America.

Special Japanese naval task forces were formed, the 1st and 2nd South Seas Squadrons, and on 7 October 1914 the first landings were made in the Palaus at Koror. There was little resistance.

The Imperial Japanese Navy moved to eliminate German naval power in the Pacific. The Imperial German Navy's East Asiatic Squadron – comprising six major warships – was the main threat. But the small German squadron was vastly outgunned and outnumbered by the allies – and with no safe harbour for it in the Pacific, the squadron left the Pacific, rounding Cape Horn and heading homewards to Europe via the Atlantic.

With the Imperial German Squadron, and thus all German naval power, having disappeared from the Pacific, the IJN quickly seized the German possessions in the Mariana, Caroline and Marshall Islands – including the Palau groups.

Japan then moved to ban any foreign ships from entering the waters of her new possessions – and this included ships of its allies in the Great War.

The two South Seas Squadrons were disbanded, and control of the new island territories was transferred to a new IJN body based in Truk – the Provisional South Seas Defence Force. Naval Districts were established at Truk, Palau and elsewhere, and the IJN took over the administration of the islands, promulgating legislation, initiating public building works and beginning a process designed to colonise the islands and convert their inhabitants to the Japanese way of life.

The hostilities of World War I were finally halted by the Armistice of November 1918 – and the terms of a final settlement were belatedly agreed seven months later with the Treaty of Versailles of 28 June 1919. The victorious Allies established the League of Nations under the Versailles Treaty – and the League granted Japan a formal South Pacific Mandate to administrate the former German Pacific Islands north of the equator.

In terms of this mandate, the Caroline and the Marshall Island groups were both awarded to Japan in 1920. There were provisions built into the mandate that prohibited Japan from establishing military or naval bases, from erecting fortifications and from making military use of the islands. No open door trade policy was provided for, however, and Japan's trade monopoly continued – the islands had been effectively closed to the outside world.

America was deeply alarmed at the League of Nations policy on Japan and strongly opposed Japanese administration of the islands. President Woodrow Wilson, who had been a driving force behind the creation of the League of Nations, insisted that the islands should be militarily neutral and accordingly refused to recognise the Japanese mandate over the islands, and Congress refused to ratify the Versailles Treaty. The United States would not be part of the League of Nations, and American isolationism began.

In 1920, the bureaucrats of the Civil Affairs Bureau took over control from the naval officers of the IJN Provisional South Seas Defence Force, and set up its HQ in Koror. In 1922 the South Seas government was formed and began to govern all aspects of the Palauan way of life – the islands were progressively becoming Japanese. The Nippon Yusen Kaisha shipping line (NYK) was awarded a government contract to provide a steamship service between the Japanese home islands and the main ports in the South Seas. This service would enable the import of the vast quantities of natural resources vital to Japan's expansionist aims to the Japanese home islands. Palau was becoming a focal point for Japanese commercial shipping in the South Seas.

On the outbound leg from Japan, freighters would carry cargoes of coal, construction materials, plant and equipment and passengers.. On the return leg, the same ships would carry back to Japan natural resources deposits such as the aluminium ore known as bauxite, which was the world's main source of aluminium and vital for aircraft manufacture. Vast quantities of lignite – a combustible brown sedimentary rock known as the lowest form of coal – were carried back. Mined phosphate minerals were also carried back to Japan for use in agriculture and industry, along with other local products such as fish, copra (the dried meat or kernel of the coconut, used to extract coconut oil), coconut oil and tropical fruits.

By the mid-1920s, Japanese immigration to the South Seas had increased substantially – and more shipping routes were soon established. In 1935, with the development of the long-range Kawanishi H6K flying boat, commercial aviation came to Palau and the South Seas. The H6K made her maiden flight between Yokohama and Palau.

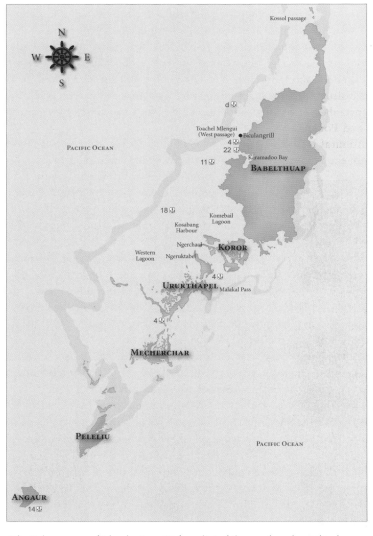

The Palau group of islands. See p32 for a list of the numbered wrecks shown.

In 1933, despite the terms of the League of Nations Mandate which prohibited the establishment of military bases, as a growing militarism took hold of Japan the Imperial Japanese Navy began making preliminary general surveys of the South Seas islands for potential naval and air bases. In 1936, following up on the results of those preliminary surveys, detailed surveys began to establish exact locations for airfields, coastal defence gun batteries and AA gun emplacements, naval anchorages, fuel and ammunition storage facilities and radio and command facilities. The Caroline Islands had been identified as an important line of defence in the event of war, with Palau having the most favourable strategic anchorages in the western Carolines.

During 1937, tensions heightened between the USA and Japan and the prospect of war loomed large. With the results of the 1936 surveys now available, Japan embarked on a secret project to militarise the Palau Islands by building ports and fortifications, viewing the islands as unsinkable aircraft carriers. Then, in 1939, Japan began to set up major airfields that would give long-range reconnaissance ability, as well as the potential for long-range air strikes against distant British and American holdings.

In 1940, the main body of the Imperial Japanese Navy arrived at Palau and the rate of development of naval facilities increased so that it could fulfil the role of an advance shipping and refuelling port. Barracks and additional shoreside facilities were built to handle fuel, ordnance and general naval supplies. Seaplane bases were also constructed for long-range reconnaissance aircraft and for Zero variant seaplane fighters.

On 5 November 1941, just one month before Japan would begin her Pacific War, Palau, Truk and Ponape in the Caroline Islands were formally approved as naval supply stations for Admiral Isoruku Yamamoto's Combined Fleet, along with other bases spread out throughout the South Seas in the Marshall and Mariana Islands.

Japanese coastal defence gun emplacement in rock cave on north shore of Ngerchaol.

On 7 December 1941, Japan initiated the Pacific War with her surprise attack on Pearl Harbor, intended to disable the American Pacific Fleet as her planned advance exploded southwards into the South Seas. Naval operations against the Philippines and Netherlands East Indies began simultaneously with the Pearl Harbor raid, with the carriers and amphibious assault units of Admiral Takahashi's powerful 3rd Fleet staging from Palau for the invasion of the Philippines.

Following the Philippine operations, Admiral Nagumo's 1st Air Fleet was based in Palau – and from here its four aircraft carriers, supported by the battleships and heavy cruisers of the 2nd Fleet, left to make a massive strike against Port Darwin in the Northern Territory of Australia on 19 February 1942. It was the largest single attack ever mounted by a foreign power on Australia.

From the surprise Pearl Harbor raid right up until Palau was neutralised in March 1944 by Desecrate 1, Palau's importance as a convoy gathering point and refuelling hub grew. Great naval warships came and went whilst her anchorages were thronged with merchant shipping of all shapes and sizes, some moving forward with men and supplies to the front at New Guinea and Rabaul whilst others were returning to the Japanese home islands to collect further cargoes. Land-based aircraft from her new airfields and seaplanes from her new seaplane bases crisscrossed the skies.

Chuuk Lagoon, as Truk Lagoon has been known since 1990, is a great natural harbour ringed by a protective reef some 140 miles in circumference and 40–50 miles in diameter. The atoll rises up from the deep blue oceanic depths of the western Pacific just north of the equator and to the north-east of New Guinea. It is some 1,165 miles almost directly east out into the Pacific from Palau.

The then Truk Lagoon was initially the IJN's 4th Fleet Base and became the Combined Fleet's forward base from 1942 until 1944. (The Japanese Combined Fleet had been formed during the 1904–05 Russo-Japanese War, and comprised a unified command for the then three separate fleets of the Imperial Japanese Navy. The 1st Fleet had been the main battleship fleet, the 2nd Fleet a fast, mobile cruiser fleet and the 3rd Fleet a reserve fleet of obsolete vessels. By World War II the Combined Fleet had become synonymous with the Imperial Japanese Navy, and consisted of battleships, aircraft carriers, cruisers and all the ancillary craft that made up the main fighting strength).

By Easter of 1942, however, with the Battle of the Coral Sea and the Battle of Midway Japan had lost significant battles, and had been forced to abandon its offensive strategy and concentrate on holding onto its most vital gains. At this time, the heavily fortified Truk Lagoon served as a safe, sheltered and well-protected forward base for the Imperial Japanese Navy's main battle fleet. Super-battleships such as the *Yamato* and *Musashi* as well as strategically vital aircraft carriers, cruisers, destroyers, tankers and submarines, along with countless minor vessels such as tugs, gunboats, minesweepers and landing craft, all thronged its waters.

In addition to the front-line battle fleet, a large number of naval auxiliary transport ships worked as tenders for the fleet and its submarines, carrying naval shells, ammunition, torpedoes, stores, spares and everything else needed to keep a battle fleet operational. Other auxiliaries carried munitions, tanks, trucks, land artillery, beach mines and the like, all destined to fortify Truk's land defences and to resupply troops there.

The Allies had suspected Truk was being used as a fortified anchorage but as Truk had been closed to foreigners for decades, little was known about the scale of the operation – until Allied victories against the Japanese brought them closer to Truk, with their capture of the Marshall Islands in 1943. From there they could stage to assault Truk Lagoon.

As Truk became vulnerable, Palau became the HQ for the IJN 2nd Fleet, and Admiral Koga began dispersing units of the Combined Fleet from Truk out of range of US land-based and carrier aircraft. The battleships *Nagato* and *Fuso* and escort destroyers left Truk for Palau on 1 February 1944, and the super-battleship *Yamato* along with other battleships, cruisers and destroyers left Truk on 3 February 1944.

Nevertheless, when the first overflight by US Navy Liberator long-range reconnaissance aircraft took place on 4 February 1944, the sight that met the American aviators' eyes was astonishing. Large elements of the IJN fleet lay below – battleships, cruisers, submarines, carriers, all lay at anchor along with a huge number of vulnerable naval auxiliaries, merchant supply ships and tenders. US military planners immediately started planning a fast carrier raid.

With the US overflight being detected, Japan knew that Truk Lagoon was now imminently susceptible to a raid; the remaining heavy IJN warships immediately left the lagoon – some steaming west, bound for Palau, whilst others headed for Singapore or Japan.

A US naval assault force of battleships, cruisers and nine aircraft carriers carrying more than 500 combat aircraft was immediately put together and designated Task Force 58. It approached Truk Lagoon undetected and took station some 90 miles off Truk on the evening of 16 February 1944.

The following day, Operation *Hailstone* began with a dawn Grumman F6F Hellcat fighter sweep of the lagoon. In one of the greatest aerial dogfights of World War II, Japanese air power was destroyed in a few hours. With US air superiority quickly established, throughout 17 February and into the following day, the US carriers launched wave after wave of Curtiss Helldiver and Douglas Dauntless dive-bombers and Grumman Avenger torpedo-bombers escorted by Hellcat fighters to attack the now vulnerable shipping and land fortifications. They met limited AA fire from the lightly armed merchant ships below and from the island land defences. It was a one-sided battle – and more than 50 ships were sent to the bottom of the lagoon over the two days of Operation *Hailstone*.

With Truk neutralised as a naval and air base, the American military machine was soon advancing westwards towards Palau. Operation *Desecrate 1* would take place on 30 and 31 March 1944 – just six weeks after the massive US strike against Truk. The same Fast Carrier Task Force 58 would repeat the success of Operation *Hailstone* – sinking a large number of Japanese vessels and destroying Palau as a naval and air base that could wage war against the Allies.

Today, whilst Truk Lagoon is the most famous wreck-diving location in the world, Palau is perhaps most famous in diving circles for its beautiful world-class coral reefs, vertical walls, sea life and blue holes; there is also its famous landlocked Jellyfish Lake, where you can snorkel amongst a thick soup of non-stinging jelly fish which, with no natural predators in the Lake, lost their unnecessary ability to sting aeons ago. It is a fascinating – almost unbelievable – sight, and an uncanny sensation to be amongst them and have your skin brushed by jellyfish that would in my own part of the world induce severe stings.

These beautiful and amazing sights alone attract countless divers to Palau – and such is the rich beauty of the diving there that the Japanese World War II wrecks almost take a back seat – with divers usually making but a couple of wreck dives on the more popular wrecks during the course of their diving holiday. But the *Desecrate 1* shipwrecks lying in the waters of Palau are a fascinating record of a brutal episode of history, and one that deserves more attention than it has had.

Many of the wrecks were relocated by local diver Francis Toribiong, who in the early 1970s opened Palau's first dive shop, Fish 'n Fins in Koror, and pioneered Palauan diving. Today diving in Palau is a huge business, and much of that is down to the early work done

by Francis who was the first to popularise such world-class dive sites as Blue Corner, Peleliu Corner and the Ngemelis Wall.

In the 1980s Francis dived with Klaus Lindemann – whose name is also synonymous with Truk Lagoon – finding and documenting the lost Japanese shipwrecks of *Desecrate 1*. Klaus Lindemann published the first edition of his definitive book, *Desecrate 1*, in 1988 – with an updated second edition being published in 1991.

The other great name in literature about Truk Lagoon and Palau's wartime legacy is that of Dan E. Bailey, who published his thoroughly researched book *WWII Wrecks of the Kwajalein and Truk Lagoons* in 1989 and then, as more information became available, published the definitive historical guide *World War II Wrecks of the Truk Lagoon* in 2000. He also published *WWII Wrecks of Palau* in 1991 – it is a triumph of original first-hand detective work and primary research. In the intervening 25 years since, however, little more has been written about the Palau shipwrecks – they have almost been overlooked in favour of the beautiful scenic diving that Palau offers.

Hard though it may be to believe today, Palau was a brutal battlefield during 1944 and 1945, and today its beautiful waters hide the scattered remains of countless ships and combatant aircraft. I have always believed that to understand and appreciate a shipwreck you need to understand the historical context in which the ship met its end. I have thus summarised the build-up to *Desecrate 1* as well as the actual raids themselves.

Many of the *Desecrate 1* shipwrecks had salvage work carried out on them in the post-war years. Some wrecks were completely removed; others were partially salved before operations were ended. Some were dismantled underwater, whilst others were blown up to allow easy access and lifting of the valuable metal – leaving today nothing but a debris field. The salved metal was sent to Korea for use in the Korean War – but in an ironic twist of fate, the vessels carrying the salved metal were lost in a storm in the South China Sea and none of the metal reached its destination.

But many shipwrecks were not touched by salvors, and on other wrecks salvage operations were ceased for safety reasons when munitions were encountered. Several salvage divers lost their lives in the 1950s as underwater salvage works detonated wartime

Amongst Palau's Rock Islands. (Author's collection)

munitions. The wrecks that have been partially salved are still fascinating – each with its own story to tell.

The purpose of this book is to give the diver visiting Palau on a diving holiday, concise information that will allow them to understand the wrecks that can be dived. I have not attempted a complete historical listing of all the ships sunk in Palau during the raid, and have deliberately omitted those wrecks that were removed or heavily salved to leave but a debris field today. I have also not included wrecks which although historically interesting are unlikely to be dived or which are well outside the easy dive boat range from the main dive centres – such as Ngaruangl Atoll, which lies some 50 nautical miles north of Koror and has a number of minor wrecks around it which have been salved, such as the *Samidare*. I also have not included many of the other numerous small craft strafed and sunk around the islands. Many have never been located; others left no record and remain unidentified.

So here is my contribution to Palau's world-class shipwreck diving – I hope this lifts a veil on the wonderful wrecks of Palau.

Good diving
Rod Macdonald

## AUTHOR'S NOTES:

1. The metric system has been used for modern-day details such as depths for diving purposes – but for wartime references I have used the imperial system then in use.
2. If you venture deep into the wrecks you may well come upon human remains. Please treat these remains with respect – they are people, and many will still have sons, daughters, and grandchildren alive. Please do not touch, move or disturb the remains in any way.
3. Koror State Government requires that you buy a diving permit. This can be purchased via your chosen dive centre on arrival and there are several permutations possible. The world-famous Jellyfish Lake can be covered by the Koror State Rock Islands Permit.

4.  If you wish to do a battlefield tour of Peleliu Island (which I would recommend), a separate Peleliu State Permit is required – again this can be purchased via your dive centre.

5.  You are required to carry your dive permit with you at all times when out on the lagoon's waters. Koror State Rangers travel around the lagoon by fast speedboat and will come alongside dive boats from time to time to inspect dive permits. There can be a substantial fine levied if you cannot produce it or do not have one. I have seen it happen.

6.  Palau law requires that you carry a delayed deco bag/SMB with you when diving.

7.  A passport valid for a minimum of six months is required to enter Palau.

8.  A departure tax (US$50 at time of printing) is payable at the airport when leaving Palau.

# BOOK ONE

## War

# CHAPTER ONE

# War in the Pacific

As the closing years of the 19th century gave way to the 20th century it was a time of great industrial change. Japan, a small island country with limited natural resources of its own, was determined to become a modern industrial nation and avoid the fate of China, where by the middle of the 19th century European powers had forced the weakened Chinese empire to open its doors to trade. The Chinese coast had become dominated by European trading posts such as Hong Kong and Shanghai.

The opening up of Japan to Western trade in the 19th century had to an extent put Japan on a similar path. Japan's leaders, however, did not want Japan to become, like China, an economic plaything of the great Western powers, and set out to modernise; and the pace of that change was extraordinary. Japan admired and envied the naval power and dominance of Great Britain, and Japanese naval reform was largely based on the Royal Navy template. Over time, Japan grew in power and influence – but, being an industrial nation with little natural resources of its own to feed its growing industry, became heavily dependent on imported raw materials.

The proximity of China and Russia on the Asian mainland to the west had always been a threat to Japan's security. Under the Treaty of Beijing in 1860, Russia acquired the island of Sakhalin from China along with a large Pacific coast maritime province adjacent to northern Japan. China had just lost the Opium War with Britain – and war weary and weakened, was now unable to defend the region. Shortly afterwards the first buildings of the present-day port city of Vladivostok were erected.

In the 1890s, Russia began building the Trans-Siberian Railway to Vladivostok. There was no economic justification for building the railway – it was an overtly strategic endeavour which would allow Russia to transport and maintain a large army near its Pacific coast. Fear of Russia became a dominant feature of Japanese foreign policy from then on.

In 1896, Russia signed an alliance with China against Japan and took a lease on Port Arthur, a strategically vital Chinese Manchurian port to the south of Korea. In 1899, Russia began building a branch of the Trans-Siberian railway to Port Arthur and continued to build up its military strength in Manchuria, basing its Pacific Fleet at Port Arthur. Russia had obvious territorial ambitions, which Japan viewed with grave concern.

Britain and Japan signed a defensive alliance in 1902 – and in 1904, to pre-empt the Russian threat, Japan began the Russo-Japanese War against Russia with a surprise attack on the Russian fleet at Port Arthur. Japanese troops from Korea landed on the Manchurian coast and swiftly cut off Port Arthur. In a series of fierce land battles Russian forces were pushed northwards across Manchuria. Port Arthur fell to Japan after a bloody siege in January 1905.

Russia was forced to send its Baltic Fleet half way round the world to relieve its beleaguered troops in Manchuria; it left European waters in late 1904 – passing Singapore *en route* on 8 April 1905.

The final land battle of this brutal war was fought at Mukden in February and March 1905 between 330,000 Russian troops and 270,000 Japanese. With more than 600,000 combatants it was the largest battle for 100 years and was the largest modern-era battle fought in Asia before World War II. After long and heavy fighting, the Russian army broke off and withdrew northwards – allowing Mukden to fall into Japanese hands.

Victorious on land, the Japanese however found themselves unable to secure the complete command of the sea that their land campaign depended upon, as the Russian naval squadrons at Port Arthur and Vladivostok remained active. The Japanese fleet finally brought the Russian fleet to battle between 27 and 29 May 1905 – the Japanese fleet under Admiral Togo won a historic victory at the Battle of Tsushima when it completely destroyed the Baltic Fleet. The battle was won by a Japanese navy created with British technical assistance, and warships built mainly at British shipyards.

The Tsarist government signed a peace treaty with Japan in September 1905, in which Japan secured the rights in Manchuria that had been Russia's – including Port Arthur and the southern section of the Manchurian railway. Japan now had vested interests and possessions in Manchuria to protect – and in 1910 it annexed Korea.

During the First World War of 1914–18, the 1902 Anglo-Japanese alliance encouraged Japan to enter the war against Germany. Japan honoured the mutual aid alliance; it declared war against Germany on 23 August 1914 and joined Britain in attacking the German-held colony of Tsingtao on the coast of China. (This was the required limit of Japan's support on the ground, as the mutual aid clause of the alliance only required it to assist Britain in operations in India and the Far East).

Once Japan had declared war on Germany, the Imperial Japanese Navy was tasked with pursuing and destroying the German East Asiatic Squadron, which consisted of six major warships under the command of Vice Admiral Maximilian Reichsgraf von Spee. The squadron consisted of the *Scharnhorst*-class cruisers SMS *Scharnhorst* and *Gneisenau*, the *Dresden*-class cruisers SMS *Dresden* and SMS *Emden*, the *Bremen*-class cruiser SMS *Leipzig*, and the *Königsberg*-class cruiser SMS *Nürnberg*. The German East Asiatic Squadron ships were already dispersed at various colonies around the Pacific on routine peacetime missions, and the outbreak of war immediately rendered them outnumbered and outgunned by the Allies in the Pacific. Von Spee commented that his squadron had no secure harbour in the Pacific, and would not be able to safely reach Germany. Resigned to his squadron's fate, he determined to plough the seas of the world inflicting as much damage as he could until his ammunition was exhausted or until he was caught by the superior firepower of the Allies. He ordered the squadron to move around Cape Horn into the Atlantic, intent on forcing its way north, but whilst attempting to run homewards, most of the squadron was destroyed on 8 December 1914 at the Battle of the Falkland Islands in which von Spee himself was killed.

By October 1914, with the German East Asiatic Squadron making itself scarce in the Pacific, the Imperial Japanese Navy had seized German possessions in the Mariana, Caroline and Marshall Islands and the Palau group. Intent on expansion – gaining territories and securing access to raw materials as Germany became vulnerable – Japan also seized German possessions in China and elsewhere in the Pacific.

After the Great War ended, the ex-German colonies in the Pacific were divided amongst the victors under the South Pacific Mandate by the League of Nations. Japan retained the conquered German colony of Tsingtao – and China was forced to relinquish other land in the area to her.

Under the South Pacific Mandate Japan was awarded Palau as a Class C League of Nations Mandate – along with the Northern Mariana Islands, the Federated States of Micronesia (including Truk) and the Marshall Islands. Under the mandate, Palau would be administered under the laws of the mandatory (i.e. Japan) as its own territory. It was a fine return for the loan of a battalion of infantry and a few naval escort vessels to Britain.

In 1921, the Washington Naval Treaty was signed – largely provoked by Japan's expansionist goals, and designed to contain them. This was a system of arms control that pegged the British Royal Navy at roughly the size of the United States Navy, and placed severe restrictions on the building of new capital ships. The treaty allowed Britain and the United States a tonnage equivalent to fifteen capital ships; the Japanese were allowed nine capital ships, and France and Italy five capital ships apiece. New battleship displacement was capped at 35,000 tons and the maximum gun barrel size pegged at 16 inches. Crippled by the huge costs of the Great War, Britain feared that it could not match Japanese and American shipbuilding programmes, and so accepted the terms of the Washington Naval Treaty. At a stroke, Britain had abandoned its cherished 19th-century two-power policy – that the Royal Navy must be equal in size to the next two largest navies in the world.

The Japanese were pointedly displeased that they had not been granted parity with Britain and the United States. However they were partly placated by a deal whereby Britain would not develop naval bases east of Singapore – and the United States would not develop bases west of Hawaii. Japan had effectively been granted control of a huge slice of the north-west Pacific.

The Great Depression from 1929 onwards, and the subsequent collapse in world trade, hit Japan's export-orientated economy hard. The economic crisis led to the Japanese military becoming increasingly convinced that Japan needed guaranteed access to new markets and raw materials on the Asian mainland. Japan's population had more than doubled, and demand was high for food, coal and materials.

During the negotiations leading up to the London Naval Conference Treaty in 1930, Prime Minister Osachi Hamaguchi had tried – but failed – to secure a better ratio of battleships for Japan in comparison to Great Britain and the USA. His failure, and subsequent settlement of the treaty, led to the Japanese people feeling that he had sold out Japanese national security – and this prompted a surge of Japanese nationalism. On 14 November 1930, there was an assassination attempt when a member of an ultra-nationalist group shot him in Tokyo Station. Hamaguchi was hospitalised for several months – he returned to office on 10 March 1931 but resigned a month later.

With Hamaguchi's firm hand no longer at the helm, a growing militarism took hold in Japanese politics. Coincidentally, just six months after Hamaguchi's resignation, the local warlord in Manchuria formally recognised the Chinese Nationalist Government in Nanking and began to obstruct the Japanese presence in southern Manchuria – which had been in Japanese possession since the 1905 Russo-Japan War. By now, after years of development, three quarters of the Manchurian economy was in Japanese control and it was a major source of coal and iron ore for Japan, as well as being an important export market.

With Japan's vital economic position in Manchuria at risk to the Chinese, on 18 September 1931 officers of the Kwantung Army (the Japanese forces in Manchuria) took matters into their own hands. Without advising either their commander-in-chief or the Tokyo civilian government, the Japanese officers staged a bombing incident on a railway they were guarding near the town of Mukden.

The Kwantung Army then claimed that local Chinese forces were responsible and launched a military campaign against them. They shelled the local Chinese garrison and destroyed the small Chinese air force. Five hundred battle-hardened Japanese troops assaulted the garrison of some 7,000 Chinese troops, mostly irregulars or conscripts. The fighting was over by the evening and the Japanese occupied Mukden at the cost of 500 Chinese dead to two Japanese dead. The Japanese then went on to occupy the major Manchurian cities of Changchun and Antung as well as the surrounding areas. The military established a puppet state, which the Tokyo civilian government was forced to rubber stamp after the event.

The aggrieved Chinese appealed to the League of Nations – of which they were members – for a peaceful solution. The League of Nations started to investigate the war in Manchuria and whilst these investigations were ongoing, Prime Minister Inukai Tsuyoshi came to power on 13 December 1931. He tried to place fiscal restraints on the military but failed – and he was also unable to control the military's designs on China. Early in 1932 a large Japanese expeditionary force was sent to Shanghai to counter anti-Japanese riots. The fighting lasted for weeks.

A *coup d'*état was staged in Japan on 15 May 1932 – launched by reactionary elements of the Imperial Japanese Navy. Eleven young naval officers assassinated Prime Minister Tsuyoshi and brought the civilian government to its knees; the military had gained control of the country. Now unchecked by a civilian administration, massive increases in Japanese military spending began –a military spending spree that would continue throughout the 1930s.

At the League of Nations Assembly in Geneva on 24 Feb 1933, the league called on Japan to withdraw its troops and restore Manchuria to Chinese sovereignty. The Japanese delegation, in defiance of world opinion, dramatically withdrew from the League of Nations and, grandstanding, walked out from the hall – unwilling to accept the assembly's report. Japan's isolation from the community of nations had started.

It seemed that the world was once again descending into chaos. In Italy, the Fascists had seized control in the 1920s. In Germany, the Nazi Party came to power – with Hitler being appointed Chancellor in 1933. Nazi Germany left the League of Nations that year and repudiated the military clauses of the 1919 Treaty of Versailles. In 1935, Italy invaded Abyssinia (now Ethiopia) and in 1936, the Spanish Civil War broke out.

In June 1935, in an effort to control the worsening military situation, an Anglo-German naval treaty was negotiated in which Britain agreed that Germany could build a fleet of up to 35 per cent of the Royal Navy's surface tonnage. Although not clear at the time, with the rebirth of the German Fleet it had just become unlikely that the Royal Navy could send a large naval force to the Far East to counter the growing Japanese threat.

A number of old general naval treaties were due to expire in 1936, and negotiations began in 1935–36 for a new round of treaties. Militant Japan however withdrew from the negotiations – leaving in tatters the system of naval disarmament instituted after the Great War under the Treaty of Versailles.

As this increasing militarism overtook Japan in the 1930s, the Imperial Japanese Navy had begun preliminary surveys in 1933 of the mandated South Seas islands, to identify potential fleet and air bases. Palau and the larger Caroline Islands group were identified as the first line of defence in the Pacific in the event of hostilities.

There was a proviso in the Versailles Peace Treaty of 1919 (which covered the mandating of the German island colonies to Japan) that 'no military or naval bases shall be established, or fortifications erected in the territory'. However, in a major contravention of the League of Nations Mandate, the Imperial Japanese Navy began construction of airfields, fortifications, ports and other military projects in the mandated islands – viewing the islands as unsinkable aircraft carriers with a critical role to play in the defence of Japanese home islands against a potential invasion by their main perceived enemy, the United States of America.

In 1937, as tensions rose between the USA and Japan, the IJN began to secretly militarise the Palauan Islands and in 1939 they started constructing airfields that would allow long-range air attacks against US and British Pacific territories..

Kwajalein Atoll in the Marshall Islands, more than 2,000 nautical miles out into the Pacific to the east of Palau, would go on to become a major base which supported the attack on Pearl Harbor – just over 2,500 nautical miles further north-east towards America. Palau itself would be used to support the campaign to take the Philippines, whilst Truk Lagoon in Micronesia, more than 1,100 nautical miles out into the central Pacific to the east of Palau, would be used as a base for the amphibious landings on Tarawa, Makin and Rabaul.

The militarily aggressive Japanese government was determined to follow a policy of expansion called the Greater East Asia Co-Prosperity Sphere. Central to that policy was the extension of Japanese power and the acquisition of an empire similar to those of the European powers. Japan's lack of its own oil resources was a critical vulnerability and caused Japan's rulers to eye the oil-rich Dutch East Indies (now Indonesia) with particular interest.

Throughout the 1930s Japan had engaged in an undeclared border war with its old enemy, Russia, which started with a number of minor incidents from 1932 onwards but escalated into a bitter undeclared border war from 1935 onwards.

Despite its commitments with the unofficial border war with Russia, on 7 July 1937 Japan assaulted a crucial access point to the Chinese city of Beijing – and started the Second Sino-Japanese War. The Japanese invaded north China and went on to capture Beijing itself as well as Tianjin – showing great brutality to Chinese soldiers and civilians alike. The Battle of Shanghai in August 1937 was the first of some 22 major engagements fought during this war – and was one of the largest and bloodiest. Eventually, defeated Chinese troops were forced to retreat along the Yangtze basin towards the Nationalist capital of Nanking, 200 miles upriver from Shanghai – all the time being pressed by Japanese mechanised columns and aircraft. The Japanese forces soon arrived outside Nanking.

On 8 December 1937 the Japanese ordered the Chinese army defending Nanking to surrender by noon on 10 December. Come 10 December, when the Chinese defending forces had not surrendered, the Japanese attack began. After two days of resistance the Japanese successfully took the city on 13 December.

As soon as they had entered the city, Japanese troops embarked on an officially condoned terror campaign against the civilian population in and around the city – which became known as the Rape of Nanking.

What had begun as an operation to round up and kill Chinese soldiers turned into a drunken orgy of murder and rape. Bodies were dumped in the Yangtze River – washing up downstream on the banks. Japanese soldiers used Chinese prisoners for public displays of bayonet practice before crowds of horrified onlookers. There were beheading competitions and the gang rape of thousands of women, who were shot after being raped. Chinese propagandists claimed at the time that some 250,000 people were killed at Nanking – Western observers put the numbers in the tens of thousands. The indiscriminate total war of the Second Sino-Japanese War would continue through to the end of World War II.

Japan's other enemy, the Soviet Union, began to aid China, hoping that by keeping China in the war with Japan this would stop Japan from invading Siberia. This policy led to Japan becoming engaged in larger-scale military confrontations with Russian forces along the Manchurian–Siberian frontier – fighting which would last until an armistice was declared in September 1939.

Japan, with scarce raw materials and resources of its own, had largely depended on American exports of oil and iron. Ironically, it was American trade and exports throughout the 1930s which had largely underpinned Japan's war industries and allowed Japan to wage its wars of aggression. But American tolerance of Japanese aggression was wearing thin.

American public opinion turned sharply against Japan when on 12 December 1937, Japanese aircraft sank the US Navy gunboat *Panay* at anchor in the Yangtze River. Two months later the US consul in Nanking was attacked and American property looted.

Contrary to what it sought to achieve by securing its own resources in Manchuria and China, Japan's China Policy, far from making Japan self-sufficient by securing raw materials, was in fact making it more dependent than ever on imports from the West. The American and British lack of response to Japan's war in China did much to make Japanese leaders believe that Western democracies were weak and lacked resolve. Meanwhile, as the war in China dragged on, Japanese troops were becoming battle-hardened and ruthless.

On 26 July 1939, after continued attacks by the Japanese military on American citizens and the encroachment on American interests in China, the United States withdrew from the US–Japan Treaty of Commerce and Navigation which had regulated trade between the two countries.

On 1 September 1939 Germany invaded Poland – and finally triggered World War II.

In November 1939, as war in Europe erupted and Japan made ready for its Pacific War, the IJN 4th Fleet was organised to protect Japan's Pacific island territories and those that it intended to seize as its government initiated its plan to create Japan's Greater East Asia Co-Prosperity Sphere – or empire.

In 1940, the IJN 4th Fleet was tasked to set up the necessary land, sea and air facilities for the Combined Fleet, and established its HQ on Truk. The Inner South Seas theatre was divided into four sectors, each with its own base force. Koror in Palau was assigned as HQ for the 3rd Base Force.

....................

In the spring of 1940, conscious of the developing Japanese threat, and in a move that would have great significance – unforeseen at the time – the US Pacific Fleet moved its main base from California further west into the Pacific – to Pearl Harbor in Hawaii. It was now unknowingly within range of the naval units from Japan's forward bases at Truk and Kwajalein.

In June 1940, just a month after the Fall of France to Germany, Japan (an ally of Germany since 1935) demanded that the Japanese troops in China be allowed to move into the northern part of French Indo-China (modern-day Vietnam and Thailand) and establish military bases there. France had controlled Vietnam since the latter part of the 19th century, but with the fall of France to Nazi Germany in 1940, the French hold on Indo-China was weak. Japan was asserting its interest in direct dominance in the region – and the French Governor-General, under the power of the Nazis, had to agree.

On 2 July 1940 in an attempt to curb Japanese aggression US President Roosevelt signed the Export Control Act, which authorised the president to either licence or prohibit the export of essential defence materials. On 31 July, exports of aviation motor fuels, iron and steel were restricted.

Then on 16 October 1940, in a move clearly aimed at Japan, an American embargo was placed on all exports of scrap iron and steel to destinations other than Britain and the nations of the Western hemisphere. Japan had essentially boxed itself into a corner and its leaders determined that it must gain control of the badly needed supplies of oil, tin and rubber in the European colonies of South East Asia. Japan had to free itself from its dependency on Western imports and the pressure the Western powers were applying with their economic sanctions.

....................

In April 1941, Japan ceased to regard Russia as its main enemy, and signed a non-aggression neutrality pact with the Soviet Union. With the Russian threat removed, Japan could now shift its focus southwards. The same month, under German and Japanese pressure, the Vichy government in France allowed Japan (which already had military bases in the north of Indo-China) the use of air and naval bases in southern Indo-China.

On 22 June 1941 Germany invaded the Soviet Union and with Russia (with who, despite the recently signed neutrality pact, Japan had a long history of conflict) now concentrated on fighting off the Nazis. Japan was free to consider a more aggressive policy in South East Asia.

At the Imperial Conference in Tokyo on 2 July 1941, Japan determined to 'construct the Greater East Asia Co-Prosperity Sphere, regardless of the changes in the world situation'. Japan resolved to continue the war in China, to await developments with Russia and to prepare for an expansion into South East Asia.

On 14 July 1941 the French authorities in Indo-China were given a set of Japanese demands. With little room to manoeuvre, the demands were accepted on 23 July – and the first of tens of thousands of Japanese troops began to arrive in the region. Japanese warships were stationed at coastal ports, and air force units were stationed around Saigon.

Once the Japanese had established themselves in southern Indo-China, they were closer than ever to Singapore, the Philippines and Dutch East Indies. Without firing a shot, the Japanese had secured bases only 450 miles from Malaya and 700 miles (little more than the length of mainland Britain) from Singapore. These British possessions were now well within range of Japanese bombers and Japan soon had over 400 land-based aircraft stationed in Indo-China and 280 carrier-based aircraft available in addition.

America reacted to this latest demonstration of Japanese aggression on the Asian mainland on 25 July 1941 by beefing up the previous year's export controls to a full embargo – banning the export to Japan of the oil and other materials that had been fuelling the Japanese war machine for years. During the 1930s Japan had imported half its oil from America, but by 1940–41 it was importing 80 per cent of its oil from America and 10 per cent from the East Indies. Japan had been stockpiling oil – but only had sufficient for 18 months' usage at normal rate.

On 26 July 1941 Japanese assets in the USA were frozen, preventing the Japanese from obtaining the dollars they needed to buy American goods. Commercial relations between America and Japan were now at an end. Britain and Holland followed suit with trade embargoes on Japan from their colonies in South East Asia. Japan was now isolated from the West and desperately in need of raw materials to keep its expansionist war machine operating.

Japan had boxed itself into an untenable position – and Britain and America knew that the Japanese might well try to escape the stranglehold of the embargoes by going to war. For their part, the Japanese felt that to save their empire they must take measures to secure the raw materials of the South Seas.

Throughout the 1930s, Japan had been building closer relations with Germany, and so, with Germany at the peak of its power, and faced with crippling trade embargoes by America, Britain and the Netherlands from July 1941 onwards, Japan must have felt that the moment was ideal for it to form an alliance with Germany. Japan formally entered the Axis Pact with Germany and Italy on 27 September 1941; in the pact, the three countries agreed to aid each other if one of their number was attacked by a power not involved in a current conflict.

Membership of the Axis Pact for Japan ensured that Germany recognised that East Asia was a Japanese sphere of influence. Germany and Italy intended to establish a New Order in Europe – Japan would do likewise in Greater East Asia.

Germany, for its part, hoped that Japan would restrain America and allow her forces to deal a final knockout blow to Britain, whilst the Axis Pact enabled Japan's leaders to consider the possibility of simultaneous war with America and Britain more seriously. Meanwhile, Japan's entry into the Axis Pact led America and Britain to increasingly view Germany and Japan as a joint threat.

Between 1921 and 1941 the combat tonnage of the Japanese Navy had doubled, while that of the British and American navies had only increased modestly. By 1941 the Japanese fleet was more powerful than the combined Pacific Fleets of Britain and America and was far better prepared for combat; it bristled with well-designed and well-armed modern ships – and well-drilled and well-exercised crews. The number of carriers and battleships had been substantially increased after 1936 with the last additions being the super-battleships *Yamato* and *Musashi* in 1940 – each displacing 63,000 tons and carrying massive 18.1-inch main guns, the largest ever installed on a battleship.

In 1941 the Japanese fleet had 10 battleships to 9 American. Japan had 10 aircraft carriers to 3 US carriers, 18 heavy cruisers to 12 US, 17 light cruisers to 9 US, 111 destroyers to 67 US and 64 submarines to 27 US; Japan was superior in every naval category.

At the Japanese Imperial Conference on 6 September 1941, in the presence of the emperor, it was decided to complete war preparations by the end of October. Meantime, Japan would continue negotiations with the USA in an attempt to end the trade embargo. If Japan did nothing, the slow strangulation of the trade embargoes would cause the country to collapse in a few years for lack of raw materials. If the embargoes could not be lifted, Japan would go to war – its leaders believing it had a 70–80 per cent chance of initial victory. A successful war against the Western powers would allow Japan to seize the raw materials of South East Asia – in particular the oil of the Dutch East Indies.

During the closing months of 1941, America and Japan tried to negotiate an agreement to end the trade embargo – but the USA, friendly towards China, would not agree to supply Japan with the oil it so badly needed unless Japan withdrew its forces from the Asian mainland of China, Korea and Manchuria.

On 14 October Army Minister General Hideki Tōjō, a name that would become infamous during the war to come, told the Japanese Cabinet that widespread troop withdrawals in

China were not acceptable to the military. On 16 October the cabinet resigned, unwilling to launch another war.

The day after the government resigned, General Tōjō became Prime Minister of Japan – he would also continue as War Minister. As the army had become dictator of Japan, Tōjō, the army representative, was now in charge of the entire population.

The Japanese army and navy both wanted war for their own reasons. The navy was concerned about the diminishing oil reserves – and the army believed that American aid to China would increase and undermine its position there. Japan would pursue the diplomatic negotiations to end the embargo – but only until midnight 30 November.

At a Japanese Imperial Conference on 1 December 1941, with no end to the embargo agreed, General Tōjō advised that war was necessary to preserve the Japanese Empire. Orders were sent out to military commanders that hostilities would commence on 8 December (7 December east of the International Date Line).

Japan's war planners hoped to quickly build an empire so large that the Western powers would not be able to countenance the cost of retaking it. Japan also hoped that its Axis partners, Germany and Italy, would prevail over the Soviets and Britain in Europe, and that thereafter Japan might be able negotiate peace with an isolated United States; anti-war rhetoric and political divisions very apparent in America encouraged the Japanese in this view. The Japanese plan however depended to a large degree upon Germany winning in Europe. It was a gamble where they didn't hold all the cards.

The Japanese military knew that there was only had a limited chance of winning a prolonged war with America, but the move of the US fleet to Hawaii in the spring of 1940 had opened up the possibility of a pre-emptive knockout strike. If Japan could destroy the main American offensive weapon, its Pacific Fleet, in one blow, it might buy enough time to forge a viable Pacific empire.

The commander-in-chief of Japan's Combined Fleet, Admiral Yamamoto Isoroku, had a background in naval aviation and had noted the recent success of British carrier-launched biplanes against the Italian fleet at Taranto on 11 November 1940.

Japan had been developing a powerful new torpedo that could be dropped from an aircraft to run in shallow waters, such as near Hawaii. If an attack on the US naval base at Pearl Harbor could successfully knock out the main elements of the American battle fleet, the 11 battleships and 10 aircraft carriers of the Imperial Japanese Navy should be more than a match for any remaining Allied naval forces in the area. The Japanese battleships and aircraft carriers could be relied upon to shield the army's invasion convoys as they sailed for South East Asia.

There would be five separate Japanese operations, targeted against:
1. The US Pacific Fleet at Pearl Harbor
2. The American airfields at Luzon in the Philippines
3. The strategically important islands of Guam and Wake, and the Gilbert Islands
4. British-held Hong Kong
5. Siam (now Thailand), British Malaya and Singapore.

The plan was breathtaking in its audacity.

In advance of the deadline for operations to commence, Japanese troop transports left ports in eastern Indo-China (modern-day Vietnam) bound for selected invasion beaches in Siam and northern Malaya. Over 26,600 soldiers crammed the 19 troop transports of the first wave of ships deployed from Hainan Island, off China – destined for the invasion of British Malaya. These troop transports would sail close to the coast of Indo-China to avoid detection for their four-day journey south towards Singora in Siam. The Japanese were relying on the bad weather of the breaking monsoon to shield the convoys from British reconnaissance aircraft. They knew that if the vulnerable heavily packed troop transports were spotted and intercepted, they would be sitting ducks and the invasion would be in trouble from the start.

Other Japanese naval units moved out across the Pacific in total secrecy towards the other four targets; Pearl Harbor, the American airfields at Luzon in the Philippines, Guam and the Wake and Gilbert Islands, and British Hong Kong.

A fleet of six Japanese aircraft carriers and support ships had put to sea from northern Japan almost two weeks earlier, on 26 November, under the command of Admiral Nagumo, and had sailed across the Pacific in total secrecy towards Hawaii.

On 7 December 1941 Japan initiated its Pacific War with the surprise attack on Pearl Harbor and implemented its plan to advance southwards to seize strategic islands and create the Southern Strategic Area, possession of which would allow Japan to dominate East Asia. The Pearl Harbor attack was intended to destroy the US Pacific Fleet so it could not impede that operation.

183 Japanese aircraft were launched at 0600 from the six Japanese carriers for the first wave of the now infamous raid. Just after 0700, an American radar operator in Hawaii spotted a huge flight of aircraft to the north on his screen. Alerting his superior, he was told that the planes were American B-17s *en route* from California. There was no coordinated system of American aerial reconnaissance in place at this time.

Just after 0800 the first wave of Japanese bombers and fighters swept across Pearl Harbor – taking everyone by complete surprise. Some Japanese aircraft headed for the military airfields where hundreds of largely unprotected US planes were neatly lined up in rows. A second wave of 167 Japanese aircraft followed at 0845.

The largest Japanese group attacked US Pacific Fleet warships lined up in Battleship Row. The battleship USS *Arizona* exploded from a bomb hit at the forward magazine, killing 1,177 officers and men; 429 men were trapped inside the battleship USS *Oklahoma* as she capsized after flooding caused by torpedo strikes. The battleship USS *West Virginia* was engulfed in flames, and the battleship USS *California* sank and settled on the bottom in shallow water. The other four battleships in the port were all damaged, with the crippled USS *Nevada* being successfully beached. By the time the assault was over, eight battleships and many smaller vessels were sunk or badly damaged; 2,403 Americans had been killed and 1,178 wounded.

Although an apparently stunning tactical success for Japan, strategically the attack was less significant. The vast fuel dumps for the Pacific Fleet had not been damaged, and the powerful American aircraft carriers, which had been away at sea that day, had not been located or damaged. They would play a pivotal role in the re-conquest of the Pacific at Japanese strongholds such as Truk and Palau.

Instead of launching a third wave to destroy the American fuel dumps and vital repair facilities, which would have rendered the whole base at Hawaii useless, and rather than hunting down the four now vulnerable American carriers, Admiral Nagumo withdrew his fleet to safety. Hawaii would remain a powerful naval base, a submarine and intelligence base which was later instrumental in Japan's defeat. Rather than crippling American naval power in the Pacific for long enough to allow Japan to secure its position, the raid had left

Hawaii – and American naval power in the Pacific – largely intact. The attack now brought America into the war in the Pacific and Asia.

Japanese forces had also gathered for an assault on British Hong Kong, which had only a garrison of six battalions, artillery and some volunteer units. As the siege of Hong Kong Island began, the small garrison was not expected to hold out long.

In the Philippines, despite intelligence having been passed to American forces about the raid on Pearl Harbor, the US Army Air Force was still caught by surprise as Japanese carrier-launched aircraft swooped in from the sea on the opening day to find US bombers and fighters parked wing to wing in neat rows at their air bases; many were destroyed on the ground in the opening attacks. Simultaneously, Japanese troops were landing at several points along the Philippine coastline.

Back off southern Siam, at about 0220 on 8 December, the main Japanese invasion troop convoy anchored off Singora, just north of the Malay border with Thailand. Japanese assault troops went ashore by landing craft, and the light Thai resistance ended after just a few hours. The Japanese advance down the Malayan peninsula was dramatic and speedy, and the British fortress of Singapore would fall on 14 February 1942.

# CHAPTER TWO
# The Japanese Naval Base of Palau

A major airfield construction programme had begun on Palau in 1939 that would enable long-range air strikes against American and British Pacific holdings. Then, in June 1940, the IJN 4th Fleet had established its HQ at Truk, tasked with developing the air and sea infrastructure necessary for the Combined Fleet to operate throughout the Inner South Seas. The whole operational area was divided into four sectors, each with its own Base Force. Koror in Palau was set up as the HQ for the 3rd Base Force.

The sheltered anchorages inside the Palau lagoon had been identified by the Japanese as some of the most suitable in the whole western Carolines and so pre-existing plans were implemented to create a major strategic forward shipping facility and fuelling station. Fuel and ammunition storage facilities were constructed along with docks suitable for merchant ships. IJN destroyers and submarines could use the shoreside docks and workshops whilst larger naval units would anchor offshore and be victualed by lighters

Palau's air capability was beefed up to allow handling of large numbers of land based aircraft as well as seaplanes. Coastal defence gun batteries were installed both in elevated positions as well as in caves down at the water level, to protect important shipping passages and anchorages. A major airfield was installed at the southern Palauan island of Peleliu, and a seaplane base at Arakabesan. Plans were developed for further airstrips on Babelthuap.

On 5 November 1941, just one month before Japan would begin her Pacific War with the surprise attack on Pearl Harbor, Palau, Truk and Ponape in the Carolines were formally approved as supply bases for Admiral Isoruko Yamamoto's Combined Fleet along with bases in the Marshall and Mariana Islands. Admiral I. Takahashi's 3rd Fleet, an amphibious force of carriers, cruisers and destroyers, with the battleships and heavy cruisers of the 2nd Fleet providing cover, staged from Palau for the invasion of the Philippines. Following the successful Philippines and Netherlands East Indies operations, as well as being an important shipping centre and convoy gathering point, Palau also became an important base for air reconnaissance operations and for staging of amphibious forces for other invasion operations.

Admiral C. Nagumo's 1st Air Fleet was based in Palau – and its four carriers sortied from Palau to strike against Port Darwin in the Northern Territory of Australia, again supported by the battleships and heavy cruisers of the 2nd Fleet.

As the Pacific War developed in the years following Pearl Harbor, Palau became an increasingly important staging and refuelling post for merchant shipping moving in convoy between Japan and the distant perimeter garrisons such as New Guinea and Rabaul. Palau became an important strategic port for the New Guinea operation and became a base for three naval escort squadrons. The 1st Escort Squadron of destroyers, mine sweepers, sub chasers and gunboats covered the vast spaces between Palau, the Philippines, East Indies and Japan.

| | | |
|---|---|---|
| 1  IJN *Akashi* | 9   IJN *Iro* | 17  IJN *Sata* |
| 2  IJN *Amatsu Maru* | 10  *Kamikaze Maru* | 18  *Teshio Maru* |
| 3  *Bichu Maru* | 11  *Kibi Maru* | 19  IJN *T.I* |
| 4  Auxiliary Subchasers | 12  *Nagisan Maru* | 20  Type F Unidentified *Maru* |
| 5  *Chuyo Maru* | 13  *Nissho Maru No.5* | 21  *Urakami Maru* |
| 6  Diahatsu Landing Craft | 14  USS *Perry* | 22  IJN *Wakatake* |
| 7  *Gozan Maru* | 15  *Raizan Maru* | |
| 8  The Helmet Wreck | 16  *Ryuko Maru* | |

 **JAPANESE AIRCRAFT WRECKS OF PALAU**

| | |
|---|---|
| a  Aichi E13A Jake | b  Mitsubishi A6M Zero Fighter |
| c  Mitsubishi A6M Zero Fighter | d  Vought F4U Corsair |

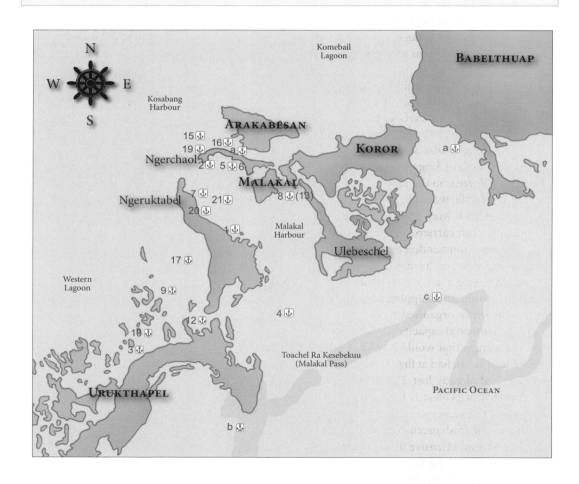

Chart of Malakal Harbor. For wrecks outwith the immediate harbor area see chart on p12.

The first strikes of the Japanese offensive of December 1941 had been stunningly successful and had cost the Japanese only relatively light casualties. The apparent weakness of American and British military power had in Japanese eyes been demonstrated by victories such as the attack on Pearl Harbor and the subsequent Fall of Singapore a few months later. As a result, the Japanese military determined to embark on a second offensive aimed at seizing Tulagi in the Solomon Islands and Port Moresby on the southern tip of Papua New Guinea. Success in this second offensive would give Japan mastery of the air above the vital Coral Sea – which lies between north-east Australia and the bounding island groups of New Caledonia and Vanuatu to the east and the Solomon Islands and Papua New Guinea to the north. Gaining control of these strategically important bases would prevent an Allied build-up of forces in Australia and would secure Japan's southern flank.

If those assaults were successful, then in a second phase to this operation the IJN Combined Fleet would cross the Pacific to annihilate the remains of the American Pacific Fleet and capture Midway Island and the western Aleutian Islands. A ribbon defence anchored at Attu, Midway, Wake, the Marshall Islands and the Gilbert Islands would be set up – followed by the invasion of New Caledonia, Fiji and Samoa to isolate Australia.

Japanese military commanders felt that with the American fleet crippled at Pearl Harbor, these new Japanese conquests could be made impregnable. It was hoped that, tiring of a futile war, the Americans would negotiate a peace that would leave Japan as masters of the Pacific.

The Pacific War would be the greatest naval war in history with mastery of the vast expanses of the Pacific the prize – but unknown to most at the time, it was to be a time of great change in naval warfare. The end of the era of the battleship had already been heralded on 10 December 1941 with the sinking, in one action, of the brand new British battleship HMS *Prince of Wales* and the battlecruiser HMS *Repulse* with great loss of life, almost 200 miles north of Singapore in a massed attack by 85 Japanese torpedo- and high-altitude bombers. Whereas in the past naval warfare had focused on the big guns of battleships, this war in the Pacific would be different – it would be an air war at sea. The Battle of the Coral Sea from 4 to 8 May 1942 would be the first of these new-style actions, fought entirely between aircraft carriers, in which no ship sighted the enemy.

Japanese commanders however failed to understand that their plans to carve out a Pacific empire depended on having an adequate sea supply system to support the distant perimeter – and on having the naval and air power required to protect the consequent long lines of communication and shipping supply. Japan's merchant tonnage was in fact insufficient and too inefficiently organised to meet these sea supply requirements. In addition, it did not have the industrial capacity or manpower necessary to build the large numbers of additional merchant ships that would be required to service and supply the distant perimeter.

Whilst Japan had at first a clear numerical superiority in both aircraft and pilots, by April 1942 it had already lost 315 naval planes in combat with another 540 lost operationally. With a lack of protected fuel tanks, when a Japanese aircraft was hit, even by small arms fire, it had a tendency to burst into flames with the loss of both the aircraft and the crew. The quality of the fresh green crew replacements was noticeably lower.

The second offensive would fatally overextend Japanese military capabilities.

The Battle of the Coral Sea heralded the beginning of the new era – one in which air power projected from aircraft carriers would dominate naval warfare. Despite heavier losses for the Americans, the Battle of the Coral Sea was an American strategic victory, with heavy damage being sustained by the Japanese carrier *Shōkaku*, the light carrier *Shōhō* and heavy loss to aircraft from the carrier *Zuikaku*.

The bitter defeat by American forces in the decisive outcome of the Battle of the Coral Sea led to the retreat of the Japanese fleet and the abandonment of its amphibious operation to take Port Moresby. Both damaged Japanese fleet carriers would be kept out of the Japanese battle order for the Battle of Midway just a few weeks later in early June 1942 – and this turned out to be a decisive disadvantage. Four Japanese carriers, *Akagi*, *Kaga*, *Sōryū* and *Hiryū* (all part of the six-carrier force that had attacked Pearl Harbor six months earlier) and one heavy cruiser were sunk at Midway – for the loss of just one American carrier, USS *Yorktown*.

From the Battle of Midway onwards, Japan's expansionist aims were ended – and in fact, Japan had by now already lost the ability to win the war. Japan did continue to try to secure more strategic territory in the Pacific – but the cumulative effect of the Battles of the Coral Sea and Midway had reduced its ability to undertake major offensives. The Battle of Midway paved the way for US landings on Guadalcanal from 7 August 1942 to 9 February 1943, and for the bitter Solomon Islands campaign.

The summer of 1943 marked the end of the period in which the USA had been strategically on the defensive in the Pacific War. The US position in the Aleutian Islands was secure, vital supply lines to the south and south-west Pacific were protected by air and naval bases in the Solomon Islands and New Guinea. Japanese forces were being slowly driven back.

By the end of 1943, Japan had lost important forward naval and air bases and suffered attrition of its naval and air forces to such an extent that it prevented it from building up its offensive power for further assaults. US forces however were by now building and strengthening rapidly towards a level that would permit a major offensive – although they still lacked advanced positions from which essential Japanese supply lines could be attacked or the Japanese homeland be threatened.

American commanders determined that US forces would advance westwards, taking a number of Japanese holdings which they could use to launch major raids against Japanese key positions such as Truk and the Marianas. America aimed to seize control of the Gilbert and Marshall Islands and secure a staging area for an attack on the Caroline Islands.

The Japanese were well aware that there would be an eventual American attack on the Gilbert and Marshall Islands area, and in May 1943 to defend this outer line had prepared the Z Plan, in which the Combined Fleet based at Truk would assist land-based aircraft and troops garrisoned in the islands.

During the summer of 1943, the Japanese position in the Solomon Islands deteriorated to such an extent that the Z Plan had to be modified by removing the Bismarck, Gilbert and Marshall Islands from the vital areas that its powerful fleet would defend. Notwithstanding that the fleet would not assist in the Gilberts and the Marshalls, land-based island garrisons would be reinforced so that they could put up a prolonged resistance. Plans were developed to redeploy land-based aircraft from flank areas to meet any attack as it developed.

Japan also had to consider the possibility that the Allies would accelerate their attacks in the Solomon Islands or New Guinea areas, where Japanese forces were already losing ground slowly. The USA held the initiative – it had a choice of several widely separated objectives in a theatre of war whose geography allowed full use of its superior naval and air power.

By September 1943, Japanese High Command had completely abandoned its offensive strategy and was consolidating its positions into a defensive perimeter known as the 'Absolute National Defence Sphere'. This perimeter extended from Timor to Western New Guinea to Truk to the Marianas. As part of this Defence Sphere, the Japanese army would be deployed in numbers to build up, fortify and strengthen all key islands in the Caroline and the Marshall Islands.

Approximately 40 battalions of 2,000 men each were reorganised from various units in Japan, Manchuria and the Philippines into South Sea Detachments, and amphibious brigades were moved into the islands. Each island garrison was tasked to resist the Allies independently until reinforcements arrived – making it possible to free up most of the Combined Fleet for the 'Decisive Battle' advocated by Admiral Koga, the commander-in-chief of the Imperial Japanese Navy. He wanted to engage and annihilate the US fleet in one massive confrontation, a decisive battle – and his attempts to do so were based on the belief that the Allies would attack the Inner South Seas first.

Initial attempts by the Japanese to confront US naval forces in the Decisive Battle failed, and in early November 1943, US carrier aircraft badly damaged the heavy cruisers *Mogami*, *Maya*, *Takao* and *Atago*, which were forced to withdraw to Truk for repair. Allied air attacks against the now vulnerable Japanese stronghold at Rabaul caused heavy losses to Japanese aircraft, and most of those left undamaged were pulled out and sent to Truk for reorganisation. No further attempts to send Combined Fleet naval units to Rabaul would be made – the Rabaul garrison of approximately 90,000 Japanese military personnel would be left cut off and isolated until the end of the war.

Up until the fall of the Gilbert Islands and the Marshall Islands in late 1943/early 1944, the Palaus had been well to the rear of any forward combat operations, being used mainly as a shipping assembly and refuelling base from where troops and naval units would be deployed to the front line in the south-west and central Pacific.

However, with the fall of the Gilberts and attacks on outposts such as Kwajalein, strategically vital island garrisons of the Absolute National Defence Sphere such as Palau would be reinforced by the IJA and held at all costs. The Japanese army thus took over the defence of Palau as part of its overall responsibility for defence of the central Pacific islands. Lieutenant General Hideyoshi Obata of the IJA 31st Army headquartered in Guam was given command.

When it appeared that the Palau Islands would become the focus of possible US amphibious landings, the IJA 35th Division was initially assigned to their defence. Allied advances in New Guinea, however, forced the Japanese to divert the majority of the 35th Division to Western New Guinea, and the 14th Division was then ordered to Palau.

The 14th Division was a battle-hardened major army unit that had previously been deployed in Manchuria against Chinese and Soviet forces. They were ordered to defend the Palaus and Yap atoll to the last man. The division arrived on Palau on 24 April 1944 and its HQ was established at Koror. Together with the 1st Amphibious Brigade and other IJA service personnel already on the islands, a total of nearly 35,000 troops had been stationed in the Palaus, and a further 10,000 on Yap.

The Japanese deployed some 25,000 troops on the main island of Babelthuap, which it was believed would be the primary objective for any Allied assault. A further 10,500 troops were stationed on the southern island of Peleliu and 1,400 on Angaur. The army requisitioned civilian buildings that were required for military purposes, dispossessed local inhabitants from their land and quickly began to further fortify the island defences.

Japan determined to depart from the previous strategy of trying to stop US amphibious troops on the invasion beaches. The softening-up 'Spruance haircut' pre-invasion naval and air bombardment, lasting a number of days, had been catastrophic for the Japanese defenders in previous Allied amphibious assaults, and that tactic was abandoned.

This time, in place of the beach defence strategy there would only be light Japanese resistance on the landing beaches as a delaying tactic. The main bulk of the Japanese defensive garrison would weather the bombardment deep below ground in pre-prepared caves and fortified shelter positions. A naval bombardment would cause them little difficulty – and once the US troops were ashore and moving inland, a sustained campaign could be waged from the relative safety of these almost perfect defensive positions.

The Japanese dug out natural caves, extended and enlarged them and dug smaller passages to tunnel entrances situated at strategic positions that gave a good field of fire over the surrounding terrain. Other man-made caves and tunnels were dug out to make an interconnecting system. Gun emplacements were set up and rooms carved out of the tunnels to serve as medical stations, ammunition and munitions stores; command posts and communication centres were set up. In the high limestone ridges of the southern island of Peleliu alone, a honeycomb of some 500 caves was created. Other tunnels were dug deeper into a larger underground system through which troops could quickly be deployed or withdrawn as circumstances dictated. Larger tunnels allowed for artillery and heavy weapons to be moved from one position to the next.

The cave systems such as at Peleliu were built on multiple levels and featured hidden escape routes. Sharp 90-degree changes of direction were built in that would give infantry protection from US rifle fire as well as from artillery and grenade blasts and the much-feared flame thrower. Water, food and ammunition were stockpiled for a prolonged campaign. Beer was also kept in large quantities to ease the rigours of cave life; Japan aimed for the bulk of its troops hidden in reserve to survive the pre-invasion naval and air bombardment of the landing beaches. Once the Allied troops were ashore, Japanese troops could emerge from their hidden positions and choose their time to counter-attack the American invaders.

The aim was to delay the American thrust in the western Pacific by prolonging the defence of the islands. This cave defence strategy would culminate in the 73-day-long Battle of Peleliu in September to November 1944, which would leave some 9,800 US ground troops killed or wounded and some 2,900 IJA troops still missing in action to this day, most still inside the cave complexes sealed up or collapsed and destroyed by the Americans. It was a brutal, bloody battle – one that was called the toughest battle of the Pacific campaign by veteran marines.

# CHAPTER THREE

# Rainbow 5: Operations Galvanic, Flintlock and Catchpole

## AMERICAN FORCES ADVANCE WEST ACROSS THE PACIFIC

American efforts to break Japanese military and diplomatic codes, code-named Operation *Magic*, had been ongoing since the 1920s – and during the 1930s an extensive network of listening stations had been set up in the Pacific. As part of this operation, in 1942, during the run-up to the Battle of the Coral Sea, the US cracked a minor Japanese code – and a US radio monitoring station on Hawaii picked up the Japanese harbourmaster at Truk Lagoon routinely transmitting in this code. US Intelligence was able to monitor the coded transmissions, establishing the names of the Japanese aircraft carriers and the times they left Truk Lagoon – critical intelligence of huge significance in the Battle of the Coral Sea itself. Even after the battle, the Truk harbourmaster continued a strict regime of radioing arrival and departures of ships.

After the Battle of Midway, Admiral Nimitz and General MacArthur determined that Japanese forces should be kept off-balance by an aggressive counter-offensive and in 1943 they planned a systematic annihilation of the Japanese Pacific garrisons. It had by then become obvious to US strategists that Truk was a main staging area for Japanese supplies of men and machines into the southern Pacific. Truk supplied the former German colony of Rabaul on Papua New Guinea, some 700 nautical miles south of Truk, which had been mandated to Australia after World War I but successfully invaded by Japan in 1942. Rabaul had become the main base for Japanese military and naval activity in the South Pacific. From Rabaul, Japanese troop reinforcements had been sent to reinforce the Guadalcanal garrison holding out against the American attempts to take the island.

During the 1920s and 1930s the US Joint Army and Navy Board developed a number of colour-coded strategic war plans to meet perceived hypothetical war scenarios. War Plan Orange was a series of many contingency plans for fighting a war with Japan alone, whilst War Plan Red was a plan for a hypothetical war against Britain and Canada. Following the events in Europe in 1938 and 1939, US war planners realised that the USA faced the possibility of war on a number of fronts against multiple enemies and thus developed a new series of war plans, the Rainbow plans, a word play on the multiplicity of the previous colour-coded plans.

Rainbow 5 formed the basis of American strategy in World War II, assuming that the USA was allied with Britain and France and providing for American offensive operations. Rainbow 5 was based on the Plan Dog memorandum of 1940 that set out the main options for dealing with a two-front war against Germany and Italy in Europe and Japan in the

Pacific. The US Navy basic war plan – Rainbow No. 5 – was finalised in May 1941 and set out the general tasks assigned for the Navy; these included the destruction of Axis sea communications in the Western Atlantic, in the Pacific area and in the Far East area as well as preparations to capture other strategic goals such as the Marshall and Caroline Islands.

The US Central Pacific Force was created for these offensive operations, and included aircraft carriers, battleships and an amphibious force. Long-range, fast carrier striking task forces were crucial to these American naval plans. The Central Pacific Force was redesignated the 5th Fleet in March 1943.

The US 3rd Fleet had been formed on 15 March 1943 under the command of Admiral William F. Halsey, and the ships of the 3rd Fleet formed the basis of the 5th Fleet – the Big Blue Fleet. Command of the 5th Fleet was given to Admiral Raymond A. Spruance – who alternated command with Admiral Halsey to allow the other admiral and his staff to plan for future operations. When the 5th Fleet was under the command of Admiral Halsey it was called the 3rd Fleet – and this nomenclature helped confuse the Japanese into thinking there were actually two separate fleets.

Seizure of the Gilbert Islands by simultaneous attacks on Nauru, Tarawa and Makin would be followed by capture of the Marshall Islands. Next up would be Ponape, the last Japanese position to protect Truk from any westward advance. Destruction of the naval and air power of Truk would be the next target. The Carolines controlled the central Pacific – and Truk controlled the Carolines. In order to take Truk, the seizure of other Japanese strongholds to the south-east of the Carolines would be required, as would the reduction of Japanese bases as far as Woleai, Yap and Palau.

A successful conquest of the Palau Islands would give US forces a naval base and airfields from where they could directly threaten Japan's most important holdings, the Philippines, just over 500 nautical miles away to the west.

The Allied timetable to implement their Rainbow 5 plan formulated during 1943 provided for an assault of the Marshall Islands on 1 January 1944. This would be followed by the seizure of Ponape on 1 June 1944 and then the seizure of Truk on 1 September 1944. Palau would be assaulted on 31 December 1944.

(In the event, the Marshall Islands were seized ahead of schedule in November 1943, and Truk was not invaded but was neutralised by Operation *Hailstone* in February 1944, then bypassed. The main Palauan island of Babelthuap was not invaded, but US ground troops went ashore at the two southern Palauan islands of Peleliu and Angaur, three months ahead of schedule in September 1944.)

The most vulnerable strategic Japanese-held islands and atolls in these island groups would be assaulted, taken and used for airstrips and US fleet anchorages. Better-defended atolls, strategically unimportant islands or those where heavy casualties had to be expected would not be invaded; they would be neutralised by air strikes and rendered useless to the Japanese. This was the eventual fate that awaited the Japanese garrison at Truk.

## OPERATION GALVANIC: TARAWA AND MAKIN, 1943

The joint chiefs directed Admiral Chester Nimitz to prepare plans for the first offensive operation of Rainbow 5, amphibious assaults against Tarawa and Makin in the Gilberts, code-named Operation *Galvanic*. Tarawa and Makin were to be taken by November 1943. The Marshall Islands would be taken in a following operation in early 1944.

The Northern Attack Force, Task Force 52, sailed from Pearl Harbor, refuelling at sea *en route* to attack Makin, the most northern of the Gilberts. The Southern Attack Force, Task Force 53, sailed on 16 November from New Zealand for Tarawa.

The third column was the Fast Carrier Force's Pacific Fleet (Task Force 50), the predecessor of Task Forces 38 and 58.

At this time there was little hard intelligence about the Japanese forward base capabilities at Truk – it had been closed to outsiders since the end of World War I – but its possibilities exerted a strong pull on American strategic thinking. It was known that Truk was a large air base, and intelligence sources reported up to 300 Japanese aircraft based there. The lagoon had also been reported by US listening posts to be busy with surface warships. Accordingly, three US submarines were tasked to take station off Truk and report on any sortie by Japanese warships – it was not yet appreciated just how crippled the Japanese Combined Fleet was as a result of the losses of the carrier-based aircraft used during Japan's defence of Rabaul. The loss to Japan of these carrier aircraft would be pivotal in the eventual US air strikes against Truk – when those aircraft were not available to repulse the American aerial assault.

## THE BATTLE OF TARAWA, 20–23 NOVEMBER 1943

The amphibious assault on Tarawa was the first time that US amphibious forces had faced determined enemy opposition. The 4,800 Japanese defenders were well dug in, well supplied and well prepared – and they fought with fanatical determination almost to the last man against an assault force of some 18,000 US Marines. Only 1 officer and 16 men surrendered out of the entire force of 4,800.

The US Marine Corps suffered some 3,300 casualties with almost 1,000 marines killed in action during the 76 hours of the battle. The severe losses encountered in Tarawa were a terrible blow and caused US commanders to reassess future amphibious assaults. If Tarawa was supposed to have been a minor operation, what would strongholds such as Truk involve?

As part of Rainbow 5, America wanted to get into strategic positions in Formosa (now Taiwan), Luzon and China that would allow direct bombing of the Japanese homeland. The Joint Chiefs of Staff determined that the most feasible approach to do so was by way of the Marianas, the Carolines, Palau and Mindanao. It was recognised however that the large, easily defendable and rugged southern Mariana Islands would take a heavy toll on any US amphibious assault forces. There was not yet any support available from Allied land-based aircraft – as no airfields were held in range. All assault operations would therefore have to be exclusively sea-based. Any Allied operations in the Mariana Islands however would be open to attack by Japanese medium bombers protected by fighters flying from Japanese airfields in Iwo Jima.

Although initially a land invasion of Truk had been called for, in the light of the costly Tarawa experience a decision was made to depart from the strategic plan, and neutralise but not invade Truk and other Caroline Islands targets. The Palau Islands would also have to be neutralised as naval and air bases at this stage, as Japanese aircraft from air bases there could threaten US naval units.

The US occupation of Saipan, Tinian and Guam was scheduled to commence on 15 June 1944 and the occupation of the Palau Islands scheduled to start on 15 September 1944, with the objective being to control the eastern approaches to the Philippines and Formosa and to establish US fleet and air bases there.

If this could be accomplished it would allow the very long-range bombing of Japan itself to begin.

## OPERATIONS FLINTLOCK AND CATCHPOLE: JANUARY–FEBRUARY 1944

The Marshall Islands campaign was designated Operation *Flintlock*, and involved attacks on seven islands, bypassing many more, in nine phases, the main phase being the capture of Kwajalein and Majuro Atolls. Kwajalein lay just under 1,000 nautical miles east of Truk Lagoon – whilst Truk itself lay just over 1,000 nautical miles to the east of Palau. A decision was made that Nauru, a small island of just eight square miles with an airfield (held by the Japanese since August 1942), would not be invaded as it was too close to Truk – which likely harboured the Japanese Combined Fleet. Contingency plans were drawn up for a possible sortie of the Combined Fleet from Truk but Nauru would be neutralised and then bypassed and 'left to wither on the vine'. Once the Gilbert and Solomon Islands had been taken, it was believed that Nauru would be useless for the Japanese and therefore could simply be bypassed.

A second phase to the Marshall Islands campaign, Operation *Catchpole*, would involve the capture of Eniwetok and remaining islands.

Operations *Flintlock* and *Catchpole* would develop lessons learned from the earlier Operation *Galvanic* of November 1943 – and US forces were better prepared for what they could now expect to face.

On 31 January 1944, as a softening-up for the amphibious assault, the big naval guns of battleships, cruisers and destroyers along with carrier-based aircraft gave the low-lying Kwajalein Atoll island a Spruance Haircut. After bitter fighting but comparatively few casualties, Kwajalein was secured on 3 February 1944. Next up after Kwajalein – Truk.

In the face of this powerful, seemingly irresistible, US onslaught, the Japanese command effectively wrote off the Marshall Islands – the island garrisons were ordered to fight a holding action to delay US progress as much as possible.

Japanese aircraft losses were at a critically high level following the ill-fated deployment of carrier aircraft to defend Rabaul – and Japanese commanders now considered the remaining air cover as inadequate for Combined Fleet operations at sea.

At the start of the war the Japanese Zero fighter had been virtually untouchable by Allied aircraft, giving Japanese aircraft air superiority. However, the latest new American fighters rolling off the production lines and entering combat now totally outclassed the Zero and other Japanese aircraft, which were all based on now outmoded 1930s designs. Allied air power now grew to dominate all encounters with Japanese aircraft.

Although several Japanese carriers had been lost to enemy action, there were still Japanese fleet carriers available – but heavy losses of experienced pilots and their outdated planes made them ineffective. With insufficient air cover, there was no alternative but for the Combined Fleet to hole up in the perceived safety of the Truk Lagoon fortress. The Combined Fleet warships were now virtually immobilised at Truk Lagoon.

In the face of the American onslaught, the Japanese had been pushed into a defensive role – a situation they had never planned for with their early offensive strategy. Their Defence Sphere perimeter was pierced – then crushed. Their small garrisons on the outer

Pacific islands, at best designed to harass American supply lines and gather intelligence, were obliterated.

On 5 January 1944 14,000 IJA troops arrived to consolidate Truk's defences against a possible US land invasion that Japanese Intelligence believed would possibly be made around 21 February 1944. Three of the five passes into the 140-mile circumference barrier reef of Truk Lagoon were mined. The remaining two navigable passes, one to the north and one to the south, were protected by coastal defence guns and Kaiten suicide units. As Truk now became vulnerable to Allied attack, Admiral Koga, based in Truk, began dispersing units of the Combined Fleet westwards, away from the American advance to safety. Some 2nd Fleet naval units were sent west towards Palau, which was at this point still out of range of US land-based and carrier aircraft. Palau became the 2nd Fleet HQ.

The battleships *Nagato* and *Fusō* and escort destroyers left Truk westbound for Palau on 1 February 1944, and the super-battleship *Yamato*, along with other battleships, cruisers and destroyers, left on 3 February 1944. Admiral Koga remained at Truk aboard his flagship, the battleship *Musashi*.

# CHAPTER FOUR

# Truk Lagoon

## OPERATION HAILSTONE, 17/18 FEBRUARY 1944

Truk was Japan's forward naval and air base, lying just over 1,000 nautical miles east of Palau. During the early part of World War II, although aware of Truk's strategic location, the Allies knew very little about it and its importance to Japan. But they knew of its excellent natural defences – Truk became known as the 'Gibraltar of the Pacific'.

The Battle for the Coral Sea confirmed American suspicions that Truk was a major harbour for the Japanese Imperial Navy. It was believed that there was also a large air base with up to 300 Japanese aircraft based there. But little else was known.

In early 1944, the Japanese began actively building up Truk's defences against an anticipated American amphibious assault. Anti-submarine netting was placed around docks and key anchorages – and coastal defences and AA installations were also increased significantly. Heavy naval coastal defence guns were set in fortified emplacements and in caves on strategic island peaks and promontories.

Now on its back foot, much of the Japanese Combined Fleet had retreated and gathered in their perceived stronghold of Truk Lagoon – amidst frantic efforts to fortify Truk's defences. The scene was set for the showdown.

On the evening of 3 February 1944 two American long-range PB4Y Liberator photo-reconnaissance planes rose into the air from their small Stirling Island airfield in the Solomon Islands for a 2,000-mile round trip to overfly Truk Lagoon and photograph Japanese shipping and land fortifications. The Liberator had four Pratt & Whitney radial engines that gave it a top speed of 300mph – fast for such a big aircraft, and almost as fast as the Japanese Zero fighter. In addition to being a fast aircraft, the Liberator was also well armed, bristling with six turrets holding twin M2 Browning 0.50-inch machine guns. Armour-plating protected the pilot, and it had a service ceiling of 21,000 feet.

After their long flight, the two huge Liberators arrived undetected over Truk Lagoon early the next morning, 4 February 1944. Scattered cloud cover

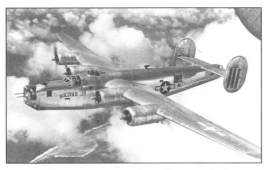

Truk Lagoon was overflown by two USAAF Consolidated B-24M Liberator reconnaissance aircraft on 4 February 1944. Truk's secret was out.
(National Archives)

partially obscured some of the shipping below but through gaps in the cloud it was still possible to take a number of photographs from a height of 20,000 feet.

The US aircraft were spotted; the Dublon Island shore AA battery opened up, soon followed by other shore batteries and some naval AA guns. Caught napping with no patrolling fighters in the air, the Japanese scrambled two or three fast and agile Zero fighters and Rufe seaplane fighters while the battleship *Musashi*, at anchor below, fired on one of the Liberators. Japanese pilots ran to their aircraft as ground crew prepared them for flight – but it would take time to get airborne and climb to 20,000 feet to attack the US aircraft. But the Zeros had a ceiling of more than 30,000 feet and a top speed, slightly faster than the Liberators, of 330mph.

After spending 20–30 minutes overflying and photographing shipping and land fortifications in the lagoon, the two US aircraft turned unscathed to head back to their distant Solomon Islands airbase at full speed – knowing that Japanese fighters would be coming after them.

Belatedly, the hastily scrambled Japanese fighters climbed up from their airfields and started to chase after the US aircraft but as their edge of speed over the Liberators was only slight they were unable to make up the ground on the US aircraft and catch them in time. The Liberators were able to outdistance the Japanese fighters and return the precious film to the Solomon Islands airfield.

The US reconnaissance overflight was enough to convince Admiral Koga, in charge of the Japanese Combined Fleet anchored below in the lagoon, that an attack by the Americans was now imminent and that his Combined Fleet of battleships, aircraft carriers, cruisers, submarines and ancillary craft, the main fighting strength of the Imperial Japanese Navy, was in danger.

Admiral Koga knew that Admiral Nimitz, in charge of the American Central Pacific Fleet, was converging on Truk from the Gilbert and Marshall Islands campaign, and that Nimitz could not bypass Truk without attacking; Nimitz could not leave Truk' s formidable defensive and offensive capabilities to his rear, allowing the Japanese to mount air attacks from behind the Allied front, for its submarines to put to sea, for its warships to attack Allied vessels. Koga believed that the Americans would next attack the Philippines, Guam and Saipan, all to the west of Truk.

Accordingly, on 10 February 1944 he ordered Admiral Kurita's 2nd Fleet to move west to the naval stronghold of Palau. Admiral Ozawa's valuable carrier fleet was sent to the great harbour of Singapore, seized from the British in February 1942 – and much further to the west.

Two of the Japanese carriers in the southerly 6th Fleet anchorage upped anchor and headed south across Truk Lagoon to the South Pass through the barrier reef. Three other carriers anchored in the westerly Combined Fleet anchorage also weighed anchor and proceeded to leave the lagoon through South Pass. The super-battleship *Yamato* and a number of escort cruisers left the lagoon soon after the carriers.

As Admiral Kurita's 2nd Fleet set out on the 1,000-nautical-mile voyage to Palau, Admiral Koga left Truk bound for Japan aboard his flagship, the super-battleship *Musashi*, with four carriers, a number of escort cruisers and destroyers, and several fleet supply ships.

Admiral Koga also ordered part of the 4th Fleet under way from its anchorage to the east of Dublon Island. But not all of the ships' captains had yet been given their sailing orders, and many ships remained in the 4th Fleet anchorage – such as the light cruisers

*Naka, Agano* and *Katori*, the ex-auxiliary cruisers *Aikoku Maru* and *Kiyosumi Maru*, the submarine tenders *Rio de Janeiro Maru* and *Heian Maru* and the destroyers *Fumizuki, Tachikaze, Maikaze, Oite* and *Nowake*, together with an assortment of tankers and cargo vessels.

There was a frantic rush to move fuel from tankers to the shore-based installations and to finish the general re-supplying of the Truk base. The vast cargo holds of the tens of freighters at anchor in the lagoon held valuable cargoes of war munitions, torpedoes, shells, anti-invasion beach mines, tanks, trucks, field artillery and the like, all destined to fortify Truk's land defences against an amphibious assault by the Allies.

The US reconnaissance photographs also revealed the land fortifications of the Japanese stronghold in astounding detail. These photographs permitted the drawing up of a well-coordinated plan of attack on Truk. Suddenly, from not knowing what shipping was at Truk Lagoon before the overflight, it now became instantly clear that nearly all of the Japanese Combined Fleet had been at Truk.

The *Musashi* was clearly identified, along with 2 aircraft carriers, 20 destroyers, 10 cruisers, 12 submarines and more than 50 other surface vessels. US high command immediately advanced plans to attack shipping in the anchorage – the original plan had been for an attack on 15 April 1944.

There was a division of opinion amongst American staff as to whether an amphibious land assault on Truk should be made – or whether Truk should simply be neutralised without a full assault. The overwhelming majority decided against a land assault, as Truk's geography is very much in favour of the defender. It was decided that the next American target for an amphibious assault would be Eniwetok, as its capture would provide an airfield and harbour to support attacks on the Mariana Islands to the north-west. Eniwetok Atoll lay in striking distance of any Japanese aircraft stationed in Truk, and accordingly Operation *Catchpole* (the Eniwetok invasion) and Operation *Hailstone* (the Truk raid) would be coordinated attacks.

Commander-in-Chief of the United States Pacific Fleet Chester Nimitz placed command of the Truk and Eniwetok striking force with Admiral Spruance, who was in charge of the 5th Fleet at that time. Expecting to possibly engage a large section of the Japanese Combined Fleet based in Truk, Admiral Spruance quickly created the Fast Carrier Task Force, Task Force 58, stripping down the enormous force that had gathered for the recent amphibious assault on Kwajalein Atoll. He organised the striking force with six of the newest

Task Force 58 carriers move in line astern towards Truk Lagoon. (National Archives)

and fastest battleships available – with six heavy cruisers, four light cruisers and twenty-seven destroyers for support.

The Fast Carrier Task Force would go on to be the main striking force of the US Pacific Fleet from January 1944 through to the end of the war in August 1945. Naval air power was now dominant, and capital ships, once the main weapon of a fleet, now simply provided support and protection for the carriers.

With Admiral Spruance in overall command of the 5th Fleet, Admiral Mark Mitscher was given operational control of the nine carriers of Task Force 58, made up of *Enterprise*, *Yorktown*, *Essex*, *Intrepid* and *Bunker Hill* along with the four light carriers *Belleau Wood*, *Cabot*, *Monterey* and *Cowpens*. The Carrier Task Force could launch more than 500 combat aircraft.

Task Force 58 was divided into several smaller task groups – each built around three to four aircraft carriers and support vessels such as screening destroyers, cruisers and battleships. The ships of each task group sailed in a formation centred on the carriers – the supporting battleships and cruisers sailing relatively close by to add their AA fire to that of the carriers themselves and counter any surface attack. Screening destroyers operated further out, providing AA fire and defence against submarines. The primary defence of the task group against air attack was the group's own fighter cover.

Task Group 58.4 would soften up Eniwetok whilst Task Groups 58.1, 58.2 and 58.3 would raid Truk. Task Group 50.9, consisting of two battleships along with heavy cruisers and destroyers, would detach from Task Group 58.3 to make a counter-clockwise sweep around the lagoon as the air attacks went in, in order to destroy any enemy vessels that attempted to leave the lagoon.

A US submarine wolf pack was sent to patrol the waters outside Truk Lagoon with orders to remain submerged until the attack – when the submarines would surface as required to rescue any US aviators downed outside the lagoon. The submarines *Tang*, *Sunfish* and *Skate* were tasked to operate south and south-west of the lagoon whilst the *Sea Raven* and *Darter* would be stationed north. The *Aspro*, *Burrfish*, *Dace* and *Gato* would cover the remaining exits from the lagoon. American aviators downed inside the lagoon would be rescued by Kingfisher floatplanes and flown out to the submarines.

In complete contrast to the cockpit armour and protected fuel tanks of the American aircraft, Japanese aircraft had no armour and, worse, unprotected fuel tanks that burst into flames when hit – literally falling from the sky with pilots trapped in the flaming wreck. Faced with American air superiority, Japanese surface vessels rarely had a chance to return to a battle area to search for survivors, so the rate of attrition of Japanese front-line pilots was far higher than for American pilots. Japan paid a heavy price for not better protecting their experienced pilots, as replacements were increasingly green, not battle-hardened, and no match for the experienced American aviators.

American aircraft factories had just started to produce the B-29, an bomber with a flying range of some 3,000 miles, almost the exact distance from Saipan to Tokyo and back. If Guam and the Northern Mariana Islands such as Saipan and Tinian could be taken, their airfields would allow air strikes directly against the Japanese homeland. The Japanese stronghold of Truk, situated some 600 miles south-east of Guam and Saipan, could not be left to operate as a base from which to harass US efforts from the rear.

As the task groups moved towards Truk on 10 February 1944 the US submarine *Permit* reported that heavy ships, believed to be the battleships *Nagato* and *Fusō*, had left Truk –

but the Americans were unaware that by now the majority of the IJN warships had in fact left the lagoon, leaving just a few lighter IJN warships there, along with naval auxiliaries, cargo vessels and tankers. Most of the vessels at anchor in Truk were armed merchantmen.

Every day, unaware of the approach of the American carrier force, more and more Japanese freighters were arriving from Japan or from other beleaguered Japanese strongholds. Supply ships setting off from Japan to reinforce outposts like the Solomon Islands reached Truk – only to learn that the Allies had overrun their destinations.

On the morning of 15 February the Japanese fleet monitoring unit intercepted a radio message from a US carrier pilot to the US carrier *Essex*. The Japanese now knew for certain that at least one carrier was somewhere out there in the vast expanses of the Pacific. An American attack was now suspected and a number of Japanese aircraft were deployed in a search pattern around the lagoon – but the Americans already knew the Japanese search patterns from previously intercepted radio transmissions and took precautions to avoid known search areas.

Just after midday on 15 February, Grumman F6F Hellcat fighters of a combat air patrol shot down a single Japanese long-range reconnaissance Betty bomber some 40 miles due west of the task force. The Betty was shot down so quickly that the crew didn't have time to transmit a warning radio message back to Truk. Another Japanese reconnaissance aircraft was also intercepted and shot down without being able to signal Truk HQ.

When the Betty bomber and the second aircraft from the Japanese air patrol failed to return, at 0230 on 16 February Vice Admiral Koboyashi, Commander of the 4th Fleet, ordered the Truk defences to their highest state of alert. At 0500, five Japanese reconnaissance aircraft took off from Moen airfield but they failed to locate any American forces during their patrol and so at 0900 the alarm status was reduced to a regular alarm. After 12 hours, when no attack had come and there was still no sign of the enemy, the alarm was cancelled. Japanese forces were stood down and returned to a state of normal preparedness.

The 53 US warships of Task Force 58 closed on Truk completely undetected and took up station 90 miles east of the lagoon on the evening of 16 February 1944. Each of the nine carriers supported two air groups comprising a combination of Grumman Hellcat fighters, Douglas Dauntless dive-bombers and Grumman Avenger torpedo-bombers. The two air groups would alternate combat duties to minimise aircrew fatigue, and over the two days of the coming Truk raid, 30 waves of attacking aircraft would continuously bomb and strafe any shipping they encountered and destroy shore facilities. Operation *Hailstone* was scheduled to commence before dawn the following day, 17 February 1944 – designated Dog-Day Minus One.

American commanders knew that they had to gain air superiority before committing to an aerial bombing and torpedo attack on the shipping and land installations. Thus, the opening move of the assault would be an initial fighter sweep to destroy Truk's airfields and aircraft.

Just over one hour before dawn on 17 February 1944, between 0440 and 0454 (local time), the first 12 Grumman Hellcat fighters of a combined group strike force of 72 Hellcats, started to take off from the Task Group 58.1 carrier *Enterprise*. Their launch was timed so that they would arrive over Truk at 0600, just as the sun's first rays were bringing light to the lagoon. Sunrise was at 0609 – sunset would come at 1804. Similar squadrons of Hellcats prepared to take off from the other four strike carriers, *Yorktown*, *Essex*, *Intrepid* and *Bunker Hill*.

The Hellcats from the four light carriers, *Belleau Wood*, *Cabot*, *Monterey* and *Cowpens*, would provide combat air patrols above the warships of the task force at their holding point 90 miles outside the lagoon to deal with any Japanese attack that might materialise – and to act as a reserve force should the need arise.

Task Force 58 carrier USS *Enterprise*.
(National Archives)

The 12 *Yorktown* Hellcats would join the 12 *Enterprise* Hellcats for the low attack sweep at an altitude of 6,000–8,000 feet. The 12 Hellcats lifting into the air from *Essex* would carry out a sweep at 10,000 –15,000 feet along with the 12 Hellcats from *Intrepid*. The 24 Hellcats from *Bunker Hill* would conduct a high-altitude sweep at 25,000 feet.

Once airborne, the groups of 12 strike fighters flew to designated rendezvous points outside the lagoon, where they formed up into their combined striking groups and moved off towards Truk low and fast from a northerly direction at about 1,000 feet above sea level – to avoid Japanese radar. Once they were about 15 minutes' flying time from Truk, the strike groups of Hellcats started to rise up to their designated patrol altitudes.

At 0520, Japanese radar based in Truk detected the approach of a large formation of aircraft, and the Truk commander, Vice Admiral Kobayashi, ordered the highest state of alarm. An initial Japanese analysis of the radar reflections concluded that a large land-based bomber formation was approaching Truk – it wasn't believed that such a large force could be solely carrier-based fighter aircraft.

After about 46 minutes of flight, at about 0600, the first of the 72 Hellcats swept into the skies at 8,000 feet above the two northerly sea passages into the lagoon, North Pass and Northeast Pass. They made an unchallenged circular run around nearly the whole lagoon before encountering any enemy fighters. Once alerted, however, Japanese fighters scrambled and made to rise into the air, striving to quickly gain enough altitude to attack the successive groups of Hellcats that were now arriving over Truk.

As well as dealing with enemy fighters, the Hellcats had been tasked to strafe Japanese airfields to destroy enemy aircraft before they could get into the air, and render the airstrips unserviceable; Japanese air strength had to be sufficiently degraded to allow the slower more vulnerable dive-bombers and torpedo-bombers that would soon follow on to do their job.

The large airfield at the north end of the largest and most northerly island, Moen Island (now Weno), was strafed. From there Hellcats swept south to strafe the seaplane base at the southern end of Moen Island before moving on to Dublon (now Tonoas), the next-largest island just to the south. Other Hellcats vectored further south to strafe the airfields on the much smaller islands of Eten and Param – it was only here that they encountered any airborne enemy planes.

Although Japanese radar had detected the approaching formation about half an hour before the first aircraft reached the fringing coral reefs of the huge lagoon, there were problems with Japanese command and communications. As a result, Eten airfield only learned of the incoming US strike some ten minutes before strafing fire swept the runway and the mass of stationary, parked fighters. The first target, the larger Moen Island airfield, received no warning at all of the attack – the first indication of it was when the Hellcats swept over the runway destroying the valuable Japanese aircraft on the ground.

Having been stood down from highest alert the day before, when at 0530 highest alert was initiated again, most Japanese pilots were in town or in bed – some on different islands from their planes. Japanese aircrew scrambled to get to their aircraft and get airborne as fast as possible – whilst all the time, Hellcats were strafing their immobile Zeros and Nakajima Ki-44 Tōjō and Nakajima A6M2 Rufe seaplane fighters. Desperate to save as many aircraft as possible, officers ordered aircraft mechanics and technicians to take off and head north. On Eten Island airstrip, absent pilots arriving by boat from other islands were beaten up by their second commanding officer. As the local Trukese population on the islands realised the expected attack was now happening, many of them took to caves in the hills.

On the aircraft carrier-shaped Eten Island airfield, there was a congestion of planes that had been offloaded from supply ships – many of which had not yet been assembled. As the Hellcats swept overhead on their strafing runs they found Japanese fighters lined up wingtip to wingtip – easy prey. Many Japanese aircraft started their motors and attempted to take off – but they were shot to pieces as they taxied along the runway, or shot down as they laboured into the sky after taking off.

Despite these losses on the ground, some 80 Japanese fighters finally gained enough altitude to take on the Hellcats – and the sky was soon filled with swirling fighters as dogfights broke out in what would become one of the greatest all-fighter aerial battles of World War II.

In the early days of the war, the Japanese Zero fighter had been untouchable by most other aircraft and superior to the early US fighters, being more manoeuvrable with a rate of climb three times more rapid than any US plane in theatre at the time. The Zero (Allied reporting name Zeke) was by now however simply outclassed by the Grumman F6F Hellcat.

The 12 battle-hardened Hellcats from the *Enterprise*, covering the lowest altitude layer at 8,000 feet where it was expected the heaviest enemy opposition would be, encountered about 47 enemy aircraft rising to intercept them from Moen and Param airfields and the Dublon seaplane base. As the great fighter battle now took place in the skies above Truk, combat reports being fed back from the fighters and other observer planes to their carriers revealed that the Japanese warships that the two Liberator reconnaissance aircraft had spotted 12 days before were nowhere to be seen; the main elements of the Imperial Japanese Navy – the battleships, battlecruisers and carriers and most of the other heavy warships – had escaped the trap and vanished.

Immediately following the initial fighter sweep, successive carrier group strikes of Douglas Dauntless dive-bombers and Grumman Avenger torpedo-bombers, protected by Hellcat fighter escorts, were readied for take-off to attack the vulnerable shipping in the lagoon. In all, six waves of aircraft would lift off from each of the carriers – forming up in the air for six coordinated group strikes spread throughout the day.

Torpedo- and dive-bombers started attacking Japanese shipping in the north Dublon anchorage where some 15 ships were spotted – as well as shipping in the Eten anchorage to the south, where another 15 ships were seen. On the land, airfields, barracks, ammunition and fuel supplies were attacked – on these early raids however, the large land-based fuel tanks would not be attacked. They would be left until later in the day to avoid smoke obscuring the selection of targets.

Just after 0700, Strike 1B aircraft were launched from *Enterprise* and *Yorktown* for the second combined group strike of the day – tasked to target enemy warships, giving priority to battleships, then carriers, heavy cruisers and light cruisers. As they sped towards the lagoon, they attacked two Japanese cruisers about 35 miles north-west of North Pass. These were left damaged and smoking. Another group of warships was spotted about 10 miles north-west of North Pass and also attacked.

Now that air superiority had been achieved, Task Group 50.9, consisting of two battleships and some heavy cruisers and destroyers, detached from Task Group 58.3 and proceeded to make its counter-clockwise sweep around the lagoon to intercept any Japanese vessels trying to leave the lagoon. (It would rendezvous again with Task Group 58.3 early the next morning.) During this sweep, the Japanese cruiser *Katori*, damaged several hours earlier by strike aircraft, was spotted on fire and listing from the earlier air attacks but still under way with her two escort destroyers and minesweeping trawler some 40 miles outside the lagoon.

The TG 50.9 battleships *New Jersey* and *Iowa* along with the cruisers *Minneapolis* and *New Orleans* and the destroyers *Burns* and *Bradford* engaged the Japanese squadron. The US destroyers screening the valuable capital ships fired six salvoes of torpedoes at *Katori* but missed. *Katori* replied with her own torpedoes – which also missed.

The battleship *Iowa* then closed with *Katori* and fired 59 16-inch shells and 129 5-inch shells at the stricken cruiser – quickly straddling her. After being under attack by *Iowa* for just 13 minutes, *Katori* sank stern first.

The last strike, 1F, from *Enterprise* was launched between 1510 and 1520 against aircraft and installations at Moen airfield. The last strikes from *Bunker Hill*, operating with *Cowpens*, were launched around 1520, tasked with degrading Eten Island airfield to render it unserviceable during the night – a time when the task force was potentially vulnerable. Quarter-ton bombs with time-delay fuzes of two to six hours were dropped on the airfield. (Days later, as other time-delay bombs dropped on Param Island airfield were collected by Japanese ground staff, they started to explode – the huge explosions being heard and felt on the neighbouring islands of Dublon and Moen.)

At 1800, as dusk fell over the lagoon and the last US aircraft were returning to the task force, there were reported to be only one Japanese fighter and four other aircraft left in action.

Seven American aviators, who had been shot down over Truk and plucked from the water by Japanese vessels, were taken to Dublon where, in the first of a series of war atrocities, they were killed by firearms and samurai sword.

Although the IJN Combined Fleet had escaped, total air superiority had been achieved. Nevertheless, due to suspected minefields, shore batteries and kamikaze suicide units, the Task Force 58 ships remained well away from the lagoon in open water, protected by their own air support from the carriers *Belleau Wood*, *Cabot* and *Monterey*.

In total, during the first day of the raid some 56 Japanese aircraft had been shot down, with 72 aircraft destroyed on the ground and 225 damaged. The heavily bombed airfields had been rendered useless to the extent that not one Japanese plane would rise to meet the American attackers the following day. Twelve large Japanese ships were believed sunk, with eight others reported as heavily damaged.

At 0207, during the darkness of the early hours of 18 February (code-named Dog-Day), the first radar-guided night torpedo attack was launched from *Enterprise* against Japanese shipping in Truk Lagoon, with twelve Grumman Avenger torpedo-bombers. This night raid would be extremely successful – for the loss of one Avenger bomber in the darkness, eight Japanese ships would be destroyed and five damaged.

Just over an hour before dawn, at about 0455, as on Dog-Day Minus One, a combined group Hellcat fighter sweep was launched from *Enterprise*, *Yorktown*, *Essex* and *Bunker Hill* – timed to arrive over the lagoon just before dawn. The mission for the 57 Hellcats was to seek out and destroy any remaining Japanese airborne opposition and destroy any enemy aircraft found on the ground.

*Enterprise* Hellcats made further strafing runs against Moen, Eten and Param Island airfields before turning to strafe shipping targets. *Yorktown* Hellcats strafed Moen No. 1 airfield without encountering Japanese fighters over the target – destroying nine Nakajima B5N Kate torpedo-bombers, four Mitsubishi G4M Betty bombers and one Zeke.

Ten strafing runs were then made on Eten airfield, where more aircraft were caught on the ground, destroyed and set on fire. The Hellcats then attacked other targets of opportunity such as merchant shipping, pillboxes, destroyers and minesweepers.

As with the attacks of the previous day, immediately following the initial fighter sweep squadrons of Dauntless dive-bombers and Avenger torpedo-bombers escorted by other Hellcats rose into the sky from the carriers, ready to start pounding the beleaguered shipping in the lagoon. Following the previous day's strikes, the remaining serviceable Japanese fighter aircraft were unable to use the runways that were pockmarked by bomb craters from the last attacks of the previous evening. Not one Japanese fighter rose to meet the US air groups – however, accurate AA fire was encountered.

A second group strike launched from the carriers between 0645 and 0700. The third and final group strike was launched from the carriers *Enterprise*, *Bunker Hill* and *Monterey* between 0845 and 0930. By the time aircraft from these last strikes of the day were returning to their carriers, a further 27 ships had been damaged.

In all, over the two days of the assault, according to US figures, between 250 and 275 aircraft had been destroyed, the seaplane base at Moen had been put out of action, 90 per cent of the atoll's fuel supply had been set on fire and all the other airfields and installations were damaged to differing extents. In all, 45 Japanese ships had been sunk – over 220,000 tons of shipping – a two-day record for the entire war.

Rear Admiral Michio Sumikawa, Chief of Staff of the 4th Fleet, reported that there had been 365 aircraft on Truk at the time of the attack and that 235 aircraft had been destroyed on the ground.

The two days of the Operation *Hailstone* raids had achieved all their objectives. Japanese air power had been virtually obliterated, airstrips had been left unusable, and land fortifications were largely smashed. Truk was left as an impotent, demolished enemy base, which the American forces were then able to simply bypass.

The Japanese still believed that an amphibious assault might take place and so the reinforcing and fortification of Truk continued after Operation *Hailstone*. By the end of March 1944, over 30,000 troops had been stationed there.

By mid-April 1944, all construction work on the land defences was complete and those radar units that had been inoperative during Operation *Hailstone* were now in service. For future Allied raids, advance warning was given and valuable equipment could be got under cover and fighters scrambled into the air.

As with Rabaul, Truk would be bypassed and the defenders left isolated and cut off – but any possible resurgence of Japanese air strength at Truk however would still require to be neutralised. As the unstoppable westwards US march across the Pacific gained momentum, the Allies had to ensure that the Japanese in Truk were prevented from getting aircraft airborne to bomb Allied shipping and attack the Allied forces massing in the increasing number of US-held territories such as Eniwetok (north-east of Truk), and the Solomon Islands to the south.

After the Truk raid, Task Force 58 split up, with some ships going on to strike at the Marianas, and *Enterprise* along with the anti-aircraft cruiser *San Diego* and four destroyers going to Majuro.

Just six weeks after Operation *Hailstone*, Task Force 58 would be reformed to assault the Palau Islands on 30 and 31 March 1944 – Operation *Desecrate 1*.

# CHAPTER FIVE

# Operation Desecrate 1

## THE FIRST AIR ASSAULT ON PALAU, 30/31 MARCH 1944

The Japanese regarded the islands of Palau and the Marianas as forming the principal strongpoints in a chain of islands that were their last eastern line of defence.

From the US perspective, Palau and the Mariana Islands were a direct threat to any Allied assault on the Philippines. They gave the Japanese land based air-cover to support naval operations by the large and powerful Japanese Combined Fleet. If Palau and the Marianas could be seized, they would give the Allies bases from which the new long-range US bombers could strike directly at the Japanese home islands. In the summer and latter part of 1944, the Americans would assault these targets sequentially, securing first the Marianas and then Palau on their way to the Philippines.

As naval units of the Combined Fleet headed towards Palau after the US photographic reconnaissance flight of 4 February 1944, it became clear that Palau's role as a rear staging area would now radically change – Palau would now be thrust into the forefront of the action and urgent preparations had to be made. Large quantities of war supplies, bunker oil, munitions and coal were immediately despatched there, and ammunition dumps in Koror, Arakabesan and Peleliu were fully stocked up with fuel; water was stockpiled on Malakal.

The Commander-in-Chief of the Combined Fleet, Admiral Koga, had determined after the 4 February overflight that Truk was now in a much too exposed location for the Combined Fleet, and gave up Truk as a major naval base. On 10 February he left Truk in the battleship *Musashi* for Japan and all the other major IJN vessels also left shortly afterwards, bound for Palau, Japan or Singapore. Those supply ships at Truk that could leave were ordered to Palau.

Admiral Koga liked to base himself at a forward base so that he would be present whenever a fleet operation developed that required his attention – hence his presence at Truk. When he became aware that US long-range bombers could reach Truk, he decided to withdraw to the comparative safety of Palau – where he could remain close to the action.

Directly after the overflight, he returned to Japan from Truk aboard his flagship, the super-battleship *Musashi*. Then on 20 February 1944 the *Musashi* departed Japan with Admiral Koga on board, bound for Palau. As a result of the losses to the 2nd Fleet, *Musashi* gave up its position as independent flagship and was assigned to the 2nd Fleet, which at that point then consisted only of *Musashi*, five or six cruisers and several destroyers. The 2nd Fleet did not have any carriers, but several ships and tenders operated with it – including the repair ship *Akashi*, the oilers *Sata* and *Iro*, and the flying boat tender *Akitsushima*.

The two battleships *Yamato* and *Nagato* came and went from Palau towards the end of February and early March. The Japanese fleet based in Palau maintained a high state of readiness and carried out training exercises inside Palau Lagoon.

Peleliu, the small island to the south of the main Palau island of Babelthuap, was the base for the Japanese Air Flotilla 26, one of two flotillas of its Air Fleet 14, which had suffered heavy losses of aircraft and crew in the defence of Rabaul. It was still in the process of regrouping, and a programme had been started to train new pilots to make up for those lost at Rabaul.

Palau had been selected for the next US fast carrier raid after Truk as the Palauan Islands were only 700 miles north-west of Hollandia, the target of a forthcoming US operation. American strategic planners considered it necessary to deny the Japanese the use of

The powerful Japanese airbase on the southern Palauan island of Peleliu. (National Archives)

Palau as a naval and air base for one month so its aircraft and warships could not threaten the Hollandia operation.

The US formulated a two-pronged plan for the Palau strikes. Whilst any Japanese naval units, aircraft and merchant shipping found there would be destroyed, US carrier aircraft would also drop mines in the Palauan shipping channels and approaches to deny the Japanese use of the great harbour for the required one month period. The main Palauan islands were surrounded by a fringing barrier reef through which there were only three main channels that led to its harbours and anchorages. They would be effectively sealed off and the Palauan harbours closed.

The mines would be laid in two distinct phases. Initially, as the first strikes went in, aerial mines would be dropped with parachutes from Grumman Avenger aircraft in the three main channels through the reef. This timing was designed to prevent enemy shipping escaping from attack in the lagoon; these were moored magnetic mines with arming-delay periods of less than an hour.

In the second phase, hard-to-detect ground mines with arming delays of up to one month would be dropped in the most important anchorages and channels inside the Palau Lagoon and also in the approaches, to close off the islands to the Japanese for one or two months after the air strikes. The arming delay periods for the mines would prevent the Japanese from clearing the shipping channels for a month after the raid – but they would also be uncertain for some time after that if all had been cleared. The Japanese had no clear idea of how the American mines operated, and in fact had no equipment available in Palau to sweep the mines.

Twelve US submarines were sent to patrol around Palau and intercept any Japanese vessels that might try to flee Palau as the 5th Fleet approached and attacked.

The date for the US raid on Palau was set as 1 April 1944.

The US Pacific 5th Fleet was under the general command of Admiral Raymond Spruance – whilst the four task groups of the Fast Carrier Force, Task Force 58, were under the command of Rear Admiral M.A. Mitscher. Admiral Spruance produced an operations plan whereby three of the four carrier groups of Task Force 58 would be used to attack Palau and the less important bases of Woleai, Yap and Ulithi. The powerful task force was assembled from 5th Fleet ships staging at the eastern Majuro Atoll anchorage and others operating elsewhere in the South Pacific.

Task Group 58.1: Following the Truk raid, the battle-hardened *Enterprise* had patrolled the New Hebrides island chain, and then taken part in the unopposed landing in Emirau. A Catalina flying boat dropped a container with her new orders onto her flight deck on 26 March; she immediately turned to the north-east and sped to join Task Force 58. The *Independence*-class flat-top *Cowpens* joined TG58.1 the following day, with its battle-hardened and much respected Air Group 25. The carrier *Belleau Wood* completed the task group, along with the cruisers *Santa Fe*, *Mobile*, *Biloxi* and *Oakland* and a screen of destroyers.

Task Group 58.2 was comprised of the carriers *Bunker Hill*, *Monterey*, *Hornet* and *Cabot*, escorted by the battleships *Iowa* and *New Jersey*, the cruisers *Wichita*, *San Francisco*, *Minneapolis*, *New Orleans*, *Boston* and *Baltimore*, and a destroyer screen

Task Group 58.3 comprised the carriers *Yorktown*, *Princeton*, *Lexington* and *Langley* with the battleships *Massachusetts*, *North Carolina*, *South Dakota* and *Alabama*, along with the cruisers *Louisville*, *Portland*, *Indianapolis*, *Canberra* and *San Juan* and a destroyer screen.

The ships assembled at Majuro Atoll sortied on the 23 March 1944 and rendezvoused with the units coming from the South Pacific on 26/27 March. Once assembled, the massive combined task force started to move towards Palau: it would be refuelled *en route* by oilers and protected by routine combat air patrols and anti-submarine patrols.

On 25 March, approximately 700 miles from Truk, it was believed that a distant Japanese search plane had spotted the task force. Another Japanese search plane was spotted the following day as the task force was being refuelled after rendezvous with fleet oilers. But despite being in range of air bases on Truk, Woleai, Palau and Papua New Guinea, no attack would be pressed home by the Japanese until 29 March.

As the Task Force had now likely been spotted, Admiral Spruance determined to strike immediately against Palau. The element of surprise had been lost and thus there was no point in the planned circuitous, clandestine approach. He brought forward the attack by two days from 1 April to 30 March to allow the Japanese as little time as possible to prepare and reinforce; Task Force 58 would make a straight push directly towards Palau at an increased speed of 22 knots so as to reach their planned launching position by 30 March 1944. Each of the carriers maintained an eight-plane combat air patrol and a four-plane anti-submarine patrol from just before sunrise at 0515 local time to sunset at 1806 local.

Initially unaware of the gathering of the massive task force and its clandestine approach to Palau, the Japanese Combined Fleet HQ was in the process of being moved to Koror on Palau. (It would officially be installed there on 29 March 1944 – just one day before *Desecrate 1*.)

Once the US force had been detected, Admiral Koga sent his main naval units away from Palau, moving them northwards to be ready for a larger naval surface engagement. The super-battleship *Musashi*, along with other units of the 2nd Fleet and a convoy of merchant ships, retired from Palau northwards on the evening of 29 March.

There were many Japanese army transport ships and merchantmen in Palau at this time; however there were problems with communications – and some vessels were not in a position to react in time. Many ships' captains felt that in the open sea their ships would be more vulnerable to attack by US aircraft, submarines and surface vessels; they chose to remain dotted throughout Palau's scattered jungle-covered islands, some nosing their vessels close to shore in the hope that the islands and terrain would give them some protection from raiding aircraft.

A convoy was hastily made up to steam through Toachel Mlengui, the West Passage through the fringing reef. The ships of the convoy were able to escape Palau, slipping past the patrolling US submarines through the hole left in the screen formation by the loss of the submarine USS

Japanese Mitsubishi G4M Navy Attack Bombers – Allied reporting name Betty – skim the waves as they make a low altitude attack on US shipping. (National Archives)

*Tullibee.* She had been patrolling off Palau on 26 March when her own torpedo, which had run a circular course, struck her.

As no orders came from the Imperial Japanese Army HQ, the IJA army transport vessels remained anchored in Palau. Most of the precious naval tankers and oilers present were vessels that had been damaged elsewhere by torpedoes or bombing attacks and were not in any condition to make good an escape.

Few orders were issued to the Japanese air forces in Palau – notably those in the large southern airfield at Peleliu. There were no orders issued for withdrawal or reinforcement –just a simple order to fight as hard as possible.

On 29 March, the task force detected two Japanese long-range reconnaissance Betty bomber aircraft approaching from the direction of Palau. One was spotted visually at 1329 ship's time at a distance of about 7 miles as it flew towards the carrier *Enterprise*, almost skimming the waves at 100 feet.

Once the Betty had been spotted, a combat air patrol of eight F6F Hellcats split into two divisions, and swooped down on it from 6,000 feet, clocking 385 mph and reaching shooting distance after a chase of about three minutes. The first Hellcat division bracketed the Betty – with two approaching from the left and two from the right – whilst the Betty's only evasive manoeuvre was to weave from right to left.

As the fighters began their second run at the Betty, a ball of fire from its unprotected fuel tanks appeared on the starboard wing and grew until the wing and part of the fuselage were on fire. The plane then crashed into the water in a fireball – its fuselage and wings disintegrating. The forward part of the fuselage continued to float for about 15 minutes and the smoke could be seen from the distant *Enterprise*. The other Betty was shot down at 1730 ship's time after managing to strafe a US ship.

At sundown, just as the CAP was being recovered to the carriers for the night, a flight of Japanese aircraft attacked the US formation. The carrier was forced to take evasive manoeuvres before the last US fighter had landed. The pilot was ordered to ditch his Hellcat off the *Fletcher*-class destroyer *Dortch*, and the pilot was picked up. The US ships returned AA fire and drove off the attackers. There were no casualties from this incident, but an unlucky fighter pilot on *Cowpens* was swept overboard when the retractable wing of a Hellcat suddenly swung open during a sharp turn on deck. He could not be found and was listed missing presumed dead. The Japanese aircraft had disappeared from US radars by

2000 local time. Meantime, intelligence reports were being received that Japanese warships were fleeing Palau.

At 2037 ship's time, TG58.3 was attacked by six Japanese aircraft from the south-east that had been picked up by radar some 25 miles out. The Japanese formation split into two, with aircraft approaching the task group from both port and starboard. The ships of the TG58.3 screen commenced AA fire at 1850, and within one minute one plane had caught fire and crashed starboard of the group. Three minutes later, a second plane was shot down.

An early morning attack by Japanese torpedo-bombers was anticipated for the next day, 30 March, so four CAP night fighters and two picket planes were launched – but no contact developed.

By 0300 local time on 30 March, the strike groups of Task Force 58 had arrived at their various designated holding points 65–110 miles south of Palau and were turning into the wind in readiness to begin launchings.

## 30 MARCH 1944: K-DAY

Following the template used during Operation *Hailstone* at Truk, night fighters were initially launched to act as a CAP around the task force during the early morning launches of Hellcats for the initial fighter sweep. Each of the carrier task groups was allocated a number; thus Task Group 58.1, comprising *Enterprise*, *Cowpens* and *Belleau Wood*, was designated Carrier Task Force 1.

Task Group 58.2, comprising the carriers *Bunker Hill*, *Monterey*, *Hornet* and *Cabot*, was designated Carrier Task Force 2. Task Group 58.3, comprising the carriers *Yorktown*, *Princeton*, *Lexington* and *Langley*, was designated Carrier Task Force 3.

Each of the successive group strikes throughout the day were designated A, B, C, D etc. Thus group strikes would be coded Strike 1A, 1B, 2A, 2B and so on.

With the CAP patrolling above, at 0430 local time 72 Hellcats began launching from the Task Force 58 carriers for the initial fighter sweep, the launch being timed so that the Hellcats would be over the target by 0600 local time, just before sunrise.

After more than an hour's flight from the south, the Hellcats began to approach Peleliu at around 0545 with the various strike groups assigned to patrol at different altitudes. The initial fighter sweep would be followed by successive waves of Grumman Avenger torpedo-bombers and Curtiss Helldiver and Douglas Dauntless dive-bombers, escorted by more Hellcats. The major Japanese airfield on the southern Palauan island of Peleliu was high on the list of targets. Peleliu was subsequently found to be the only serviceable airfield; an airstrip had been cleared on each of Ngesebus and Babelthuap Islands but the fields were not yet operational. There were submarine and seaplane bases on Arakabesan Island and a seaplane base on Koror

The battle-hardened Hellcats from TG 58.1 carriers *Enterprise*, *Belleau Wood* and *Cowpens* were given low cover and ground attack assignments where the most enemy contact could be expected – they would be in the thick of the battle whilst other air groups kept the intermediate and high altitudes clear.

As the Hellcats of one division of *Enterprise* Air Group 10 dived to strafe Peleliu Airfield, they found many Betty bombers parked up on the airfield – but none of the anticipated dangerous Japanese fighters. It was assumed that, knowing that the Task Force 58 aircraft were approaching, the Japanese fighters had already taken off. The Hellcats made several strafing runs and shot up the Bettys, which burst into flames when hit. They received limited AA fire from the ground.

After the attack runs, the division swung north over Urukthapel (just to the south of Koror Island) and spotted some fifteen freighters, one oiler, one destroyer and a hospital ship in the anchorages. After continuing north they located the unfinished airfield at the south of Babelthuap and then returned to Peleliu, where they encountered some of the missing Japanese fighters which had taken off previously. A dozen or more Zekes and Nakajima A6M3-32 Zero floatplane variant (Allied reporting name Hamp) were observed. The American aviators reported the Zekes as extremely manoeuvrable but that their tactics were to shy away from a pitched battle with the flights of Hellcats – the Zekes seemed to prefer to attack US aircraft when they were single or damaged.

At one point a number of Zekes closed on the division commander, Lt Cmdr. W.R. Kane, who had become separated from his division. He spent ten minutes or so trying to shake the Zekes off his tail, but after damaging one Zeke, first one and then the other of his 0.50-inch Browning machine guns stopped firing. The Zekes continued to pursue him, but when they arrived just 100 feet short of the Peleliu runway both pilots broke off the engagement. Kane's wingman got on the tail of another Zeke, shooting it down; then another Zeke was shot down in flames. It is believed that many Japanese aircraft at Peleliu were well dispersed and camouflaged, and that a substantial number were not destroyed in the initial fighter sweep.

Meantime, the other division of *Enterprise* Hellcats was dogfighting with Zekes and strafing ground targets. Further north on Babelthuap, an oil storage facility near a barrack was set on fire; the phosphate plant in Angaur was strafed and began to smoke. AA fire from land-based batteries was poor and largely ineffective.

An old Japanese destroyer was attacked and sunk some 20 miles out of the Toachel Mlengui passage. In total, US aircrew reported that some 35 ships had been spotted in the various Palau anchorages below them.

During the fighter sweep a total of some 35 Japanese aircraft were reported shot down, with two Hellcats shot down and three others damaged by AA fire and Japanese aircraft. One Hellcat was bracketed by two Zekes from above after a strafing dive, and was hit in the engine. The Hellcat started to lose power, and by the time it had laboured back to *Enterprise* the engine was smoking and about to cut out. The engine was replaced and the damaged engine was thrown overboard – the other damage was all repairable on board. The Hellcats were back on their carrier by 0724.

Strike 2A was launched just after 0530 local time from *Enterprise* and *Belleau Wood*, with Hellcats lifting off just ahead of the Avengers and Dauntlesses they were to escort, the primary objective being to destroy shipping. Six of the Avengers carried a single torpedo each, three set for a depth of 8 feet and three for a depth of 12 feet, for use against warships and shipping. The other aircraft were loaded with fragmentation clusters and incendiary bombs, all fuzed with no delay, for use against land targets. The Avenger torpedo aircraft carrying bombs instead of torpedoes were assigned to attack the seaplane bases.

Once up in the air, the flights of aircraft proceeded in formation to their designated strike areas. One division proceeded to a point about 15 miles west of Kossol Passage to the north of Babelthuap, where it had been reported that several ships were on their way out of the lagoon, among them one or two light cruisers.

*PB-31* under attack off Palau on 30 March 1944. (National Archives)

The US pilots recognised the first speeding warship as an old destroyer, and Hellcats immediately began strafing runs to silence her AA fire before a section of Dauntless dive-bombers began to attack. One 1,000lb bomb was a near miss at the bow that lifted the bow up in the water, but the others were further off. One of the Dauntlesses made a perfect dive on the ship but didn't pull out of the dive as expected and continued until it impacted into the water and disintegrated – the aircraft must surely have been hit by AA fire.

Another Dauntless took small-calibre AA fire hits to its engine, which started to smoke. The aircraft developed an instability, and the pilot had to turn to nurse it back towards the carrier. On the way, the plane started to lose altitude and it had to be ditched 20 miles southwest of Angaur. The crew safely got off and were picked up three hours later by a destroyer.

Further dive-bombers continued the attack after the first division's bombs were used up. One was a hit at the stern, and the ship immediately slowed drastically from its high speed to about 8 knots – desperately making for a rainsquall in the distance, which might cloak its position. After further attacks the destroyer was seen to be moving in circles – a classic indication of a jammed rudder. Six Grumman Avengers started their attack with a torpedo hit about midships that caused a huge plume of white water to erupt some 20–30 metres high. They were followed by aircraft from *Yorktown* before the destroyer finally succumbed, broke in two and sank.

Two smaller ships were spotted steaming west of Kossol Passage, attempting to escape the carnage. They were heavily strafed and one blew up from an apparent ammunition secondary explosion whilst the other ship started to burn.

When the group was about 8 miles west of Koror, six Avengers loaded with bombs peeled off and, joined by fighter cover from *Belleau Wood*, attacked the air bases at Koror and Arakabesan.

At Koror, bombs were dropped on warehouses and other buildings although no planes were spotted other than two anchored floatplanes. The seaplane base on the western side of Arakabesan, the site of the present Palau Pacific Resort, was peppered with bombs from four aircraft, and direct hits were scored on repair and shore facilities which caused fires to break out. Two Type 95 Nakajima E8N reconnaissance floatplanes (Allied reporting name Dave) were sunk, along with two Rufe Zero variant seaplane fighters.

The Japanese Nakajima A6M fighter-bomber – Allied reporting name Rufe. (National Archives)

22 CV12-3 30MAR44 1525-11K20 6 3/8 2000E11 MAI

Burning Japanese shipping in Malakal Harbor and Urukthapel anchorage on K-DAY National Archives)

Just after 0800 (local), Strike 2B launched 12 *Enterprise* Hellcats to escort 11 dive-bombers and Avenger torpedo-bombers tasked to attack targets of opportunity. Whilst all the Avengers of Strike 2B carried 500lb GP bombs, one Avenger was allocated for a photographic mission.

The strike group bombed and strafed shipping in Malakal Harbor before heading for Kossol Passage to the north of Babelthuap, where a possible battleship had been reported by a previous strike. The flight arrived in the location at 0900, but there was no battleship to be seen – so after a brief search, the bombers and torpedo planes split up. The pilots observed a total 15 oilers, freighters and cargo ships; eight in the Malakal anchorage as well as several among the small islands of the Urukthapel anchorage. Many ships were anchored close inshore and alongside the small islands.

At the Malakal anchorage, Douglas Dauntless dive-bombers and Avengers bombed and strafed the repair ship *Akashi* and other merchantmen. A tanker near the north shore – most likely the *Amatsu Maru* – received several hits. A medium freighter on the south shore was also hit, and a ship in open water west of Peleliu was also strafed along with several other small ships at Koror. There was little AA fire and no airborne aircraft were encountered.

The Avengers, carrying four 500lb bombs dived at an angle of 50-60 degrees from a height of 8,000 feet swooping down to 2,000 feet as they attacked a large ship in the Malakal anchorage, one of eight found there – most likely the *Urakami Maru*. The first aircraft missed but the following aircraft hit the target; the ship immediately began to smoulder and settle. After further attacks on shipping, including possibly the *Nagisan Maru* west of Urukthapel, the flight turned around and began to climb to safety for the return to the carrier. On the return run, one Avenger dropped its bombs on a freighter hugging one of the small islands off Urukthapel reporting a hit and the ship sinking. Other aircraft attacked a small freighter

Dive bombing in Palau Harbor – combat photo. (National Archives)

whilst others again attacked the grey fleet repair ship *Akashi* – but missed. An old destroyer was attacked at the southern part of Urukthapel anchorage – it immediately started to list from two close misses and one hit at the stern. The ship sank quickly in shallow water – its outline visible from the air. The planes reformed about 5 miles west of the lagoon at about 0950 and headed back to the *Enterprise*.

Meantime, eight Hellcats and six Avengers had been launched from *Belleau Wood* for Strike 2B just after 0800 local time – although only six Hellcats went to the assigned target, as two, along with a cruiser's floatplane, were detached for a search mission for a downed aircraft. The six Hellcats arrived at the Toachel Mlengui Pass around 0915 and started strafing runs on a freighter grounded on a reef on the east side of the pass near its southern end – possibly the *Teshio Maru* – setting it on fire. They then joined the other aircraft attacking shipping at the Urukthapel anchorage.

By 0939 (local), with the Americans now having total air superiority, the *Enterprise* and *Belleau Wood* Dauntless dive-bombers and Avenger torpedo-bombers were able to attack at will – with escorting Hellcats able to break off to strafe ground targets of opportunity. Peleliu Airfield was strafed again along with two freighters near Angaur. Ten Hellcats and eight Dauntless dive-bombers from *Enterprise* combined with eight Hellcats and two Avengers from *Belleau Wood* for Strike 2C, an attack on Peleliu Airfield; its aircraft, buildings and hangars were soon ablaze.

At 1145 local time for Strike 2D six escort Hellcats rose into the air from *Enterprise* followed by their charge of ten Dauntless dive-bombers and six Avenger torpedo-bombers. The flight joined a further eight *Belleau Wood* Hellcats and six Avengers, and headed to the Malakal and Urukthapel anchorages to attack shipping. The strike groups strafed Peleliu, hitting a Betty and a Val, before moving north and strafing the ships in the western anchorages and knocking out a lighthouse at Toachel Mlengui (West Pass) set high on a mountain plateau at Babelthuap, a radio station, and hitting a freighter grounded on a reef south of West Pass, near to Karamado Bay, most likely the *Kibi Maru*. The *Nagisan Maru* was attacked and three hits scored, one in the bridge and two at the stern. When the flight broke off the attacks about 20 minutes later, she was seen to be smouldering and going down by the stern. Hits were also scored on a large oiler believed to be the *Amatsu Maru*, with a hit in the engine room spaces aft that caused a large explosion. Hits were also scored on a medium tanker outside the claws of the Malakal anchorage, believed to be the *Asashio* or *Akebono Maru*, and another medium freighter believed to be possibly the *Kamikaze Maru* or *Gozan Maru*. Two Nakajima A6M2-N Rufes were set on fire at Koror along with a hangar.

At 1420 local time, *Enterprise* again launched Avengers, Dauntlesses and Hellcats for Strike 2E, the fifth group strike of the day; several of the aircraft were heavily loaded with 1,000lb bombs fuzed with delays of several hours. These would be dropped on Peleliu Airfield to deny the Japanese the opportunity of repairing it overnight. Then 15 Hellcats launched from *Belleau Wood* along with eight Avengers, each loaded with four instant fuze 500lb bombs. The group was joined by eight Hellcats from *Cowpens* for subsequent attacks on shipping in the Malakal anchorage, where a freighter and an oiler were hit along with smaller vessels. Two large ships anchored either side of the northern tip of Urukthapel were attacked. By this time, five ships were observed burning in the Malakal anchorage, with four more damaged.

Strike 2E also included a photo mission of four Hellcats with 500lb bombs and a photography-equipped Avenger launched from *Enterprise*. Two of the Hellcats had a 45-minute duel with a Nakajima Ki-27 Nate, a small old monoplane which ducked in and out of clouds as it frantically outmanoeuvred the two far faster and more heavily armed American fighters. Eventually it was shot down, but as the pilot made to bail out, his parachute caught the tail assembly of the Nate and he was taken down with his plane to crash below.

This was the last flight from TG58.1 *Enterprise*, *Cowpens* and *Belleau Wood*, and as soon as their aircraft were recovered the group started to move northwards in preparation for strikes against Yap and Ulithi. *Enterprise* herself had flown 221 sorties, claiming five enemy aircraft shot down, one oiler, one large transport and three medium freighters sunk – and nine freighters, three destroyers and one minelayer damaged.

.....................

Task Group 58.2 comprised the four carriers *Bunker Hill*, *Hornet*, *Monterey* and *Cabot* along with the battleships *New Jersey* and *Iowa* – the largest battleships ever built by the USA – and the cruisers *Baltimore* and *Boston*. The Carrier Task Force had positioned itself about 75 miles south of Angaur Island on the morning of 30 March. The launch of her 12 Hellcats for the initial fighter sweep began in darkness at 0430 (local) along with the launch of Mining Group No. 1 comprising four Hellcats and three Grumman Avengers. The launch was timed so that the aircraft would be over their targets just as the sun was coming up at 0600.

Whereas TG 58.1 Hellcats had been assigned a patrol zone of 8,000 feet for ground attack and low-altitude operations, TG 58.2 *Bunker Hill* pilots had been assigned the patrol zone above, from 14,000 to 20,000 feet. Approaching the Palaus from the south, they attacked and strafed Peleliu Airfield.

Just as the Hellcats were pulling up from their attack, the division was attacked by 12 Zekes at 3,000 feet – and a series of violent dogfights broke out. During the fighter sweep,

Grumman TBF Avenger fitted with aerial mines for dropping in Palau's shipping channels. (National Archives)

twenty-six Zekes would be encountered over Peleliu and Angaur Islands with three Zekes shot down in dogfights and another two Zekes probable kills.

Once Japanese air cover had been sufficiently degraded, the TG58.2 aircraft flew a number of sorties against shipping and ground targets. When they arrived over Koror they encountered heavy 20mm and 40mm AA fire, with heavy concentrations over Arakabesan, where the seaplane base was situated.

For the first time in action, carrier-based aircraft would lay aerial mines. These would be air-dropped with two main objectives; firstly, to prevent shipping inside Palau Lagoon escaping the US attacks and secondly, to deny the Japanese use of Palau's anchorages for a period in excess of one month, to allow the US Hollandia operation to take place uninterrupted.

The first objective of sealing the lagoon would be accomplished by air-dropping buoyant Mark 10 magnetic mines, which were chained to a heavy anchor that had a release mechanism that would operate after the pre-set period of one hour and allow the mine to float up until the chain or tether from the anchor stopped it at the correct depth. These mines had an explosive charge of 420lbs and would be spaced at roughly 200-yard intervals to prevent a sympathetic detonation following a mine nearby detonating.

To achieve the second objective of denying the anchorages to the Japanese, Mark 25 magnetic ground mines with fuze delays of up to one month would be dropped in important channels and shipping choke points in the lagoon. These negatively buoyant mines were designed to sit on the seabed and although they were the same size as the tethered mines, because they did not require a heavy anchor and release mechanism, they could accommodate a much heavier 1,274lb explosive charge. These mines were very hard for the Japanese to sweep, so they could never be sure if they had completely cleared an area.

TOP: The ex-*Momi*-class 2nd class destroyer, *Patrol Boat 31*.

BOTTOM: *PB-31* finally disappears from sight, sinking into abyssal depths. (National Archives)

The Grumman Avengers of the first mining groups took off at 0445 local time, heavy with their large mines and protected by their own fighters, with their arrival over the lagoon timed for sunrise at 0600. Flying at a speed of 180 knots at just 200 feet, they were very vulnerable as they made their mine-laying runs. Some would lay a minefield of tethered magnetic mines in the southern arm of the channel that leads to Toachel Mlengui (West Passage) to prevent ships in that anchorage escaping. Other aircraft would lay mines off the seaward side of Malakal Pass, which leads from the east through dangerous reefs into Malakal Harbor itself.

The escort Hellcats began intensive strafing of all ships encountered in the vicinity of the air-drop, to protect the lumbering Avengers from AA fire. Up at West Passage, Hellcats attacked the IJN destroyer *Wakatake*, the ex-destroyer *Patrol Boat 31*, a subchaser, an auxiliary subchaser, the freighter *Teshio Maru* and the other ships of a large convoy spotted and attacked by several strike groups as they attempted to leave the lagoon through West Passage. The auxiliary subchaser was forced to stop at the mouth of Karamado Bay, where it was later destroyed by Douglas Dauntless dive-bombers. *Teshio Maru* ran aground on the west side of the reef bordering the northern part of the channel and was later repeatedly attacked. *Patrol Boat 31* managed to run through the pass into open water but was later sunk by dive-bombers and torpedo-bombers. *Wakatake* took refuge in Karamado Bay to the east, where she was subsequently sunk.

Mining Group No. 1X launched nine Avengers laden with mines and escorted by eight Hellcats, from *Bunker Hill* at 0900 local time, tasked to lay their mines between Arakabesan and Ngargol Islands.

A total of 33 magnetic ground mines were detailed for the entrance channels with another 15 around the approaches and anchorages of Arakabesan Island and its seaplane base.

.....................

At 0545, TG 58.2 Strike 1B launched 8 Hellcats and 18 dive-bombers from *Bunker Hill*, tasked to destroy enemy shipping in conjunction with strike aircraft from the three other carriers of the task group and an observer group. Although the flight found Palau and Koror partially obscured by cloud, merchant shipping was located and attacked by the dive-bombers amidst heavy AA fire. It was difficult to get clear IDs of ships attacked due to heavy AA fire and the partial cloud cover, but hits were observed on a large freighter in the north of Urukthapel Bay, possibly the *Nagisan Maru*, plus an oiler, possibly the *Iro*, and several other ships.

Strike 1C of eleven Hellcats and nine dive-bombers launched at 0900, tasked to destroy enemy shipping in Palau Harbor and attack land installations on Angaur Island. Aircraft from *Hornet* also joined the attack.

Next, 15 Hellcats, 12 dive-bombers and 6 Avengers launched from *Bunker Hill* at 1115 for Strike 1D, and were soon followed by similar aircraft from *Hornet*, *Monterey* and *Cabot*, loaded with 1,000lb GP bombs and rockets; they were tasked to hit shipping in the anchorages and, further, to strafe Peleliu Airfield.

The final minelaying operation by Mining Group No. 2 and Strikes 1E and 1F against shipping and land installations launched at 1500 local time.

The aircraft of the TG58.2 light carrier *Cabot* were assigned anti-submarine patrol and combat air patrol duties. They only participated in one offensive strike against shipping in Palau, on 30 March. Eight Hellcats and three Avengers loaded with four 500lb bombs got four hits on the fleet oiler IJN *Sata*: one hit forward and three others aft of the bridge.

The light carrier *Monterey* contributed 12 Hellcats to the initial fighter sweep assigned to cover the high-altitude layer from 20,000 to 25,000 feet, launching in darkness at 0440. *Monterey* also launched three torpedo-bombers for Strike 1A, each armed with a 2,000lb GP bomb that was fuzed for instant detonation. They flew with 18 Helldivers and 12 Hellcats from *Bunker Hill* and 11 Hellcats and 18 Helldivers from *Hornet* to attack shipping in the Urukthapel anchorage of the Western Lagoon. In this strike, the large tanker *Akebono Maru* was hit near the bow, setting her ablaze from stem to stern. She motored slowly into a sheltered bay just to the north-east of the anchorage and beached, her fo'c'sle still smoking. She sank on the afternoon of the second day coming to rest stern down on a sloping seabed with her bow thrust high, sticking out of the water.

In the afternoon of 30 March, *Monterey* sortied other strike groups of aircraft and two photographic missions comprising four escort Hellcats for one Avenger mounted with a camera.

.....................

Task Group 58.3 comprised the carriers *Yorktown*, *Princeton*, *Lexington* and *Langley* with the battleships *Massachusetts*, *North Carolina*, *South Dakota* and *Alabama* along with the cruisers *Louisville*, *Portland*, *Indianapolis*, *Canberra* and *San Juan* and a destroyer screen. It took station 119 miles south of Palau Harbor in the early hours of 30 March 1944, and turning into the wind assumed cruising formation to begin flight operations. For the initial fighter sweep, her Hellcats were tasked with patrolling the intermediate level of 10–15,000 feet.

As with the other two task groups, her strike aircraft took part in group strikes throughout the day against shipping and land targets and also carried out a number of mining group operations.

In all, six attacks, A–F, were flown by TG 58.3 on 30 March, designated K-Day, against shipping and ground installations, a total of 454 sorties including patrols.

.....................

More than 30 Japanese aircraft had been damaged or destroyed on the ground on Peleliu Airfield and Arakabesan Island Seaplane Base during the initial fighter sweep, with an additional 28 aircraft reported destroyed throughout the day by the strike groups. Few serviceable aircraft remained.

As a result, Japanese aircraft were scrambled from other islands and rushed to Palau. Twelve Betty bombers were despatched from Saipan and arrived in the late afternoon – immediately taking off to attack the US task force. They scored little success however, due to the intense AA fire thrown at them from the task group's individual screens of battleships, cruisers, destroyers, and from the carriers themselves. None of the task force ships were damaged.

The US combat air patrols of eight Hellcats had flown routinely throughout the day to protect the carriers: four planes circling the carriers at 5,000ft and four more at 10,000ft. Around 1700, they were ordered to intercept an unidentified incoming contact about 50 miles away from the carriers.

As they closed the contact, they spotted 10–12 Japanese aircraft, which they identified as Nakajima B6N torpedo-bombers (Allied reporting name Jill) or Yokosuka D4Y dive-bombers (Allied reporting name Judy). All but one of the aircraft were quickly shot down – the one surviving aircraft, a Judy, continued to head towards the task force at speed.

Two of the Hellcats, capable of a top speed of 380mph, turned to chase after the Judy – which had a fast top speed for a dive-bomber of 342mph. The Judy had closed to within 10 nautical miles of the task force by the time the two faster and more agile Hellcats were close enough to engage. The Judy was hit and exploded. As with most Japanese aircraft, the

Judy had sacrificed armour and fuel protection for speed – it was a design weakness that the Hellcats would exploit to great advantage during the Pacific War.

As the two Hellcats turned to head back to their carrier they spotted two more Judy dive-bombers hugging the waves as they closed on the task group. Two more Hellcats soon joined the chase and one was able to open fire at extreme range of 1,000 metres. This caused the Judys to drop their heavy bombs and leave the contact unscathed.

That night, more than 50 Japanese fighters arrived at Peleliu from Saipan in the evening. The scene was set for an aerial fighter duel the following morning.

...................

That evening, *Enterprise* went to general quarters when it appeared she was about to be attacked by Japanese torpedo planes. The carrier launched a night fighter but no contact was made and no attack developed.

The first day of Operation *Desecrate 1*, on 30 March, seemed to have completely degraded Japanese air cover and given total air superiority to US aircraft. Action reports throughout the day and the results of photo-reconnaissance missions revealed that most of the shipping found in the lagoon had been sunk or badly damaged.

As Task Group 58.1 broke off to sortie against Yap and Ulithi, Task Groups 58.2 and 58.3 readied to attack the Palaus again the following day.

## K-DAY PLUS ONE, 31 MARCH 1944

As with K-Day, an initial fighter sweep was once again launched in darkness around 0430 (local) timed for arrival above Palau at dawn. Following the departure of TG 58.1 the night before, this time there would be a reduced number of 60 Hellcats. The groups of strike aircraft from the remaining Task Groups 58.2 and 58.3 carriers rendezvoused *en route* at 7,000ft – but as the air groups formed up to proceed to Palau, a Betty bomber approached. The Hellcats immediately attacked it – the Betty took a hit that caused the starboard engine and unprotected fuel tank to burst into flame. The Betty streaked through the sky before falling from the sky to disintegrate in the water.

*Princeton* Hellcats were soon strafing Peleliu Airfield, where five Zekes were found on combat air patrol. Two were shot down and three escaped into cloud cover, allowing the attacks to proceed on the airfield. From there the flight was vectored to attack the airfield under construction on the main island of Babelthuap.

The high-altitude patrol of *Yorktown* Hellcats at 20,000 feet spotted six Japanese aircraft circling below them, at the top of a cloud layer at about 7,000 feet. With the advantage of height, the Hellcats dived down at great speed to attack, shooting down two Hamps and four Zekes.

US pilots reported a total of 60 Japanese planes airborne during the initial fighter sweep on K-Day Plus One – these being the fighters that had arrived from Saipan the evening before along with the few serviceable aircraft that had survived the previous day's attacks. The sky turned into a swirling mass of individual dogfights with aircraft harrying or being chased in every direction. The Japanese aircraft were no match for the modern US aircraft and appeared to give up the offensive, scattering to save themselves and dipping into cloud cover where they could.

Whilst the strike groups were assaulting Palau, combat air patrols of eight Hellcats patrolled the air space around the carriers throughout the day: four planes circling the carriers at 5,000 feet and four more at 10,000 feet.

As the initial fighter sweep was going in over Palau – and before the dive-bombers and torpedo-bombers launched, at 0530 Strike 1A-2 from TG 58.2 carrier *Bunker Hill* launched an air target observer aircraft along with three escort fighters to identify targets for subsequent attack by the dive- and torpedo-bombers. The Observer found that there were few ships left in seaworthy shape in the anchorages below – most of the shipping was already damaged or disabled in some way. There were just two ships in Malakal Harbor that appeared undamaged. The shipping would be attacked again – and then most aircraft in the strike would bomb land installations before flying south again to attack Peleliu Airfield *en route* back to the carriers in their southern holding position. As Avengers bombed the airfield, Hellcats strafed Japanese aircraft spotted inside protective revetments.

Strike 1A-2 from TG 58.2 carrier *Hornet* launched at 0535, with 12 Hellcats and four Avengers loaded with one 1,000lb bomb and two smaller bombs on the wing racks – assigned to attack shipping and land installations. Nine Avengers from TG 58.2 carrier *Monterey* also took part in Strike 1A-2. They carried a selection of bomb types; 100lb fragmentation bombs, incendiary bombs and 100lb GP bombs. This was the last strike of *Monterey* aircraft against Palau.

At 0540, implementing the second strategic objective of the operation, to deny Palau to the Japanese for at least 30 days, the first of several mining missions launched from *Hornet*. Five Avengers took off, each carrying a single Mark 25 ground mine with delayed arming – escorted by eight Hellcats.

Strike 3A-2 from Task Group 58.3 carriers *Yorktown* and *Lexington* launched just after 0600, and comprised a total of 46 aircraft, namely 20 Hellcats, 14 Dauntlesses and 12 Avengers. *Langley* provided anti-submarine and combat air patrols, and her aircraft did not take an active part in the strikes on Palau.

At 0800, a second strike (1 B-2) launched from *Hornet* with five Helldivers, each loaded with two 500lb bombs in the bomb bay and two 100lb bombs on wing racks. They were tasked to attack shipping and land targets.

A second mining mission with six torpedo-bombers was then launched from *Hornet*, the aircraft arriving over their target – the shipping channel between Babelthuap and Koror Islands – at about 0920. The escort fighters went in ahead of the Avengers and strafed AA batteries on Arakabesan and Koror Islands, allowing the Avengers to drop their mines from 400 feet at 200 knots. With this mission successfully completed the aircraft returned safely to the carrier.

Just after 0800, 12 Dauntless dive-bombers launched from *Lexington* escorted by ten Hellcats for Strike 3B against remaining shipping and land installations. As Japanese AA fire had now been largely suppressed, it was decided to arm the Hellcats with 500lb or 1000lb bombs – the powerful aircraft could easily carrier-launch with such a payload and it gave the strike groups more hitting power. Ten of the Hellcats would carry a 500lb GP bomb with a very short-delay fuze of 4–5 seconds to allow a masthead attack. The 12 Douglas Dauntless dive-bombers each carried a more powerful 1,000lb bomb.

Strike 3C-2 launched from *Lexington* at about 1030 as *Desecrate 1* was drawing to a finale – this was the penultimate strike from *Lexington*, with 39 aircraft. Nine Hellcats again carried 500lb bombs, with a number of Dauntlesses with 1,000lb bombs and 13 Avengers, most carrying a Mark 25 magnetic ground mine with arming delays of up to 30 days. These would be laid in the main channel leading north up the west side of Babelthuap Island to Toachel Mlengui West Passage. This time no AA fire was encountered and few strafing targets were found.

Strike 3D was *Lexington*'s final strike of the day and was again directed at hitting the airfields and land infrastructure. On their return south to the carriers the aircraft again hit Peleliu Airfield with long-delay-fuzed bombs to deny the airstrip to the Japanese. The aircraft had returned and completed landings by 1554, whilst the carrier was already speeding on its way away from Palau to Woleai to deliver its next strike. With some 1,426 sorties carried out, the Task Force 58 air operations against Palau had ceased.

...................

TG58.2 moved towards Woleai at sunset and operations began there at 0646 ship's time (+2 hrs local) on 01 April, with 193 sorties being flown. The raid on this small Japanese island would be called off after the third strike for lack of targets, and Task Group 58.2 moved off towards the US Navy's eastern base at Majuro.

## AFTERMATH

Six weeks before, after the US photographic overflight of Truk, the Commander-in-Chief of the Combined Fleet, Admiral Koga, had left Truk for Japan on 10 February aboard the battleship *Musashi* – immediately before Operation *Hailstone* on 17/18 February. On 20 February, after reports of the Truk raid, he set off from Japan in *Musashi* for Palau to establish his Combined Fleet HQ in Koror. It was officially installed there on 29 March 1944 – just one day before *Desecrate 1*.

On Palau, Admiral Koga survived the two days of gruelling US air attacks on 30 and 31 March. When a lull came on the evening of 31 March he decided to leave Palau aboard his HQ Kawanishi H8K flying boat – Allied reporting name Emily. He perhaps believed that the two days of US air attacks were a softening-up operation and that a large naval bombardment would follow, presaging an amphibious landing by US Marines.

With Palau's air ability now totally degraded and with a consequent lack of reconnaissance intelligence, he was no doubt unaware that the lull in the late afternoon of 31 March was in fact the end of the American operation. Unbeknown to him, Task Force 58 was already withdrawing at high speed northwards to strike at Yap and Ulithi. The huge American task force was moving north as fast as possible to get out of range of any Japanese torpedo aircraft which might mount a feared and potentially devastating night torpedo attack.

As Admiral Koga boarded his flying boat that evening, his staff boarded a second Emily. A third aircraft would act as escort. The Emilys lifted up from Palau's battered landscape and turned due west in the direction of Davao, some 625 miles away in the Philippines, where he intended to set up his new HQ. But on the way there, the aircraft ran into a severe tropical depression and became separated.

The Commander-in-Chief of the Combined Fleet, Admiral Koga, died that

Kawanishi H8K flying boat – Allied reporting name Emily.

night when his plane crashed in a heavy storm near Davao. His whereabouts remained a mystery for a time – his plane simply disappeared and was never seen again. The second Emily, with several staff officers, became separated and crash-landed at about 0200 on 1 April in waters 450 miles north of Davao, off Cebu in the Philippines. Locals heard an aircraft engine spluttering for some time before it faltered – and then stopped as the giant flying boat plunged into the sea and exploded.

They got into canoes and paddled out to the site, where a group of 12 survivors was found about 3 kilometres off the shore, swimming for shore and towing the dead body of one of their colleagues. The majority of the Emily's occupants had survived and said that their aircraft had been shot down by AA fire from a submarine. Those survivors were subsequently captured by Filipino guerrillas led by an American.

A blackened wooden box washed ashore held a quantity of military papers, including two Japanese operational maps detailing bases, landing fields and other facilities in Indo-China, Hainan, the Philippines and southern China. The Japanese mounted a massive effort to find and recover the prisoners and the intelligence documents before they fell into US hands.

Meanwhile, the guerrillas took the prisoners to the interior of Cebu and held them for ten days, until intense Japanese rescue efforts forced them to surrender. The survivors turned out to be high-ranking Japanese officials led by Vice Admiral Shigeru Fukodome, Chief of Staff of the Combined Fleet. Before surrendering, the guerrillas had placed the captured papers inside two empty mortar shell containers and sent them to a rendezvous with an American submarine for onward transmission to US Intelligence.

Once delivered to US Intelligence in Australia, the documents were found to contain important information about the Japanese defence in the Philippines and other areas. They revealed the weakness of Japan's central Philippine defences; Leyte stood out as the soft underbelly of the Japanese position and was poorly defended. Once this was confirmed by other American intelligence operations, this precious intelligence led to the acceleration of the American return to the Philippines from December to October 1944 and to a change of landing site from Mindanao to Leyte.

......................

During *Desecrate 1*, more than 40 Japanese ships were sunk or damaged. The ex-*Momi*-class destroyer *Patrol Boat No. 31*, the destroyer *Wakatake* and at least eight IJN subchasers, auxiliary subchasers and picket boats had been sent to the bottom. The valuable tankers and oilers *Iro*, *Sata*, *Ose*, *Akebono Maru*, *Amatsu Maru*, *Asashio Maru* and *Unyu Maru No. 2* had all been sunk, and the tanker *Hishi Maru No. 2* damaged. The loss of so many tankers and oilers at Palau was a crippling blow to the Combined Fleet and to Japan's ability to sustain its war effort. The shortage of tankers and oilers after *Desecrate 1*, coming so soon after the loss of the oilers *Fujisan Maru*, *Hoyo Maru* and *Shinkoku Maru* at Truk six weeks earlier, severely limited the range of the fleet and degraded Japan's ability to transport oil from the Netherlands East Indies to the empire.

The fleet repair ship *Akashi* had been sunk along with the fleet aircraft transport *Goshu Maru*, the torpedo-boat tender *Kamikaze Maru*, the netlayer *Nissho Maru No. 5* and the submarine tender *Urakami Maru*, along with many requisitioned freighters such as *Akita*

*Maru No. 3*, *Bichu Maru*, *Chuyo Maru*, *Gozan Maru*, *Hokutai Maru*, the two ships named *Kibi Maru* and *Nagisan Maru*.

A claimed 110 Japanese aircraft were shot down over Palau, with no air opposition encountered on the other islands. A further 15 Japanese aircraft were also claimed as severely damaged, probably downed. The US ships shot down four Japanese aircraft with AA fire. Including the aircraft destroyed or severely damaged on the ground in Peleliu Airfield, Arakabesan Seaplane Base, Koror, Woleai and elsewhere, US pilots claimed a total of 214 Japanese aircraft rendered unusable to the Japanese – but the total claimed has never been formally agreed.

The sea approaches and exit routes for shipping to Palau had been successfully mined. Palau Harbor was blocked until it could be swept – and sweeping was made difficult by the extensive use of the ground mines, which self-activated at irregular intervals. The underwater terrain made it impossible to successfully sweep for ground mines.

The TF58 AA screen had proved to be very effective against Japanese air attacks, in particular the feared torpedo night attack. The principle of the initial fighter sweep had again been proved sound, successfully eliminating air opposition over the target, as had been done at Truk and Saipan beforehand.

The fighter escort for the vulnerable minelaying Avengers was crucial to the successful mine drop. Japanese AA fire was intense but had been successfully suppressed by repeated strafing by Hellcats as the Avengers made their 180-knot drops from 200 feet.

Seven US aircraft had been lost in combat and others operationally to landing accidents, forced ditchings and the like. Eight US pilots and ten crewmen had been killed or reported missing in action.

Some Japanese aircrew and aircraft were withdrawn to Davao in April and May, where rebuilding the decimated air groups began. Other surviving pilots were evacuated to Saipan, where more aircraft were sent to allow the reconstitution of Japanese air strength to begin.

The war moved onwards – towards Japan.

# CHAPTER SIX

# Operation Forager

## THE MARIANA AND PALAU ISLANDS CAMPAIGN, JUNE 1944

The islands of Palau and the Marianas formed the principal strongpoints in a chain of islands that Japan's military regarded as the last line of defence to the east. For the Americans, they represented important targets for several reasons: Palau was a barrier to the Philippines, and the Marianas afforded the Japanese land-based air cover and an ability to strike at US operations. Conversely, if the Marianas could be taken then they would give the Americans airfields from which they could deploy the new Boeing B-29 Superfortress heavy bomber against Japan itself.

In the campaigns of 1943 and the first half of 1944, the Allies captured the Solomon Islands, the Gilbert Islands, the Marshall Islands and the Papuan peninsula of New Guinea. This left the Japanese holding the Philippines, the Caroline Islands, the Palau Islands and the Mariana Islands.

Given progress to date, the American joint chiefs thought it now possible to accelerate the Rainbow 5 timetable of pending operations. On 13 June 1944 they asked General Douglas MacArthur and Admiral Chester Nimitz for their opinions on bringing forward the operations timetable by bypassing, and not assaulting, some of the previously selected targets – and choosing new targets that would allow strikes to be made against the Japanese home islands earlier.

General MacArthur favoured the recapture of the Philippines followed by the seizure of Okinawa and a subsequent attack on the Japanese mainland. Admiral Nimitz, on the other hand, championed a more direct strategy of bypassing the Philippines, seizing Okinawa and Formosa and using them as staging areas to launch direct air strikes at the Japanese home islands. This would be followed by a subsequent invasion of the southernmost home islands.

Both strategies included the invasion of the Palauan island of Peleliu, but for different reasons. As the two great US commanders formulated their views, the planned Mariana and Palau Islands campaign, code name Operation *Forager*, would continue.

The Mariana and Palau Islands campaign followed the Gilbert and Marshall Islands campaign, and was intended to neutralise Japanese bases in the central Pacific, support the Allied drive to retake the Philippines, and provide bases for a strategic bombing campaign against Japan. The Americans planned to assault the Marianas island by island – and then take Palau on their way to the Philippines.

In July 1944, President Franklin D. Roosevelt travelled to Pearl Harbor to personally meet both commanders and hear their competing arguments. He decided to go with General MacArthur's strategy, but before General MacArthur could retake the Philippines, the Palau

Islands, specifically the southern islands of Peleliu and Angaur and the potent air threat they posed, would need to be neutralised and the islands taken. A US airfield would be installed to protect General MacArthur's right flank.

In June 1944 (almost three months after *Desecrate 1* had temporarily degraded Palau as a naval and air base, and a month before General MacArthur's strategy to retake the Philippines had been approved), Operation *Forager* began, with Saipan being assaulted first, followed by Guam and then Tinian. The location of Saipan made it a logical and crucial first target – as, with Saipan in American hands, Guam and Tinian would be cut off from support from the more northerly Marianas Islands.

A great naval bombardment of Saipan began on 13 June 1944 – with 15 battleships firing some 165,000 shells. The bombardment was followed by landings of US Marine amphibious forces, which began at 0700 on 15 June. Some 71,000 US troops of V Amphibious Corps, which comprised the 3rd, 4th and 5th Marine Divisions, along with the 2nd Marine Division and the 27th Infantry Division, landed on Saipan, fighting their way ashore at first, against more than 30,000 well-dug-in Japanese troops.

Once the US Marines had started landing on Saipan, this triggered the pre-prepared Japanese contingency plans. The Japanese were aware that US control of the Marianas Islands placed their home islands in range of the new long-range US B-29 Superfortress heavy bombers. The Imperial Japanese Navy thus determined that the time had come for the long-awaited Decisive Battle. An IJN fleet counter-attack was ordered, and three large fleet carriers, two converted carriers, four light carriers, five battleships, thirteen heavy cruisers, six light cruisers, twenty-seven destroyers and twenty-four submarines sortied to attack the US Navy 5th Fleet, which was supporting the landings at Saipan.

At 1835 on 15 June 1944, a Japanese carrier and battleship were spotted coming out of the San Bernardino Strait by the American submarine USS *Flying Fish*. An hour later another Japanese battleship and a heavy cruiser were spotted coming up from the south. Task Force 58 was ordered to move west of Saipan into the Philippine Sea to intercept.

The subsequent Battle of the Philippine Sea took place between 19 and 20 June 1944 – and was nicknamed the Great Marianas Turkey Shoot by American aviators for the severely disproportional loss ratio of Japanese to US aircraft. On the first day of the battle, four Japanese air strikes launched 373 carrier aircraft, but only 130 returned to their carriers. US submarines sank two Japanese carriers – and all this for the loss of just the 23 US aircraft that were shot down.

On the second day, some 240 US aircraft were launched late in the day for an all-out counter-attack at extreme range on the Japanese fleet, which was spotted about 275 miles away moving west at 20 knots. This was right at the limit of Task Force 58's strike range, and daylight was already starting to fade. When the Japanese fleet was found, it was actually 60 miles further away than had been anticipated. Nevertheless, the US attack was pressed home. One Japanese carrier was hit and sunk whilst three more carriers and a battleship were badly damaged by bombs. Twenty US aircraft were lost.

After the lengthy strike, it became clear that most of the US aircraft turning to head home towards their carriers were running dangerously low on fuel. They would have grave difficulty finding their carriers and then landing quickly in the pitch darkness of a tropical night. They had no fuel to allow them to search for the carriers and then make perhaps several attempts to land.

So at 2045, as the first of the US aircraft began to arrive back, knowing that the US aviators would have difficulty finding their carriers and getting down quickly, Admiral Marc

Mitscher, in charge of TF 58, ordered his carriers to switch on their lights and be fully illuminated. Searchlights were shone directly upwards into the night – visible like lighthouses for many miles – despite the risk of attack by Japanese night fighters and submarines. US picket vessels far out in the protective screen fired star shells to help the aircraft locate the task force.

Despite this, as they started to near the task force, one by one aircraft started running out of fuel and were forced to ditch. Some 80 of the returning aircraft were lost, some even crashing on the flight deck as their fuel gave out just as they were coming in to land. Adding these to the combat losses meant that some 100 US aircraft had been lost in total on Day 2 of the battle. Over the coming days approximately three quarters of the downed aircrews were rescued from the sea. Meanwhile, by the end of the second day, the Japanese had lost more than 435 carrier aircraft, three carriers and some 200 land-based aircraft.

The Battle of the Philippine Sea had indeed been a decisive battle – but not the battle that the Japanese had hoped for. Japanese naval forces had been decisively defeated, with heavy and irreplaceable losses to their carrier-borne and land-based aircraft. Task Force 58 had destroyed some 90 per cent of the Japanese carrier air groups, and the Japanese only had enough pilots left to form an air group on one of their light carriers. As a direct result, at the Battle of Leyte Gulf a few months later, their carriers were used solely as decoys. Successful US landings on Guam and Tinian followed in July 1944.

## OPERATION *SNAPSHOT*: PHOTO RECONNAISSANCE AND SECOND PALAU AIR ASSAULT, 25–27 JULY 1944

As part of the Operation *Forager* Mariana and Palau campaign, Fast Carrier Task Force 58 would once again be tasked to strike against the Palaus, in July 1944. Its primary objective would be to obtain complete photographic coverage of the islands in preparation for the planned land invasion of Palau – it was still envisaged at this time that all the major Palau islands would be assaulted and taken. The proposed invasion beaches at Babelthuap, Arakabesan, Koror, Angaur and other islands were to be photographed in detail. Any enemy shipping or aircraft encountered would be destroyed and ground installations would also be hit.

Whilst Task Group 58.1 raided Ulithi and Yap, the Palau attack would be carried out by Task Group 58.2 carriers *Wasp*, *Franklin*, *Monterey* and *Cabot* and Task Group 58.3 carriers *Bunker Hill*, *Lexington* and *San Jacinto*, again under the overall command of Vice Admiral Marc A. Mitscher in his flagship *Lexington*. The Task Force 58 carriers would be protected by the battleships *New Jersey*, *Washington*, *Indiana*, *Alabama* and *Iowa*, along with a screen of cruisers, destroyers and submarines and combat air and anti-submarine patrols.

The task groups took up a holding station some 120 miles north-east of Palau, and on 25 July 1944 launched an initial fighter sweep of Hellcats against airfields in Peleliu, the Arakabesan seaplane base, Ngesebus and Babelthuap.

*Wasp* Hellcats caught and destroyed eight single-engine floatplanes and an Emily flying boat at the Arakabesan seaplane base, where AA fire was intense and two US aircraft were destroyed. Three single-engine aircraft were strafed at Babelthuap Airfield. Composite group strikes of Hellcats and dive- and torpedo-bombers would then follow against shipping, AA positions and ground installations.

During the three days of strikes, fuel installations on Malakal were bombed and set afire again as they had been in March during *Desecrate 1*. An ammunition dump in Malakal was blown up and a radio station was destroyed on Koror, along with buildings and storage facilities. A fuel dump in Ngesebus was set ablaze and the phosphate plant and bauxite open mine in Babelthuap was destroyed and rendered useless. The carrier *Franklin* had armed her 16 Hellcat fighters with rockets, and these were used in limited dogfights against Zekes on the first day of the strikes and against land targets and shipping. After the first day no further airborne enemy fighters were encountered.

At Peleliu Airfield thirteen single-engine and eight twin-engine aircraft were destroyed whilst at Ngesebus eight aircraft were bombed and destroyed. Those Japanese fighters encountered aloft were shot down.

Flights of four Hellcats and three Avengers each were sent out in a three-sector search assigned to an area stretching 80 kilometres in all directions from Palau. A small Japanese Navy minelayer, *Sokuten*, was discovered and promptly sunk 25 nautical miles north of Babelthuap.

On 27 July the 1,500-ton *No. 1*-class armed fast transport *T. 1* was sunk along with several other smaller vessels. *T.1* had been spotted moored close to and parallel with high cliffs and camouflaged with nets and a dense matting of branches and foliage in an attempt to render it undetectable from the air. Other vessels were moored in small bays and similarly camouflaged. When the US aerial reconnaissance photos were studied back on the task force vessels, it became clear that the cliffs had man-made artificial straight lines where none should be; funnel openings and outlines of hulls were spotted amongst the foliage. Once targets were identified, strikes were sent in. Ships still beached or disabled from the *Desecrate 1* raid, such as *Teshio Maru* and *Hokutai Maru*, were hit again.

By the late afternoon of Day 3 of the raid, 27 July, the Palau objectives had been accomplished and the two task groups were ordered to retire to the Saipan area. Task Group 58.1 joined them as it returned from the Ulithi and Yap raid on 29 July.

Saipan had been secured after bitter fighting earlier in July. The Second Battle of Guam ended on 10 August 1944 with US forces retaking the American island that had been seized by Japanese forces at the outset of the war almost three years earlier, in December 1941. The Battle of Tinian was fought between 24 July and 1 August 1944. These conquests now allowed the USA to construct airfields on Saipan and Tinian that would then allow B-29 Superfortress strategic bombers to conduct missions against the Japanese mainland until the end of World War II – including the nuclear attacks on Hiroshima and Nagasaki.

Following their landings in the Mariana and Palau Islands, Allied forces would continue their successful campaign by landing in the Philippines in October 1944 and in the Volcano and Ryukyu Islands at the beginning of January, 1945.

## OPERATION *STALEMATE II*: INVASION OF THE PALAUS AND THE BATTLES OF PELELIU AND ANGAUR, SEPTEMBER–NOVEMBER 1944.

To secure the eastern flank for US forces preparing to attack Japanese forces in the Philippines, in September 1944 Operation *Stalemate II* saw US Marine and Army forces landing on the Palauan islands of Peleliu and Angaur – Peleliu alone was occupied by about 11,000 Japanese 14th Infantry Division troops.

The Battle of Peleliu raged from September to November 1944 and saw US Marines of the 1st Marine Division, and later soldiers of the US Army's 81st Infantry Division, assault the island to capture the airstrip. The commander of the 1st Marine Division predicted that the island would be secured within four days; however Japanese defenders, well dug into pre-prepared and heavily fortified cave defences, offered stiff resistance. The battle lasted over two months and was called the toughest battle of the war for the marines.

As a result of heavy losses during the US assaults in the Solomons, Gilberts, Marshalls and Marianas, the IJA had decided to abandon its previous tactic of trying to stop the American assault on the beaches. Instead, a limited beach defence holding action would take place to disrupt the US amphibious assault whilst the majority of the IJA forces would be secure in a prepared defensive position further inland. Heavily fortified bunkers, gun positions and cave systems would form an interlocking honeycomb system through the natural terrain.

The Japanese defence of Peleliu was focused around Peleliu's highest feature, Umurbrogol Mountain. Rather than being a mountain, as its name suggests, it was a collection of hills and steep ridges running north–south along the middle of Peleliu that overlooked a large portion of the island – including the crucial airfield. An estimated 500 interconnecting caves and tunnels were prepared, becoming an almost unassailable defensive position.

Japanese engineers added sliding armoured steel doors to the caves and built multiple openings to accommodate both artillery and machine gun emplacements. As a defence against the feared flamethrowers and grenades, cave entrances were built slanted, with internal corners and walls angled at 90 degrees to give troops protection from artillery and grenade blasts. This interconnecting honeycomb of caves and tunnels allowed the Japanese to quickly evacuate or reoccupy positions as need be.

The Japanese defenders were well equipped with portable and easily concealed Type 97 81mm and Type 96 150mm mortars. These rapid-fire mortars could be fired out of caves or slit trenches, and the 81mm had a range of 2,800 metres. The Type 96 150mm mortar was the largest mortar in the IJA, and had a range of 3,900 metres. In addition the Japanese used the natural protection of high cliffs and caves to dig out and install artillery gun emplacements in elevated positions that commanded views over large areas of land below where US forces would require to operate. A number of 20mm AA cannons were installed and a light, mobile anti-infantry tank unit was brought to readiness, along with 20mm AA cannons being installed to ward off attack runs from US aircraft.

Wherever they could, the Japanese used the natural features of the terrain to their advantage. At the north end of the anticipated US western landing beaches a coral headland projected outwards and had a field of fire directly down the beach – this feature would come to be known as 'The Point' by the US Marines who would land here. The Japanese blasted emplacements for 47mm anti-tank guns and 20mm cannons into the coral. Once the guns were installed, the positions were sealed shut leaving only a slender horizontal firing slit. Similar reinforced concrete gun emplacements were set up all along the tree line overlooking the two-mile stretch of potential landing beaches. These reinforced concrete bunkers were covered in coral and foliage, and were almost impossible to detect.

Thousands of beach obstacles for landing craft and amphibious tanks were set up, as had been done with the Normandy landing beaches in Europe. Hemispherical anti-invasion beach mines (such as those seen in the foredeck holds of *San Francisco Maru* in Truk Lagoon today) were dug into the sand, and in addition heavy artillery shells were buried upright with their fuzes exposed and ready to detonate when run over. A sacrificial IJA infantry

Reinforced concrete Japanese firing position overlooking Orange Beach, Peleliu. (Author's collection)

battalion was deployed along the beaches in these pre-prepared bunkers and firing positions to harass the first waves of US invaders and delay their advance inland.

Whilst the Japanese had departed from their previous beach defence strategy, the American amphibious assault would take place in the same fashion as previous assaults – despite suffering some 3,000 casualties during two months of Japanese delaying tactics at the Battle of Biak in the New Guinea campaign.

US planners selected the two-mile-long string of beaches to the south-west of Peleliu for their main amphibious assault. These beaches lay only about one mile away from the target, the major airfield inland, and would allow a direct push and assault. All along the beaches, coral reef flats only a few metres deep extended out for a several hundred yards to the coral reef drop-off offshore.

The 1st, 5th and 7th Marine Regiments would make the assault, with the 1st Marines landing at the northern end on one of the White Beaches. The 7th Marines would land at the southern end on Orange Beach 3, and the 5th Marines would land in the middle on Orange Beaches 1 and 2. The 1st and 7th Marines would drive inland guarding the right and left flanks of the 5th Marines as they assaulted and seized the airfield, which was located about a mile inland. The 5th Marines were tasked to drive right across the slender island, essentially cutting it in half. The 1st Marines were to push north into the Umurbrogol mountain area whilst the 7th Marines cleared the southern end of the island. The army's 81st Infantry Division was held in reserve at Angaur, to the south of Peleliu.

Loading operations for the assault group began at five widely separated staging posts, but finally on 4 September 1944, the US Marines LST assault ships departed their Solomon

Japanese pillbox protecting Peleliu airfield. (Author's collection)

Islands staging post of Pavuvu, just to the north of Guadalcanal. The assault group set off, protected by its screen of heavy warships, anti-submarine-warfare (ASW) equipped destroyers, minesweepers and aircraft, for the long slow insertion passage of some 2,000 nautical miles at the group speed of 7 knots. Faster transports left later – all due to rendezvous during the early hours of Peleliu D-Day, by which time the fire support group would have been softening up the landing zones for three days.

The navy's underwater demolition team, an elite special-purpose force, went in first, reconnoitring the beaches and waters just offshore, locating reefs, rocks and shoals that would interfere with landing craft and using explosives to demolish Japanese underwater obstacles. The development and deployment of the demolition team had followed on from the Battle of Tarawa in November 1943, when aerial reconnaissance had incorrectly led planners to believe that dangerous coral reefs and flats were submerged deep enough to allow assault landing craft to pass right over them safely. In the event, the landing craft foundered on the shallow reefs – and the heavily laden US Marines were forced to abandon their landing craft in chest-deep water some 1,000 yards from shore, terribly exposed to Japanese fire. They suffered heavy casualties.

On 12 September the pre-invasion naval bombardment of Peleliu began as the battleships *Pennsylvania*, *Maryland*, *Mississippi*, *Tennessee* and *Idaho*, the heavy cruisers *Columbus*, *Indianapolis*, *Louisville*, *Minneapolis* and *Portland*, and light cruisers *Cleveland*, *Denver* and *Honolulu*, led by the command ship USS *Mount McKinley*, opened up with their big guns on the tiny island, which is only six square miles in size. The punishing pre-invasion bombardment lasted three days – only pausing to allow air strikes from the three

Fortified Japanese command building on Peleliu which took a direct hit from a shell from the battleship USS *Mississippi*. (Author's collection)

fleet carriers, five light aircraft carriers, and eleven escort carriers of the attack force to take place.

The Americans were of course unaware of the new Japanese defence tactic, and the initial US assessment of the pre-invasion bombardment was that it had been a success. The navy thought they had run out of targets to hit with their big guns. The reality was, however, very different. The IJA battalion assigned for the beach defence delaying tactic were heavily dug in in their deep fortified bunkers and firing posts – they were virtually unscathed. Whilst obvious military targets above ground such as fortified buildings, command and communications centres were taken out, the Japanese troops and their infrastructure sheltering in the deeper cave complexes inland were not affected to any great extent. The bombardment may have destroyed aircraft and buildings surrounding the airfield, but the main bulk of the Japanese troops maintained strict firing discipline to avoid giving away their positions, patiently waiting in their caves and bunkers, ready to attack.

The Japanese had deployed mines around Angaur, Peleliu and the Kossol Passage entrances, where US forces were likely to assemble during any amphibious assault. Underwater demolition team frogmen detected Japanese mines during their clandestine operations, and mines were detected during reconnaissance by US submarines. The American submarine USS *Batfish* sunk the Japanese minelayer *W22* and detected another.

On 13 September a US minesweeper unit swept Kossol Passage to the north of Palau whilst other units swept around Angaur and Peleliu in the south.. The destroyer USS *Wadleigh* struck a mine and was heavily damaged whilst the minesweeper YMS-19 also struck a mine and sank. The minesweeper USS *Perry* struck a mine and sank while sweeping along the south-east coast of Angaur.

On the morning of 15 September just after 0800, US Marines began their amphibious assault, moving towards the shore from their mother ships in their landing craft – a combination of tracked landing vehicles (LVTs) and amphibious trucks (DUKWs or 'Ducks'). The 1st Marines would hit White Beaches 1 and 2 in the north section of the south-western landing beaches. The 5th and 7th Marines would land to the centre and south on Orange Beaches 1, 2, and 3.

LEFT: On 15 September 1944, as the three-day-long pre-invasion softening-up Spruance Haircut bombardment hits Peleliu, the first waves of US Marines are inbound in their LVTs and DUKWs. (National Archives)

RIGHT: Waves of US Marines head for the west Peleliu invasion beaches of White Beach and Orange Beach. (National Archives)

As the vulnerable landing craft packed full of US Marines approached White and Orange beaches, the Japanese opened the steel doors guarding their dug-in gun positions on the coral promontories projecting out to the north and south of the beaches on each flank. The Japanese then opened up with their 47mm anti-tank guns and 20mm cannon positions. The exposed marines were caught in a vicious artillery crossfire and by 0930, accurate Japanese fire had destroyed 60 LVTs and DUKW amphibious trucks.

The 1st Marines began their landings at 0832 but were quickly bogged down on the beaches by heavy fire, whilst the 7th Marines to the south faced a cluttered Orange Beach 3, with natural and man-made obstacles that forced the LVTs to approach in column.

The 5th Marines in the centre made the most progress on the first day, using cover provided by coconut groves. They pushed towards the airfield, which was only a mile or so inland. There as they reached the outskirts of the airfield they were met with the first Japanese counter-attack as a company of 13 Japanese light anti-infantry tanks raced across the airfield towards them. The marines engaged the Japanese counter-offensive with tanks and howitzers, and called in support from offshore naval guns and dive-bombers. The Japanese tanks and escorting infantrymen were quickly decimated.

As the daylight began to fade at the end of the first day, the marines were ashore in great strength and held their two-mile long invasion beach – but they had only managed to push inland by about a mile in the centre. To the north end of the beach, the 1st Marines had become bogged down by heavy resistance and had made little progress. Already 200 marines lay dead with 900 wounded.

As daylight of day two of the operation came, the 5th Marines in the centre assaulted and overran the airfield, taking heavy casualties from IJA infantry and from artillery that dominated the area from the Umurbrogol highlands to the north. Once they held the airfield they pushed across to the east side of the island.

With the airfield finally secured, the 5th Marines were sent to capture the tiny island of Ngesebus, just a few hundred metres to the north of Peleliu and connected to Peleliu by a small causeway. Ngesebus harboured many Japanese artillery positions and was the site of an airfield that was still under construction. The 5th Marines commander elected to make a shore-to-shore amphibious landing, believing that the Japanese would have been aware of the obvious route to take the island across the causeway and would have made careful preparations.

A coordinated pre-landing bombardment of the island began on September 28 – carried out by army 155mm (6.1-inch) guns, naval guns from the ships offshore, howitzers from the 11th Marines and strafing runs from VMF-114's Corsairs. The assault LVTs opened up with their own 75mm (2.95-inch) weapons as they approached. The naval bombardment here had

Looking from Peleliu across the causeway to Ngesebus island. (National Archives)

successfully degraded the Japanese positions to the extent that the island quickly fell with relatively light US casualties.

After capturing The Point, the 1st Marines moved north into the Umurbrogol pocket, soon to be named 'Bloody Nose Ridge' by the marines. Rather than being a mountain or a ridge, it was a series of ridges honeycombed with some 500 interconnecting caves and firing positions. The 1st Marines mounted several assaults but as they sought to press their attack higher they became trapped in crossfire in the narrow paths between the ridges.

As they pressed higher, they took increasingly heavy casualties to accurate Japanese fire. Japanese snipers began to target stretcher bearers. Once night fell Japanese troops stealthily infiltrated the American lines to attack the marines in their foxholes as they slept. The marines soon began to dig two-man foxholes so that one marine could sleep as the other stood guard.

When the 1st Battalion of the 1st Marines attacked Hill 100, over six days of fighting the battalion suffered 71 per cent casualties as they ran out of ammunition and were forced to fight with knives, bayonets and their bare hands.

The stalemate continued and by October 1944, the 7th Marines had suffered 46 per cent casualties by the time they were relieved by the 5th Marines under the command of Colonel Harold D. Harris. Pushing from the north, he adopted siege tactics, using bulldozers and flamethrower tanks to seal IJA troops in their caves or burn them out of their defensive positions.

Some of the caves had been hewn downwards so that any attackers would be silhouetted as they approached; however this feature was used by the Americans to their advantage – US bulldozers rolled 55-gallon drums of aviation fuel into the caves and then set the fuel on fire. On 30 October, the US Army 81st Infantry Division took over command of Peleliu operations from the battered marines. Using the same tactics, they took another six weeks to reduce the Umurbrogol Pocket and secure Bloody Nose Ridge.

The normally jungle-clad terrain has been almost completely deforested.

After two months of the most bloody defence, on 24 November Colonel Kunio Nakagawa, commander of the Japanese forces on Peleliu, proclaimed, 'Our sword is broken and we have run out of spears.' He solemnly burned his regimental colours and then performed ritual suicide. On 27 November, the US Army declared the island secure, ending the 73-day-long battle. (Colonel Nakagawa was posthumously promoted to lieutenant general for the valour he had displayed on Peleliu; his remains were discovered in a cave complex in 1993.)

The reduction of the Japanese pocket around Umurbrogol Mountain has been called the most difficult fight that the US military encountered in the entire war. The 1st Marines Division had been so badly degraded that it was not deployed in action again until the invasion of Okinawa on 1 April 1945. In one month the 1st Marines took casualties to more than one third of its strength, some 6,500 men. The 81st Infantry Division suffered 3,300 casualties. IJA losses were estimated at 10,000 killed in action. The battle has caused much post-war controversy, as with the airfields, anchorages and shore works of Palau neutralised, the Japanese garrison, many holed up in their cave complexes, had no means to interfere with US operations in the Philippines. At the end of the day despite the huge numbers of US troops killed or wounded, Peleliu airfield was not used operationally by the US, nor were Palau's anchorages used as a US staging point. Instead Ulithi Atoll was used as a staging post for the invasion of Okinawa. The brutal Battle of Peleliu was overshadowed by General MacArthur's return to the Philippines and the battle was largely overlooked until recent times. The new Japanese defensive strategy would be repeated at Iwo Jima and Okinawa.

US war memorial to the fallen near Orange Beach, Peleliu. (Author's collection)

On the recommendation of Admiral William F. Halsey, Jr, the planned amphibious assault of Yap Island in the Caroline Islands was cancelled. Halsey had previously recommended that the landings on Peleliu and Angaur be cancelled and that the marines and infantry be deployed to Leyte Island instead – but had been overruled by Nimitz.

The substantial Japanese garrison and civilian population on the largest Palauan island of Babelthuap was bypassed – there was no land invasion. With most of the towns and villages reduced to rubble, many of the remaining Japanese and civilians took to the jungle and hills. In the coming weeks and months, only a few Japanese submarines and fishing vessels were able to take food and supplies to the beleaguered inhabitants. With the shipping passages and harbours mined and American air power completely dominant, no Japanese ships could reach Palau. The Japanese garrison troops had effectively been cut off from Japan itself, as had other bypassed garrisons such as Truk and Rabaul. Palau began to starve, and martial law had to be declared.

The IJA moved to seize much of Palau's supplies of food to feed its troops, along with houses to billet its troops and gardens that could be used to grow food – causing great resentment amongst local Palauans. As starvation threatened, both troops and locals did what they could to grow food. Sweet potatoes, the root vegetable taro, grown for its edible corn and leaves, and other vegetables were all cultivated where they could be grown. The lagoon itself held bountiful supplies of fish but fishing by boat was dangerous due to repeated US air attacks. Any livestock on the islands was soon eaten. Local tropical fruits such as bananas, breadfruit, mangoes and coconut were all eaten extensively and became scarce. There was simply not enough food to go round, and starvation and disease set in. Leaves, lizards, rats and roots were soon being eaten. By the end of the war, more than 2,000 troops of the stranded Japanese garrison on Babelthuap would be dead, along with some 500 Palauans.

With Palau neutralised, Admiral Nimitz's strategy of island hopping continued. Rather than attacking the Imperial Japanese Navy in force, his aim was to capture and control strategic islands along a path that would bring US bombers within range of the Japanese home islands and pave the way for a possible invasion of Japan.

By early 1945, leapfrogging US forces led by Task Forces 38 and 58 had advanced as far as Iwo Jima and Okinawa, the carrier aircraft repelling sustained attacks from Japanese kamikaze aircraft as well as providing close air support to the US troops fighting on the ground. US forces had now advanced to within 340 miles of mainland Japan – but at great cost. On Okinawa alone during 82 days of fighting some 100,000 Japanese troops and 12,500 US troops were killed with, in addition, 50–100,000 Okinawan civilians being killed. But by now US forces were nearing their aim for the next stage of the war – the invasion of the Japanese home islands.

Less than a year would pass from the Operation *Hailstone* raids of 17/18 February 1944, until American B-24 and B-29 bombers lifted off in February 1945 from captured airfields on Saipan and Tinian for the first of many bombing raids against the city of Tokyo itself. In the first raid alone, 88,000 people are estimated to have died, with 41,000 injured.

On 8 May 1945 Germany finally surrendered. Japan was now left to fight on alone – but steadfastly refused to surrender. On 6 August 1945, the American Boeing B-29 Superfortress bomber *Enola Gay* left Tinian in the Marianas to drop the first nuclear bomb, Little Boy, on Hiroshima; 70,000 to 80,000 people were killed – some 30 per cent of the population – with 19,700 injured and 170,000 rendered homeless.

On 9 August 1945 a second nuclear bomb, Fat Man, was dropped from the B-29 bomber *Bockscar* on the city of Nagasaki, a secondary target, with similar devastating effect. The original target had been the city of Kokura but on the day of the attack it was obscured by cloud. The third target would probably have been Tokyo itself. The combined shock of these events caused Emperor Hirohito to intervene and order the Supreme Council to accept the terms the Allies had laid down in the Potsdam Declaration for ending the war. A cease-fire was arranged for 15 August 1945, and the occupation of Japan by the Allies began on 28 August 1945. The Empire of Japan formally surrendered unconditionally to the Allies on 2 September 1945. The war was over at last.

Some pockets of Japanese resistance on small Pacific islands however refused to surrender. Some Japanese troops might simply never have heard of the surrender – others would not surrender until ordered to do so by their superior officers who had perhaps been killed, captured or disappeared. A group of 35 IJA soldiers survived amongst the caves of Peleliu, hiding for 18 months before surrendering in April 1947. In another case, Second Lieutenant Hiroo Onoda had taken to the hills in Lubang Island in the Philippines when the Allies landed. He continued a campaign as a Japanese holdout, initially living with three fellow soldiers and carrying out guerrilla activities, killing local Filipino inhabitants and

Top: Knocked-out Japanese HQ buildings at Peleliu airfield. (Author's collection)
Bottom: Knocked-out US LVT near the foot of Bloody Nose Ridge. (Author's collection)

being involved in several shootouts. One of the four left the group in 1949 and surrendered in 1950. In 1952, letters and family pictures were air-dropped, urging the three remaining Japanese soldiers to surrender – but they believed this was a trick. One Japanese soldier was shot and killed in 1954, and local police killed another in 1972 whilst he was burning rice collected by farmers as part of his guerrilla activities.

In 1974 Onoda met a young Japanese man, Norio Suzuki, who was travelling the world and amongst other quests was searching for him. They became friends, but although urged to surrender, Onoda said he would not surrender until he received orders from a superior officer. Suzuki returned to Japan with photographs of Onoda and himself.

Despite the passing of some 30 years, on learning of Onoda's position, the Japanese government located Onoda's former wartime officer and flew him to Lubang Island. Here he finally met Onoda, formally relieved him of his duties and ordered him to surrender, using commands he had last used during World War II. Onoda ritually turned over his sword, his rifle, ammunition, hand grenades and a dagger.

Private Teruo Nakamura was the last known Japanese World War II combatant to surrender – emerging from his hidden retreat in Indonesia in December 1974. Two other Japanese soldiers, who had joined communist guerrillas at the end of the war, fought in southern Thailand until 1991.

To this day there are still some 2,600 IJA troops listed as missing in action in Palau – most still inside some of the 200 caves that have remained sealed since 1944. Archaeologists are now carefully and painstakingly opening up and investigating these cave systems. Some are still booby-trapped, and most still hold dangerous ordnance. Every now and then, a cave sealed since 1944 is opened to be examined – and inevitably the remains of missing IJA troops are discovered.

US LVT Amtank (amphibious tank with 75mm howitzer) at the foot of Bloody Nose Ridge.
(Author's collection)

# CHAPTER SEVEN

# Post-war Salvage of the Japanese Shipwrecks

At Kwajalein, Rabaul and Truk, the Japanese had anchored most of their large transport and merchant ships in deep water. As a result, after the US air raids had sent their ships to the bottom it was found that the ships were out of reach of Japanese salvage gear. The ships and their precious cargoes of war materials were completely lost to the Japanese, who did not have the heavy dive and salvage gear to bring up cargo on a large scale from those depths.

In Truk, a huge amount of war supplies went to the bottom – desperately needed shells, ammunition, beach mines, tanks, trucks – but all could have been salvaged and reused if the ships had been sunk in shallower water. Many of the ships had sunk with just one torpedo hole in their hull, and could have been repaired and reused if they had beached or sunk in shallow water. But most of the ships lay too deep – and so the ships, still filled with their cargoes, were left to lie on the bottom for eternity (to the benefit of today's divers).

Learning from these hard lessons, the Japanese used Palau's shallow-water anchorages, where the ships' bottoms would be close to the soft seabed. If the ships were hit and sunk, it was hoped that they could then be repaired, refloated and reused – and their precious war cargoes saved.

After Operation *Desecrate 1*, it was found that parts of some of the sunken ships' superstructures were standing proud of the water in the southern part of the Malakal anchorage. Towering masts rising well above superstructures projected from the water, marking the resting places of other vessels. Some of the casualty vessels – such as *Bichu Maru* and *Ose Maru* – had rolled over to one side or the other as they sank, ending up on the seabed resting on their beam, and this made salvage very difficult. The tankers *Iro* and *Sata* were left untouched by salvors in the deeper water of the Urukthapel anchorage; they had already been damaged in action and were in Palau for repair. They still held their inflammable cargoes of oil, a major fire hazard. The *Kamikaze Maru* and *Nagisan Maru* also held dangerous cargoes, such as the Long Lance torpedoes on *Kamikaze Maru*, so they had been anchored well away from the main Malakal Harbor anchorage.

The merchant ships not anchored within the confines of the Malakal Harbor anchorage were mainly dispersed in the Western Lagoon amongst the multitude of bays and channels west of Urukthapel Island, where the nearby steep walls of the numerous rocky islands provided a degree of protection against US air attack. The natural geography of these bays, channels and islands – for which Palau is now justly famous – formed sheltered anchorages, but these restricted areas gave little room for big supply ships to manoeuvre. For the attacking US aircraft, the terrain made the use of torpedoes extremely difficult, with the steep cliffs close to the ships preventing the aircraft from flying masthead attacks. They were forced to fly higher and this reduced the accuracy of their bombing.

There were some notable torpedo successes, such as the massive IJN oiler *Sata*, which lay in a large bay not far from her sister oiler *Iro*. This bay opened to seaward to the west and had allowed a clear attacking torpedo run; *Sata* was hit on the port side of her engine room, which faced to west and rolled over and sank.

However, despite all the Japanese efforts to save the ships and cargoes, at the end of the day, their new tactics did them little good. All the ships that were camouflaged and seeking shelter hard up against cliffs were eventually sunk – most often by near-miss bombs, the shock of which burst hull plating. Direct hits with 500lb or 1000lb bombs were catastrophic, particularly with engine room hits and the fires that followed. In some cases delayed-fuzed bombs exploded underneath the keel of a ship, breaking its back. Several of the ships that were strafed or bombed had secondary explosions of munitions or fuel cargo.

After the raids, the Japanese military closely surveyed the ships to recover anything which had not been spoiled by immersion or damaged in the attacks, and limited military salvage work took place.

After the war, in about 1950, several propellers were taken off the wrecks – they were easy to remove and very valuable. During the Korean War and afterwards, prices for non-ferrous metals were high, and concentrated salvage efforts by several salvors took place, which involved an American company, Micronesia Salvage (which mainly collected scrap from the land), a local company, Sakuma Salvage, and two Japanese companies, Nanshin and Fujita Salvage. Nanshin had the heavy equipment to refloat ships; freighters and tankers under 1,000 tons had their top hamper such as masts, superstructures and winches cut off, and were then lifted to barges by a large floating crane. Many of the shallow wrecks in the Malakal anchorage were removed in this way.

Nanshin wound down its operation on the 1950s, and Fujita Salvage took over. They clinically worked the wrecks using Japanese hard-hat divers and three small boats equipped with an air pump for the divers and acetylene cutting torches and dynamite. The divers would work all day, being taken to the surface, using in-water decompression, once or twice a day for food and drink. There was no recompression chamber, and in-water recompression was used for decompression sickness; unsurprisingly, several divers suffered terrible cases of the bends, with several fatalities recorded.

Fujita worked on some 27 Japanese wrecks including the *Akashi*, *Akebono Maru*, *Amatsu Maru*, *Asashio Maru*, *Goshu Maru*, *Gozan Maru*, *Hokutai Maru*, *Kamikaze Maru*, *Kibi Maru*, *Matsuei Maru*, *Ose*, *Raizan Maru*, *Shinsei Maru No. 18*, *T.150*, *Urakami Maru* and several ex-whaler auxiliary subchasers. Fujita's divers systematically dismantled the wrecks, using underwater cutting equipment to strip out propellers, condensers, masts, kingposts and amidships superstructures – before cutting the vessel down to the mud line if commercially viable. The scrap metal was lifted to barges and then taken ashore where it was further cut down for transport to Japan. The tanker *Akebono Maru* had been beached during the air raids and as Japan was very short of tankers after the war (due to the high wartime rate of attrition by US submarines), she was refloated and recommissioned.

There was no concentrated salvage attempt on the tankers *Iro* and *Sata*. An attempt to lift the tanker *Amatsu Maru* was abandoned – but 8,000 gallons of oil were recovered from it by using flexible large black rubber hoses connected into the wreck's tanks and pumping it out. Salvors then began to cut the wreck down, firstly by removing her masts along with her winches, anchors and chain from the bow. Work had started on removal of the propeller, but operations ceased after a diver was killed whilst cutting hull plating when his acetylene torch ignited some flammable material, causing an explosion. This was seen as a bad omen and work on the vessel ceased.

Salvage operations also ceased on the *Kamikaze Maru* after the superstructure had been taken off and the hull cut down; the foredeck Hold No. 2 held a large number of very dangerous Long Lance torpedoes and their high-pressure oxygen propellant tanks. On the large 4,500grt cargo steamer *Urakami Maru*, only the propeller, condenser and some 1,300 tons of metal were taken off due to the amount of munitions encountered and the dangers they posed.

When Fujita Salvage ceased operations, local salvors took over, using crude blasting techniques that have left many of the wrecks badly damaged or scarred.

It is said that the ships transporting the scrap metal recovered from the Japanese wrecks sank in a storm *en route* to Korea; whatever actually happened, none of the salvaged metal made it there.

# BOOK TWO

## The Shipwrecks of Palau

# The Shipwrecks of Palau

1. IJN *Akashi*
2. IJN *Amatsu Maru*
3. *Bichu Maru*
4. *Ch 6*, *Ch 10* and *Ch 12*; *Cha 22*, *Cha 26*, *Cha 52*, *Cha 53* and *Showa Maru No.5*
5. *Chuyo Maru*
6. Daihatsu Landing Craft wrecks
7. The Helmet Wreck
8. *Gozan Maru*
9. IJN *Iro*
10. *Kamikaze Maru*
11. *Kibi Maru*
12. *Nagisan Maru*
13. *Nissho Maru* No 5
14. USS Perry
15. *Raizan Maru*
16. *Ryuko Maru*
17. IJN *Sata*
18. *Teshio Maru*
19. IJN *T.1*
20. Type F standard ship – unidentified
21. *Urakami Maru*
22. IJN *Wakatake*

## AIRCRAFT WRECKS OF PALAU

1. Aichi E13A IJN seaplanes – Allied reporting name: Jake
2. Mitsubishi A6M Zero fighters – Allied reporting name: Zeke
3. Vought F4U Corsair

## OPERATION DESECRATE 1: US TASK FORCE 58 STRIKE AIRCRAFT

1. Curtiss SB2C Helldiver bomber
2. Douglas SBD Dauntless dive-bomber
3. Grumman TBF Avenger torpedo-bomber
4. Grumman F6F Hellcat fighter

# 1. IJN Akashi

IJN Akashi-class Auxiliary Repair Ship (1939)

## MALAKAL HARBOR

The 10,500-ton IJN *Akashi*-class auxiliary repair ship was laid down at the Sasebo Naval Yard on 18 January 1937 as the first IJN vessel to be designated as a repair ship under the 2nd Fleet Replenishment Programme of 1937. She was 507 feet long with a beam of 67 feet and a draught of 18 feet. She was launched on 29 June 1938, and after fitting out was completed she was placed on the Reserve List on 31 July 1939.

IJN *Akashi*-class Auxiliary Repair Ship *Akashi*.

With her two diesels driving two shafts, she could make a creditable 19 knots, and she carried a crew of 650. She resembled contemporary British submarine depot ships and was flush-decked with two low exhaust stacks amidships.

A few months after being placed on the Reserve List, on 15 November 1939 *Akashi* was assigned to the Combined Fleet, with Captain (later Vice Admiral) Miyazato Shutoku, the former commanding officer of the *Naka*, being appointed her chief equipping officer.

Following her assignment to the Combined Fleet, from November 1939 through to March 1940 the *Akashi* was fitted out for her specialist role as a repair ship with a 23-ton crane, two 10-ton cranes and two 5-ton cranes installed fore and aft to handle the transfer of spare parts and stores. A tool room, repair shop, machine shop and assembly plant were installed along with facilities for metal working, casting and forging custom parts. She was then fitted with two 5-inch 40-cal dual-purpose guns and smaller AA guns. She was the only specifically designed repair ship completed by Japan – the other two ships of her class ordered simultaneously, plus two other similar repair ships of the *Mihara* class, were subsequently cancelled.

Once her fitting-out works were completed, she was commissioned into the Imperial Japanese Navy as a fleet repair ship on 10 March 1940 under the command of Captain Shutoku – who would later go on to become CEO and first CO of the super-battleship *Yamato*.

Just a few months later, in June 1940, Vichy France ceded airfields, and agreed to the admission of Japanese troops and the establishment of military bases, in northern Indo-China – modern-day Cambodia, Laos and Vietnam. In July 1940, America responded by placing a ban on the export of steel, scrap metal and aviation fuel to Japan. Tensions were rising to boiling point.

Starboard quarter view of IJN *Akashi*.

On 11 October 1940 at Yokohama, *Akashi* and 97 IJN warships gathered in Tokyo Bay for the Imperial Naval Review; Emperor Hirohito, accompanied by Vice Admiral Yamamoto Isoroku, CINC Combined Fleet, boarded the battleship *Hiei* for the annual review whilst more than 500 aircraft thronged the sky above. The *Hiei*, escorted by the cruisers *Takao*, *Kako* and *Furutaka*, then passed amongst the fleet's ships, inspecting them.

In July 1941 Japanese and Vichy French authorities reached an agreement that extended Japanese use of air facilities and harbours into southern Indo-China. *Akashi* participated in the occupation operation.

On 25 September 1941 Captain (later Rear Admiral) Fukuzawa Tsunekichi assumed command of *Akashi*, and in December 1941 she moved from Kure in Japan to Palau, arriving there on 2 January 1942. She quickly moved on to Davao in the Philippines, where she provided emergency repairs for the destroyer *Inazuma* following a collision with the storeship *Sendai Maru*, and then attended to the destroyer *Hatsuhara* after a collision with the light cruiser *Nagara* on 25 January in the Celebes (now Sulawesi).

During February 1942 *Akashi* undertook engine repairs on the auxiliary water carrier *Koan Maru* before moving on to Celebes and then to Ambon, where she provided repairs for several battle-damaged warships before departing Ambon back to Kure in Japan, where she was dry docked for maintenance works to be carried out.

On 28 May 1942 she departed Kure in Vice Admiral Kondo Nobutake's 2nd Fleet Midway Invasion Force, arriving at Truk on 4 June 1942. At Truk, she provided temporary repairs for the cruiser *Mogami*, which had been damaged on 5 June 1942 in a collision with the cruiser *Mikuma* and also by US bombs in the Battle of Midway. Later that month she also completed emergency repairs on the destroyers *Asashio* and *Arashio*, both damaged by bombing and strafing at Midway.

Based in the forward naval base of Truk Lagoon, she carried out frequent repairs in Truk's Repair Anchorage on damaged naval vessels from July 1942 until the Operation *Hailstone* air assault on Truk on 17/18 February 1944. During this time she repaired bomb- or torpedo-damaged destroyers such as *Hagikaze*, *Yugiri*, *Shirakumo*, *Kagero*, *Minegumo* and *Urakaze*, along with seaplane tenders, the light cruisers *Jintsu*, the escort carrier *Taiyo*, the fleet carrier *Shōkaku* (hit by 1,000lb bombs) and the battleship *Yamato*. She was herself damaged in the Battle of Guadalcanal and several other contacts.

When the Operation *Hailstone* air raids began at dawn on 17 February 1944, *Akashi* was anchored in Truk's Repair Anchorage west of Dublon and north of Fefan Island. Nearby were the destroyer *Fumizuki*, the transports *Kiyosumi Maru*, *Kensho Maru*, *Tonan Maru No. 3* and *Yamagiri Maru*, the tanker *Hoyo Maru* – all were undergoing or awaiting repairs by *Akashi*.

She survived the two-day air raids, although her speed was reduced to 12 knots by damage sustained in them. A few days later, at 0400 on 20 February 1944, she departed Truk bound for Palau with the destroyers *Akikaze* and *Fujinami* during the Combined Fleet's redeployment.

She arrived at Palau on morning of 24 February and anchored in Malakal Harbor. She initially carried out repair work on her own damage before shortly afterwards beginning repairs on the torpedo-damaged *Bichu Maru*. Those repairs were completed on 28 March 1944.

*Akashi* is moored (top of shot) between small islands close to the north shore of Ngeruktabel in Malakal Harbor. The Type F refrigerated vessel is moored stern to, opposite the words 1,000ft. (National Archives)

During Operation *Desecrate 1*, on 30 March 1944, the *Akashi* was anchored in Malakal Harbor, off the northern side of Urukthapel Island. She was moved to shallower water, closer to shore in a cove. An important US target, she sustained numerous direct hits and near misses by bombs, torpedoes and rockets, taking at least seven hits on her stern, two on her port bow, one on her forward superstructure, two amidships and another aft of her stack which caused a fierce fire. She sank by the bow in shallow water on a shelving bottom – her bows sank into slightly deeper water than her stern, and she came to rest with her bows submerged, but with her bridge, crane tops, masts and stern proud of the water. She remained like this for several years after the war, allowing locals to free dive into her innards to salvage what they could.

In 1954, Fujita Salvage under the authority of the Palau government began its salvage work on the Palau wrecks, systematically dismantling them for scrap. At 507 feet in length with a displacement of 10,500 tons, *Akashi* was a large and valuable wreck sitting in very shallow water, and so was a prime target for them. The *Akashi* was cut into sections and then lifted from the bottom – in all Fujita was able to recover some 4,500 tons of scrap metal.

## THE WRECK TODAY

Today all that remains of the *Akashi* is a long depression in the shelving seabed marking where she lay, and a substantial debris field – the combined results of the punishing US air attacks and the attentions of Fujita Salvage. The seabed is in 12–15 metres, and there are many recognisable sections of ship strewn around, such as forced-draught ventilators, frames, and torn and bent sections of steel shell plating. Depressions in the seabed resembling the effects of bomb hits can be made out here and there around the area.

With so many world-class wrecks to choose from, the remains of *Akashi* are little dived.

SHIPWRECK – THE ESSENTIALS

| | |
|---|---|
| Type: | *Akashi*-class auxiliary repair ship |
| Built: | 1937–39 |
| Displacement: | 10,500 tons |
| Dimensions: | Length 507 feet; beam 67 feet; draught 18 feet |
| Propulsion: | 2 diesels, 2 shafts |
| Date of loss: | 30/31 March 1944 |
| Cause of loss: | Bombed, torpedoed and rocketed at anchor by Task Force 58 aircraft |
| Depth to seabed: | 10–15 metres |
| Location: | Malakal Harbor – north shore of Urukthapel Island |

# 2. IJN Amatsu Maru

Type 1TL Standard Merchant Tanker (1943)

## MALAKAL HARBOR WEST ENTRANCE

The *Amatsu Maru* was laid down in Nagasaki by Mitsubishi Zosensho as yard number 911. She was a 10,567-ton Type 1TL Standard Merchant Tanker built for Nippon Kaiun KK of Tokyo. *Amatsu Maru* was launched on 23 March 1943 and was a big ship – 526 feet long overall with a beam of 65 feet 7 inches and a draught of 29 feet 10 inches. Her geared steam turbine and machinery were situated aft – as with

Type TL merchant tanker similar to IJN *Amatsu Maru*.

all tankers – and gave her a service speed of 13 knots, a top speed of 18 knots and an operating radius of 10,000 nautical miles. She could carry a cargo of 105,000 barrels of oil (a barrel being 35 imperial gallons). She had a prominent 'economy' hull shape, long and almost pointed at the stern, and fully loaded she displaced 14,500 tons. She was fitted with a single 2-ton cargo boom.

Approximately 12–15 of the Type TL and TL (Modified) vessels had been built by July 1944 – and the class included the *Kyokuei Maru, Kyuei Maru, Miri Maru, Nampo Maru* and *Okikawa Maru*. The class had a slender bridge forward of amidships and a stern superstructure housing her machinery.

There were a number of Japanese standard ship designs throughout the latter part of World War II. During the pre-war 1930s, Japanese ships had been built to modern fast designs; however, with Japanese sea-lanes enormously extended soon after the outbreak of war and with the successful degradation of its existing shipping stock by US submarines, Japan realised that it had to radically boost ship production.

Before 1941 there was no actual or effective standardisation of Japanese ship types, for while shipbuilding was subsidised by the Japanese government, ship design was largely determined by shipping requirements and individual ship builders. Japanese pre-war shipping requirements resulted in a standardisation of general types of ship rather than the adoption of set individual designs. Freighter design concentrated on diesel-powered vessels of 5,000–6,000 grt with superstructure amidships, cruiser sterns and hulls designed for speed – and few engines-aft freighters were built. Tanker design called for fast 10,000-ton vessels with cruising speeds of 17 knots and top speeds of 19 knots.

Conscious of the stress to its merchant shipping capacity that the war was bringing, Japan began work on new modern standard ship designs in 1942. However, with approximately

Artist's impression of the Type 1TL merchant tanker *Amatsu Maru*.

two years required to design and begin building new types of standard ship, construction of the newer designs of standard ships would only start in early 1944. Therefore, in the interim, to boost its merchant fleet to service its far-flung Pacific garrisons, Japan started a programme of mass standard ship production using older, tried and tested pre-war designs. Cargo capacity, range and speed of construction would be given paramount importance – whilst the actual speed of the ships themselves was given less importance. An emphasis was placed on engines-aft freighters, which gave more economical operation – but it may be that there was a shortage of facilities for forging the far longer propeller shafts required for engines-amidships vessels, in which a shaft must run half the length of the vessel to the propeller itself.

Older steam turbine and reciprocating engines were generally fitted – as opposed to more modern, faster, cleaner diesel engines. This perhaps indicates a shortage of manufacturing facilities for building the more complicated diesel engine – there were also practical considerations such as availability of engine types, and facilities for casting or forging parts. The use of the older style of steam engine in new ships may perhaps be an indication that Japan realised that it might be forced to depend on coal rather than oil for fuel in the future.

The new welded hull designs were angular, with a broad beam relative to length – this was a sacrifice of speed for a larger cargo capacity. To speed up construction, flat 'economy' hull surfaces were adopted where possible in place of smooth sculpted steelwork. This economy measure resulted in a loss of 2–3 knots compared to traditional smooth hull shapes.

The 2nd War Standard Programme came into force at the end of 1942 and was characterised by the abandonment of many traditional ship features thus allowing greater speed of construction and mass production of shipping with maximum economy of building materials. The majority of ships built during the war were ordered under this programme, and they included uncased funnels and a counter stern, a total lack of camber on decks, a reduced number of transverse frames, and the absence of double-bottom compartments.

Between December 1941 and July 1944 some 125 standard ships were built to a number of different designs. The number in the standard type refers to the year of construction, with Type 1 being a 1943 build, Type 2 being 1944 and Type 3 being 1945. The letter in the standard type refers to the actual type or specification of ship and went from A, B and C onwards. *Amatsu Maru* was a Type 1TL tanker, the 1 denoting her as a 1943 build.

The tankers of the early part of the 20th century were of relatively simple construction – basically being a long steel box divided into a series of compartments. The forward spaces were designed to carry water and dry cargo such as oil in drums. The after spaces held water, bunker fuel, cargo pumps and the ship's engines. Between these two end spaces, the rest of the tanker was divided on a gridiron plan into cargo compartments or tanks. This extensive subdivision, with sometimes as many as 33 compartments, gave tankers exceptional strength and stability. The war years showed that tankers could stay afloat despite several breaches of the hull beneath the waterline.

In hot weather, the oil cargo in a tanker expands and in cold weather it contracts. If the ship's tanks were completely sealed this expansion and contraction of the cargo would create a vacuum and allow dangerous internal pressures to build up. To let the cargo breathe, small pipes ran from the top of each tank to the ship's masts – running up to flameproof venting outlets high above the deck and safely away from any possible causes of ignition. At the bottom of the cargo tanks, a system of heating coils was installed through which steam was passed if the cargo was heavy grade oil, which required heating to enable it to be pumped.

Each cargo tank could be filled and emptied independently of the others so that different types of oil could be loaded into separate tanks and discharged without being cross-contaminated. Numerous valves linked each cargo tank to a system of pipelines inside the ship that led to the ship's pumps. Another set of pipelines led up from the pumps on to the tanker's deck, where they were conveniently located for connecting to shore pipelines for loading and discharging; the pump room was a small control deckhouse usually set on the main deck just in front of or abaft of the midships bridge superstructure. The ship's pumps were primarily used for pumping the cargo out of the ship to shore storage tanks and for pumping ballast water in or out of the ship. Shore pumps were used for pumping oil cargo aboard from the land.

The deck of a tanker was a continuous weather deck only penetrated by small raised cargo hatches, one for each tank, which were fitted with watertight steel lids – and kept dogged down and sealed when the ship was loaded.

Rising above the weather deck were three superstructures – the fo'c'sle, the midships bridge superstructure and the poop or stern deckhouse.

The fo'c'sle spaces were used to store ship's equipment, such as the chain locker, the lamp room etc. The midships superstructure held the bridge, the chart room, the radio room, store rooms and officer accommodation. The stern deckhouse held the accommodation for the rest of the ship's company, the mess room, galley, refrigerated space and steering gear.

A fully laden tanker would lie deep in the water and in rough seas the weather deck would be continuously swept by seawater. The tanker would thus become a three-island ship with only its three superstructures visible from any distance. To allow the crew to pass in safety from each of the three islands when decks could be awash, an elevated catwalk called a flying bridge connected all three superstructures on most tankers. In the case of the Type TL tankers the flying bridge ran along the port side of the hull from the aft machinery superstructure to the bridge forward of midships. The flying bridge however was absent from the bridge to the fo'c'sle.

*Amatsu Maru* had a prominent flat economy hull and long, almost pointed, stern. Many of the class had their foremast abaft the bridge superstructure. The distinctive stern, the location of the foremast and the absence of a forward flying bridge were all distinctive features that helped US pilots identify them as Type TL targets.

*Amatsu Maru*'s career at sea would be short-lived. She was launched on 23 March 1943 at a time when the war had already turned against Japan – she was fitted out afloat and completed on 10 June 1943. Such was the pressing need for tankers that just five days later, on 15 June 1943, she had departed Sasebo for Takao, Formosa – where she arrived on 22 June. She was under repair at Takao until 30 July 1943, and from there she moved to St Jacques in Indo-China.

On 12 October 1943 *Amatsu Maru* departed the southern Japanese port of Moji in a convoy consisting of her sister Type 1TL standard merchant tanker *Kyokuei Maru*, the IJN seaplane tender *Sanuki Maru*, and the IJN transports *Nankai Maru*, *Mizuho Maru*, *Aobasan Maru*, *Fuso Maru* and *Manila Maru*, escorted by the destroyer *Asakaze* and the IJN *kaibōkan* escort vessel *Tsushima*. (For more information about *kaibōkan*, see Chapter 4, Section *Ch 6*.) The convoy arrived at Takao in Formosa on 16 October 1943 before departing for Samah on Hainan Island in the South China Sea two days later, on 18 October. The convoy departed from Samah on 24 October bound for Singapore – arriving there on 30 October.

On 3 November 1943 *Amatsu Maru* departed Singapore in convoy to return to Takao, again with her sister Type 1TL standard merchant tanker *Kyokuei Maru*, plus a number of freighter transports, and again escorted by the *kaibōkan Tsushima*. Five days later off the Philippines, the convoy was attacked as dawn broke by the American submarine USS *Bluefish*, which successfully torpedoed and sank the valuable tanker *Kyokuei Maru*. *Tsushima* was detached to rescue survivors but was then unable to relocate the convoy, which had to proceed unescorted.

The following morning the American submarine USS *Seawolf* made three separate attacks on the convoy but all were unsuccessful due to defective Mark 14-3A torpedoes. The remainder of the convoy arrived at Takao on 10 November 1943.

On 7 December 1943 *Amatsu Maru* was formally requisitioned by the Imperial Japanese Navy, assigned directly to the Combined Fleet and ordered to Moji. From there she departed in convoy for Takao with the 1TL Standard Merchant Tanker *Ominesan Maru* and the smaller 5,135-ton Type 1TM Standard Tanker *Zuiho Maru*, the IJN seaplane tender *Kagu Maru*, a number of transports and escorted once again by *Tsushima*. *En route* the convoy was attacked by the American submarine USS *Aspro*, which fired four torpedoes. All missed or were evaded, and the convoy was able to proceed unscathed – reaching Takao later that day.

The following day she departed Takao for Singapore, where she arrived on 21 December. From December 1943 until March 1944 she operated on a regular supply run between Moji, Takao and the large Japanese naval base at Singapore where oil and supplies were desperately needed. With the virtual abandonment of Truk as a forward naval base following the Operation *Hailstone* raids of 17/18 February 1944, much of the Combined Fleet had moved westwards to Palau and Singapore, so there was an increased need for oil for the naval units there.

On 5 March 1944 *Amatsu Maru* arrived once again in Singapore, and on 16 March she departed Singapore bound for Palau in an escorted convoy consisting of the 5,266-ton Type

*Amatsu Maru* moored just to the south of Ngerchaol in Malakal Harbor takes a near miss whilst an unidentified freighter is also hit nearby on 30 March 1944. *Chuyo Maru* is just out of shot to the right. (National Archives)

View aft from a Douglass Dauntless dive-bomber towards Malakal Harbor. Ngerchaol is to the left and Ngeruktabel to the right – the claws of Malakal harbor. *Amatsu Maru* can be seen under attack.

1TM Standard Merchant Tankers IJN *Yuho Maru* and *Asashio Maru* and the war prize fleet oiler *Ose* (ex-*Genota* – requisitioned by British Ministry of War Transport and captured by raiders *Aikoku Maru* and *Hokoku Maru* in the Indian Ocean on 9 May 1942). The small convoy arrived safely at Palau on 27 March with its valuable cargoes of oil for the naval units stationed there – just as Task Force 58 was closing at speed on Palau; Operation *Desecrate 1* was only three days away. *Amatsu Maru* anchored on the north side of Malakal Harbor not far from the western entrance between the long promontories of Ngerchaol to the north and Ngeruktabel to the south that form the distinctive claws around the anchorage.

During the morning of 30 March, *Amatsu Maru* was bombed by Douglas SBD Dauntless dive-bombers from USS *Enterprise* on Strike 2B. Hits by 1,000lb bombs were reported around the fantail and at the bow – one bomb had struck her or been a near miss at the stern on the starboard side, causing a fire to take hold in the engine room.

About an hour later, another section of Douglas SBD Dauntless dive-bombers attacked her during Strike 2C and she took a direct hit amidships, which caused a large explosion and the loss of ten of her crew. Hit now by at least three 1,000lb bombs she sank slowly by the stern – and aerial reconnaissance photographs taken early the following day, 31 March, show her down by the stern with only her bow, foremast and the top of her bridge superstructure showing above the water. She remained in this half-sunken attitude for some months – Operation *Snapshot* aerial photo-reconnaissance images taken on 26 July show her still in this condition. She subsequently sank completely into just over 40 metres of water, coming to rest on an even keel.

Fujita Salvage surveyed *Amatsu Maru* in the 1950s, when it was found she still held her partial cargo of oil. Some 8,000 gallons of oil were successfully recovered at that time by using large black flexible rubber hoses to connect into her oil tanks. It was initially considered that she could be raised intact – however that plan was subsequently abandoned

The wreck of the 10,567grt Type 1TL merchant tanker *Amatsu Maru* sits upright in 41 metres of water. She is a massive, structurally intact shipwreck lying in an area of generally good visibility and depths of about 30 metres to her main deck.

TOP: Control panel inside *Amatsu Maru*. Photo © Richard Barnden, Unique Dive Expeditions.
BOTTOM: The safe of *Amatsu Maru*. Photo © Richard Barnden, Unique Dive expeditions.

and more minor salvage works began. Both masts were taken away to reduce the danger to shipping, and the anchor windlass and anchors were removed from the fo'c'sle deck. The engine room was blasted open and the engine lifted out.

The salvage works were however abandoned when a diver using an acetylene torch ignited a pocket of trapped gas. The resulting explosion killed both the diver and his tender. Taking this as a bad omen, further salvage work on this vessel was abandoned.

## THE WRECK TODAY

Today the wreck of the *Amatsu Maru* rests perfectly upright on an even keel in about 41 metres of water with the main deck at 30 metres and the top of the bridge superstructure at about 24 metres. She is a massive, largely intact wreck – so much so that it took me a good 50 minutes to swim completely around her non-stop to video her. Her open spaces such as her main decks seem to disappear in every direction, dwarfing a diver. Her fo'c'sle appears huge, and the swim aft from her bridge to her stern superstructure seems to go on forever.

This large wreck lies in an area of relatively good underwater visibility – with 25–30-metre vis about the average. Located inside the northmost claw of Malakal Harbor, she is just ten minutes' boat ride away from several dive shops, such as Sam's Tours' fantastic dive centre; you can head out to dive her, have the day's first dive lasting 1–2 hours, and still be back at Sam's by 1100 for an early lunch. She is so large that it will take several dives to get to know her well – there is so much to explore in areas such as her bridge superstructure and stern superstructure that you could easily spend an entire dive in each of these areas alone. She was a welded ship, and her welded deck and hull plates are still clearly discernable.

Starting at her bow, her soft-nosed raked stem is very evident – she has a massive bow that dominates divers and disappears into the slightly milky vis that you get near the bottom on wreck dives inside the harbour and in some of the small bays outside.

The raised fo'c'sle is ringed by coral-covered guardrails with a small section of raised gunwale at the very tip of the bow. Bollards and forced-draught ventilators are dotted around the deck, along with some large flexible rubber hoses perhaps left from the salvage works. Evidence of the small-scale salvage work can be seen here, with the anchor windlass and most of the anchor chain being removed, but a section of it is snagged on twin bollards and runs forward past where the windlass would have been sited, towards the twin hawse pipes on the centre line. Both anchors have been salved and are no longer present on the wreck.

A single door in the centre of the fo'c'sle bulkhead at main deck level allows access into the fo'c'sle spaces and is flanked on either side by a fixed set of steps that lead from the main deck up to the fo'c'sle deck. Inside the fo'c'sle are large reels of cable.

Dropping down from the fo'c'sle to the well deck, sturdy gunwales run along either side of the deck. With the ship's substantial beam of 66 feet, the opposite gunwale can just be made out on good days. Fixed pipes for loading and unloading the foredeck oil tanks below criss-cross the deck and lead to more major loading/offloading athwartships pipes situated just in front of the bridge superstructure. Each has a circular turn valve on top of the side pipe connector that would have given control of the flow of oil on or off the vessel. Several small raised deck hatches allowed access for the crew from the weather deck down to the oil cargo tanks situated forward of the bridge superstructure. Being a Type TL tanker there is no flying bridge here on the foredeck, and the foremast has been removed by salvors. More

AMATSU MARU

Looking up from the bottom of the *Amatsu Maru* pump room abaft the bridge superstructure to the open skylights in the distance. Photo © Richard Barnden, Unique Dive expeditions.

large flexible black rubber hoses lie strewn about the foredeck – again perhaps used by the salvors and simply abandoned.

The bridge superstructure still stands – rising up for several levels almost 10 metres from the well deck to the highest navigating bridge deck. Open doorways at either side of the well deck allow entry to the lowest deck level of this superstructure, which is lined with cabins with portholes. A raised deck access hatch is situated close to this doorway to allow crew emerging from the doorway to the foredeck to descend below to the oil cargo tanks themselves. Outboard of the doorways at the gunwales, fixed steps lead up to higher promenade walkways that run down either side of the superstructure at shelter deck level and have cabins leading off inboard.

On the next deck level up, and beneath the bridge itself, can be found the radio room with the radio equipment still *in situ*. All internal wall divisions are now burnt or rotted away, creating a wide-open space.

The intense fires that ravaged *Amatsu Maru* following the 1944 air strikes have also consumed all wooden deck and wall materials of the superstructure and have now left the skeletal framework of the higher deck levels exposed in places. The bridge itself, situated at the highest level, can be entered in a number of ways through open doorways and between the exposed structural beams of the roof – the navigational instruments are now absent. Guardrails line the outer edges of the higher deck levels and are now covered in corals. A section of the original port wing docking position is still present.

The promenade deck walkways ring right around the back of the superstructure and, mirroring the foredeck layout, fixed stairways lead down from them to the main weather deck with access doorways to the deckhouse and raised deck cargo tank access hatches nearby. The gunwales that protected the foredeck, which had no flying bridge and could be swept by seawater in a poor sea, give way to a flush deck with guardrails here on the main deck between the bridge superstructure and the aft machinery superstructure. This deck was less likely to ship any sort of sea and was thus less dangerous for crew who could use the flying bridge in poor weather. Mooring bollards and bitts for springs are dotted around the outer deck here.

Immediately aft of the bridge superstructure stands the pump room – a one-storey small deckhouse from where the loading and unloading of the oil cargo was controlled. It has a pitched roof set atop it similar to an engine room, with two part-open skylights on each pitch and at each aft corner a forced-draught ventilator. A raised walkway leads aft from the promenade deck of the bridge superstructure along the centre line of the vessel to the top of the pump room, where a hatch and steps allow access below. At main deck level on the aft-facing bulkhead of the pump room, an open doorway allows access into its innards and a staircase grating winds down through several deck levels to the very bottom of the ship.

The main deck again has oil pipes running across it both athwartships and fore and aft, and several cargo tank deck access hatches. A large, flexible rubber hose lies jumbled on the deck – most likely left by the salvors. The flying bridge connecting the bridge superstructure to the sterncastle is still intact, and runs fore and aft just inboard from the port side of the main deck at a depth of about 30 metres. In places, fixed steps lead up to it from the main deck. Further twin flexible hoses are still connected to the ship's valves outboard on the port side of the flying bridge. It is as though the salvors just stopped whatever work they were doing immediately the explosion occurred and left their pipes lying around in places on the wreck – some still connected to valves. A number of cargo hatches dot the main section of the deck and the port side of the flying bridge – their lids are all removed, no doubt due to the salvage works in the 1950s.

The main deck of this large tanker, between the bridge superstructure and the sterncastle, is a massive long section of open decking. The deck is sagging noticeably by 1–2 metres along the centreline and in the middle; the deck plates are opening up fore and aft along their welded joins for quite some distance. A small section of her main mast is still left *in situ*.

Finally, after quite a swim, the sterncastle at main deck level comes into view with two open doorways leading inside, and two sets of fixed steps leading up at either side to its roof at shelter deck level where a guardrail runs along. The flying bridge connects with the top of this deckhouse, where there is a broad expanse of open shelter deck before another deckhouse rises up a further level – accommodating the roof of the boiler and engine rooms further aft. Guardrails again ring around its edges and two large forced-draught ventilator funnels stand near its leading edge – the depth to this higher deck level is about 26 metres.

TOP: This closed box on top of the bridge superstructure of *Amatsu Maru* may well have held ready-use ammunition for AA guns. (Author's collection)

BOTTOM: Looking towards the port bridge wing above brain corals that adorn the top of the bridge superstructure. The wooden deck planking was burnt away during wartime fires. (Author's collection)

Immediately aft of the two forward ventilator funnels there is a large jagged hole some 20 feet square, where it looks as though salvors have cut away the roof to rip out the boilers or condensers. The decking around sags downwards into the hole.

Promenade walkways run along either side of this deckhouse towards the fantail. The wood of the decking and the roofing of the spaces on either side of the fireproof steel walls of the engine casing has all been consumed by the fires, leaving only the structural beams.

The large banded funnel has collapsed to port and now, partly flattened, rests on top of the deckhouse, projecting slightly forward along the top. It is so big that divers sometimes fail to recognise what they are looking at. The pipework for its steam whistle runs up the side.

Aft of the funnel is a second and much larger black rectangular ragged hole where salvors have cut away the roofing of the engine room to rip out the valuable non-ferrous engine and associated fitments. The cut-away sections of roof have just been dumped on the adjoining deckhouse roof. Two sets of lifeboat davits in the swung-out position (indicating the crew were able to abandon ship) dot either side of the deckhouse roof.

The aft section of the ship, although structurally intact, shows much damage from a combination of the 1,000lb US bombs and the fires that resulted – and from the subsequent attentions of salvors. On the starboard side of the hull a near miss has buckled and blown in the shell plating of the hull, allowing divers to pass through.

At the aftmost end of the sterncastle towards the fantail, a large open hatch allows easy access down into the deckhouse where the steering gear and quadrant are housed. There is no stern gun. Mooring bollards and forced-draught ventilators dot around the edges of the deck here as it sweeps towards the fantail.

Dropping over the very stern of the ship the large rudder and four-bladed propeller can be found at seabed level of 41 metres – such is the orientation of the ship that the rudder is almost completely clear of the seabed.

I loved diving this huge tanker – there is so much to see that she needs several dives to really take her in and allow time to explore gems such as her steering gear and the pump room. She is a world-class shipwreck and one of the 'musts' of Palau diving.

## SHIPWRECK – THE ESSENTIALS

| | |
|---|---|
| Type: | Type 1 TL Standard Merchant Tanker |
| Built: | 1943 |
| Tonnage: | 10,567 grt |
| Displacement: | 14,500 tons (loaded) |
| Dimensions: | Loa 526ft 7in.; beam 65ft 7in.; draught 29ft 10in. |
| Propulsion: | Geared steam turbine – single shaft |
| Date of loss: | Exact date unknown, but post July 1944 |
| Cause of loss: | Bombed at anchor by Task Force 58 aircraft on 30 March 1944 |
| Depth to seabed: | 41 metres |
| Least depth: | 24 metres – top of bridge |
| Location: | North side of Malakal Harbor – just inside western entrance. |

# 3. Bichu Maru

Type 1B standard cargo vessel (1943)

## WESTERN LAGOON – NORTH-WEST SHORE OF URUKTHAPEL ISLAND

The 4,667grt naval transport *Bichu Maru* was built by Ishikawajima Zosensho of Tokyo for Nippon Yusen Kaisha in 1943 and was one of approximately 16 Type 1B ships built by Japan that year. She was 387 feet long with a beam of 52 feet and a draught of 24 feet. Powered by a coal-fired turbine she had a service speed of 11 knots, a top speed of 14 knots and an operating radius of 7,500 nautical miles.

The 4,667grt Type 1B freighter *Bingo Maru* – the same standard type as *Bichu Maru*.

Standard ships such as *Bichu Maru* were all built to a simple standard design at a time when Japan saw the need to quickly build large numbers of ships to make up for those sunk in action and thus allow the continued transport of the huge volumes of materials and supplies needed to fight its war in the Pacific.

Japan began work on new modern standard ship designs in 1942 with the 1st War Standard Programme, which included different types of specialised vessels as well as cargo vessels and tankers. The various classes did not vary in any great respect from their peacetime equivalents and they were intended to be economical vessels suitable for post-war use.

With approximately two years required, however, to design and start building new types of standard ship, construction of the newer designs of standard ships would only start in early 1944. In the interim, to boost its supply fleet to service its far-flung Pacific garrisons, in 1941 Japan started a programme of mass standard ship production using older, tried and tested pre-war designs. Between December 1941 and July 1944, some 125 standard ships were built to a number of different designs.

The 2nd War Standard Programme was initiated at the end of 1942, and was characterised by the abandonment of many common ship's features to facilitate mass production with the greatest economy of building materials. The majority of ships built during the war were ordered under this programme, and they featured a total lack of camber on decks, a reduced number of transverse frames, an absence of double bottoms, uncased funnels and counter sterns.

The 3rd War Standard Programme was initiated in September 1943 and included seven classes with improved compartmentation and higher-powered machinery giving greater speed to counter submarine attack. But only six of these large ships were eventually completed (along with 36 coasters) before the end of the war.

From 1943 onwards, Japanese standard ships were allocated a number which referred to the year of construction. Type 1 was a 1943 build, Type 2 being 1944 and Type 3 being

1945. The letter in the standard type refers to the actual type or specification of ship and went from A, B, C etc. onwards; the design of the individual types varied from year to year. *Bichu Maru* was built in 1943 and is thus a Type 1B standard ship.

During the age of initial recreational diving exploration of the *Desecrate 1* wrecks at Palau in the 1980s and 1990s, when the main wrecks were being relocated and identified, doubts emerged as to whether the wreck known locally as *Bichu Maru*, resting in a small bay on the north-west side of Urukthapel Island, was in fact that ship. Some sources proposed that it was the *Gozan Maru* or possibly the *Hokutai Maru*. Having researched all three of these ships for this book, I can well understand the confusion. For the purposes of this book, however, the evidence suggests to me that the wreck known locally as the *Bichu Maru* has been correctly identified, and that the *Gozan Maru* is the wreck in Malakal Harbor that was dismantled by Fujita Salvage in the 1950s and is now only a debris field of parts left over from that commercial work.

A lot is known about most Japanese ships built or acquired before the war – most were registered with Lloyd's Register of Shipping in London. But once the veil of the secrecy of war had descended, many Japanese ships were built without the Allies being aware. Of course any new ships built after the war had started were not registered at Lloyd's of London – the UK was the enemy of Japan. Consequently, *Bichu Maru* is not registered at Lloyd's.

US Intelligence had collated all the information they had on Japanese ships and types of ships into a number of wartime classified military briefing documents, which were mainly declassified in the 1970s. The *Bichu Maru* is not listed in the restricted American wartime intelligence dossier *Japanese Merchant Ships Recognition Manual* ONI 208-J (Revised). This now declassified dossier was being collated by the Division of Naval Intelligence in 1943 when *Bichu Maru* was being built, and was distributed in 1944. This document is a fascinating source of information about all Japanese merchant shipping known at the time and was intended to provide Allied submarine, air and surface forces with recognition data to facilitate successful attacks on the Japanese merchant fleet. *Bichu Maru* is not mentioned.

She is however listed in the restricted American wartime Division of Naval Intelligence briefing document *Standard Classes of Japanese Merchant Ships ONI 208-J (Revised)* issued the following January. This document, declassified on 3 May 1972, gives profile drawings for each known class of Japanese ship – the ships being graded A, B, C and D to indicate their evaluated accuracy. *Bichu Maru* is listed in this document as a Type B ship, which the US document classifies as generally a long ship of 410 feet having a split superstructure similar to a tanker, with a slender bridge forward of midships and a larger superstructure holding her machinery at the very stern. The engine room and funnel of these tanker-like freighters is at the very stern – they were often misidentified as tankers by US aviators. US Intelligence believed that some 30 Type B ships including *Bichu Maru* were built.

The wreck known locally as the *Bichu Maru* at Palau however has a composite superstructure amidships that holds both the bridge and the engine room in the middle of the ship. That at first sight seems to suggest that the *Bichu Maru* is not our wreck – however the American intelligence document *Standard Classes of Japanese Merchant Ships* does state that some of the Type B ships 'are possibly of engines-amidship construction', allowing the possibility that *Bichu* is indeed a Type B.

Records show that some 16 Type 1Bs were built in 1943 with a composite superstructure amidships, five holds set two fore and aft of the superstructure, and a stoke hold in the gap between bridge and engine casing – such as the *Hanakawa Maru* wreck at Truk Lagoon and similar to the smaller Type 1C freighters. Another wreck at Palau, the *Urakami Maru*, is also Type 1B freighter.

The fog of war has produced much confusion about *Bichu Maru*. The *Dictionary of Disasters at Sea during the Age of Steam* by Charles Hocking notes that *Bichu Maru* was bombed and sunk off New Guinea on 29 December 1943. The authoritative *Warships of the Japanese Imperial Navy, 1869–1945* by Hansgeorg Jentschura, Dieter Jung and Peter Mickel, and published by Arms and Armour Press, London, in 1977 is able to list the identities of 12 of the 16 Type 1B freighters built in 1943, but has question marks about the identity of several of those. *Bichu Maru* is not mentioned, but could be one of the four unknowns.

After the war, a compilation of the wrecked ships left at Palau was made. This compilation shows the ships' names, their positions and major damage, but the positions were not plotted correctly and some of the ships' identities were assigned incorrectly. The NYK vessel *Bichu Maru* is however listed as being sunk at Palau and in the 1950s when Fujita Salvage made their initial surveys of the wrecks, the *Bichu Maru* was listed as being salvageable in depths of 16–20 metres. The wreck known today as the *Bichu Maru* today at Palau sits in 28 metres of water

The late Klaus Lindemann in his authoritative book *Desecrate 1* published in 1988 lists the *Bicchu Maru* (sic) as being sunk at Palau at an unknown location, and consequently gives no diving details. He does however give a detailed description of a wreck he calls *Gozan Maru* situated in a sheltered bay, and I suspect he is referring to the wreck known today as *Bichu Maru* – his description is a dead ringer for our *Bichu Maru* and his wreck location fits the current wreck.

On my last visit to Palau whilst researching this wreck, we made a rough measurement by tape measure of the *Bichu Maru*'s beam and this came in at 50 feet – not far off the standard 52 feet of a Type 1B beam. The discrepancy no doubt is a testament to the inaccuracy of my measuring ability and perhaps a slight sagging of the hull. Although the correct identity of the wreck known as *Bichu Maru* has caused much confusion over the years, having measured the beam of wreck at 50 feet rules out the suggestion that it is the smaller *Gozan Maru*, which had a beam of 43 feet 7 inches.

In addition, Fujita Salvage records indicate that its workers dismantled the *Gozan Maru* lying in 15 metres of water in Malakal Harbor at position 07° 19' 36" N, 134° 25' 50" E. I can see no reason to doubt this statement; Fujita Salvage was a professional commercial salvor which would have had lots of local information, and would have found much on the wreck, from bells to makers' plates and identifying crockery, to confirm its identification. A debris field today lies at Fujita's position for the *Gozan Maru*, and I think the old question mark about the wreck we call *Bichu Maru* being possibly the *Gozan Maru* or indeed the *Hokutai Maru* is now cleared up.

After construction in 1943, *Bichu Maru* entered service as an IJA cargo ship – but her sea career would be relatively short. The American submarine USS *Silversides* attacked and torpedoed her on 29 December 1943 off New Guinea. This is no doubt the origin of the reference in *The Dictionary of Disasters during the Age of Steam* by Charles Hocking to the effect that *Bichu Maru* was bombed and sunk off New Guinea on 29 December 1943. (The USS *Silversides* was commissioned just a few days after the Pearl Harbor attack of 7 December 1941 and would go on to sink 30 Japanese vessels including 23 major Japanese ships – a total tonnage of approximately 90,080, the third highest total for any US Navy submarine – during 14 combat patrols in the Pacific during World War II. She is still on patrol today, beautifully preserved at the USS *Silversides* Submarine Museum at Muskegon Lake Channel near Lake Michigan, USA.)

*Bichu Maru* had temporary repairs made to her following the torpedo attack by USS *Silversides*, and on 10 March 1944 she arrived alongside the repair ship *Akashi* at Palau for more permanent repairs to be carried out. Two weeks later,

*Bichu Maru* (top right) is moored close to the west shore of Ngeruktabel Island seeking shelter from US aircraft from its high hills. (National Archives)

on 28 March 1944, the repairs on *Bichu Maru* were deemed complete and she was moved away from *Akashi*, no doubt to free up space for other damaged ships to be repaired. When the *Desecrate 1* air raids began on 30 March 1944, *Bichu Maru* was still in Palau, at anchor in a small bay close to the nearby jungle-covered steep slopes of the west side of the northern shore of Urukthapel Island.

Four US dive-bombers attacked her – scoring near misses, but no hits. Moored so close to the steep sides of Urukthapel Island, she was a hard target to hit for the American aviators.

Bombs from a second attack run were seen to hit and produce explosions and start fires aboard. One bomb either went straight into foredeck Hold No. 2 and blew out the starboard side shell plating of the ship – or else was a delayed-fuze near miss that continued its trajectory and detonated under the keel. Either way, a large hole beneath the waterline allowed the empty hold to quickly fill with seawater. It is known that where ships were 'light' (in that they didn't have their holds filled with cargo), the empty holds, as big as swimming pools, could flood with a massive amount of water very quickly – and this could drag a ship under in minutes. Where a hold was filled with a cargo of, say, timber, far less water could get into the hold, and the ship would remain afloat longer. Another bomb appears to have hit the top of the superstructure towards port around Hold No. 3. Mortally wounded, she started to sink, heeling to port.

The wreck, known as *Bichu Maru*, was located about 1984 by Francis Toribiong after an aerial search based on US combat photos.

## THE WRECK TODAY

Today the large wreck of the cargo vessel *Bichu Maru* lies well heeled over onto her port side in 28 metres of water in the Western Lagoon, about 100 metres from the steeply plunging jungle-clad hillside of Urukthapel Island's north-western shore. A scattering of rock islands around the island's shore creates a natural amphitheatre with several entrances and exits, and makes this a very sheltered anchorage – albeit one with little room to manoeuvre. In the large bay directly to the north through a wide channel can be found the wrecks of the two massive *Shiretoko*-class fleet oilers, *Iro* and *Sata*.

There is a least depth of 15 metres down to the uppermost starboard side of the wreck. She is a world-class wreck dive and in common with other Palau wrecks in small bays, the

The wreck of the 4,667grt naval transport *Bichu Maru* lies in 28 metres of water. She is a large, structurally intact wreck that clearly shows the scars of her demise in the vicinity of Hold No 2.

visibility is crystal clear on her uppermost parts but usually a bit cloudy the nearer you get to the seabed – much depends on what state of tide you dive.

*Bichu Maru* had been moored close to the steep jungle-covered slopes of Urukthapel to try and get some protection from US aircraft, which consequently couldn't attack her from the south. Being light, she sunk quickly just as she was anchored, with her bows pointed obliquely towards the shore. The pile of her port anchor chain on the seabed at her bow shows she sank almost vertically, at speed. The higher starboard anchor remains tight in its hawse.

The uppermost starboard side of the wreck is bathed in sunlight, with blue good visibility the rule. Her welded shell plating is very visible. She has a slightly raked bow with a soft nose as opposed to the plumb stem of older ships. There is no gun platform evident on the fo'c'sle deck – the space being dominated by her anchor windlass from which her anchor chains run out through hawse pipes.

Two forward-facing doors in the fo'c'sle bulkhead allow access into the fo'c'sle spaces, and fixed steps are set either side of the bulkhead allowing access to the higher fo'c'sle deck. The lower port side of the vessel is engulfed by a build-up of sediment which largely conceals the port gunwale.

There are two foredeck holds set in the well deck, with high coamings. Some of the hatch cover beams for Hold No. 1 have been jarred loose as the ship hit the seabed and have slipped so that their port ends rest on the seabed. Others have tumbled at different angles. The lower tween deck hatch cover beams remain in place.

The foremast originally rose from a masthouse set in between the two foredeck hatches and had two cargo-handling winches set fore and two aft and square-braced derrick booms leading from short kingposts either side of the mast, fore and aft across both holds. The foremast, which still has ladder rungs welded to it, has lost the topmast above its crosstree and now juts out almost horizontally to port several metres off the seabed to finally rest on the port arm of its crosstree on the seabed at 28 metres.

Beneath the foremast, the large circular jumbo derrick boom, used for lifting heavy loads, runs parallel along the seabed from the masthouse to where it would have been secured above the crosstree. The smaller square-braced derrick booms, used for everyday cargo handling, that ran forward over Hold No. 1 are still secured to the short kingposts either side of the foremast but their derrick heads have swung loose from their mounts and fallen to port, the booms now angled down towards the seabed from their kingposts. The square-braced port derrick boom, which extended aft from the masthouse over Hold No. 2 lies flat on the seabed aft of the jumbo derrick boom.

The starboard side shell plating near the very bottom of Hold No. 2 has been blown out by a bomb hit or near miss. Jagged sections of hull plating around the hole are smoothly bent and deformed, revealing the force of the blast. The hold still has its hatch cover beams in place at both main deck and tween deck levels, and although some are jumbled up it is possible to look directly into the hold and see right out through the bottom. Both holds are empty – the ship had been in Palau for repairs and any cargo would have been removed before she came in. The hatch cover beams at both main deck and tween deck level create an eerie, atmospheric space to explore.

The bridge superstructure had three levels with the upper level being the flying bridge – the open area on top of the pilot house or main bridge which provides unobstructed views of the fore, aft and sides of the ship and served as an operating station for the ship's officers.

Looking up from the bottom of a cargo Hold through the tween deck hatch. Photo © Richard Barnden, Unique Dive Expeditions.

The spaces below would have held radio rooms and crew or officer accommodation. Much of the wooden decking and flooring has been burnt away in fires, giving the superstructure a largely open, skeletal appearance with only structural sections of the engine casing and beams and girders remaining.

An accessible promenade deck walkway runs along the higher starboard side of the composite superstructure with cabins opening off. Bathed in sunlight, it is profusely covered with coral and throngs with abundant fish life. The superstructure itself now leans forward and is sagging and collapsing downwards leaving the lower port side of the deckhouse, and the port promenade deck walkway, crushed and unsafe to enter. The telemotor pedestal for the helm lies fallen from the bridge on the seabed just forward of the superstructure – the helm itself is missing, the wooden spokes no doubt consumed by fire.

Immediately behind the main bridge section of the composite superstructure, and still on top of the superstructure between the bridge and smokestack is situated the smaller hatch for Hold No. 3 – the coaling hatch, which took the coal for her engine. The forward edge of the coaming for Hold No. 3 has been smoothly and seemingly effortlessly bent back upon itself – evidence of a bomb explosion close by during the attack.

The bridge superstructure is split from the superstructure holding the boiler and the engine rooms below by a goalpost-kingpost pair which now angles downwards at 45 degrees towards the seabed as the superstructure has sagged. Derrick booms project forward from its base and would have been used to work the hold. Forced-draught ventilators, their cowls long gone, are dotted around.

Immediately aft of the goalpost kingposts is a large hole where the smokestack once stood – the narrow, impressively tall stack of the coal-burning vessel has fallen to lie flat on the seabed. It has no commercial owner's markings on it, but fixed ladder rungs run up to its top. There are several lifeboat davits here at either side of the boat deck – all are in the swung-in position.

The engine room itself is a wide open space easily accessed and in which the inner engine fitments, the steam turbine, crankshaft and prop shaft can be found ringed by catwalks. In the extended superstructure there are two entrances into the galley, which still contains many pots and pans.

Immediately aft of the collapsed smokestack amidst a maze of forced-draught ventilators, some still with their cowls, stands the immediately recognisable pitched engine room roof with two large ventilators still standing at each aft corner. The pitched roof had large skylights – one on the starboard side is open, the others closed. An open-sided covered walkway runs along the aft edge of the superstructure and connects to the promenade deck walkways either side. Now horizontal doorways from the starboard promenade deck walkway allow access into the engine room and cabins. The engine room superstructure comes to an end and gives way to a now horizontal drop to the aft well deck, the aft-facing bulkhead studded with portholes at its lowest level.

There are two large aft deck holds – both empty of cargo and with high hatch coaming. The hatch cover beams for Hold No. 4 at main deck and tween deck level are still present and a section of curved hull plating lies over the forward edge where it was blown during the attack.

In a mirror image of the foredeck setup, a mast house is set on the main deck between Holds Nos. 4 and 5 from which the main mast rose, flanked by two short kingposts. The masthouse has two aft-facing doors, forced-draught ventilators and two cargo winches

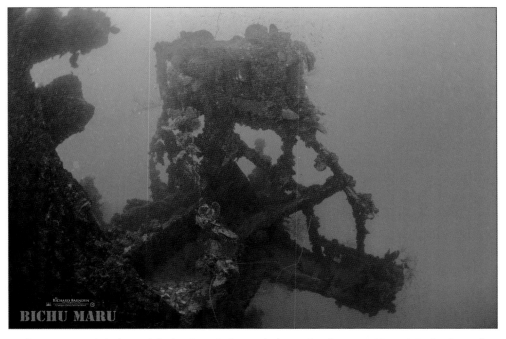

Looking up toward the base of the bandstand aft gun platform of *Bichu Maru*. Photo © Richard Barnden, Unique Dive Expeditions.

set fore and two more set aft of it. Square-braced derrick booms run fore and aft over both holds from the short kingposts either side of the mast – the booms now angled down towards the seabed. The main mast itself has fallen at 45 degrees so that its highest end now rests on the seabed.

The hatch cover beams for Hold No. 5 are missing at both main deck and tween deck level. Two sets of fixed steps lead from the aft well deck up to the poop deck where a short stumpy 3-inch defensive stern gun is still mounted high up on a large now skeletal platform – with its barrel pointing forward and to starboard. The gun seems particularly small for such a grand platform.

There is a large expanse of poop deck between the stern gun and the fantail, and this is studded with mooring bollards and winches, plus a hatch allowing access down to the steering gear compartment. At the auxiliary steering position, a ship's telegraph stands close to the stern. The fantail appears narrow, cut off and blunt in economy fashion.

The large square-topped rudder and part-buried three-bladed propeller remain *in situ* – evidence that this wreck was never touched by salvors.

## SHIPWRECK – THE ESSENTIALS

| | |
|---|---|
| Type: | Standard Type 1 B cargo vessel |
| Built: | 1943 |
| Tonnage: | 4,667 grt |
| Dimensions: | Length 387 feet; beam 52 feet; draught 24 feet |
| Propulsion: | Steam turbine – single shaft |
| Date of loss: | 30 March 1944 |
| Cause of loss: | Bombed at anchor by Task Force 58 aircraft |
| Depth to seabed: | 28 metres |
| Least depth: | 15 metres |
| Location: | North-west shore of Urukthapel Island, Western Lagoon |

# 4. Ch 6, Ch 10 and Ch 12; Cha 22, Cha 26, Cha 52 and Cha 53; Showa Maru No.5

## THE SUBMARINE CHASERS, AUXILIARY SUBMARINE CHASERS AND PICKET BOATS RECORDED AS SUNK IN PALAU DURING WORLD WAR II

A scour through Japanese records reveals that some three larger subchasers, *Ch 6*, *Ch 10* and *Ch 12*, four smaller auxiliary subchasers, *Cha 22*, *Cha 26*, *Cha 52* and *Cha 53*, the converted auxiliary subchaser *Showa Maru No. 5* and many picket boats were all sunk in and around Palau during World War II.

Whilst the wreck of an unidentified auxiliary subchaser near the Malakal Pass at Kesebekuu Buoy No. 6 has been known about for many years and is dived fairly regularly, little is known about the fate and whereabouts of the others. During our 2015 dive expedition to survey the Palau wrecks we were very privileged to be taken by Sam's Tours to two new small wrecks of auxiliary subchasers which had only been found in the last year and only dived once or twice, and whose identities were unknown at the time we dived them.

A summary of the fates of the subchasers and auxiliary subchasers lost at Palau during World War II is as follows:

1. *Ch 6* is recorded as beached at Babelthuap on 30 March after the TF58 *Desecrate 1* air attack. She was deleted from the IJN Active List on 10 October 1944.

2. *Ch 10* is recorded as wrecked and abandoned on 2 May 1944 through stranding in the Palaus at 07° 20' N, 134° 30' E, which is east side of the Koror about the same latitude as Malakal Harbor.

3. *Ch 12* is recorded in some sources simply as lost 'off the Palaus' in August 1944 – 'cause unknown'. Other sources have her arriving at Palau escorting a convoy on 5 August 1944. On 13 August 1944, whilst escorting a convoy east of Mindanao, just after 0900 the convoy was attacked by USS *Bluegill* at 06° 17' N, 126° 10' E – that is some 60 nautical miles south of Palau. There is no further information on *Ch 12* after this date, so it is likely that she was either sunk or severely disabled. Either way, if lost 'off the Palaus' – or at the position 60 miles south – then it is clear that she was sunk outside the lagoon in abyssal depths and she can be discounted from attempts to establish the identity of subchasers and auxiliaries in the lagoon. She was deleted from the IJN Active List on 30 September 1945.

4. *Cha 22* (launched 30 May 1943 and completed on 20 June 1943) was reported sunk at position 07° 30' N, 134° 30' E by Task Force 58 aircraft. That puts her up beside West Pass – but this position tends to be a generic one given by the Japanese for a number of vessels that were part of the large convoy PATA-07 that was making to leave the lagoon

through West Passage but which were attacked and all sunk in the first raids of Day 1 of *Desecrate 1*.

5. *Cha 26* (launched 1 May 1943 and completed 1 June 1943) is recorded as sunk by TF 58 aircraft during Operation *Desecrate 1*, but no position is given. Given she was leading convoy PATA-07 as it made to leave through West Passage there is every likelihood that her wreck is up beside West Passage or outside the lagoon in abyssal depths.

6. *Cha 52* was reported as sunk on 25 October 1944 – also up at West Passage at position 07.30, 134.30E.

7. *Cha 53* is listed as sunk by TF58 aircraft on 30 March 1944 but no position is recorded for its sinking. It is possible that this is the vessel, attacked by eight *Belleau Wood* aircraft just off the western shore of the southern part of Urukthapel Island, was set on fire by strafing and sunk and subsequently salvaged. There is no confirmation of that – it's just a best guess at present.

8. *Showa Maru No. 5* is simply listed as 'Sunk 30 March 1944 at Palau by TF 58 aircraft'. Two other former whalers (used as auxiliary subchasers) were also sunk.

9. Picket boats or auxiliary patrol boats. During the war, Japan requisitioned a large number of fishing vessels for picket boat duty, many with the primary duty of observing the sea to the east of mainland Japan and providing early warning of any US task force attempting to close on the Japanese homeland islands. With their high rate of attrition, the Imperial Japanese Navy intended to build 280 purpose-built picket boats – but due to a lack of wood and raw materials fewer than 30 would be completed by the end of the war.

Vessels identified are:

a) *Hakko Maru*. The 150grt guard boat was sunk at Palau by TF 58 aircraft on 31 March 1944.

b) *Ibaraki Maru*. The 150grt auxiliary patrol boat was sunk at Palau during *Desecrate 1* at an unknown location.

c) *Seiei Maru No.2*. The small 113grt guard boat is listed as sunk at Palau on 30 March 1944.

Here's as much information as I have been able to glean from sparse historical references and from diving those unidentified auxiliary subchasers that have been located to date – and my best guess about identities of the known wrecks.

## CH 6: SUBMARINE CHASER

In 1921 the Washington Naval Treaty was signed between the major maritime powers – largely provoked by Japan's expansionist goals, and designed to contain them. This was a system of arms control that pegged Britain's Royal Navy at roughly the size of the United States Navy and placed severe restrictions on the building of new capital ships – battleships and battlecruisers. The treaty allowed Britain and the United States a tonnage equivalent to 15 capital ships; the Japanese were allowed nine capital ships, and France and Italy five capital ships apiece. New battleship displacement was capped at 35,000 tons and the maximum gun barrel size was limited to 16 inches.

The Japanese were pointedly displeased that they had not been granted parity with Britain and the United States – however they were partly placated by a deal whereby Britain would not develop naval bases east of Singapore and the United States would not develop bases west of Hawaii. Japan had effectively been granted control of the north-west Pacific.

Japan had started preparing for an offensive war in the Pacific in the 1920s. Saddled with a lesser number of capital ships due to the Washington Naval Treaty, it specifically developed new types of sea-going destroyers. These would be armed with the new powerful Long Lance torpedo that, it was hoped, would be able to degrade the US Pacific Fleet as it crossed the Pacific to campaign against Japan. Japan's focus was on an offensive war – it had not contemplated fully or prepared for a defensive war such as it would be forced to fight after the Battles of Midway and the Coral Sea in 1942.

With a focus on developing an offensive naval capability, Japan gave little attention in the 1920s and 1930s to how it would protect its sea transport vessels. A very small percentage of the resources and finance allocated for warship construction was allocated to vessels that could protect its merchant fleet. The Imperial Japanese Navy failed to foresee the protracted nature of the coming war and failed to recognise that it would inevitably need to protect its supply ships over a vast area. The Imperial Japanese Navy's obsessive fixation on the Decisive Battle monopolised the design and construction of its ships, armaments and preparations; naval training focused on tactics for an offensive war and left Japan blind to the possibility that destruction of the empire's commercial shipping might also be decisive.

Just before the London Treaty of 1930, the Imperial Japanese Navy did briefly consider building a sizeable force of specialised craft for commercial shipping protection – but for budgetary considerations the plan was abandoned.

The net result of this lack of attention to protecting its commercial shipping was the construction of only four *kaibōkan* coastal defence vessels – originally designed for fishery protection and security in Japan's Kurile Islands. These *kaibōkan* vessels could fulfil the role of general naval escort, and were able to perform coastal defence duties such as minelaying, minesweeping and anti-submarine patrols. It is staggering that to protect the vast maritime commerce required for its empire, only four ships of this class were laid down – and even these were reduced in displacement from 1,200 tons to 860 tons, due to a portion of the funds set aside to build them being diverted to help defray the costs of the super-battleships *Yamato* and *Musashi*. These *Shimushu*-class *kaibōkan* vessels were broadly similar to British and American destroyer escorts.

Once the four *Shimushu*-class vessels had been built, the Imperial Japanese Navy was sufficiently impressed enough with them to order 14 more such vessels of an improved *Shimushu* design –but construction of these vessels took so long that none were operational by the time Japan launched its Pacific war.

The *kaibōkans* were tough, capable sea-going vessels designed to withstand the stresses of operating in the north Pacific – but their feeble armament and low number of depth charges carried, none of which could be thrown forward, made them a less potent threat. In addition their top speed of less than 20 knots was slightly slower than the topside speed of the US submarines they were to hunt. They were less than ideal as anti-submarine vessels.

In addition to the four *kaibōkans*, the Imperial Japanese Navy began the construction of a number of other vessels ostensibly for peacetime civilian duties but which could be quickly converted to serve as naval escorts in time of war. The Imperial Japanese Navy also converted several torpedo boats and older destroyers for escort work, and developed a new breed of subchaser.

It was only in 1931 that Japan decided to protect its fleet with anti-submarine craft – after it became aware of the build-up of the US submarine fleet following World War I. Japan's first 210-foot-long subchaser was ordered under the 1931 Fleet Supplementary Programme.

The 2nd Fleet Supplementary Programme of 1934 and the 3rd Fleet Supplementary programme of 1937 produced subchasers with a long, low bridge superstructure. Further programmes of 1941and 1942 produced modified versions of 160 feet in length with a beam of 22 feet.

Subchasers were given the prefix *Ch* and an identifying number – as in *Ch 1*, *Ch 2* etc. Eventually 64 purpose-built subchasers were ordered, most during the pre-war years. The first 300-ton displacement, twin-shaft IJN subchasers were 210 feet long with a beam of 19 feet 5 inches, and were powered by diesel engines which gave them a speed of 21 knots. They were the smallest naval units in the Imperial Japanese Navy but nevertheless were large vessels that looked like proper warships – unlike the auxiliary subchasers, which were much smaller, often converted trawlers.

The first class of these purpose-built subchasers was the *Ch 1* class of two units. Completed in 1933, they were armed with two 40mm AA guns, two 7.7mm machine guns and two depth charge throwers, and carried 36 depth charges. They were found to suffer from excessive top weight as a result of trying to keep within the tonnage limits imposed by the 1930 London Naval Treaty. In 1934 the top-heavy torpedo-boat *Tomodzuru* capsized in a storm, and this disaster forced the redesign and rebuilding of the subchasers with a ballast keel and additional permanent ballast.

The 2nd Fleet Supplementary Programme of 1934 produced experimental, slightly smaller and slower craft of the same basic design – but with 146-foot-long hulls and a beam of 15 feet 9 inches. The manoeuvrability of the first of these was poor in trials and new rudders were fitted

The 3rd Fleet Supplementary Programme of 1937 produced vessels of the *Ch 4* class – also known as the *Ch 7* class. These 291-ton vessels were 184 feet 5 inches long with a beam of 18 feet 4 inches, and twin shafts powered by two diesel engines gave them a top speed of 20 knots. Completed in 1938–39, they had a long, low bridge superstructure, were armed with two 40mm AA guns and carried 36 depth charges. Further programmes of 1941 and 1942 produced modified versions of 160 feet in length with a beam of 22 feet. In 1944, three 25mm AA autocannon replaced the two 7.7mm machine guns, and Type 13 radar was fitted

*Ch 6* was laid down at the Sakurajima Iron Works shipyard in Tsurumi on 7 May 1938 under the terms of the 3rd Fleet Supplementary Programme of 1937. She was launched on 2 June 1939, and fitting out afloat was completed by 20 May 1939.

On 7 December 1941, the very first opening day of Japan's Pacific War, she was assigned to take part in the invasion of the northern Philippines, departing Mako in the Pescadores in the late afternoon. On 10 December 1941, she took part in the landings at Vigan in the Philippines. On 22 December 1941 she was operating in Lingayen Gulf, and by January 1942 she was patrolling from Davao.

In February 1942, she formed part of the invasion force for Java in the Netherlands East Indies and participated in the landings near Batavia (now Jakarta). The following month she participated in the capture of Surabaya, Java.

Following these operations she was assigned to convoy escort duties in places such as Borneo and Ambon, calling frequently at Palau, Balikpapan and Truk. On 12 November

1943, ten of her crew were killed during an air attack on Surabaya, and her operational ability was degraded for a time.

On 30 November 1943 *Ch 6* departed Balikpapan with a second convoy escort vessel, escorting three tankers to Truk via Palau. On 3 December, the American submarine USS *Tinosa* sighted the convoy and attacked – hitting the heavily laden tanker *Azuma Maru*. As the tanker slowed and settled into the water, *Tinosa* approached on the surface to finish her off – but was repulsed by accurate fire from the stricken tanker's deck guns, which forced the American submarine to crash-dive. Undeterred, *Tinosa* continued the attack submerged, launching more torpedoes at *Azuma Maru*. The beleaguered tanker was hit again, and blew up and sank. The remainder of the convoy continued to Palau and arrived there on 4 December.

After several more convoy escort runs, TF 58 aircraft bombed and disabled *Ch 6* and damaged many other ships, at 07° 30'N, 134° 30'E, and she is noted as being beached at Babelthuap. She was removed from the IJN Active List on 10 October 1944.

So far, none of the remaining wrecks at Palau have been identified as *Ch 6*. As a sizeable military wreck of 184 feet 5 inches with twin shafts, she would be easy to recognise and if lying in diveable water would surely have been found by now. It may be that she sank outside the lagoon, or if she remained beached after *Desecrate 1* was dismantled post war.

## CH 10: SUBMARINE CHASER

(For general information regarding subchasers, see *Ch 6* above.)

The subchaser *Ch 10* was laid down at the Sakurajima Ironworks shipyard in Osaka on 16 September 1938 and launched on 31 January 1939. After fitting out afloat she was completed on 15 June 1939. She displaced 309 tons and was 184 feet 5 inches long with a beam of 18 feet 4 inches. Twin shafts driven by two diesel engines gave her a top speed of 20 knots. She was fitted with two 40mm AA guns and carried 36 depth charges.

In December 1941 *Ch 10* was assigned to the Philippines Seizure Force, and participated in the landings at Vigan on the west coast of Luzon in the Philippines. In January 1942 she formed part of the Borneo Invasion Force; with its rich petroleum resources at Tarakan, Balikpapan and Banjarmasin, Borneo was a prime target for Japan and was poorly defended by Britain and Holland. Japan, desperate to secure the natural resources it badly needed to prosecute its war, needed an assured supply of fuel. Borneo also stood on the main sea routes between Java, Sumatra, Malaya and Celebes, and control of these routes was vital to Japan's expansionist aims. The main Japanese objectives were the oilfields at Miri in the Sarawak region, and Seria in Brunei. Yet despite the rich oil supplies, the Sarawak region had initially no Allied air or sea forces to defend it; it was only in late 1940 that Britain deployed a limited number of troops and artillery. After the attack on Pearl Harbor on 8 December 1941, the oilfields at Miri and Seria and the refinery at Lutong were quickly demolished.

Once *Ch 10*'s duties in Borneo were finished she took part in the blockade of Manila Bay until the fall of the island bastion of Corregidor on 6 May 1942. With its network of tunnels and 45 coastal artillery guns, 23 batteries of mortars and some 72 AA gun emplacements, Corregidor was one of four Allied island fortresses in Manila Bay that formed the harbour defences of Manila and Subic Bays. These fortified islands were protected by minefields across the entrance to Manila Bay, and had denied the Japanese the use of Manila Bay, the finest natural harbour in the Far East. *Ch 10* was assigned to the Kure Guard Unit based at Saeki, Japan, from 1 May through till September 1942.

In October 1942 she was assigned to the 4th Base Force at Truk, where she conducted regular anti-submarine patrols and sweeps throughout the remainder of the year and into 1943. By August of that year she was operating on convoy escort duties around Rabaul and Palau before undergoing repairs in Yokohama in November. Once repaired, on 5 December 1943 she departed Moji on convoy escort duty, bound for Takao in Formosa.

On 15 April 1944 she departed Tokyo, escorting a large powerfully protected convoy of transports bound for Truk via Chichi Jima, along with the subchaser *Ch 12* and several destroyers, minesweepers and minelayers. On 23 April 1944 she arrived at Saipan and then on 1 May 1944 while nearing Palau she ran aground, along with three *Maru* transports on the north tip of the Palau atoll. By the following day *Ch 10* had been wrecked and is recorded as abandoned at approx. 07° 20' N, 134° 30' E. The other vessels were refloated successfully.

*Ch 10* has never been formally located or identified in Palau. As a 184 foot 5 inch-long twin-shaft military vessel she would be easy to recognise. Interestingly, Fujita Salvage reported salving a subchaser in 7 metres of water at position 07° 18' 41" N, 134° 27' 24" E. That position is just 1.5 nautical miles further north and a little to the west of the wartime position approximate for *Ch 10* being abandoned. The Palau nautical charts are known to be quite inaccurate, so it is a good possibility that this is the same vessel.

## CHA 22: AUXILIARY SUBMARINE CHASER

*Cha 22* was launched on 30 May 1943 and was completed on 20 June 1943 as one of more than 200 auxiliary subchasers built by 16 commercial shipyards specialising in the construction of fishing craft. These vessels were then equipped for war duties by the naval dockyards at Yokosuka, Kure, Maizuru and Sasebo; they were mainly constructed of wood, with 4mm armour on the bridge and engine rooms. They were initially equipped with one 7.7mm machine gun, and carried 22 depth charges

At approximately 85 feet in length, these auxiliary subchasers were much smaller than the 185-foot-long IJN subchasers. The auxiliary subchasers displaced just 135 tons compared to the 300-ton displacement of the subchasers. Whilst the subchasers were usually twin-shaft, the auxiliaries, being much smaller and simpler craft, were powered by a single diesel engine; there is no confusing the subchasers with the auxiliaries.

In 1943, the auxiliary subchasers were re-armed, with two 13.2mm AA guns being added. In 1944 and 1945 the 13.3mm guns were replaced by 25mm AA autocannon. Whilst the larger subchasers had the prefix *Ch* and an identifying number, the auxiliary subchasers had the prefix *Cha* with their identifying number.

The auxiliary subchasers were much smaller, slower and more poorly armed than the purpose-built subchasers. The auxiliaries were in fact largely ineffective vessels, only good for harbour and coastal patrol work. With a lamentable service speed of just 11 knots, their feeble armament and low freeboard made them ineffective as sea-going anti-submarine-warfare vessels.

The first *Cha 1* class of auxiliary subchasers had a design based on the two IJN diesel-engined 'tugs', *Eisen No. 1182* and *No. 1183*, which had been built during 1940. Just 85 feet 4 inches long, they had a beam of 18 feet 4 inches and were fitted with a single shaft driven by a diesel engine that developed their 11 knots service speed. These vessels were of wooden construction with 4mm armour on the bridge and engine rooms, and the intention was that they could be converted after the war for use as fishing vessels. They required a crew of 23.

After trials of the two *Eisen* tugs, the Imperial Japanese Navy ordered an initial batch of 100 similar vessels as auxiliary subchasers to be built by the 16 commercial fishing craft shipyards. The *Cha 1*-class vessels built in 1943 were initially armed with one or two 13.2mm AA guns, and they carried ten depth charges. In 1944 and 1945 the 13.2mm AA guns were replaced by 25mm AA autocannon.

In addition to the large numbers of such purpose-built small vessels, after the fall of the Netherlands East Indies in 1942, 30 Dutch patrol boats and small minesweepers were captured. Most had been scuttled – but the Japanese had them refloated and converted to auxiliary subchasers.

In the early part of the 20th century, Japanese commercial fishing had mainly been dependent on the warm Japan Current that runs through the cold Pacific waters along Japan's southern and eastern coast and brings essential nutrients and an abundant supply of fish. However with advances in boats and technology, in the years following World War I, Japanese trawlers had started to venture further. By the 1930s, Japan had one of the largest fishing industries in the world. Many sturdy sea-going deep-sea trawlers and fishing boats of the large fishing fleets were requisitioned for military purposes, and many smaller coastal *Maru* freighters were also assigned for work as auxiliary subchasers.

Woefully short of destroyers and frigates, the Imperial Japanese Navy thus converted a ragtag band of smaller vessels into often ineffective auxiliary subchasers, minelayers, minesweepers and netlayers to escort their convoys. Some of these vessels formed a picket boat network around the Japanese home islands; being poorly armed and unable to defend themselves, these boats often fulfilled their role simply by being sunk and failing to report as scheduled, thus alerting Japanese command. It was picket boats that spotted the two US carriers, *Enterprise* and *Hornet*, approaching Japan for the famous Doolittle Raid on 18 April 1942 and sent warning messages to Japanese command. As a direct result, once the carriers had been spotted, the US bombers had to be launched ahead of schedule and from a greater distance.

But despite the belated Japanese attempts to create a convoy protection fleet, the number of ships assigned for escort duty for Japan's long and vulnerable supply routes was wholly inadequate for the defence of its shipping. Not only was the *quantity* of these vessels wholly inadequate, but their weapons and equipment were also largely ineffective for escort tasks. They were equipped with no forward-throwing anti-submarine warfare (ASW) weapons, and their main armament deck gun was usually inferior to the larger deck guns of the enemy submarines they would confront on the surface. Even when attacking a US submarine, their depth charges were often ineffective because they were set too shallow. The Japanese had initially severely underestimated how deep US submarines could dive to when attacked, and their depth charges exploded impotently far above. The Japanese only learned of this well into the war from loose words by an American congressman.

Japanese anti-submarine warfare capability had not developed much since the Great War – much of which had been acquired from Great Britain and Germany at the time. In the 1920s they undertook their own research on hydrophones and in 1930 imported the American MV-type hydrophone, which they reverse engineered to produce their own version. The WWII Japanese hydrophones however were poor in comparison to those of the Allies and had a limited detection range of only 1,000 yards throughout the entire Pacific War.

By the time war broke out Japanese ASW had made some progress and some 20 destroyers were fitted with the Type 93 sonar. Destroyers were the most formidable warships the Japanese had both for ASW and convoy escort but Japanese naval tactics made it reluctant to release destroyers for either of these roles.

Thus, at the beginning of the Pacific War, the IJN was simply poorly structured for naval escort work, both in its philosophy and doctrine as well as with its ships and crews. The Japanese psyche simply failed to let its leaders foresee and understand the protracted nature of a Pacific War that would inevitably require the protection of its sea transport over a vast area.

In the run-up to war, Japanese naval thinking was obsessively focussed on securing and winning the Decisive Battle – and this obsession led to its resources, its ships and men being channelled in the direction of an offensive war. Japan was blind to the possibility that a significant attrition and degradation of its commercial shipping might also be equally decisive, but in a different way. From British and American statements advocating limitations on submarine construction at the 1930 London Naval Conference, Japan had concluded that submarine warfare was a weak point of the US Navy. This led to Japan's fatal and erroneous conclusion that the possibility of an effective submarine war being waged by the US against it was minimal.

*Cha 22* is reported sunk at position 07° 30' N, 134° 30' E by Task Force 58 aircraft. That puts her up beside West Passage – but this is often a generic position given by the Japanese for a number of vessels part of the large convoy PATA-07 that when making to leave the lagoon through West Passage were attacked and all sunk in the first raids of Day 1 of *Desecrate 1*. To date *Cha 22*'s wreck has not been located or identified.

## CHA 26: AUXILIARY SUBMARINE CHASER

(For general information regarding auxiliary subchasers, see *Cha 22* above.)

*Cha 26* was launched on 1 May 1943 and completed on 1 June 1943. Displacing 135 tons, she was 85 feet 4 inches in length with a beam of 18 feet 4 inches. She was a small-displacement vessel and her single shaft powered by a diesel engine gave her a service speed of just 11 knots.

Just nine months after her completion she was in Palau in March 1944 as the approach of Task Force 58 and its imminent strike against the Palau Islands developed.

A large convoy, PATA-07, was formed up in the Western Lagoon to try to flee Palau on the evening of 29 March 1944, before the anticipated imminent US strike, and escape to Takao, Formosa. The convoy included the 1941-built transport *Kibi Maru*, along with the fleet oiler *Akebono Maru*, the auxiliary transport *Goshu Maru*, the IJN requisitioned 2,838grt Standard Type 1C steamers *Raizan Maru* and *Ryuko Maru*, and the IJA transports *Teshio Maru* and *Hokutai Maru*.

The convoy was escorted by *Patrol Boat 31*, the IJN second-class destroyer *Wakatake* and the auxiliary subchaser *Cha-26*. Picket boats and the *Wakatake* led the convoy. At the far southern end of the convoy, several other freighters were congregating, waiting their turn to join.

Although the convoy had been scheduled to leave the Western Lagoon on the evening of 29 March, there were problems in organising such a large convoy so quickly, and departure was delayed until first light at 0500 the next morning. Simultaneously, 70 miles to the south, the first initial fighter strike groups of Grumman F6F Hellcats were lifting off from their carriers and forming up into their strike groups to head north towards Palau. Convoy PATA-07 and initial fighter sweep Hellcats were completely unaware of each other at this point.

As the first rays of light filtered over the eastern horizon, the ships of the convoy started to leave the anchorages of the Western Lagoon. In line astern, they moved north up the west side of the main Palau island of Babelthuap in the main narrow deep-water channel that leads up towards Toachel Mlengui – the West Passage through the fringing barrier reef. On either side of the channel, light green/brown coral reef flats just a few metres deep flanked the azure blue waters of the deep shipping channel. There is little room to manoeuvre for a large ship in the channel.

As *Lexington*, *Bunker Hill* and *Monterey* F6F Hellcats swept at speed over the southern Palau islands, they all spotted the northbound convoy. Such valuable targets were given priority and soon *Bunker Hill*'s Avenger torpedo-bombers swept in to attack the lead ships as F6F Hellcats from *Lexington* strafed and met limited AA fire from the ships' own defences. Meantime other Grumman Avengers started air-dropping mines in the shipping channel in West Passage to block it – and seal the convoy ships in the lagoon.

As the TF58 aircraft started to attack the convoy, the Japanese ships began to take evasive manoeuvres and having no doubt seen the mines being air-dropped and West Passage effectively sealed off, the convoy dissolved and the ships scattered. But with little room to manoeuvre in such a narrow channel, during the contact *Kibi Maru* ran aground on the western side of the channel whilst *Teshio Maru* grounded on the eastern side. The *Hokutai Maru* successfully came about and headed back south towards Malakal Harbor.

All the merchant ships of PATA-07 would be sunk over the two days of the air raid -as would the escort destroyer *Wakatake*, which was sunk west of Babelthuap in Karamadoo Bay near West Passage.

There is no record of *Cha 26*'s actual fate, but she may have been sunk around West Passage or may have made it in the convoy's vanguard out of West Passage and been sunk in deeper water.

## CHA 52: AUXILIARY SUBMARINE CHASER

(For general information on auxiliary subchasers, see *Cha 22* above.)

*Cha 52* was another small 135-ton displacement 85 foot 4 inch-long auxiliary subchaser with a diesel engine driving a single shaft and giving her a top speed of 11 knots. She was fitted with one 7.7mm machine gun, and carried 22 depth charges when built; in 1943 two 13.2mm AA machine guns were added and latterly 25mm autocannon.

She was not a casualty of Operation *Desecrate 1*, but was reported sunk six months later on 25 October 1944, up at West Passage at position 07° 30' N, 134° 30' E, as the battle for Peleliu raged further south.

## CHA 53: AUXILIARY SUBMARINE CHASER

(For general information on auxiliary subchasers, see *Cha 22* above.)

*Cha 53* was a small 135-ton displacement 85 foot 4 inch-long auxiliary subchaser with a diesel engine driving a single shaft and giving her a top speed of 11 knots. She was fitted with one 7.7mm machine gun, and carried 22 depth charges when built; in 1943 two 13.2mm AA machine guns were added and latterly 25mm autocannon.

In *Warships of the Imperial Japanese Navy 1869–1945* by Jentschura, Jung and Mickel, *Cha 53* is listed as simply 'Sunk 30 March, 1944 at Palau by aircraft from US TF 58'. No position is given in this authoritative book.

In *WWII Wrecks of Palau*, author Dan Bailey records that an intercepted Japanese message reported that *Cha 53* had been beached and damaged at Palau as a result of the TF 58 air raids. He narrates that eight *Belleau Wood* aircraft attacked such a small beached vessel just off the western shore of the southern part of Urukthapel Island, setting her on fire by strafing as she lay stranded between two small rock islands. Later she was photographed with only her bow showing above the water. Dan Bailey dived the site based on those combat photos, and reports in his fine book that only a small debris field remained; it appeared that salvors had dismantled her.

## SHOWA MARU NO. 5: CONVERTED AUXILIARY SUBMARINE CHASER (EX-WHALER GALICIA)

Artist's impression of the auxiliary submarine chaser *Showa Maru No. 5* (ex-whaler *Galicia*)

The 218grt steel whaler *Galicia* was built in 1924 by Smiths Dock Co. Ltd in Middlesbrough, England, for Hvalfangersisk Antarctic A/S. She boasted an ice-breaker bow, and was 110.4 feet long with a beam of 23.1 feet and a draught of 13.1 feet. She was registered in Tonsberg, Norway – at that time Norway was the pre-eminent whaling country. *Galicia* was powered by a vertical triple-expansion steam engine built by Smiths Dock Co. Ltd, – with cylinder diameters of 14 inches, 23 inches and 39 inches.

From 1909 onwards, Toyo Hogei KK (the Oriental Whaling Co.) had been one of Japan's great whaling companies, and in the 1930s it was pivotal in the greatest decade of whale slaughter in history; in 1931 alone, more than 37,000 blue whales were massacred in the Southern Ocean.

During the 1930s, as this slaughter continued and as whale catches diminished in Japan's coastal waters, Japan looked to Antarctica, beginning to use large factory ships to convert the whales caught to oil, and also sending refrigerator ships to freeze and transport the meat back to Japan. By capitalising on both the meat and oil products of whales, Japan continued to outperform other whaling nations.

The auxiliary subchaser *Showa Maru No. 5*.

In 1934 Toyo Hogei KK was renamed Nippon Hogei KK, and in 1935 the whaler *Galicia* was taken over by Nippon Hogei KK, the whaling department within Nippon Suisan KK. She was renamed *Showa Maru No. 5* and registered in Tokyo.

In 1935 the Geneva Convention for the Regulation of Whaling was ratified, but Japan and Germany refused to sign – thereby effectively becoming the first two outlaw whaling nations. The sale of whale oil helped Japan finance its activities in Manchuria and its invasion of China in 1937. In the years leading up to World War II, Germany purchased whale oil from Japan, and both nations used whale oil in their preparations for war. In 1937 more than 55,000 whales were slaughtered.

At that time, Japan was the greatest fishing country in the world, and almost all of its overseas and domestic fishery was in the hands of four large companies and their various subsidiaries. The largest of the four, and perhaps the largest fishing company in the world, was the owner of *Showa Maru No. 5*, Nippon Suisan KK – the Japan Marine Products Co. Ltd, which had subsidiary companies operating in Argentina, Formosa, Borneo, the Philippines, Manchuria and Korea. It also operated fishing vessels and floating canning and processing factories in waters near Kamchatka and in the Bering Sea. (All of its Antarctic whaling factory vessels and half of its fishing fleet would be destroyed in the war.)

With the outbreak of war in the Pacific in 1941, *Showa Maru No. 5* was requisitioned from Nippon Suisan KK and assigned to the 3rd Base Force in Palau as part of Subchaser Division 55, along with the 216-ton *Ganjitsu Maru No. 1* (1926) (which would be sunk on 14 January 1943 east of Mindanao by USS *Searaven*) and the 222-ton ex-steam whaler *Showa Maru No. 3* (ex-*Leslie* 1926), (which would later be sunk on 30 May 1944 by a mine east of the northern Kurile Islands).

In the end, almost all of Japan's civilian fleet of whale killers that could be spared from essential fishing were converted to auxiliary subchasers for war use. Built for heavy-duty work in inhospitable seas, they proved to be extremely valuable ships with great endurance, seaworthiness, speed and towing power – designed to be able to tow several killed whales back to the factory ship for processing. Their towing power was better than that of most naval vessels of comparable size.

The whalers were fitted out for anti-aircraft, minesweeping and ASW escort duty – with deckhouses being enlarged to house 30–40 officers and men, the foremast being moved abaft the bridge and bow gun platforms, AA guns, depth charge racks and minesweeping gear added.

Another view of an auxiliary subchaser showing different aft deck layout.

A typical example of war alterations would be a 3-inch gun on the fo'c'sle and six 7.7mm or 13mm machine guns. At least eight depth charges would be ready on the stern launching racks, with a number of reloads stored below. Minesweeping floats and paravanes would be carried for both high-speed single-ship sweeping and low-speed twin-ship catenary sweeping with the sweep wire slung between the two ships. Some whalers were fitted out with radio direction finder (RDF), hydrophonic gear and degaussing coils.

*Showa Maru No. 5* escorted convoy PATA-06 as it left Palau on 24 March 1944. Once the convoy was safely away, she was detached from the convoy and returned to her base in Palau on 27 March 1944, just days before the US assault.

Japanese records list *Showa Maru No. 5* as simply 'lost at Palau' during *Desecrate 1*.

Fujita Salvage also lists *Showa Maru No. 5* as 'sunk at Palau'. Fujita's records narrate that it worked three unidentified 'whalers': one at 07° 18' 01" N, 134° 27' 22" E in 10 metres of water; another at 07° 17' 59" N, 134° 27' 24" E in 13 metres of water; and the third at 07° 17' 55" N, 134° 27' 25" E in 8 metres of water. All of these positions are in or about the Malakal Harbor area of Koror, but despite extensive searches I have not been able to trace the identities of these vessels.

## PICKET OR AUXILIARY PATROL BOATS

Japan used many requisitioned fishing boats for picket boat duty, and it is known that convoy PATA-07 was led by several picket boats as it proceeded north in the main shipping channel up the west side of Palau on 30 March 1944 in an attempt to break out of the lagoon through West Passage. Being relatively small, unimportant vessels, there is little information about them.

Japan laid out plans to build 280 new picket boats in 1944–45, but in the end only 27 were completed and of those, five were lost during the war, with most surviving. Many of the planned picket boats were still under construction and uncompleted at war's end. These purpose-built auxiliary patrol or picket boats were 238 tons, with a length of 93 feet 6 inches and a beam of 20 feet. They were powered by diesel engines and could make 9 knots. They were fitted with four Type 96 25mm AA autocannon, and carried 12 depth charges, early warning radar and Type 3 active sonar.

A selection of miscellaneous other small types of vessel were used as guard boats or auxiliary patrol boats. Vessels of this category identified as sunk at Palau during *Desecrate 1* are as follows:

a)  The 150grt guard boat *Hakko Maru*, built in 1940, was sunk by TF 58 aircraft on 31 March 1944.

b)  The 150grt guard boat *Ibaraki Maru*, built in 1932 by Mitsubishi Zosen Hikoshima Zosensho, was laid down on 12 December 1931, launched on 25 January 1932 and completed on 30 April 1932. She was requisitioned on 1 October 1941 and sunk at Palau during *Desecrate 1* on 30 March 1944 at an unknown location. She was removed from the Navy List on 10 May 1944.

c)  The 113grt guard boat *Seiei Maru No. 2*, built in 1925 on Osaka for Kazutaro Ogata, was sunk by carrier-based aircraft at Palau on 30 March 1944.

....................

The unidentified auxiliary subchaser and picket boat wrecks of Palau located to date are:

**(i)  Toachel Ra Kesebekuu Channel Buoy No. 6 wreck, Malakal Pass**

The wreck of a small auxiliary subchaser of about 85 feet in length sits on her keel in 23 metres of water, hard up against the very westernmost side of the narrow Malakal Pass that leads from the Eastern Lagoon through expansive coral flats to busy Malakal Harbor. This is a tidal dive in a busy shipping channel with strong currents, so it is a must to carry a delayed deco bag to mark your position topside – this channel is heavily used by small boats and several will likely pass by during your dive.

The dive boat usually drops divers in shallow water some considerable distance up-current in advance of slack water. Divers descend in free water – not following a shotline down. Once on the sloping seabed, divers can drift down the channel with the current until the wreck appears. The strong current here brings clean, clear water, and as a result the small vessel can be seen sitting on its keel from quite a distance.

The bow has a trawler or whaler's pronounced flare, with a large horn some 2–3 metres long, used for handling ropes or nets. The port anchor is still in its hawse, and on the fo'c'sle deck the anchor windlass and a gun platform can be found – the gun itself is missing. The wooden decking is almost all gone – consumed by woodborers or perhaps a wartime fire during the attack.

There is a bomb hole in the starboard side amidships into the aft section of the vessel. The base deckhouse beneath the wheelhouse remains – but the wheelhouse above would have been made of wood and has disintegrated or been burnt away. The small engine room is located immediately aft. The smokestack has corroded away and disappeared.

Between the wheelhouse and the stem are four square hatches, with three round hatches either side; these will be hatches to fish and ice holds from her days as a trawler. A small head or latrine can be located.

The stern is rounded with a small aft deckhouse. Post-war salvors have removed the propeller. The rudder is swung out to port and has largely rotted away, leaving only the reinforcing bands.

This vessel is so close to the west side of Malakal Pass that it is not hard to believe that possibly she had beached or stranded on the reef and later slid down off the reef into deeper water. She could possibly be *Cha 53* – as *Chas 22, 26* and *52* all appear to have been sunk further up, beside West Passage. Alternatively she could be a picket or auxiliary patrol boat.

## SHIPWRECK – THE ESSENTIALS

| | |
|---|---|
| Type: | Auxiliary Submarine Chaser |
| Built: | 1939–1944 |
| Displacement: | 135 tons |
| Dimensions: | Length 85ft 4in.; beam 18ft 4in. |
| Propulsion: | Single shaft – diesel engine |
| Date of loss: | 30/31 March 1944 |
| Cause of loss: | Strafed by Task Force 58 aircraft |
| Depth to seabed: | 23 metres |
| Least depth: | 20 metres |
| Location: | Malakal Pass – near Toachel Ra Kesebekuu Buoy No. 6. |

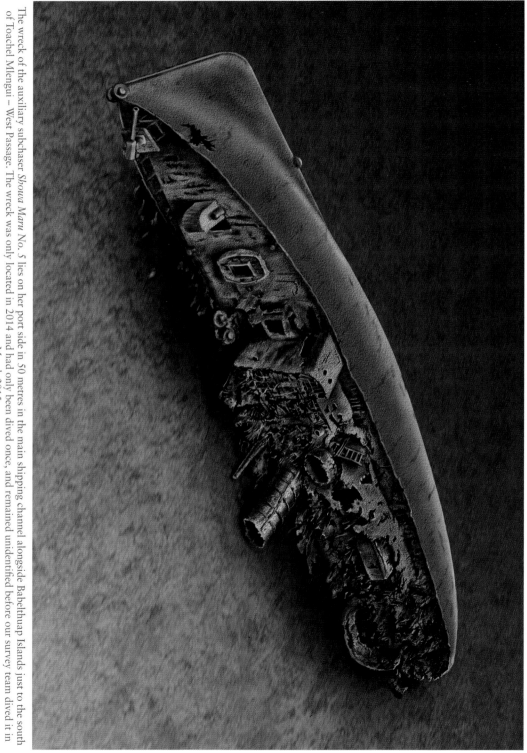

The wreck of the auxiliary subchaser *Showa Maru No. 5* lies on her port side in 50 metres in the main shipping channel alongside Babelthuap Islands just to the south of Toachel Mlengui – West Passage. The wreck was only located in 2014 and had only been dived once, and remained unidentified before our survey team dived it in March 2015.

## (ii) Toachel Mlengui – West Passage wreck, Bkulangriil: Showa Maru No. 5?

During our 2015 expedition to survey the Palau wrecks for this book, we were very privileged to be taken by Sam's Tours north up to West Passage to dive a new small wreck that had only been found in the previous six months in 50 metres of water on the eastern side of the main shipping channel, not far from the small settlement of Bkulangriil. It had only been dived once before – at the time when it was found.

Sam's Tours took us right up beside a lateral channel marker on the east side of the channel, and once our group of six divers were all prepped to dive, we all simultaneously rolled over backwards off the dive boat and started to make a free descent down towards the steeply shelving eastern side of the shipping channel. The current started to drift us southwards.

We were aware that the wreck lay in 50 metres of water and so we spread out in line abreast at about 40 metres as we drifted south – to cover as much of the reef as we could. The minutes ticked by as we drifted along the face in beautiful clear underwater visibility of about 50 metres. Then suddenly, at about Minute 10, the wreck of a small vessel lying on its port side in 50 metres of water with its bows facing north towards us came into view. At this point we had no idea what sort of vessel we were now to be diving on.

At the very tip of the bow on the fo'c'sle deck was a fairlead and roller for handling nets or wires. I moved around to my right towards the now vertical foredeck, and immediately came to a 80mm (3-inch) bow gun set almost right at the bow – perhaps 10 feet back from the stem. The gun was set on top of a four-legged skeletal platform. Subchasers had 80mm bow guns fitted as standard – so immediately I was starting to think this wreck was *Ch 10*, as by the end of the war most auxiliary subchasers were fitted with much smaller 25mm autocannon. I noticed a blast hole through the starboard side of the gunwale high up – this was clearly a war wreck, which had seen action – it was also bows to the north – the direction in which convoy PATA-07 had been heading as the US aircraft swept overhead.

Immediately aft of the gun platform, the deck was flush – there was no raised fo'c'sle. Aft of the gun itself there was a raised aft-facing companionway doorway with small forced-draught ventilators either side leading down into the foredeck spaces. Close behind was a sizeable, slightly elevated, rectangular hatch into the foredeck spaces that was big enough to accommodate a diver, and allowed views inside. Here were stored depth charges, their fuzes and 3-inch shells for the bow gun. This vessel was already starting to look like a steam trawler – and these hatches would have allowed access to the fish hold if this vessel had indeed been a trawler during her civilian days.

Immediately aft of the foredeck hatch, down at seabed level on the port side of the deck was set a large powerful steam-driven windlass, possibly used for working nets or booms or, if she had been a whale catcher in her pre-war days, for hauling in harpooned whales and towing them to the fleet factory ships.

Just behind the windlass, the square frontage of a sturdy steel bridge superstructure was found, with portholes facing forward and a small raised structure at its base with two hatches or skylights. The bridge superstructure had survived the contact relatively well; however ventilators and other structures from its roof had fallen, to litter the seabed. At the back of the bridge superstructure a now horizontal doorway on the starboard wing of the bridge at main deck level allowed views inside. Its armoured doorway had fallen backwards, to lie flat against the now horizontal side of the boiler room and engine room superstructure.

Abaft the bridge, the superstructure returned inwards on both sides to form a more slender deckhouse with square hatches on its top opening down into a boiler room with open circular apertures from which forced-draught ventilators had fallen.

The bow of *Showa Maru No. 5* with bow gun and combat damage to the higher starboard gunwale.
(Author's collection)

The circular base for the funnel was present, and the tall slender funnel of a coal-burning vessel had collapsed to the seabed, where it lay outwards at right angles to the wreck. Behind the funnel opening the structural ribs and frames of the deckhouse were buckled and twisted, exposing the large boiler and the engine room. Initially I thought this was the work of salvors but when I spotted the valuable vertical triple-expansion steam engine still present on the centre line of the vessel, that ruled out salvage. Con rods led from the bottom of the engine to the crankshaft and to a single prop shaft.

Moving further aft, the damage increased as the stern came in sight – the devastating effect of being hit by US aerial bombs. This was a very small vessel – and the aft part of this vessel had been almost completely demolished by the bomb. Sections of hull shell plating lay strewn about amidst torn and bent pipes and structures. Any of the crew in the vicinity of the boiler room, engine room or aft spaces would have been killed instantly by the force of this explosion.

I popped up to have a look at the aft section of hull here. There was no damage to the bottom, so the bomb had exploded as it hit the topsides of the vessel, wrecking the after part of the ship but not blowing through as far as the bottom of the ship.

Immediately aft of the engine block, which was still suspended fore and aft on the centre line of the vessel, after another 15–20 feet of debris, the rounded fantail of the stern appeared. I moved out over the fantail to check for the rudder and propeller or twin shafts. Once behind (and under) the fantail, I found that the vessel had a single shaft and that the usual smooth rounded lines of her fantail were all crumpled up.

TOP: Looking forward along the starboard side of the superstructure to the starboard bridge wing entry door. The door itself lies flat on the superstructure. (Author's collection)

BOTTOM: The tall funnel of a coal burner lies flat on the seabed. A doorway into the starboard superstructure can be seen top right. (Author's collection)

TOP: A circular ASW sonar array pod projects downwards for several feet on the keel strip towards the bow. (Author's collection)

BOTTOM: Although *Showa Maru No. 5* rests on her port side, her rudder and prop are 90 degrees out of position. The stern of the ship hit the bottom so hard as she sank that her prop shaft was broken and a section of her keel was bent out of alignment. She clearly went down quickly by the stern. (Author's collection)

Moving further under the keel, I found that the rudder stock and post had been bent 90 degrees out of position with such force that in a vessel lying on its port side the stock now descended vertically to the seabed and the three-bladed propeller was sitting on its boss with all three blades flat on the seabed. It was immediately clear that the devastating bomb hit on the after part of this small vessel had sent it to the bottom stern first very quickly; the stern of this vessel had hit the seabed with such force that the prop shaft was broken or bent – and the rudderstock skewed 90 degrees out of normal alignment.

I popped round to the keel side of the wreck and found a single keel strip on a gently rounded bottom with no bilge keels. There was no damage whatsoever to the keel.

About 25 feet aft from the bow, on the keel strip itself, was a circular sonar pod about 3 feet in diameter. Looking along the clean lines of the entire length of this small vessel, I thought the length was more than the 85 feet of the purpose-built auxiliary subchasers – but it certainly wasn't the 184 feet of a subchaser. I felt the length was more like about 120 feet – the sort of length of the many wrecks of steam-driven Icelandic deep-sea trawlers we see in the North Sea. The subchasers, in addition to being much larger than the auxiliaries, were all diesel engines and twin shaft – they were clearly ruled out. The purpose-built auxiliary subchasers were also all diesel engine vessels – so this steam-driven vessel does not appear to be any of *Cha 22*, *Cha 26*, *Cha 52* or *Cha 53*. This small vessel had a triple-expansion steam engine and a single shaft.

Convoy PATA-07 was led by a number of picket boats; however as this wreck was a triple-expansion steam-driven vessel she could not be one of the 280 purpose-built diesel powered auxiliary patrol or picket boats that Japan started building in 1944. Also, she doesn't look like a requisitioned fishing boat used as a picket boat – she is too well constructed with too much steelwork, and she has an ice-breaker bow.

My best guess is that this is the ex-whaler *Showa Maru No. 5*. This small wreck is clearly that of a converted auxiliary subchaser – she has an acoustic sonar pod attached to her keel like modern sub-killer vessels. She is also, by her design, a former steel whaler.

Such is the fog of war that the records are so vague at this distance in time. But was *Showa Maru No. 5* escorting convoy PATA-07 north up the west side of Palau to West Passage in its early morning bid to escape before the imminent US attack – just as she had escorted convoy PATA-06, one week before, as it had left Palauan coastal waters. She is not listed by name, but may simply have been one of the picket boats mentioned in the convoy records.

Having an acoustic sonar pod on her keel, it is likely that that was in use and that she therefore would be at the vanguard of the convoy and would have been one of the first vessels to approach West Passage. Her wreck is almost level with West Passage, whereas the convoy stretched all the way south to Kosabang Harbor.

She has clearly been bombed – taking a catastrophic hit in the stern.

The clues all fit – but there has been no clincher of an ID as yet on this recently found wreck. Something may yet be found to clear this up – but in the meantime, it is my best guess that the auxiliary subchaser found up beside West Passage during 2014 is that of *Showa Maru No. 5*, the former whale-killer *Galicia*.

Lloyd's Register of Shipping records the cylinder diameters for *Showa Maru No. 5* (ex-*Galicia*) as being 14 inches, 23 inches and 39 inches. Cylinder sizes are very specific to individual engines and ships, and are used as a good way of identifying a wreck. The way to do it is quite simple:

1. Measure the cylinder lids of the wreck's triple-expansion engine.
2. Measure the distance from the outside of the lid to the middle of the nearest lid-retaining bolt. The bolt is situated in the middle of the cylinder jacket.
3. Multiply the distance at No. 2 above by 4. This gives the total thickness of both walls of the cylinder jacket.
4. Deduct the calculated measurement at No. 3 above from the diameter of the cylinder lid at No. 1 above. The resulting three figures, one for each cylinder, will give you the diameters of the three cylinder bores themselves.

If the measurements and calculations bring out cylinder sizes of 14 inches, 23 inches and 39 inches, then it would be fairly safe to say we have got a positive ID on this wreck!

To be continued ...

## SHIPWRECK – THE ESSENTIALS

| | |
|---|---|
| Type: | Converted Auxiliary Submarine Chaser – ex-whaler |
| Built: | 1924 |
| Tonnage: | 218 grt |
| Dimensions: | Length 110.4 feet; beam 23.1 feet; draught 13.1 feet |
| Propulsion: | Single shaft – vertical triple-expansion steam engine |
| Date of loss: | Believed 30 March 1944 |
| Cause of loss: | Strafed and bombed by Task Force 58 aircraft |
| Depth to seabed: | 50 metres |
| Least depth: | 42 metres |
| Location: | West Passage – near Bkulangriil |

### (iii) Bay south of Urukthapel Island

On the way back to Koror from a day's battlefield tour of Peleliu, our dive boat with Sam's Tours was able to divert into a bay on the south side of Urukthapel Island, where we'd had reports of a small wreck found parallel to and hard up against the steeply shelving south side of the island. It had only been located and dived very recently for the

first time. We motored into the bay and started an echo sounder search along the steep jungle-clad slopes of Urukthapel Island. After 30 minutes of searching a familiar shape appeared on the bottom trace on the sounder – it was time to dive.

All the divers in the group entered the water together and descended towards the wreck down the shotline. It was immediately evident that although there was little current on the surface, the current was strong down on the

A steam trawler similar to the unidentified auxiliary steam trawler located in 2014 in a small bay on the south shore of Urukthapel Island.

The wreck of an unidentified ex steam trawler auxiliary subchaser lies in 24 metres of water close to the south shore of Urukthapel Island. She has been partially salved post war.

wreck. It was a very noticeable trait in diving this wreck that due to localised eddies and swirls in the bay, the current varied in direction and strength incredibly, almost from minute to minute and at different depths. Visibility was a fine 20–30 metres – not bad for a small tidal bay.

As I reached the wreck I found a small steel vessel lying on its port side parallel to the shelving side of the island in 24 metres of water with both anchors run out along the seabed – not surprising given the strength of the currents we were encountering – she probably had a kedge anchor out or a wire fixed to the rocky shore less than 50 metres away to hold her in position. The top of the stem sported a wide fairlead for ropes or cable handling.

I moved aft from the bow and found that she had a raised fo'c'sle still ringed with remnants of her guard rails – there was no gunwale. Twin squared-off hawse plates for her two anchor chains were set in the deck, but although her chains were still run out on the seabed there was no chain in either hawse pipe, and it appeared that the anchor windlass itself was missing – presumed salved. The chains would have been cut and now free from the windlass, the ends no doubt just ran out from their hawse pipes and fell to the seabed. Immediately aft of the hawse pipes down on the port side there was a high-velocity projectile penetration scar on the deck – and a few feet aft was another similar wound, presumably from strafing.

Still on the fo'c'sle deck, just in front of the aft bulkhead, a large, sturdy V-shaped horn several feet high was set in the very middle – this would have been used for handling nets, cables or booms.

Fixed steps lead up from the main deck to the fo'c'sle deck either side of an open doorway into the fo'c'sle spaces. A complete pristine porthole had been unbolted from the hull and carefully placed upright (and ready to lift) on a now flat piece of the port side of the vessel. This looked as though it had been done aeons ago, to judge by the coverage of growth, which now welds it onto the section of ship. A flat section of steel plating has also fallen to partially cover it – whoever set it there to be collected later never came back for it. On the starboard side under the cover of the fo'c'sle deck was a fixed wash hand basin.

Moving over the well decayed foredeck, I estimated the beam as being only 20 feet – she was a small wreck. It looked as though the foredeck had been wooden, as the decking was now almost completely gone, allowing open views into her innards. I spotted a minesweeping paravane stowed below decks here – she was definitely a war wreck.

Fore and aft of the cut-off stump of a foremast, there were a couple of rectangular raised square hatches on the foredeck – these were the fish hold and ice hold hatches from her civilian days; she had been a trawler. Aft of the hatches the wooden decking appeared to have been burnt away to now expose her framing around the large fish hold. Moving further aft, I could see a large rectangular opening directly in front of the bridge running from one side of the ship to the other. The holds had many 0.5-inch-thick ceramic tiles lying around – perhaps insulating tiles for the ice hold.

Moving aft over the foredeck, I came to the remnants of her wheelhouse, which was well smashed up and collapsed to port. The topmost section of the lower bridge level was made of steel and still had a starboard side door into it. The higher wheelhouse deck level would have been made of wood and was completely gone – now just random spars and struts of her skeleton lying about on the seabed.

The rudder has been cleanly cut off and the prop removed by post war salvors. (Author's collection)

Aft of the bridge superstructure the tall narrow funnel of a coal-burning vessel, which had risen from a lower deckhouse abaft the bridge, had fallen to lie flat on the seabed with a large spar lying diagonally across it at its top.

Immediately aft of the smokestack, a large single boiler had fallen from its mounts on the centre line of the vessel, and now lay on the seabed, exposed and almost in free water. Sections of the uppermost starboard side of the deckhouse had collapsed down onto it. I could by now see right to the end of the vessel, and it was clear that her wheelhouse and engine machinery were situated at the after end of the ship.

Moving aft of the boiler there was a gaping hole where the engine would have been. Here the shell plating of the uppermost starboard side of the hull had been cleanly cut right down to the internal frames of the bottom of the ship. The area around the engine room was a mass of tangled and bent steel spars and plates, and it was obvious that the area here had been cut away and blasted open by salvors and the valuable engine lifted out.

At the very stern her auxiliary steering gear could be found directly above the rudder.

I moved round the heavily damaged fantail of the vessel and underneath the keel to check the rudder and prop. Here I found that the rudder had been neatly cut away and the propeller unbolted and removed, leaving the shaft still *in situ*.

This appears to be the wreck of a steam trawler being used as an auxiliary patrol boat or auxiliary subchaser. Although a minesweeping paravane was spotted on the wreck, that was common to most Japanese vessels, small or large. There was no indication of any bow gun or sonar sub-chasing gear that would nail her as an auxiliary subchaser, although that possibility cannot be ruled out. I look forward to hearing of her identity in due course once some vital clue emerges.

## SHIPWRECK – THE ESSENTIALS

| | |
|---|---|
| Type: | Picket or auxiliary patrol boat |
| Built: | Unknown |
| Displacement: | 185 tons approx. (author) |
| Dimensions: | Length 125 feet approx.; beam 22 feet approx. (author) |
| Propulsion: | Single shaft – vertical steam triple-expansion engine |
| Date of loss: | Believed 30/31 March 1944 |
| Cause of loss: | Strafed by Task Force 58 aircraft |
| Depth to seabed: | 24 metres |
| Least depth: | 20 metres |
| Location: | South side of Urukthapel Island |

# 5. Chuyo Maru

Amakasu Maru No. 1-class cargo vessel (1941)

## WEST MALAKAL HARBOR

The 1,941grt Standard Type D coastal freighter *Chuyo Maru* was one of some 40 vessels of the *Amakasu Maru No. 1* class, built before the Pacific War. They were built to an engines-aft design with the characteristic tall, slender funnel of a coal-burning ship, a slender bridge deckhouse set forward of amidships with goalpost kingposts abaft, foremast on the

The *Amakasu No. 1*-class Type D coastal freighter *Chuyo Maru*.

fo'c'sle and main mast on the stern castle. These were characteristic features of the class that aided identification by US forces.

The small steamer *Chuyo Maru* was built by Toyo Kisen Kaisha in Tokyo in 1941 – Toyo KK also built the well-known Truk Lagoon shipwreck *Hanakawa Maru*. *Chuyo Maru* was 295 feet long overall with a beam of 40 feet and a draught of 17 feet 6 inches. The main section of the hull between the poop and bridge superstructures was a single large rectangular hold, with no tween deck, that was worked by derricks extending aft from the two kingposts abaft the bridge and another two derricks extending forward from the sterncastle. A smaller hold was set in the forward well deck between the front of the bridge and the raised fo'c'sle. Small coastal freighters like her were used extensively around the mandated islands.

*Chuyo Maru* was fitted with a 4.7-inch defensive short-barrelled gun on a platform at her stern along with depth charge throwers and depth charges in roll-off boxes either side of the fantail. The small stern gun was designed to enable her to ward off any attack by a submarine on the surface as she attempted to get away. The British Royal Navy used a similar arrangement on their merchant vessels, called a DEMS gun: Defensively Equipped Merchant Ship.

Fitted with a single screw powered by a reciprocating coal-fired steam engine, the *Amakasu Maru No. 1*-class freighters had a radius of approximately 4,000 miles at a service speed of 10 knots. The top speed was a modest 13 knots.

By the time of the *Desecrate 1* air strikes, *Chuyo Maru* was anchored in west Malakal Harbor, just to the south of its northmost claw, Ngerchaol. The large tanker *Amatsu Maru* was anchored not far away to her west – nearer the west entrance to the harbour. The large freighter *Urakami Maru* was anchored to her south. In the distance, on the north shore of the southern claw of the harbour, Ngeruktabel, the large repair ship *Akashi* was anchored close to shore.

*Chuyo Maru* is at top right in this combat photo from 30 March 1944. *Amatsu Maru* is the large vessel under attack to left of shot. *Gozan Marui* is under attack bottom left. (National Archives).

At about 1000 on 30 March 1944, the nearby tanker *Amatsu Maru*, a valuable and priority target for the US raid, was bombed by Strike 2B Douglas SBD Dauntless dive-bombers from USS *Enterprise*. *Amatsu Maru* was hit by 1,000lb bombs around the fantail and near the bow – one bomb had struck her or been a near miss at the stern on the starboard side, and this caused a fire to take hold in the engine room. Crew on *Chuyo Maru* about a quarter of a mile away must have witnessed the whole attack and wondered when their turn would come – they wouldn't have to wait long for the answer. No doubt her gunners did what they could to engage the American raiders and defend *Amatsu* and herself.

Less than an hour later, Grumman Avenger torpedo-bombers from USS *Lexington* attacked *Chuyo Maru* and another *Maru* anchored to her west with 500lb bombs. With her distinctive layout, *Chuyo Maru* was readily identifiable. The US aircrew turned away reporting that a hit had been scored on one of the ships.

Just a quarter of an hour later, another section of Douglas SBD Dauntless dive-bombers attacked *Amatsu Maru* again, and she took a direct hit amidships which caused a large explosion and the loss of ten of her crew. Hit now by at least three 1,000lb bombs, she sank slowly by the stern. The small, less valuable target *Chuyo Maru*, however, remained afloat as night's embrace brought a welcome respite in the action.

The following day, 31 March 1944, at about 0730, *Chuyo Maru* was attacked by Grumman TBF Avenger torpedo-bombers from USS *Yorktown*. One of the TBFs scored a near miss on *Chuyo Maru* on her port side amidships with a 500lb bomb – rippling her hull shell plating and causing substantial fires to break out.

About two hours later, two F6F Hellcats carrying 500lb bombs from USS *Lexington* attacked the small ship – which was still smoking from the earlier fires. In a low-level masthead attack, one bomb was a hit but failed to explode whilst a second bomb was dropped short and was a near miss on her port side. As the pilots withdrew, the ship was noted to be smoking much more heavily than before their attack.

The near-miss bomb blast on the port side took place in the immediate vicinity of her engine room, and the force of the explosion transmitting through incompressible seawater was enough to blow in the hull and spring some of her shell plates at, or just below, the waterline. The blast left a conspicuous deformation in the hull about 10 metres across, and the welding between two plates had parted over some 3–4 metres. The gap was not large, only 5–10cm wide, but being located in the engine room was sufficient to put her engines out of action and lead to her sinking slowly. The ship was not attacked again but is noted in Japanese records as having sunk at about 2000 on 1 April.

The location of *Chuyo Maru* a few hundred yards offshore in Malakal Harbor was known post-war but seems not to have attracted the attention of Fujita Salvage in the 1950s – there were perhaps other more valuable ships and cargoes for it to recover, and this small coastal freighter perhaps did not merit dismantling or refloating and scrapping. No doubt the salvage law of diminishing returns was at work. Memory of this small, seemingly insignificant, freighter passed with the years and she was soon forgotten.

In 1989, divers Klaus Lindeman and Francis Toribiong, using attack photos from the various Task Force 58 carrier air groups filed in the US Navy archives, rediscovered *Chuyo Maru*. These first divers to dive her since the war found a completely intact virgin shipwreck, still filled with everything that was on her the day she went down, from navigational instruments to the personal belongings of her crew. From the wreck's dimensions and distinctive silhouette, aided by china found aboard bearing the logo of Toyo Kisen Kaisha, the ship's commercial owners, her identity was soon confirmed.

## THE WRECK TODAY

Today the completely intact and mesmeric wreck of the small coastal freighter *Chuyo Maru* rests upright on an even keel in 34 metres of water. She is a world-class wreck that lies just a ten-minute boat ride from most of the dive shops in Koror. It is frankly amazing that she is not dived more often – as dive boats must pass over her in astonishing numbers as they head out to the more popular shark, ray and reef dives that Palau is justly famous for. Like most of Palau's wrecks, she is only infrequently visited.

The least depth down to the top of her intricately braced goalpost kingposts, which are easily visible from the surface with a mask, is 12 metres, and it is 30 metres to the main well deck. Being in Malakal Harbor, the water is crystal clear in the shallows but slightly hazy lower down on the wreck – but this cannot diminish the joy of diving such a pristine, untouched wreck.

The wreck is often marked by a buoy, with the downline attached to the cross-brace of the goalpost kingposts abaft the bridge. As these rise up to just 12 metres from the surface in such shallow crystal clear water, they are bathed in sunlight and covered in coral and encrusting sea life. They are a convenient place to start a dive, and at the end of the dive, the kingposts are readily identifiable to allow divers to ascend to the buoy line. Any decompression penalty can be pleasantly passed watching the sea life and getting fine views of the wreck below.

The goalpost kingposts abaft the bridge have intricate bracing between them – a feature unique to Japanese ships. (Author's collection)

The ship has a slightly raked bow and, being at anchor when she was attacked in 1944, her starboard anchor chain is still run out to the seabed. It is not piled up on top of itself as it would have been had she sunk quickly, and this is perhaps indicative of her very slow sinking. The port anchor is still held snug in its hawse.

Coral-covered guardrails fringe the raised fo'c'sle deck, and heavy-duty anchor chains run out to their hawse pipes from a large double steam-driven anchor windlass. Large coils of cable on single drums are positioned on both sides of the fo'c'sle deck – there is no bow gun. There are two smaller steam-driven winches mounted either side of the fo'c'sle deck, one for each derrick, still wound with the running rigging.

The foremast still stands tall – rising from the aft section of the fo'c'sle deck – it is cut off just above its crosstree and still has the remnants of steel rigging hanging from its top to securing fixtures. Square -framed cargo derrick booms with angular internal bracing struts extend aft from goosenecks on short kingposts set either side of the foremast. The starboard derrick boom runs to the deck aft of Hold No. 1, whilst the port boom drops away into the hold at first but then rises up again where it has lost its structural integrity and sagged – its far derrick head rests higher up in front of the bridge. Recessed companionway stairways, as opposed to the more common fixed steps, lead down from either side of the fo'c'sle deck to the well deck, where aft-facing doors in the bulkhead open into the fo'c'sle spaces.

Hold No. 1, forward, has a single hatch cover beam in place but is empty. This ship being a small freighter, there is no tween decks space. There are two anchors on the port side

The 1,941grt coastal freighter *Chuyo Maru* sits upright in 34 metres; a completely intact virgin wreck, she was located in 1989 by Klaus Lindeman and Francis Toribiong. The roof beams of her bridge superstructure were weakened by intense fires and now sag downwards. Note her economy stern.

of the well deck just forward of the bridge – one of which is believed to be from a fishing boat that fouled the wreck with its anchor in the 1990s.

Moving aft, the bridge deckhouse can be found rising up several deck levels with pronounced slender wings higher up. Promenade walkways ringed by guardrails pass aft down either side of the deckhouse with doors and portholes opening to the inboard spaces.

The forward-facing bottom deck levels of the bridge are studded with portholes, the majority of which are open by a small gap. The deck level, directly under the navigating bridge, held the radio and communications rooms and also has a row of portholes forward and doors to the boat deck.

The topmost level, the navigation bridge, had rectangular windows facing forward and to the side to allow unobstructed views to ship's officers. The strong, thick beams of her roof structure sag noticeably in the centre – no doubt due to the weakening effects of an intense fire. The bridge was built with wood decking covering the roof and the decks on steel supporting beams set about 4 feet apart. With the fires having consumed all wood here, only the skeletal supporting floor beams are left internally, and the substantial ship's telegraph, situated on the starboard side of the bridge, has fallen backwards to now lie face down across two of the athwartships bridge floor beams. The telemotor pedestal of the helm remains standing, securely bolted to a steel deck support on the centreline of the vessel. The helm itself has gone – no doubt burnt away. At either side of the bridge, doorways open aft to the boat deck.

On the main deck lower level of this superstructure, at the aft end, a number of china plates and cups were found bearing the Toyo Kisen Kaisha company logo, and it is likely that this area was the officers' mess.

A goalpost-kingpost pair with intricate bracing at its top – bracing that is unique to Japanese ships – stands immediately abaft the bridge deckhouse, with each kingpost having a cable drum forward of it and slightly outboard for running rigging. Rigging, encrusted with corals, hangs down from the kingpost cross-bracing, and each kingpost has a winch set abaft on the deck for working the running rigging and cargo handling. A square-framed derrick boom with angular internal bracing runs aft and downwards from a gooseneck on the port kingpost to rest its derrick head on the port side of the well deck. At the derrick head there are two stepped large circular guides for running rigging to pass through.

Aft of the bridge superstructure the large rectangular Hold No. 2 is set in the well deck – with high coaming and noticeable flanges protruding outboard for fixing the hatch cover. There is only one hatch cover beam in place at the aft end of the hatch – the other hatch cover beams have been carefully lifted off by crew and stacked on the port side of the well deck.

There is no dividing bulkhead or tween deck space in Hold No. 2 – so although *Chuyo Maru* is a relatively small ship this cargo hold appears particularly large. The hold is heavily filled with mud and sediment.

The main well deck was flush-decked and has no gunwale – but most of the guardrail remains. At the forward end of the hold, on the port side just forward of the derrick head, the hull has vertical ripples high up, and is concave lower down from a near-miss bomb blast. The guardrails are bent inwards with the deformed shell plating here – just beside where the square-braced port derrick head comes to rest on the deck.

At the very stern, the large sterncastle dominates; it houses the machinery, engine casing and steering gear. Fixed steps lead up from the well deck to the poop deck either side of the

Top: The telegraph lies face down across structural deck beams – the wood deck planking has been burnt away. Photo © Richard Barnden, Unique Dive Expeditions.

Bottom: The derrick boom from the port kingpost abaft the bridge runs aft to rest on the main deck beside the hold. Note the circular guides for running rigging. (Author's collection)

Deep in the bowels of the *Chuyo Maru* – wheelbarrows. Photo © Richard Barnden,
Unique Dive Expeditions.

forward bulkhead of the sterncastle. Just aft from the front edge of the deckhouse the main mast rises from a masthouse and ends at its crosstree. As with the foremast, the topmast above the crosstree is missing. A jumbo derrick which would have risen from the base of the main mast to be secured at the crosstree has fallen forward and broken in the process a few metres from its base.

Short kingposts are situated either side of the main mast with square-braced derrick booms used for cargo handling goosenecked to them and extending forward. The starboard derrick head rests on the main deck at the starboard side of the hold. The port derrick boom rises up at an angle of 45 degrees at first for several metres until a point where it has rotted and snapped, and then angles back downwards to rest its derrick head on the deck on the port side of the hold.

On top of the sterncastle, either side of the deck just forward of the main mast and short kingposts, sit large steam winches used for working the cargo derricks.

Abaft the masthouse there is a slender gap between it and the superimposed machinery deckhouse. Here a long and slender athwartships hatch can be found – most likely for coaling.

Abaft the masthouse, the main superimposed deckhouse holding the engine casing below and the machinery rises up to the same level as the top of the masthouse. At the leading edge of this deckhouse is the large circular opening for the smokestack, criss-crossed by beams and spars and surrounded by rotted sections of decking. An open access hatch immediately beside it still has its grated hatch cover for ventilation (and to prevent crew falling down an open hatch) flung back to one side and the second weather hatch cover flung open to the other side.

On either side of the superimposed deckhouse there are two open doorways; the forward one allows passage forward of the smokestack across gratings running athwartships to a corresponding doorway on the other side of the deckhouse. The aftmost doorway opens into smaller compartments and again allows passage to the other side. The crew messed in this area, and the remains of tables, chairs and more china and crockery can be found here. Near to these doorways, at either side of the deck, cable drums for running rigging and winches are located.

The tall, slender smokestack of a coal-burning vessel has fallen onto the port boat deck. Steel ladder rungs lead up the side of the funnel to a small lookout platform. Either side of the smokestack aperture are two small kingposts, which doubled as ventilators with derricks goosenecked to their base and used for coaling the ship. Lifeboat davits are set either side of the boat deck.

There are two pitched roofs on the top of this superimposed deckhouse; the aft one was for the engine room and the forward one for the boiler room. The forward boiler room roof has two skylights either side, which have two small portholes in the opening part. The engine room roof has three skylights either side with two portholes in each. Several of the skylights are open. There are four sets of symmetrical forced-draught ventilators dotted at each corner of the engine room roof.

The engine room, which drops down through three deck levels, has a quadruple-expansion steam engine in fine condition secured at its lowest level and rising up through the deck levels. Each cylinder lid has a pressure relief valve on top, and at one end there are bulbous projections that housed recirculating pumps at the side. The top of the photogenic engine is framed in grated catwalks, and at one end a tight, narrow stairway leads down

Ready-use ammo boxes beside the aft gun. Photo © Richard Barnden, Unique Dive expeditions

LEFT: A 'cut-off' *economy* stern similar to that of *Chuyo Maru*.
BELOW: Switching panel in the *Chuyo Maru* engine room.
Photo © Richard Barnden, Unique Dive Expeditions.

to the deck level below where a single generator is situated aft of the engine and a tools board still holds its array of large spanners. An electrical switching board with big, clunky old-fashioned brass levers can be found amidships two levels down, and a number of wheelbarrows – perhaps for moving coal – can be found in a storage space at the lowest level. The engine room is relatively large, but is heavily lined and coated with silt and rusticles which if disturbed can quickly close the visibility down – great care is needed. Up on deck at the starboard side of the engine room roof a large closed box of ready-use shells for the stern gun can be found.

The boiler room with its single boiler is difficult to enter but can be accessed from the engine room slightly aft through a forward-facing doorway.

The port side of the hull in the vicinity of the engine room has a number of plates which have been deformed over a length of about 10 metres by a near-miss bomb explosion which has split the welding between plates below the waterline, opening up a gap of 5–10 cm over 3–4 metres.

The rudimentary small 4.7-inch defensive short-barrelled dual-purpose gun used for anti-submarine and AA work sits on top of the deckhouse on a now skeletal platform that is flush with the superimposed deckhouse roof and extends in a semi-circle out over the aft deck below. Three boxes of ready-use shells are scattered at the base of

Top: Spanner rack in *Chuyo Maru* engine room. Photo © Richard Barnden, Unique Dive Expeditions.
Bottom: Turn valve in *Chuyo Maru* engine room. Photo © Richard Barnden, Unique Dive Expeditions.

TOP: The three skylights of the pitched engine room roof with a box of ready-use shells in the foreground. (Author's collection)

BOTTOM: The fallen smokestack of *Chuyo Maru*. (Author's collection)

the gun, two of them concreted together and a third slightly to starboard. The high-explosive shells were loaded by hand, and the gun could fire about eight rounds per minute.

On each side of the fantail, square rail-release depth charge roll-off launchers are situated right on the edge of the deck – each still ominously holding a single depth charge. Inboard of the depth charge boxes on the centreline of the vessel sits a windlass for a kedge anchor. Twin mooring bollards are dotted either side of the fantail, and sections of guardrail can be found.

Like many modern ships, the stern is squared off due to wartime standard ship economy building reasons. Underneath can be found the rudder, locked at 90 degrees to port, and the four-bladed propeller – again evidence that salvors did not touch this ship in the 1950s. Propellers are very valuable and relatively easy to remove.

## SHIPWRECK – THE ESSENTIALS

| | |
|---|---|
| Type: | *Amakasu Maru No. 1*-class Standard Type D coastal freighter |
| Built: | 1941 |
| Tonnage: | 1,941 grt |
| Dimensions: | Length 295 feet; beam 40 feet; draught 17ft 6in. |
| Propulsion: | Coal-fired reciprocating engine– single shaft |
| Date of loss: | 1 April 1944 |
| Cause of loss: | Bombed at anchor by Task Force 58 aircraft |
| Depth to seabed: | 34 metres |
| Least depth: | 12 metres – kingpost |
| | 30 metres – main deck |
| Location: | West Malakal Harbor |

# 6. Daihatsu Landing Craft Wrecks

## NGERCHAOL

The Imperial Japanese Navy and Army used a variety of landing craft for their operations, including the 13-metre *Chuhatsu* type, the 14-metre *Daihatsu* type, the 15-metre *Moku Daihatsu* and the larger 17-metre *Toku Daihatsu* type. These landing craft were all steel-built, with the exception of the 15-metre type, which was wooden-built. Most were fitted with bow ramps.

The 14-metre *Daihatsu* Type landing craft. Note the twin keels for stability when landing.

The Japanese navy ordered more than 3,200 of the 14-metre *Daihatsu* type – each was simply allocated an identifying number. These landing craft were used extensively by the IJA to carry troops, vehicles or cargo to a beach that had no port facilities. They had no great sea-going capability and were generally launched from larger ships close to shore.

Landing craft were used extensively throughout Japanese anchorages such as Truk and Palau to tend to anchored freighters and larger naval vessels transferring crew, cargo and stores to and from the land. The wrecks of several *Daihatsu* type landing craft can still be found in shallow water in Palau and make an interesting snorkel.

The 14-metre *Daihatsu* type landing craft was 47 feet 10 inches long with a beam of 11 feet and a draught of just 2 feet, and was used by the IJA for amphibious landings from 1935 until 1945. The *Daihatsu* was of simple construction, with a welded steel hull with wooden braces, armoured sides and a bow ramp that was lowered on hitting the beach. Twin keels gave stability when grounded, and two fins extended forward from these keels to support the landing ramp when it was lowered.

The *Daihatsu* displaced 10.5 tons when it was light and had a loaded displacement of 17 tons. Diesel engines ranging from 60hp to 150hp gave it a service speed of about 8 knots, and it had an operating radius of approximately 100 nautical miles at 7.5 knots and 50 nautical miles at full speed.

The *Daihatsu* landing craft was armed with two 7.7mm machine guns or two to three 25mm AA autocannons in a twin or triple mount. It could carry one Type 95 Ha-Go 7-ton light battle tank or 10 tons of cargo or about 70

A heavily loaded *Daihatsu* Type landing craft.

troops. It was often field-modified to carry additional weapons of up to 37mm calibre, and the crew were often protected by simple improvised armour-plating.

Allied destroyers had a difficult time dealing with the *Daihatsu* landing craft traffic in the Solomons, as the improvised armour kept US 40mm fire from being fully effective – and the small landing craft were difficult targets for bigger naval 5-inch guns because of their size and manoeuvrability. The *Daihatsus* were less boxy than the American LCTs, and this gave them better sea-keeping ability.

## THE WRECKS TODAY

The most accessible *Daihatsu* landing craft wrecks can be found in shallow water along the south side of Ngerchaol, just a few minutes, boat ride from the main Koror settlement and very close to Sam's Tours.

A local boat will take you through a narrow, shallow channel with steep cliffs either side, and over a coral bar that is nearly impassable at low water. You enter an almost hidden small cove shielded on all sides by high jungle-clad cliffs.

At the far side of this small cove in just 2–3 metres of water, two *Daihatsu* landing craft sit submerged and upright, parallel to the cliffs that tower above the cove on all sides. The landing craft lie submerged one behind the other just a few metres away from the northern cliff face with the verdant foliation of the jungle-clad slopes almost overhanging them. No doubt they would have been camouflaged against being spotted from the air – with nets and branches rendering them almost undetectable from above.

It is a pleasant snorkel to fin around these famous craft with only the well-corroded armour-plate that protected the helmsman in the steering position of one of them showing above the water nowadays.

The coxswain's rudimentary armour plate protection projects from the water. (Author's collection)

The base of a *Daihatsu* Type landing craft. Photo © Richard Barnden, Unique Dive Expeditions.

Underneath the water the sturdy, flat latticework of transverse bottom frames and struts can be seen – with only traces here and there of the less substantial side frames and sheeting. The shallow sweep of the hull to the keel can be made out underneath the flat base framing, and the engine block and part of the shaft can also be spotted.

# 7. Gozan Maru

CARGO STEAMSHIP (1919)    IJA TRANSPORT (1943)
AIRCRAFT TRANSPORT (1940)

## MALAKAL HARBOR

The 3,213grt cargo vessel *Gozan Maru* was built in 1918 and completed in January 1919 by Ishikawajima Shipbuilding Co. in Tokyo for Hashimoto Kisen KK of Uraga – who also built her triple-expansion engine. In 1920 she was sold to Kokusai Kisen KK of Uraga and then in 1932 she was sold to Kuribayashi Syosen KK. She was 305 feet in length with a beam of 43.7 feet and a draught of 27.2 feet.

The 3,213grt cargo vessel *Gozan Maru*.

*Gozan Maru* was built as a three-island steamer with the plumb stem iconic of her era, raised fo'c'sle, forward well deck with cargo holds, composite superstructure amidships housing the bridge forward and the engine room aft, an aft well deck with cargo holds, a poop deckhouse and an old-fashioned cruiser stern. She was fitted with coal-fired boilers that fed her triple-expansion engine and drove her single screw to a service speed of 9–10 knots and a maximum speed of 10–11 knots, and gave her an operating radius of approximately 9,600 nautical miles at 10 knots. Her design was very common at the time of construction, and she had at least 16 sister ships including the *Yubae Maru* which was sunk in Truk Lagoon during the Operation *Hailstone* raids of 17/18 February 1944.

As Japan's dreams of conquest exploded across the Pacific, its massive expansion brought huge demands for shipping to service the islands in its newly won Pacific Empire. As with countless other vessels, *Gozan Maru* was requisitioned for war service in 1940. The faster, larger merchant ships started to carry cargoes to the outlying garrisons, but an old-fashioned and slow medium-sized ship like *Gozan Maru* was initially used to work around the main Japanese homeland islands, not venturing out to the South Pacific island garrisons where her lack of speed might make her very vulnerable.

On 28 December 1942 she departed the port of Futtsu near the entrance to Tokyo Bay, in a northbound convoy escorted by the old 1921 IJN *Minekaze*-class destroyer *Namikaze*. The convoy arrived at Muroran on Hokkaido, the northernmost of the main Japanese islands, on 30 December 1942, where *Gozan Maru* offloaded and set off a few days later, on 1 January 1943, for the return voyage to the southern city of Osaka. She arrived in Osaka on 8 January 1943 and shortly afterwards was on her way back to Tokyo Bay.

On 13 January 1943 she departed Tokyo Bay again in a north bound convoy bound for Hokkaido in company of the auxiliary collier/oiler *Asakaze Maru*, the IJA transports *Nikko*

*Maru* and *Santo Maru* and the civilian cargo ship *Inari Maru*, escorted by the minesweeper *W-18*. The convoy arrived safely at Hokkaido on 10 February 1943.

By 21 March 1943 *Gozan Maru* was back in the northern port of Muroran, departing in a sizeable southbound convoy escorted by IJN minesweeper *W-24* bound initially for Shibaura in Tokyo Bay. The convoy continued south from Tokyo Bay, and arrived at the port of Kunisaki (on the northern coastline of Kyushu, the southernmost main island) on 24 March 1943, where it was dissolved.

After further coastal voyages around Japan, by 15 July 1943 *Gozan Maru* was back in Kyushu, departing the port of Saiki in a convoy escorted by the torpedo-boat *Hato*, the subchaser *CH-10*, the auxiliary minesweeper *Tama Maru No. 7* and IJN minesweeper *W-18*.

As the attrition of Japanese surface vessels by US submarines grew, so did Japan's need for shipping, and *Gozan Maru* was pressed into voyages further afield. Soon she was being sent to the busy and strategically important Japanese port of Takao in Formosa (modern-day Taiwan). On 17 December 1943, she departed Takao for Manila in the Philippines in a large convoy that included the present-day Palau wreck *Raizan Maru* and several other vessels, escorted by the IJN subchaser *CH-46*, the old 1922 IJN second-class destroyer *Fuyo*, the auxiliary minesweeper *Wa-7* and the auxiliary gunboat *Busho Maru*.

Three days into the dangerous blue water voyage, the convoy was attacked off Subic Bay (just to the north of Manila) at 0915 on 20 December by the American submarine USS *Puffer*. Two torpedoes from *Puffer* struck the destroyer *Fuyo*'s stern, making short work of the lightly protected World War I-era *Wakatake*-class destroyer and causing her to sink with great loss of life in just a few minutes.

But USS *Puffer* was not yet finished with the convoy. Having successfully sent the escort destroyer *Fuyo* to the bottom, just over half an hour later *Puffer* attacked the vulnerable convoy again at 0950, firing a spread of five torpedoes – but alert lookouts on *Gozan Maru* spotted her torpedoes in the water. The ships of the convoy started to take evasive action – and to their relief, one torpedo exploded prematurely and the other four missed. The remaining escorts *CH-46* and *Wa-7* counter-attacked – driving *Puffer* deep, and allowing the convoy to escape, escorted by the auxiliary gunboat *Busho Maru*. The convoy arrived safely at Manila on 23 December, where *Gozan Maru*'s supplies were offloaded, and she was almost immediately sent back to Takao in Formosa to take on further cargo.

Palau Harbor

A plume of spray from a large near-miss bomb rises 100 feet in the air as *Gozan Maru* sits amid an oil slick from a previous attack. (National Archives)

By 3 January 1944, *Gozan Maru* was departing Takao in another large convoy of IJA transports protected by the *kaibōkan* escort vessels *Tsushima* and *Miyake*. The convoy arrived at Moji in the south of Japan on 10 January.

On 26 February *Gozan Maru* departed Moji in another convoy of some nine transports bound for Takao escorted by the *kaibōkan Awaji* and the fleet storeship *Muroto*. The convoy anchored off Ssu Chiao Shan, China, on 29 February, before departing on 1 March for Takao, arriving there on 4 March.

Just a few seconds later, the splash now towers hundreds of feet high above *Gozan Maru*. (National Archives)

On 7 March *Gozan Maru* departed Takao for Palau in a convoy of 10 *Maru*s escorted by the old 1922-built IJN second-class *Wakatake*-class destroyer *Asagao*, the modern 1943-built destroyer *Hamanami* and the torpedo-boat *Sagi*. The convoy arrived at Palau on 14 March 1944. *Gozan Maru* anchored in Malakal Harbor along the north-east side of Ngeruktabel, backing into shallow water with her bow pointing away from shore.

On 30 March she was attacked and bombed by US aircraft during Operation *Desecrate 1* and set on fire. Despite the attacks and damage sustained she remained afloat as night fell – surrounded by a large oil slick. The following day, as US aircraft flew over the anchorage largely unchallenged after the initial fighter sweep, she was again attacked. When Palau was overflown by US photographic aircraft on 25 July, only the tips of *Gozan Maru*'s masts were found above the water.

Fujita Salvage Company worked the *Gozan Maru* in the 1950s, and dismantled the wreck almost completely, leaving sections of the hull bottom flush with the sand, and a debris field of bits and pieces of ship where she lay. Her remains lie in an area of very poor visibility.

## SHIPWRECK – THE ESSENTIALS

| | |
|---|---|
| Type: | Cargo steamship (1919) |
| | Aircraft Transport (1940) |
| | IJA Transport (1943) |
| Built: | 1919 |
| Tonnage: | 3,213 grt |
| Dimensions: | Length 305 feet; beam 43.7 feet; draught 27.2 feet |
| Propulsion: | Coal-fired triple-expansion steam engine – single shaft |
| Date of loss: | 30/31 March 1944 |
| Cause of loss: | Bombed at anchor by Task Force 58 aircraft |
| Depth to seabed: | 15–20 metres |
| Location: | Malakal Harbor |

# 8. The 'Helmet Wreck': Nissho Maru No. 5?

COASTAL FREIGHTER

## MALAKAL HARBOR

The wreck of an unknown Japanese auxiliary transport was discovered shortly before my first visit to Palau in 1990 – I was lucky to dive it at that time. The wreck lies in the east part of Malakal Harbor, quite close to Ulebsechel. Despite some 25 years passing since it was relocated, its identity has never been established. It has variously been known locally as the Depth Charge wreck, X-1 and the Helmet Wreck – the latter name has stuck and with its identity unknown, that is how this famous shipwreck is still known today. I believe that this wreck is in fact the coastal freighter *Nissho Maru No. 5*.

Trying to establish the identity of this wreck has led me on one of my longest, wildest wreck identification adventures to date – I have spent days researching Japanese World War II losses and have gone through the details of every single listed Japanese auxiliary transport vessel of World War II in a variety of formats both on the internet and the old-fashioned way, by poring over countless old reference books. Although I suspect the wreck is that of *Nissho Maru No.5*, as nothing definitive has ever been found on the wreck, that ID is by no means certain – it is just my best guess, and I look forward to the day when something conclusive is found on the wreck that will confirm its identity one way or the other. There is however one *caveat* to this ID; more of that later.

The Helmet Wreck – so called because of several stacks of IJA helmets in the aft hold – was rediscovered for sport diving by a group of divers, led by Dan Bailey, who were searching for two shipwrecks known from US aerial combat photos to have been attacked in the area. The search threw up this unknown wreck – they had found a virgin shipwreck, untouched since World War II, that still carried its cargo and was filled with artefacts. The wreck quickly became a 'must' for anyone diving in Palau. The wreck today is one of the most popular in Palau and is only a 10-minute boat ride from most of the dive shops in Koror.

Despite the wreck apparently having lain untouched by divers and salvors since World War II, there were no easy clues to its identity immediately forthcoming. No bell was found – perhaps the wreck had been visited by local divers in the past and it had been removed, or perhaps it had been lost in the attack. There was no lettering on the bow or stern, and no maker's plate has been found. The abundant crockery was standard issue, the sort to be found on many other wrecks in Palau, Kwajalein and Truk.

Even now, 25 years later, the identity of this wreck remains a mystery; it is a testament to the chaos of war that such a ship, filled with its wartime cargo of depth charges and aircraft parts, can be lost so easily – and that once found, official records are largely silent about its

The Helmet wreck has remained unidentified since her discovery in the late 1980s. The author believes she is the wreck of the auxiliary netlayer *Nissho Maru No. 5*, which records show was fitted with one 80mm deck gun and two depth charge racks, and carried 24 depth charges. Her aft hold is still filled with depth charges.

Coral-encrusted double anchor windlass on the fo'c'sle of the Helmet wreck. (Author's collection)

identity. Before I go on to discuss how I think I've got its identity, here is a description of the wreck.

The Helmet Wreck I had always estimated as being just short of 200 feet long, with a beam of about 30 feet and a tonnage of 1,000 grt or less. She is a small well-deck coastal cargo steamship - which sits on her keel on a sloping bottom that runs down from a depth of 15 metres at the stern to about 30 metres at the bow. She has a raised fo'c'sle with a double-anchor windlass from which both chains run out to their hawse pipes.

The port anchor is run out and the chain wraps around the stem; it is piled up on the seabed on the starboard side – so she drifted slightly as she sank. There is a dent in the stem bar just above where the chain wraps round the stem where the chain went tight as she sank. The starboard anchor is in its hawse.

The ship was built with an old-fashioned plumb stem, reminiscent of the beginning of the last century – however as her shell plates are welded and not riveted, she isn't that old; labour-intensive riveting started to be overtaken by welding in the 1930s, so her construction dates her from about the 1930s onwards. As Japan rapidly built vessels in the 1930s with a possible wartime use in mind it used old-fashioned tried and tested designs, so even though this ship looks old, it perhaps dates from just before the war.

There is no gunwale to the fo'c'sle – the guardrail that ringed it has rotted and collapsed to the deck. There is a small raised section of gunwale or spirket plate at the very bow where divers have placed a number of beer bottles, now out of context, and a brass cone-shaped object with small blades. This is a ship's log that would be towed behind a vessel – the blades were turned by the forward motion of the vessel through the water like a propeller and a mechanical counter gave a readout of the approximate distance travelled through the water for dead reckoning position fixing.

The bow of the Helmet wreck with bottles and ship's log to starboard. (Author's collection)

There are several navigation lanterns in the lamp room.

There are two cargo holds set in the forward well deck, which has a high gunwale and large rectangular vertically-barred scuppers. The foremast is set on the section of well deck in between, and is flanked fore and aft by sturdy cargo winches. A gooseneck on the mast held a single cargo boom forward and a single cargo boom aft, which rested on a cradle just in front of the bridge. The booms themselves are missing and were presumably wooden.

The forward Hold No. 1 contains several rotary aircraft engines – its hatch cover beams are missing. At one time Hold Nos 1 and 2 were separated below deck by a bulkhead, but this has now completely rotted away to leave one common space. There are numerous large ceramic containers here, and lots of beer bottles and ceramic *sake* containers scattered about – many Japanese wrecks at Truk hold large quantities of beer and *sake* bottles designed to ease the rigours of life in such hot climates. A number of the ceramic containers have been lifted out and placed out of context on the well deck around this hold.

Hold No. 2 holds depth charges, and still has a couple of its hatch cover beams in place. There are two Lewis-type machine guns – possibly mounted atop the superstructure. A searchlight has fallen down into the hold from its mount atop the bridge superstructure. The aft bulkhead of this hold has also rotted away, and divers can now get glimpses into the coal bunker underneath the bridge superstructure.

A single semi-circular derrick support, which received and stowed the derrick head from the foremast, is positioned on the centre line of the vessel in front of the bridge superstructure. A forced-draught ventilator, still with its cowl, stands on the starboard side of the deck near to a large grated scuttle in the gunwale.

The composite superstructure amidships held the bridge forward and, immediately aft, the engine and boiler rooms, with lifeboats swung in davits on the boat deck either side of the tall smokestack, so characteristic of a coal-burning vessel. The front of the superstructure is studded with two rows of portholes with two open forward-facing doorways either side of the bridge superstructure at well deck level. Sets of steps lead up outboard of these doors on either side of the well deck to the promenade deck walkways that run through the base of the bridge wings and then across the boat deck on top of the main section of superstructure at shelter deck level. The teak deck planking of the boat deck floor either side of the engine casing has been burnt away to reveal the latticework structural beams and views down into the corridors.

The lifeboat davits on either side of the boat deck are in the swung-out position – indicating that the crew had time to abandon ship. Forced-draught ventilators can be found dotted around the vicinity of the engine room roof.

The uppermost forward levels of this superstructure held the navigating bridge and chart room but this deck, made largely of wood, is now almost completely gone, apparently consumed by fire and leaving only the skeletal inner deckhouse box of the room underneath. A pipe rises up the port aft side of the steel bridge deckhouse to a tapered gear to which the helm in the now-disappeared wheelhouse above would have connected to via a corresponding gear and pipework. With the navigating bridge almost completely burnt away, this leaves

A ceramic container sits beside mooring bollards and the port gunwale of the foredeck. (Author's collection)

the large rectangular space of the deckhouse below completely open – which no doubt held the radio communication apparatus. Doors open to either side of this room into the upper skeletal bridge wings

The slightly raised outline of the engine casing, flanked by the structural lattice work of the boat deck, runs from the aftmost edge of this composite superstructure to the back of the bridge, and accommodates the engine and boiler rooms below.

On top of the raised engine casing can be found the pitched engine room roof with skylights and the remains of four forced-draught ventilators dotted one at each corner. Just in front of the engine room roof can be found the coaling hatch for the vessel's coal fuel.

Just in front of the coaling hatch is the circular smokestack base opening. The tall coal-burner funnel has collapsed and fallen to the seabed on the starboard side of the wreck leaving only a gaping black hole where it once stood with 2–3 inches of ragged steel around it.

The engine room contains a vertical triple-expansion steam engine; either side of the engine casing were situated cabins, storage rooms, heads and the like. It is possible to get into the engine room from three directions: from directly ahead, from the boiler room, and through doorways from corridors either side of the engine casing. Access does involve a bit of a wriggle along the tight corridors before a turn into the engine room itself. The engine sits fore and aft on the centre line of the vessel, surrounded by catwalks – the walls are covered with pipework and there is a large wall-mounted gauge on the port side of the forward doorway to the boiler room. A large steam pipe comes through the forward doorway into the engine room from the boiler room to the engine. The smaller high-pressure cylinder of the engine is at the front – nearer the boiler room. Each of the three cylinders has on its top a circular turn valve for regulating pressure. Steps lead up from this level to a room aft studded with portholes where more machinery and pipework is located.

In about 2014 work was carried out to render safe some of the depth charges stacked in the aft hold, as divers had been reporting that they had been leaking fluid. One depth charge has been lifted out of the aft hold and covered in a blue resin, and has been dumped at the aft side of the pitched engine room roof close to the aft hold. Divers should not interfere with this depth charge or any of the many depth charges in the aft hold.

The aft well deck has a single large hold with the main mast set aft of it, rising up through the well deck hard in front of the aft deckhouse and flanked on either side by open doorways into the sterncastle and fixed steps outboard leading up to the poop deck. The main mast rises up a long way although its topmast section is missing. It still has a gooseneck attached to it lower down – however the derrick boom itself, presumably wooden, is missing.

The aft hold is filled with a large number of depth charges, neatly stacked and rising up on the port side from the bottom level of the hold to the top of it at its foremost corner. None of the depth charges has a detonator fitted – that would have been far too dangerous for transport.

The starboard side of the hold has a massive gash in it – the cause of this ship's loss is unmistakable; a bomb came into the hold, apparently from the port direction, and exploded against the starboard side of the aft hull. The blast blew out a large section of her shell plating, almost right down to her keel. A large section of her hull plating, complete with gunwale and scuppers, has been ripped from her frames, folded almost right back on itself to aft and angled downwards to reach the seabed. The steel decking from the starboard side of the hold has been blown upwards and bent back on itself so that its end now reaches and is level with the aft gun platform.

TOP: Depth charges are still neatly stacked on the port side of the aft hold. (Author's collection)
BOTTOM: The depth charges are in some disarray on the starboard side of the aft hold beside the site of the US bomb detonation. (Author's collection)

On the port aft deck just in front of the sterncastle, two depth charges have been lifted out of the hold and encased in blue material to stop hazardous fluid leaching out. (Author's collection)

The depth charges immediately adjacent to the damaged starboard side of the hull have been thrown about and tumbled on top of each other. Initially I wondered why the bomb did not set off a secondary explosion of the munitions, but I suspect that by a quirk of fate the bomb just missed a direct impact with the depth charge cargo and struck the starboard inner side of the hull – it is clear that the full explosive force vented out through the starboard side of the ship and the bomb was not a direct hit on any of the depth charges. Hence the depth charges on the port side of the hold are still neatly stacked in rows whereas the depth charges on the starboard side are jumbled up with some having spilled out onto the seabed as the ship hit the bottom. The detonators are stored in boxes nearby at the aft section of the hold. There are two more blue encased depth charges at the port aft corner of the hold.

In the tween deck are the famous stacks of IJA infantry helmets that have given the wreck her name – along with a mixture of other general cargo such as rifles, ammunition, belts, shoes, bowls and gas masks. The helmets were moved from their original position during the depth charge works but can still be found.

A stern defensive 80mm deck gun platform had been fitted on top of the poop deckhouse when she was converted for military use; this is now a skeletal structure well covered in coral – the gun itself has fallen from its mount and lies on the platform, its barrel pointing out to port. Three boxes of ready-use ammunition can be located here, and open hatches beneath the platform no doubt allowed for the transfer of shells from storage below to the gun platform. There was no bow gun.

TOP: The stern 80mm defensive gun has fallen to port from its square mount onto the bandstand platform. Boxes of ready-use shells sit forward near the main mast. (Author's collection)

LEFT MIDDLE: Crockery on the Helmet wreck bears generic markings of an eagle on top of a globe. (Author's collection)

RIGHT MIDDLE: A half-full box of detonators for the depth charges sits on the aft gun platform. (Author's collection)

BOTTOM: Close detail of the markings on Helmet wreck crockery. (Author's collection)

There are two depth charge release boxes built into the guard railing either side of the fantail at the stern. When the ship was first found, each box had a depth charge still inside. The depth charges were however removed in 2013/14 for diver safety. The auxiliary steering position and rudderpost are mounted on the deck just forward of the fantail, with position slots laid out in a quadrant shape on the deck below. An open hatch gave access to the steering compartment below deck. The ship had a counter stern with a square-topped rudder and a single screw.

The plumb stem and her coal-fired triple-expansion engine mark her design as being from the early part of the 20th century; however the use of welding for her hull plating marks her as a post-1930s vessel built to an old design. It has never been known how this vessel came to be in Palau – but it was thought that she was probably a captured vessel, possibly a war prize.

This vessel was anchored not far from another vessel in the east part of Malakal Harbor – and both vessels were attacked and sunk during the *Desecrate 1* air raids. It appears that the second vessel was salved post-war as no trace of it remains. Somehow the commercial salvors never found the Helmet Wreck or went after more valuable ships – her propeller, the first, most valuable and easiest item to salve from a shipwreck was still visible on the wreck when it was found in 1990 but is now completely buried in the seabed.

When diving the wreck in 2015 researching for this book, I noticed the compass binnacle – a large round brass cylinder a foot or two in diameter, which held the (now missing) compass head. When I looked at the binnacle more closely I saw that there was a white-faced clinometer on the front of it. Marine clinometers are used to measure the list of a ship in still water – and the roll of the ship in rough water. They can have a simple pointer or can have a liquid-filled curved tube with an air bubble in it that works in much the same way as a spirit level. It is an important tool for a loading officer – or the captain – to see how the ship is lying in the water in port as cargo is being loaded.

When I examined the face of the clinometer I noted the needle was gone but that the curved scale was still there at the bottom along with the legend identifying the marine instrument maker:

**D McGregor & Co., Glasgow & Liverpool**

I had always gone on the assumption that this was a Japanese ship – a minor *Maru*. But D McGregor & Co. was a Scottish company that had begun manufacturing marine instruments in the 19th century in Glasgow before going on to open offices in Liverpool and London and become marine navigation instrument makers for the British Admiralty.

To find Scottish-built marine navigation instruments in the bridge of a Japanese vessel wasn't that unusual; at the beginning of the 20th century something like three quarters of all the ships built in the world were built on the Clyde, and it is well known that quite a number of vessels were made on the Clyde for Japanese interests – from three-masted sailing ships, to military vessels, to modern steamers. This wreck could be that of a vessel that had been built on the Clyde for a Japanese owner, and perhaps requisitioned into the Japanese merchant fleet as the war started. Alternatively, it could be that in the decades before the war a Japanese company had purchased an older ship built on the Clyde in the ordinary course of commerce, and that the ship had subsequently been requisitioned in the run-up to war. Another possibility, just as likely, was that the marine instruments had been taken from an older Scottish ship perhaps being broken down for scrap, and subsequently fitted to a newer Japanese ship.

TOP: The compass binnacle with white clinometer on its side has been placed on the aft bulkhead of the bridge superstructure. The scalloped gear for the ship's telegraph can just be seen to left. (Author's collection)

BOTTOM: The face of the clinometer still bears the legend *D. McGregor & Co, Glasgow & Liverpool*. The needle has corroded away from its fixing at the top but the curved scale showing degrees of tilt can still be clearly seen. Photo © Richard Barnden, Unique Dive expeditions.

The possibilities were endless – but could it be that this mystery wreck that has intrigued people for so long was a Scottish-built ship? The clinometer clue certainly merited further investigation – it would perhaps be fitting if it was a Scotsman who identified a Scottish-built ship sunk by TF 58 in Palau. This rather romantic idea set me off on a bit of a dead-end quest that would consume a lot of my time.

Of all the endless possibilities, applying Occam's Razor (that the simplest explanation is usually the right one), I decided to research Scottish-built ships owned or operated by Japan pre-war. If a ship was being built in Scotland, it was likely in those days that it would be fitted with marine instruments sourced locally.

I started to research, scrolling through endless website and online images of ships, and soon had come to a website, www.clydesite.co.uk that covered ships built on the Clyde for, or owned by, Japanese concerns. A list of ships and images appeared on my screen and I scrolled down through the list of ships and corresponding photos, discounting immediately ships of the wrong shape or with more than one funnel. I had estimated that the Helmet Wreck was less than 1,100 grt, so I discounted all ships of greater than 1,000 grt. A photograph of one ship jumped right out of the list – a ship built on the Clyde in 1899, called the SS *Josephina*. The site had a bow photo of the *Josephina* aground in 1917 – and she certainly looked like the Helmet Wreck.

I read that the 1,192grt steamship *Josephina* was built by Robert Duncan & Co., shipbuilders in Port Glasgow on the River Clyde in 1899. Her dimensions were 233.1 feet long with a beam of 34.7 feet. She was fitted with a steam triple-expansion engine built by Hall-Brown, Buttery & Co. of Glasgow and she was listed as 'Sunk 1944' – the year of Operation *Desecrate 1* – but no date or further details were given. That seemed to fit the bill; the plot thickened. I conveniently ignored that she was built before welding of ship's plates appeared and that she seemed too big a ship.

I read further, Holland Gulf Scheepvaart Maats of Rotterdam had acquired her in 1902 and then she had gone through a succession of other owners from being involved in World War I with the British Royal Navy, to owners in Bremerhaven, Panama and Shanghai, and then in 1942 had come under the control of the Japanese government.

The wild goose chase – SS *Josephina* aground in 1917. Her bow section is a spit for the Helmet wreck. (Author's collection)

On 16 February 1917, whilst being pursued by a submarine, she was put ashore at St Jean de Monts on the Vendée coast. Her cargo of coal was removed and she was refloated on 6 July 1917. The bow photo was of her aground during attempts to refloat her.

After almost 25 years of further maritime traffic, on 7 December 1941 she sailed from the Indo-Chinese Port Campha for Shanghai with a cargo of coal – but arrived in Hongay on 13 December 1941 under French guard. With the fall of France to the Nazis there was little to stop the Nazis' Axis partner, Japan, seizing a French ship, and by 22 December 1941 she was under Japanese guard and being sent to Haiphong and Saigon.

In December 1942 she was condemned in the Sasebo Prize Court in Japan, which had convened to consider whether or not the ship had been lawfully captured or seized – a proper prize court condemnation was required to convey a clear title to a seized vessel and its cargo to its new owners and settle the matter. *Josephina* now belonged to Japan.

The website concluded that she was reported as a war loss in the South Seas, which would fit. It also commented that there were other reports that she had been broken up at Hong Kong in 1945 – that most definitely did not fit.

I searched further with Lloyd's Register of Shipping, and found that the *Josephina* had been built with one deck and deep framing – and she was indeed 1,192 grt. She had been renamed several times, which was not uncommon, and had been called in her time *Grahamland* (1915), *Pollcrea* (1922), *Isabel Harrison* (1924), *Amanda* (1925), *Sturmsee* (1937) and *Essi* (1942) – after which the trail went cold. Her dimensions – 233.1 feet long with a beam of 34.7 feet – were in the right ball park – but if anything, were slightly too large. The bores of her triple-expansion engine were 18½-inch, 30-inch and 49-inch.

There was very little other information available on the *Josephina*, so I did some more digging around – searching against each of the *Josephina*'s various other later names. When I searched for the *Pollcrea* I got a hit with the well-respected shipwreck information site www.wrecksite.eu, which had the *Pollcrea* as being under the control of the Japanese government from 1942 to 1945 and having been renamed *Ejri Maru*. At last I had a possible Japanese name for this vessel.

However, nearly all my searches through the internet and all my Japanese reference books failed to turn up any more information on *Ejri Maru*. However, www.wrecksite.eu had a stern shot of the *Pollcrea* at the time of her grounding in 1917, and this seemed to show that there were two aft deck holds with the main mast positioned in between them.

The Helmet Wreck has only a single aft hold, with the main mast positioned hard against the forward bulkhead of the sterncastle and rising through the main deck from its mount. This was a serious ID problem – it was unlikely that the Japanese government had gone to the cost of reworking the aft deck layout and mast position to allow her to carry larger cargoes. This just didn't fit.

Then I noticed on reviewing the underwater video footage I had taken that the rudder is the wrong shape. The Helmet Wreck rudder has a squared-off horizontal top – compared to the black and white photos of *Pollcrea*, which show a graceful, slender, almost delicate curved rudder. The topmost section may have been damaged or become detached and fallen away, squaring it off – or alternatively it may have been a replacement rudder – the original rudder would have been damaged when she grounded. It was dawning on me that I was trying too hard to make this ship fit the bill.

On my last dive trip to Palau, Gary Petrie and I measured the beam of the Helmet Wreck and got it as 30 feet 7 inches across the foredeck immediately in front of the bridge.

303. - Renflouement du *Pobrea* sur les Côtes de la Vendée

En attendant la Marée

The deal breaker – the aft section of SS *Josephina* clearly doesn't fit the bill (Author's collection)

Dan Bailey had also measured the beam and noted it in *WWII Wrecks of Palau* as being 31 feet 4 inches, so we are in fairly close agreement that it's around 31 feet, give or take. But the beam of the *Josephina* as listed at Lloyd's is 34.7 feet – the discrepancy was just too much.

The discrepancy in the beam, the problem with the aft hold layout, the lack of riveting and the shape of the rudderstock finally forced me to face the truth. From trying to make a round peg fit a square hole, I had to conclude that the *Josephina* was not the Helmet Wreck. I had wasted all my time – it was back to the drawing board.

The cylinder bore sizes of the *Josephina* are listed at Lloyd's as 18 ½-inch, 30-inch and 49-inch. I didn't measure the cylinder sizes for the triple-expansion engine – but it is a sure-fire way of identifying a wreck. To do it, you measure the diameter of each of the three cylinder lids in the engine room. Then, measure from the outside of the lid to the centre of the nearest lid nut and multiply that distance by four. (The bolt and nut will be located in the centre of the cylinder casing, so you've measured from the outside of the casing to the centre. Doubling that measurement gives you roughly the thickness of one side of the casing. Multiplying it by four gives you the thickness of both sides.) Subtract that calculated figure for both wall thicknesses from the cylinder lid diameter measurement and you will have a pretty close figure for the cylinder bore. I became sure that the Helmet Wreck bores wouldn't tie up with the Lloyd's figures.

Reluctantly I started researching from the beginning again – this time I went through the records for every Japanese *Maru* of World War II in my reference books and looked at one of each of the many classes of *zatsuyosen* – converted auxiliary transports.

Prior to and during the Pacific War, the Imperial Japanese Navy enlisted many of Japan's merchant fleet cargo ships to transport troops, military equipment, aircraft parts and stores. In all there were hundreds of transports divided up into about 130 classes dependent on their tonnages and cargo-carrying abilities. After hours of monotonous, tedious checking I eventually spotted the name of a vessel that I was aware had been sunk at Palau but had believed to have been salvaged by Fujita Salvage and had discounted originally from this book – IJN *Nissho Maru No. 5*.

Starting to look at other sources again, I noticed that Fujita Salvage did have a preliminary salvage document that listed *Nissho Maru No. 5* as being a candidate for salvage in 28 metres of water in the 'Palau Harbor' area. When I traced a photo of this vessel and clicked on it to open it – the exact image of the Helmet Wreck jumped out of my screen. This vessel had a raised fo'c'sle with no gunwale other than a small section right at the bow – she had a guardrail. She had two foredeck holds with her foremast in between. The composite superstructure seemed right with a tall coal-burner funnel – and she had a single hold aft with her main mast set hard up against the bulkhead of the sterncastle and a single derrick extending over the hatch. The rudder shape also looked correct.

The *Nissho Maru No. 5* had a gross tonnage of 783 grt, which also seemed right. She had a length of 180.4 feet with a beam of 31.2 feet. That was pretty close to Dan Bailey's 31 feet 4 inches and not far away from my own 30 feet 7 inches. She had been built in 1935 by Ohara Zosen Tekkosho – again right, welded plates – and was requisitioned as a netlayer at the beginning of the war.

*Nissho Maru No. 5* was listed as being fitted with one 80mm deck gun and two depth charge racks carrying 24 depth charges. All these features fit with what is seen on the Helmet Wreck – aka the Depth Charge Wreck.

My best guess for the identity of the Helmet Wreck therefore is *Nissho Maru No. 5* – it nearly all fits, and perhaps Fujita didn't salvage her after all; they don't make any specific reference in their records to her other than listing her as a candidate for salvage.

But there is one apparent discrepancy; it is potentially major – but I think can be disregarded.

The Helmet Wreck has a triple-expansion steam engine. Lloyd's Register of Shipping simply states that *Nissho Maru No. 5* was fitted with 'Oil Engines'. Normally with Lloyd's entries about diesel engines there is a lot of information given – about the number of cylinders, who built the engines, whether they were two-stroke, what horsepower they developed etc. As tensions heightened between the USA, Britain and Japan in the 1930s, to conceal the true nature of its war shipbuilding programme, Japan banned Lloyd's agents from about 1934–35. Lloyd's agents did not thereafter have access to official sources and were reliant on gleaning information from builders' yards. It is known that Lloyd's information about Japanese ships of this period needs to be treated with a certain amount of caution. Thus it is a feature of Lloyd's entries for late 1930s-built Japanese ships that the usual level of information is not given, and the two simple words 'Oil Engines' are stated. Given the climate in the run-up to war it is perhaps understandable if the usual level of detail is not given – and indeed false information perhaps given. It looks to me that Lloyd's here did not have the correct information and just made an assumption. Its two-word 'Oil Engines' is thus not a deal breaker.

However, in the authoritative online resource www.combinedfleet. com it is stated that *Nissho Maru*

*Nissho Maru No. 5 – the Helmet wreck revealed?*

*No. 5* was fitted with one triple-expansion reciprocating steam engine that developed 490bhp. That fits with the archive picture of her, which clearly shows the tall smokestack of a coal-burner belching a black cloud of coal smoke, and thus contradicts the Lloyd's statement.

Hayashi's 11-volume set, *Senji Nippon Senmeiroku*, lists *Nissho Maru No. 5* as being triple-expansion steam, also contradicting the Lloyd's entry.

For more information on *Nissho Maru No. 5* see Chapter 13.

## SHIPWRECK – THE ESSENTIALS

| | |
|---|---|
| Type: | Coastal steam cargo vessel |
| Built: | Believed 1935 |
| Tonnage: | Unknown – presumed circa 750 grt |
| Dimensions: | Length 180.4 feet; beam 31.2 feet (author) |
| Propulsion: | Vertical triple-expansion engine – single screw |
| Date of loss: | 30/31 March 1944 |
| Cause of loss: | Bombed/strafed by Task Force 58 aircraft |
| Depth to seabed: | 15 metres – stern |
| | 30 metres – bow |
| Least depth: | 10 metres |
| Location: | Malakal Harbor |

# 9. IJN Iro

SHIRETOKO-CLASS FLEET OILER (1922)

## URUKTHAPEL ANCHORAGE, WESTERN LAGOON

Ten *Shiretoko*-class fleet oilers were ordered by the Japanese navy under the 1919, 1920 and 1921 Building Programmes. The class included *Shiretoko, Erimo, Notoro Ondo, Shiriya, Tsurumi, Hayamoto, Naruto, Iro* – and what turned out to be another famous Palau wreck, IJN *Sata*. All were completed between 1920 and 1924.

The 15,450grt *Shiretoko*-class fleet oiler IJN *Iro*.

The *Shiretoko*-class fleet oilers displaced 15,450 tons and had an oil cargo capacity of 8,000 tons. They were 470 feet 8 inches long with a beam of 58 feet and a draught of 26 feet 6 inches.

*Iro* herself was laid down on 2 September 1921 at Osaka Iron Works' Sakurajima factory in Osaka. She was launched and named on 5 August 1922, and fitting out afloat in Osaka was officially completed on 30 October 1922 when she was registered in the Kure Naval District.

Powered by a vertical triple-expansion engine, her single shaft gave her a service speed of 9 knots and a maximum speed of 14 knots. She could carry 1,350 tons of bunker coal and 1,000 tons of oil, and was manned by a crew of 160.

After almost 20 years of maritime duties, on 31 October 1941 in the immediate run-up to war in the Pacific, *Iro*, with her precious fuel-carrying ability, was assigned to the 4th Fleet on 31 October 1941. She was fitted with two 140mm (5.5-inch/50-cal) low-angle guns on circular bandstand platforms, one on the fo'c'sle at the bow and one at the stern. She was also fitted with two 80mm (3-inch/40-cal) high-angle (HA) AA guns and four 13.2mm machine guns.

The *Shiretoko*-class oiler *Shiryia* fitted with abeam-fuelling gear on her kingposts and a tripod on her sterncastle. This photo was taken in 1938, when despite the hostilities with China, no guns are mounted on her bandstand gun platforms at bow and stern.

Oil had been a key factor in Japan's decision to go to war with America – following the oil embargoes placed on her in July 1941 by the USA, Great Britain and Netherlands East Indies. At that time, Japan had approximately 50 merchant tankers, and the Imperial Japanese Navy had nine slow fleet oilers. Despite stockpiling oil for two years previously, with no substantial natural resources of her own Japan had to rely on imported oil from its conquered territories in southern Asia. As a result, Japan quickly requisitioned 77 merchant ships for conversion to naval auxiliary oilers.

As final preparations for the now infamous attack on Pearl Harbor were being completed, on 20 November 1941 *Iro* departed Sasebo heading south-east towards Truk and then much further east, well out into the Pacific, to Kwajalein. On 2 December 1941, the coded signal '*Niitakayama nobore* (Climb Mount Niitaka) 1208' was received from the Combined Fleet, signifying that hostilities would begin on 8 December 1941 (Japan time).

On 8 December 1941 *Iro* set out from Kwajalein, to support the invasion operations against Wake Island that would commence a few days later, on 11 December. The invasion force included the light cruisers *Yūbari*, *Tenryū* and *Tatsuta*, along with eight destroyers and two troop transport ships carrying 450 Special Naval Landing Force troops. The bold Japanese invasion operation however would not go to plan.

The light cruiser *Yūbari*, the flagship of Rear Admiral Kajioka Sadamichi's DesRon 6 (Destroyer Squadron 6) and three of the squadron's destroyers, the *Kamikaze*-class destroyers *Hayate*, *Oite* (a present-day Truk wreck) and *Asanagi* closed to 4,400 yards off Wake Island to bombard American land positions. The attack however met stiff opposition when at 0615, US 5-inch coastal defence shore batteries opened up. Accurate American gunners quickly straddled the *Yūbari* and although the flagship escaped a direct hit she was forced to open the range to 5,700 yards – but even so, although again not hit, she was straddled twice more by the US coastal protection guns.

Two miles south-west of Wake Island, the destroyers *Hayate*, *Oite* and *Asanagi* closed to bombard Wilkes Island. At 0652, *Hayate* took three direct hits from the 5-inch US shore batteries. She blew up and sank with the loss of her entire crew of 168. *Oite* also took a near miss that damaged her. The destroyers *Yayoi*, *Mutsuki* and *Kisaragi* of DesDiv 30 (Destroyer Division 30) then closed to bombard Wilkes and Peale Islands, but shore batteries on Peale Island opened up and scored a direct hit on *Yayoi*.

At 0724, 30 miles south-west of Wake, Grumman F4F Wildcats strafed the light cruiser *Tenryū*, damaging three torpedoes on her deck – another Wildcat strafed the light cruiser *Tatsuta*, hitting her radio shack with machine gun fire. The destroyer *Kisaragi* was hit with a US bomb that probably detonated her depth charges – as at 0731 she blew up and sank with her entire crew of 150.

In the face of these losses and resistance, Rear Admiral Kajioka Sadamichi ordered his invasion force to return to Kwajalein later that morning. *Iro* arrived back at Roi, Kwajalein, with the force on 13 December 1941 and after a few days' grace, on 18 December she departed Roi heading back to Yokosuka in Japan, where she arrived on 28 December 1941.

After loading valuable fuel she departed Yokosuka on 5 January 1942 bound to supply the Fleet at Truk – arriving there on 14 January. After just over a week there, on 23 January she took part in the invasion of Rabaul and Kavieng by providing refuelling support for the invasion landings and refuelling the cruiser *Aoba* at sea.

*Iro* left Rabaul on 4 February 1942 – arriving back at Yokosuka Japan on 17 February. After a quick turnaround she departed Yokosuka on 24 February, heading back south for Rabaul again where she arrived on 11 March. She left Rabaul on 15 March to head northwards back to Yokosuka, arriving there on 29 March. After lading, she departed Yokosuka on 9 April southbound once again for Rabaul – *Iro* was working hard in her vital role. She arrived at Rabaul on 28 April and immediately starting to replenish fleet naval units there.

Two days later, on 30 April 1942, the Japanese invasions of Tulagi and Port Moresby began. Rear Admiral Kajioka Sadamichi's Port Moresby Attack Force departed Rabaul with his flagship, the light cruiser *Yūbari* of DesRon 6, the DesDiv 29 destroyers *Asanagi* and *Oite*, the DesDiv 30 destroyers *Mutsuki*, *Mochizuki* and *Yayoi* and a patrol boat escorting Rear Admiral Abe Koso's Transport Force, which comprised five navy and six army transport vessels, along with the oilers *Iro*, *Goyo Maru* and *Hoyo Maru* and the repair ship *Ojima*, escorted by minesweepers and a minelayer. The attack force halted briefly at the Shortland Islands, Bougainville, off New Guinea, to set up a seaplane base. *Iro* detached from the attack force at this point, remaining at the Shortlands as a station tanker with *Keijo Maru* and a guard unit, as the rest of the attack force proceeded to its objective.

On 5 May the cruisers *Kinugasa*, *Aoba*, *Furutaka* and *Kako* of CruDiv 6 (Cruiser Division 6) arrived at the Shortland Islands and refuelled from *Iro*. The battle of the Battle of the Coral Sea ended badly for the Japanese on 8 May, resulting in the invasions of Tulagi and Port Moresby being cancelled. The attack force returned to Rabaul.

*Iro* departed Rabaul on 13 May, heading northwards back to Kure, Japan, where on arrival on 30 May she was dry docked for repairs.

Repairs completed, she was undocked on 23 June and departed Kure on a now familiar southbound passage for Rabaul – arriving there on 11 July and engaging in a fuel run between Rabaul and Truk. More runs between Kure and garrison islands were undertaken before she arrived at Truk on 15 February 1943 and then moved on to Jaluit in the Marshall Islands. On 27 February 1943 at about 0900 west of Jaluit, *Iro* was hit by one of the five torpedoes fired by the American submarine USS *Plunger* and was rendered unnavigable; *Katori Maru* took her in tow, bound for Jaluit, with *Shonan Maru No. 11* as escort.

The small group towing the beleaguered *Iro* arrived at Jaluit on 4 March 1943, and *Iro* underwent repairs for the next two months before being taken in tow on 23 May 1943 from Jaluit by the passenger–cargo ship *Okitsu Maru*, escorted by the destroyer *Oite*, the subchaser *CH-31* and the auxiliary subchaser *Tama Maru No. 5* for Saipan, arriving there on 30 May.

The convoy left Saipan on 1 June – but on 10 June 1943 south-east of Fuka Island, southern Japan, at about 0500 whilst still under tow, *Iro* was hit by two of four torpedoes fired by USS *Tinosa*. She sustained some flooding but due to her tanker's immense strength and internal subdivisions she remained afloat and the tow was able to continue. She arrived safely at Kure on 12 June 1943 after being towed some 4,600 miles by *Okitsu Maru*.

On 30 November 1943 she was dry docked for repair, and an experimental camouflage was painted on her upper works to replace the previous dazzle camouflage. The new camouflage was dark grey overall except for bow and stern, which were painted light grey to resemble a smaller oiler with a raked bow and cruiser stern.

Repairs once again completed, she departed Saeki for Palau on 8 December 1943 along with the cargo ships *Fukko Maru* and *Taian Maru* and escorted by the torpedo-boat *Hato* and the minesweeper *Yurishima*. The convoy arrived at Palau on 18 December 1943 and *Iro* departed later for Balikpapan where she loaded 8,000 tons of crude oil bound for fleet units at Palau. For the next few months she worked between Balikpapan and Palau before setting off on 15 March 1944 from Balikpapan bound for Palau in a large convoy of 21 transports and oilers with five escort vessels.

On 22 March the large convoy was picked up on radar well to the west of Palau by the American submarine USS *Tunny*, which began to close on the surface. A Japanese escort destroyer spotted *Tunny* but in poor visibility the submarine was able to evade the destroyer and continue to close on the convoy. Once in a firing position a full bow spread of six torpedoes was fired at two Japanese cargo ships – seeing hits on both vessels.

Lookouts on the conning tower of *Tunny* spotted the Japanese escort destroyer *Michishio* moving at high speed across the American submarine's stern and fired a spread of four torpedoes before crash-diving as the first of 87 depth charges were dropped. In the following four-hour-long contact, *Iro* was hit by a torpedo at the very bottom of her bow on the starboard side, well forward of her collision bulkheads. Although damaged, she was still watertight and was able to limp on to the perceived safety of Palau for repair.

As *Iro* entered Palau's Western Lagoon at dusk on 23 March 1944 through West Passage, she turned her bows south and moved down to the sheltered Urukthapel anchorage to the south of the southern claw of Malakal Harbor, Ngeruktabel. She was still carrying a very volatile and dangerous flammable cargo and for safety reasons she was being kept well clear of the vessels anchored up within Malakal Harbor itself. Her sister *Shiretoko*-class fleet oiler, IJN *Sata*, was already at anchor, undergoing repairs half a nautical mile away to her north-east for the same safety reasons.

Seven days later, at dawn on 30 March 1944, Operation *Desecrate 1* began, and the F6F Hellcats, Douglas SBD Dauntless and SB2C Helldiver dive-bombers and Grumman TBF Avenger torpedo-bombers of Task Group 58 swept over the Palau anchorages. Tankers and oilers were priority targets, and the valuable *Iro* and *Sata* were quickly spotted and identified in their sheltered anchorage just to the south of Malakal Harbor.

Three *Bunker Hill* dive-bombers attacked *Iro*, dropping six 1,000lb bombs on the ship at about 0730 (local) and reporting one hit.

The following day, 31 March, she was found to be still afloat – and was attacked by Douglas Dauntless dive-bombers. One 1,000lb bomb hit the ship on the starboard aft quarter just above the waterline and, fitted with a delayed fuze, punched straight through her shell plating. The bomb passed through a crew accommodation compartment before exploding in her engine room. The large explosion caused a fire to break out and soon clouds of black fuel smoke were billowing up into the sky from her aft section; 200 of her crew were able to escape the ship, but 50 had perished, including her captain.

Mortally wounded in her cavernous engine room area, she settled by the stern – but such was a tanker's strength and internal subdivisions that she did not go under completely. Fuel flooded out of breached compartments causing a large slick, and hundreds of 55-gallon fuel drums floated out from her dry cargo holds.

As her stern sank and grounded on the bottom, her bow rose in the air, straining at her starboard anchor chain. Her bow rose so high that the damage caused to the bottom of her stem from the earlier submarine attack by USS *Tunny* became visible. The metal of her bow was so hot from fires that white steam billowed up from it.

Half a mile away her sister *Shiretoko*-class oiler *Sata* was also attacked – she too was hit in the stern at the engine room area, this time by a torpedo. She also sank by the stern, her stern hitting the seabed and deforming slightly with her massive weight before she turned turtle and went under.

TOP: Combat photo showing the aft section of *Iro* ablaze and billowing clouds of black fuel smoke.
(National Archives)

BOTTOM: *Iro* sinks by the stern amidst a slick of fuel oil. Her bow section is hot from the intense fires that
swept her, and steam billows from her metalwork. She strains at her anchor chain and the damage to her
bow by the submarine USS *Tunny* is clearly visible. The jumbo boom from her starboard kingpost is swung
over to port; 55-gallon fuel drums from her dry cargo spaces bob in the water around her.
(National Archives)

The wreck of the fleet oiler Iro sits on her keel in just over 40 metres of water, a stunning world-class wreck dive.

Although she had settled by the stern, *Iro*'s bow and forward tanks retained their buoyancy and remained sticking up out of the water. Her cargo of fuel on fire, she burned for several days after the strike. She finally succumbed and sank nearly three weeks later on 17 April 1944, coming to rest upright on the bottom in some 40 metres of water.

Perhaps because of her depth, she received only limited salvage works from Fujita Salvage after the war.

## THE WRECK TODAY

The 470-foot-long wreck of the fleet oiler IJN *Iro* sits upright on her keel in just over 40 metres of water in the Urukthapel anchorage in the Western Lagoon – exactly where she had been at anchor when she was attacked. She is a massive, structurally intact vessel that will take several dives to fully explore, understand and appreciate. Sitting upright in an area of generally excellent 100-foot visibility, this 470-foot-long oiler with its guns, cavernous engine room and massive refuelling at sea (RAS) masts is a stunning world-class wreck – and is one of the highlights of diving at Palau.

At the very bow, her slightly raked stem defines the era of her construction. A large portion of the lower stem, about 5 metres, and part of her keel are missing – the stem bar hangs straight down without being connected to the bottom of her keel.

This is the damage inflicted by the torpedo from USS *Tunny* – and the result is a large hole, about 8 metres wide. The torpedo that punched this hole appears to have come in from the starboard side just aft of the stem bar as the entry wound is smaller here than the exit wound on the port side, where torn plating and bent metal, ribs and beams all reveal how the energy of the explosion vented out through the port side of the hull. The bottom

The bow and fo'c'sle deck of the *Iro*. (Author's collection)

of the bow stands a few metres clear of the seabed at 41 metres, and ripples in the shell plating caused by the explosion extend backwards. The starboard anchor chain runs out of its hawse and hangs down vertically before running out along the seabed at right angles to the wreck.

*Iro* carries a 140mm (5.5-inch) gun with splinter shield set on a large raised circular platform on the fo'c'sle deck that extends over the well deck below. The plating of the bandstand gun platform has corroded away to reveal the structural latticework. The gun was most likely an old gun from the secondary battery of a decommissioned Japanese battleship or cruiser; similar guns were used as coastal defence batteries ashore and can be seen at a number of locations. The barrel with its small, curved splinter shield is depressed and is pointed slightly to port off the bow.

Just forward of the gun platform sits the anchor windlass. *Iro* was at anchor when she was attacked, her starboard anchor being run out to the seabed. The port anchor is no longer present on the wreck and may have been removed by salvors. Rotted sections of coral-encrusted guardrail still ring the fo'c'sle deck.

Dropping down from the fo'c'sle deck to the forward well deck, two forward-facing doorways on the aft bulkhead of the fo'c'sle allow entry into the fo'c'sle spaces.

On the foredeck immediately aft of the fo'c'sle, on the centre line of the vessel, is a modest hatch with high coaming that opens into a large open hold with a tween deck where dry cargo would have been stored. The various levels of the hold are now largely empty, barring cargo-handling gear and cargo booms. At the very bottom of the hold, the structural beams of the hull are contorted and bent inwards – again a direct result of the large explosion in the spaces of the bow just forward. Unlike the Standard Type 1TL tanker *Amatsu Maru* which had no foredeck flying bridge, IJN *Iro* has a still-intact foredeck flying bridge set several metres in from the port gunwale.

Aft of Hold No. 1 stands the foremast, flanked by two tall kingposts which doubled as ventilators. These are connected to the mast by thick horizontal and diagonal bracing and are reinforced with a cross-bar high up. The topmost part of the port kingpost has broken and fallen inwards.

A topmast rose from the centre foremast and no doubt would have projected out of the water after she sank; it has broken or been cut away to reduce the danger to shipping. There are no cargo tank deck access hatches forward of the foremast.

Aft of the foremast and kingposts is a cluster of four small oil cargo tank hatches on the centre line, some with their ventilator lids open. A larger open hatch for dry cargo flanks this cluster of four access hatches on the starboard side.

The tubular jumbo derrick boom used for exceptionally heavy lifts runs aft from the base of the starboard kingpost. It would have no doubt been secured upright when not in use at the top of the starboard kingpost. In the action photo of her sinking by the stern, her bow raised high, the jumbo derrick can be seen passing diagonally aft from the starboard kingpost, to rest on the port side of the well deck just in front of the bridge – exactly where it remains today.

The substantial bridge superstructure is set slightly forward of amidships and is three deck levels high, the first level being the integral midships island, or shelter deck. The next level up has a steel central deckhouse flanked by skeletal wings that extend out to either side of the deck. The top deck level has a much smaller steel deckhouse and the same skeletal bridge wings arrangement. The wooden front walls of the open decks on these higher two levels have been burnt or rotted away to leave just the steel latticework structure. The bridge superstructure remains very much the open structure you see in the black and white topside wartime photos. The topmost framing has sagged or been damaged on the port side of the small steel deckhouse.

Abaft the bridge, the lower deck level is a solid steel deckhouse that extends some way aft, flush with the sides of the ship. At shelter deck level aft there are two conical mounts, one either side of the ship – most likely mounts for AA guns.

Moving aft from the bridge superstructure, the flying bridge continues aft just in from the port side of the deck with a cluster of several more cargo tank access hatches on the centre line of the ship flanked by larger open rectangular hatches in the same fashion as on the foredeck. Lifeboat davits dot the gunwales of the ship in the swung-out position on the port side, indicating the crew here had time to abandon ship. The lifeboat davits on the starboard side are in the swung-in position – those boats were never launched.

Midway between the bridge superstructure and the sterncastle, one of the most striking and characteristic sights of this wreck comes into view – the massive twin goalpost RAS masts with a latticework of horizontal and diagonal thick bracing steel cables now well encrusted with sea life. A tubular jumbo derrick boom is still goosenecked high up on the port kingpost (on the opposite side to the foredeck jumbo derrick) and runs aft until its derrick head rests on the deck beside a cluster of four more oil cargo tank access hatches mirroring the layout forward of the RAS masts– the forward two hatches are missing their lids. As with the two forward similar clusters of four access hatches, these are flanked by a larger rectangular open hatch on the starboard side that holds 55-gallon fuel drums.

The starboard square-framed derrick boom with internal angular bracing has fallen out over the starboard side of the ship so that the derrick head now rests on the seabed with the derrick heel gooseneck fittings snagged on the gunwale.

As the flying bridge approaches the sterncastle, it starts to sag, and then collapses down to the main deck as it meets the deckhouse as though the intense fires had weakened the metal.

The sterncastle begins with a narrow deckhouse set well in from both sides of the deck with guardrails along its roof. On top is a smaller superimposed deckhouse and a long covered rectangular athwartships hatch aft, which opens down towards the boiler room – no doubt a coaling hatch. This deckhouse runs back towards where the sterncastle extends out to the full width of the ship at either side, and here it is noticeable that the deckhouse roof is sagging – again weakened by fire.

The large refuelling tripod used to support RAS gear such as transfer hoses rises up for almost 10 metres on the port side of the vessel here, with a large fixed diesel oil tank athwartships on mounts inboard. Oil was most likely pumped by the ship's low-pressure pumps up to this tank which may have held high-pressure pumps to force the oil high up the transfer hoses via the tripod and over to the ship being refuelled.

The massive smokestack rising from the boiler room has fallen to port and now lies collapsed on top of the superstructure. It projects out over the port gunwale and is still ringed by conspicuous reinforcing banding. There are four forced-draught ventilator funnels dotted around the circular opening of its base, but the mushroom cowls designed to capture air and channel it down to the hot boiler and engine rooms have disintegrated. Empty lifeboat davits are dotted either side of the stack, and at main deck level beneath, cabins open off walkways and the galley can also be located.

Top: A diver brings scale to the massive fallen banded smokestack of the *Iro*. (Author's collection)
Bottom: Starboard compartment off engine room. (Author's collection)

A rectangular hatch aft of the fallen smokestack allows divers to drop into the largely open engine room. Here the large triple-expansion engine running fore and aft on the centre line dominates, with gratings and catwalks around, all jumbled up and bent out of shape by the catastrophic bomb explosion and subsequent fires. Doorways open aft to deck on either side at its highest level and stairwells drop down several deck levels. The smaller high-pressure cylinder is the furthest forward – nearer to the boiler room where the steam is created. The larger low-pressure cylinder is the aftmost. Large con rods connect the engine to the crankshaft and dwarf the diver. Spare piston rings can be found clamped onto the engine room bulkhead – failure of piston rings was a very serious problem during voyages and from time to time a piston had to be re-ringed.

On the starboard side of the engine casing a large silt-filled room appears to hold upturned beds and chests – this is no doubt crew accommodation; the officers would have messed in the more pleasant spaces underneath the bridge superstructure. On the starboard hull shell plating of this room there appears to be an entry gash for an aerial bomb – this is perhaps where the fatal bomb that mortally wounded her entered the vessel, as the hull plating is pierced and bent inwards.

A 140mm (5.5-inch) defensive gun, similar to the bow gun, is mounted on a large, now skeletal, circular platform on top of the poop near the very stern. Its large barrel, still with its semi-circular splinter shield, points aft, and there are boxes of ready-use shells nearby, one directly under the barrel. The sterncastle extends right up to the fantail, with covered promenade walkways ringing the deck level below the platform. All the wooden decking and roofing of the various spaces here has been burnt away to leave a skeletal framework. The very stern compartments hold the steering gear below decks, and on deck there is an auxiliary steering position with twin helms.

Stern defensive bandstand gun platform on the *Iro*. Photo © Richard Barnden, Unique Dive Expeditions.

55-gallon fuel drums in dry cargo space. Photo © Richard Barnden, Unique Dive Expeditions.

The rudderpost emerges from the beautiful counter stern leading down to the tall, narrow rudder below –but the propeller itself, if still present on the wreck, is well buried in deep silt and out of sight.

Degaussing cables, designed to protect against magnetic mines, still ring the hull.

The *Iro* is an amazing world-class dive with so much to see – she ranks as one of my top wreck dives anywhere. I average a 90-minute bottom dive on her, which is needed to get round her. But even then you are just scratching the surface – the *Iro* requires many, many dives to get to know her. Although she sits quite deep in the seabed, her identical sister ship, IJN *Sata*, rests just half a mile away upside down, revealing the parts you don't get to see on *Iro*.

## SHIPWRECK – THE ESSENTIALS

| | |
|---|---|
| Type: | IJN *Shiretoko*-class fleet oiler (1922) |
| Built: | 1921/22 |
| Displacement: | 15,450 tons |
| Dimensions: | Loa 470ft 8in., beam 58 feet; draught 26ft 6in. |
| Propulsion: | Single vertical triple-expansion steam engine – single screw |
| Date of loss: | 17 April 1944 |
| Cause of loss: | Bombed at anchor by Task Force 58 aircraft |
| Depth to seabed: | 41 metres |
| Least depth: | 28 metres – main deck |
| Location: | Urukthapel anchorage, Western Lagoon |

# 10. Kamikaze Maru

PASSENGER–CARGO VESSEL (1937)    IJN KAMIKAZE-CLASS DESTROYER
IJN TRANSPORT (1943)             TENDER (1941)

## URUKTHAPEL ANCHORAGE, WESTERN LAGOON

*Kamikaze Maru* was laid down as a 4,950grt civilian passenger–cargo vessel at the Osaka Iron Works in Sakurajima on 31 July 1937 for Todai Kisen KK of Osaka. She was 365.8 feet long with a beam of 54.1 feet and a draught of 29.2 feet. She was launched and named on 27

The 4,916grt passenger cargo vessel, *Kamikaze Maru*.

December 1937 and after fitting out afloat was completed on 17 March 1938. She had five sister ships all constructed in 1936–1940, the *Sanko Maru*, *Sinryu Maru*, *Sinsei Maru No. 6*, *Yamahuku Maru* and *Tenryū Maru*.

She was built to a modern design as a three-island vessel with a raised fo'c'sle and raked bow, composite bridge and engine room superstructure amidships – and a stern castle. Her forward and aft well decks were given over to cargo holds, and in between each pair of forward and aft holds goalpost kingposts rose from a mast house. A topmast was fitted on top of the cross-beam of the goalposts.

*Kamikaze Maru* was powered by a coal-fired steam turbine built by the Ishikawajima Shipbuilding & Engineering Co. of Tokyo. This gave her a normal cruising speed of 12 knots and a maximum speed of 15 knots. She could hold 900 tons of bunker coal, giving her an operating radius of 8,000 nautical miles at 12 knots.

Ownership of the vessel was transferred to Yamashita Kisen KK of Kobe on 1 August 1940 and then, less than a year later, on 3 June 1941 she was requisitioned by the Imperial Japanese Navy. She was moved to the Uraga Dock Co. yard in Tokyo, where on 29 July work began to convert her for military use, with bow and stern guns being fitted at this time.

On 15 August 1941 she was rated as an auxiliary destroyer tender or *suirai-bokan*; these were used as mother ships for destroyers and torpedo boats. The conversion works were completed on 30 September 1941, and she was assigned to Vice Admiral Nobutake Kondo's 2nd Fleet.

During the latter part of 1941 and into early 1942 she made voyages to Mako (modern-day Magong in the Pescadores Islands, between Taiwan and China), Saipan and Ponape.

Mako was a major base for the Imperial Japanese Navy and an embarkation point for the invasion of the Philippines. She returned to Yokosuka in Japan where on 14 July 1942 she was assigned to the 11th Seaplane Tender Division and started making replenishment voyages to the southern Japanese port of Kure.

In October 1943, she was re-rated as a transport, and in December 1943 she departed Shanghai in an escorted convoy for Sasebo. By early February 1944 she was in Truk Lagoon, where almost immediately after the successful US photographic overflight on 4 February 1944, IJN and merchant vessels started to leave Truk, seeking safety elsewhere in the face of an imminent follow-up US assault.

On 12 February 1944, just days before the Operation *Hailstone* raids, *Kamikaze Maru* departed Truk for Palau in a convoy consisting of the fleet oiler IJN *Sata*, the tanker *Hishi Maru No.2*, the ammunition ship *Nichiro Maru* and the stores ship *Kitakami Maru*, escorted by the destroyer *Hamanami*, the subchaser *Ch 30* and auxiliary subchasers *Takunan Maru No. 2* and *Shonan Maru No. 5*.

At 2200 on 17 February, five days into the voyage and the first day of Operation *Hailstone* at Truk, the convoy was approximately 150 nautical miles north-east of Palau when the American submarine USS *Sargo* intercepted it, and fired eight torpedoes at the primary prize, the valuable *Shiretoko*-class fleet oiler *Sata*. One torpedo struck the large 470-foot long vessel and disabled her.

Six minutes later, at 2206, USS *Sargo* fired two more torpedoes at the ammunition ship *Nichiro Maru*; one of the torpedoes triggered a catastrophic secondary explosion that caused her to sink immediately. The convoy escort vessels pressed home a depth charge attack on what they believed to be two US submarines – driving *Sargo* deep and allowing the beleaguered convoy to retire to the north-west.

Just after 0900 on 19 February 1944, the day after Operation *Hailstone* concluded, the convoy arrived at Palau. On 11 March, whilst at Palau, she was provisioned by the stores ship *Kitakami Maru*.

*Kamikaze Maru* was still present in Palau, in the Urukthapel Island area of the Western Lagoon, on 30 March 1944 as Operation *Desecrate 1* began. Her foredeck Hold No. 2 was filled with a deadly cargo of 30-foot Long Lance torpedoes, her fore ship extensively converted as a service facility for such torpedoes.

As *Desecrate 1* began, *Kamikaze Maru* worked up a head of steam to get under way. At about 0745, as IJN *Iro* was being attacked just to her north, she was manoeuvring in amongst Palau's jungle-clad small islands to the south-west of Malakal Harbor at 3 knots when six Curtiss Helldivers from *Bunker Hill* attacked her with 1,000lb and 500lb bombs. She was hit forward of the bridge and amidships – and three near misses sent plumes of white water skyward. The force of the explosion transmitting through the incompressible water buckled and damaged her plating. The hit forward of the bridge triggered a significant secondary explosion, which caused fires to break out. White smoke billowed high into the air – an indication that no fuel or gasoline was burning. *Kamikaze Maru* slewed to a stop as her crew fought to control the fire and repair the damage.

Later the same day however, just after midday she was attacked by Grumman Avenger torpedo-bombers and also hit by rockets. Attack photos show the mid and aft sections of the ship on fire with black smoke billowing high into the air. She is believed to have sunk shortly thereafter, coming to rest upright on the bottom in about 35 metres of water with the tips of her masts showing a little above the surface and marking her position.

Soon after the war had ended, local salvors are believed to have removed her easily accessible propeller and valuable condensers. Several years later, in the 1950s, Fujita Salvage began its commercial salvage operations with plans to break up the sunken vessel for scrap. As divers inspected the wreck they found the aft section of the ship heavily damaged from the attack. They also discovered the Long Lance torpedoes in Hold No. 2 and a large quantity of ammunition in Hold No. 1. From then on salvage efforts were very careful and a decision was made not to use explosives on the wreck. The superstructures were cut off by hand using acetylene torches – and about 1,000 tons of scrap metal is reported to have been lifted before *Kamikaze Maru* was left alone.

Some time later some other less professional salvage attempts were made by local salvors using explosives – where Fujita had elected not to do so. A series of small explosions were set off in various locations at the bow, alongside the fore ship, the engine room and at the stern of the ship, but one triggered a large secondary explosion as munitions on the wreck detonated. After a series of further such secondary explosions the salvors elected to work elsewhere and the heavily damaged *Kamikaze Maru* was finally left in peace.

## THE WRECK TODAY

The wreck of the *Kamikaze Maru* lies across the prevailing tidal stream, so when the tide is running the soft sediment of the seabed can be stirred up clouding visibility. She has been heavily worked by salvors – so with the potential for poor vis and a worked wreck, this is one for the wreck enthusiast and is not one for divers looking for good visibility, fine corals and fish life. The visibility varies according to the state of tide you dive, but if you can see past (or through) the poor visibility and damaged ship, and see her for what

Long Lance torpedoes in Hold No. 2 Photo © Richard Barnden, Unique Dive Expeditions.

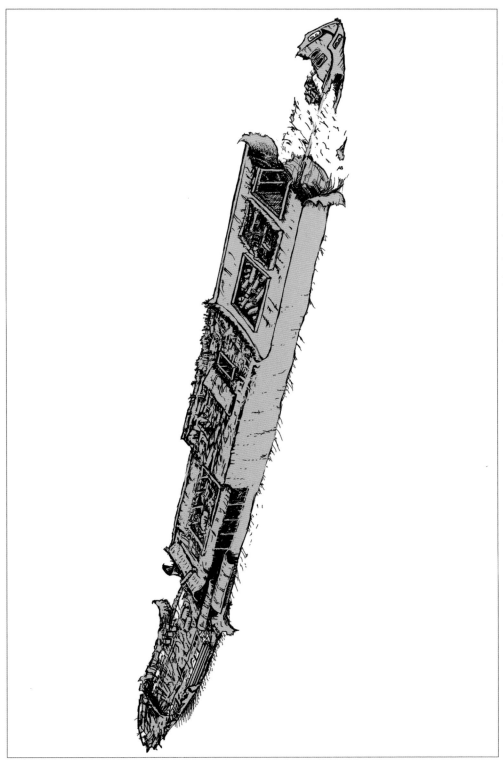

The wreck of the *Kamikaze Maru* lies in 33 metres of water in a cloudy bay. Salvors cut down most of the ship after the war but stayed well clear of Hold No. 2, which contains a number of dangerous Long Lance torpedoes.

she is and was, she becomes an interesting testament to the war and the salvage works. It is worth diving this wreck and putting up with the poor vis just to see the bow and the Long Lance torpedoes in Hold No. 2.

Large sections of the ship were dismantled and salved; superstructures were cut away by hand with acetylene torches, and there has been considerable blasting of the ship. It does not go unnoticed that the most intact area of the original ship is the foredeck Hold No. 2, which holds the powerful Type 93 Long Lance torpedoes; the salvors stayed well away from these dangerous weapons.

The ship was constructed with a soft-nosed raked bow of bent shell plating – as opposed to the stem bar seen on other older ships. The fo'c'sle has been blasted and damaged between the anchor hawses and the aft fo'c'sle bulkhead. The fore part of the ship is essentially gone from immediately aft of the deck hawse plates to the middle of Hold No. 1. The anchor windlass, which would have been situated on the fo'c'sle deck in the destroyed section, is missing, as are the anchors, chain and chain lockers – all presumably recovered to the surface. The forward tip of the bow, now free from the ship, has tilted and fallen forward and to starboard so that the rounded bow with twin fairleads on it is now only a few metres above the clay seabed. The two deck-mounted hawse plates and pipes are flanked either side of the deck by mooring cleats and twin mooring bollards.

There is a gap of several metres from the anchor hawses on the bow section to where the aft fo'c'sle bulkhead would have been – now also largely missing – and only the keel now connects the two sections. The ship resumes something of its original shape at the well deck.

The forward part of Hold No. 1 is destroyed – with hull plates forward blown out. The hold is wide open with no hatch coaming, and has an empty tween deck. The lower section of the hold contains some boxes of ammunition and wooden boxes holding twenty 250mm shells each. On deck are the remains of a mast house razed to about a metre above the deck, and the remains of the goalpost kingposts.

Hold No. 2 is also wide open and is largely intact – due to its dangerous cargo of 20-30 Type 93 Long Lance torpedoes, now in some disarray but impossible to mistake. Their very size is intimidating – and when you remember that over the years, as their high-pressure oxygen fuel cylinders finally rusted through, several of these are reputed to have spontaneously exploded, they suddenly feel even more threatening. Most are stacked flat on the bottom of the hold with their heads pointing aft, but others stand half-upright, jumbled at awkward angles. It appears that several of the oxygen cylinders have indeed corroded and blown apart

There are no warheads fitted to these torpedoes. The front of each torpedo ends where the warhead would be attached, revealing the internal rounded tops of the high-pressure oxygen cylinders used for propulsion. These oxygen cylinders were made of an alloy of nickel chromium-molybdenum steel that was originally developed for battleship armour belts. The previous Type 91 torpedoes had used compressed air as the oxidiser with an 11-foot long internal air cylinder charged to about 2,500–3000 psi – the same pressure as today's conventional scuba cylinders; compressed air, however, left a noticeable bubble trail.

The Type 93 used compressed oxygen as the fuel oxidiser in place of compressed air, with a wet-heater engine that burned a fuel such as methanol or ethanol to produce the driving force for the twin counter-rotating propellers. Compressed oxygen is dangerous to handle, but IJN engineers found that by starting the torpedo's engine with compressed air then gradually switching to oxygen they were able to overcome the explosions which

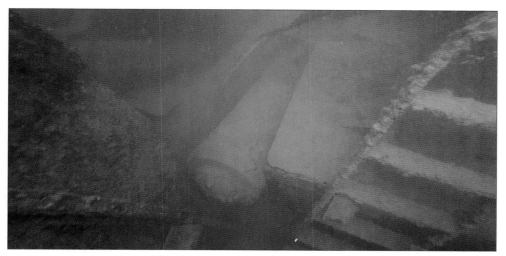

Long Lance torpedoes jam Hold No. 2 with access steps down into the hold adjacent. (Author's collection)

had hampered its use before. To conceal the use of pure oxygen from the ship's crew, the Japanese called the oxygen tank the 'secondary air tank'.

Since air is only 21 per cent oxygen and 78 per cent nitrogen, 100 per cent oxygen provides five times as much oxidiser in the same tank volume, and this greatly increased torpedo range. The absence of inert nitrogen also resulted in the emission of significantly less exhaust gas – which comprised only carbon dioxide and water vapour. The $CO_2$ combustion by-product is significantly soluble in water, and the resulting exhaust gas mixture greatly reduced the tell-tale bubbles in its track.

The Japanese Type 93 torpedo had a maximum range of about 25 miles at 38 knots and it carried a 1,080lb high-explosive warhead. Its long-range, high-speed and heavy warhead marked it as a quantum leap forward in torpedo development – and it was far ahead of any Allied torpedo of the time. The US Navy's standard surface-launched torpedo of World War II, the Mark 15, had a maximum range of just 7.4 nautical miles at 26 knots or just 3 nautical miles at 45 knots, and it carried a smaller, 826lb, warhead.

Large sets of compressors are mounted on the aft Hold No. 2 bulkhead in the tween deck, with large cylinders, associated machinery, hand wheels and gauge panels for producing high-pressure air or, more likely, the oxygen fuel for the Long Lance torpedoes.

Aft of Hold No. 2 the front bulkhead of the amidships composite bridge superstructure rises up a few metres. This composite superstructure held the bridge forward and boiler and engine rooms aft. The superstructure has however been almost totally removed by salvors, leaving a mass of bent, twisted and cut-away spars and plates, with a jumble of bent steam pipes and engine room catwalk gratings strewn about. The valuable steam turbine itself, along with the condensers and other engine room and boiler room fitments, has been ripped out of the wreck. The engine room, now a largely empty space, still drops down through several deck levels but is something of a scene of chaos. Just forward, the smokestack has fallen and now lies collapsing in upon itself athwartships.

The wrecked midships superstructure gives way to the aft well deck where the vessel regains something of a shiplike form – although it has clearly been heavily worked. The two aft holds were separated by a section of main deck with a mast house – and the coaming for

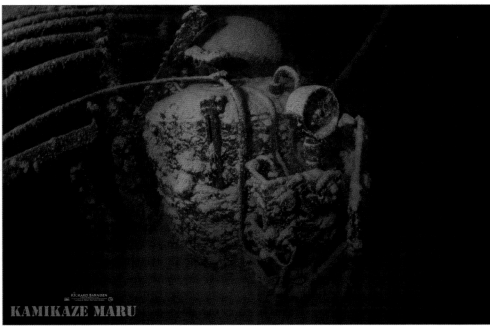

Top: Control panel in the engine room of *Kamikaze Maru*. Photo © Richard Barnden,
Unique Dive Expeditions.
Bottom: *Kamikaze Maru* engine room. Photo © Richard Barnden, Unique Dive Expeditions.

Hatch No. 3 is still recognisable. Abreast of Hold No. 3, there is explosion damage to the port side of the hull and a zigzag-shaped tear in the deck. On the starboard side the force of the explosion has blown the hull shell plating outwards and separated the hull plating from the deck and web framing. The tensioned degaussing cables which ran along the sides of the hull have been sprung off, and still under tension have come free from the side of the ship. These cables have sprung inboard and are now twisted across Hatch No. 3. Inside the hold is another set of high-pressure machinery and cylinders similar to that found in Hold No. 2 in the foredeck.

Aft of Hold No. 3, salvage blasting has deformed the main deck, which rises up in a large athwartships smooth ripple almost from one side of the ship to the other, whilst in other places sections of decking are distorted and lie at strange angles. Structurally weakened, the ship has collapsed down upon itself, so there is little depth to the hold areas.

Amidships, in the damaged depths of Hold No. 3, the shaft and shaft tunnel running aft from the engine room (just forward) are exposed. The aft bulkhead towards Hold No. 4 partly withstood the force of the explosions and is now deformed and bulging.

Hold No. 4 is well collapsed, but contains coal and a number of large drums – most are open and crushed. The remaining hull plates on the port side of this hold are blown out from an internal explosion, most likely from ammunition for the stern gun cooking off in the fires that consumed her after the attack. On the starboard side the damage is heavier and more widespread and a large part of the hull plating has been blown or cut away.

The stern is settled well into the seabed and is now only a few metres proud. The fantail is quite heavily damaged and slightly to starboard and there is a wide gap in the hull plating, most likely the effect of a salvage explosion used to blow the prop and stern shaft off. On the port side of the former sterncastle the shell plating is cut down to just a few metres off the seabed.

## SHIPWRECK – THE ESSENTIALS

| | |
|---|---|
| Type: | Passenger–cargo vessel (1937) |
| | IJN *Kamikaze*-class destroyer tender (1941) |
| | IJN transport (1943) |
| Built: | 1937 |
| Tonnage: | 4,950 grt |
| Dimensions: | Length 365.8 feet; beam 54.1 feet; draught 29.2 feet |
| Propulsion: | Coal-fired steam turbine – single shaft |
| Date of loss: | 30 March 1944 |
| Cause of loss: | Bombed by Task Force 58 aircraft |
| Depth to seabed: | 33 metres |
| Least depth: | 28 metres – main deck |
| Location: | Urukthapel anchorage, Western Lagoon |

# 11. Kibi Maru

STANDARD TYPE C CARGO FREIGHTER (1941)     IJA TRANSPORT

## WEST OF BABELTHAUP

There were two ships called *Kibi Maru* present in Palau during *Desecrate 1*. Both were Standard Type C freighters, and both were sunk in the raid on 30 March 1944 – some 11 miles apart:

1. The 2,759grt *Kibi Maru* (1941) is recorded as sunk at position: 7° 30' N, 134° 30' E.

Type C standard ship similar to *Kibi Maru*.

2. The 2,909grt *Kibi Maru* (1943) is recorded sunk at 7° 19' N, 134° 28' E.

The ship name *Kibi Maru* was a very common name for Japanese shipping – *Kibi* refers to an area or province of Japan. During the World War I era there were a number of ships produced with that name and simply given a distinguishing number, as in *Kibi Maru No. 1, No. 2* etc. By way of example, *Kibi Maru No. 16* capsized and sank during a typhoon in 1922.

Similarly, on 6 November 1941, the large 4,522grt passenger steamer *Kibi Maru* sunk after striking a mine believed to have broken loose from Russian waters whilst on a voyage between Korea and Tsuruga, Japan, with 342 passengers aboard, and this caused much public outrage.

Both the ships lost at Palau, built two years apart, were constructed under the veil of wartime secrecy, so little is known about either. The ships are not registered at Lloyd's, and do not feature in the restricted American wartime intelligence dossier *Japanese Merchant Ships Recognition Manual* ONI 208-J of 1944 (now declassified), which collated information on all Japanese merchant shipping in immense detail.

There is also no mention of either ship in the American wartime Division of Naval Intelligence briefing document *Standard Classes of Japanese Merchant Ships* ONI 208-J (Revised) declassified on 3 May 1972. Nor is either ship mentioned in the authoritative *Warships of the Imperial Japanese Navy, 1869–1945* by Hansgeorg Jentschura, Dieter Jung and Peter Mickel, published by Arms and Armour Press, London, in 1977.

Both *Kibi Marus* appear to be Type C standard well-decked medium cargo freighters. These were built as three-island ships with a raised fo'c'sle, a composite central superstructure slightly aft of midships, housing bridge, accommodation and the engine casing – and a sterncastle. The rest of the ship forward and aft of the composite superstructure was given over to cargo holds. Masts were centred in the fore and aft well decks, and the smokestack was close abaft the bridge. Variations did appear with goalpost masts, and in all the Japanese built some 30 engines-amidships Type C standard ships between 1941 and July 1944.

These 'standard ships' were all built to a simple standard design at a time when Japan saw the need to quickly build large numbers of ships to make up for those sunk in action and thus allow the continued transport of the huge volumes of materials and supplies needed to fight its Pacific War.

Japan began work on new modern standard ship designs in 1942, but with approximately two years required to design and start building new types of standard ship, construction of the newer designs of standard ships would only start in early 1944. In the interim, to boost its supply fleet to service its far-flung Pacific garrisons, from 1941 Japan started a programme of mass standard ship production using older, tried and tested, pre-war designs. Between December 1941 and July 1944 some 125 standard ships were built to a number of different designs.

From 1943 onwards, Japanese standard ships were allocated a number which referred to the year of construction, with Type 1 being a 1943 build, Type 2 being 1944 and Type 3 being 1945. A letter in the type specification referred to the actual type of ship and went from A, B, C etc. onwards. The design of the individual types varied from year to year.

The Type C freighter *Kibi Maru* dived at Palau nowadays is the vessel built in 1941 and is the northernmost of the two recorded sinking positions. Having been built before 1943 she is simply a Type C standard ship and has no identifying number. She was laid down as a 2,759grt cargo vessel in 1940 and completed in June 1941 by Nippon Kokan Tsurumi Shipyard at Tsurumi for Tochigi Kisen KK of Tokyo. She was subsequently owned by Hinode Kisen KK.

The Type C freighters were an average 320 feet long with a beam of 45 feet and a draught of about 21 feet. They were fitted with a single screw that was driven by a reciprocating steam engine and coal-fired boilers. This gave her a service speed of 11 knots and a top speed of 13 knots.

Completed just before the outbreak of war in the Pacific, *Kibi Maru* (1941) was soon being used as a Japanese army transport. Her reported sinking position at 7° 30' N, 134° 30' E, is well to the north of Malakal Harbor, about one third of the way up the west side of the main island of Babeldaob near Ngeremedu Bay *en route* to the West Passage (Toachel Mlengui) from the lagoon.

The other Type C standard ship *Kibi Maru* (1943) was built at the Tochigi shipyard in Wakamatsu for Tochigi Kissen KK of Kobe. She had a slightly larger gross tonnage of 2,909 tons, but had an identical length of 320 feet and beam of 45 feet. She was completed in February 1943 and was also taken over and used by IJA as transport. She is recorded as being sunk by US carrier-based aircraft in Malakal Harbor, off Babelthuap Island, 11 nautical miles further south than the 1941 vessel, at 7° 19' N, 134° 28'E.

As part of the research for the joint US Naval Reserve-National Park Service operation in Palau in 1988, interviews were conducted with local residents who were in Palau during the war years and those who had knowledge of post-war salvage operations by Japanese companies. Mr Fujita of Fujita Salvage, who worked some of the sunken Japanese vessels in the 1950s, released copies of the only documents still retained by him at that time on the salvage of the wrecks. Fujita Salvage records the *Kibi Maru* it worked as being sunk at 7°18.55' N, 134° 26.55' E, which coincides very closely with the wartime position for the 1943 vessel.

There are a number of records of '*Kibi Maru*' being involved in various convoy duties from 1943 onwards, but as no build year is given it is not clear which *Kibi Maru* is being referred to. The information available is set out here in the hope that it may be of assistance to future researchers. There were several references where because of the impossibility of the same vessel being essentially in two different locations at the one time it was clear that both vessels were being referred to. Being such a common ship's name there will no doubt have been several other *Kibi Maru*s active at the same time.

On 29 August 1943 *Kibi Maru* departed the port of Niigata on Japan's north-west shore, escorted by IJN minesweeper *W-23*, and moved up the north-west coast to the port of Otaru near Sapporo on the north-western side of the island of Hokkaido, arriving there on 31 August.

On 10 September *Kibi Maru* departed Saeki near Hiroshima in a large southbound convoy escorted by destroyer *Harukaze*, the torpedo-boat *Sagi*, the minelayer *Yurijima*, the auxiliary gunboat *Choun Maru* and the auxiliary patrol boat *Nitto Maru No. 12*. At 0150 the following morning, 11 September, the convoy was attacked by the American submarine USS *Spearfish* 80 miles off the Toi Promontory, the south-easternmost point of Kyushu, the southernmost of the main Japanese islands, at 30° 56' N, 132° 47' E. One vessel, *Tsuyama Maru*, was struck and was taken in tow by two vessels to Osaka for repair as the rest of the convoy proceeded.

On 8 October 1943 a *Kibi Maru* was in Palau, setting off in a convoy bound for Rabaul escorted by subchasers *Ch 23* and *Ch 24* – the convoy arrived at Rabaul on 15 October. Meantime a *Kibi Maru* is also listed as departing Palau on 13 October 1943 in another escorted convoy for Moji in Japan, arriving there on 22 October.

On 25 October 1943 that latter *Kibi Maru* is listed as departing Saeki, a port near Hiroshima in Japan's southern Inland Sea, for Palau in a convoy of IJA transports escorted by the *kaibōkan Iki* and the auxiliary minesweepers *Oi Maru* and *Tama Maru*, along with *Tama Maru No.7*.

On 17 November 1943 a *Kibi Maru* is listed as departing Truk at 0700 bound for Palau in a convoy with *Yamazuru Maru*, which was towing a *tokugata unkato* midget supply submarine. The convoy was escorted by *Patrol Boat-31* and the auxiliary subchasers *Aoi Maru* and *Tokuho Maru No. 10*, and arrived at Palau on 26 November after being plagued by submarine attacks.

On 13 December 1943 a *Kibi Maru* departed Palau for Hollandia in Dutch New Guinea (now known as Jayapura, Indonesia) along with *Fukkai Maru* and escorted by auxiliary subchaser *Cha 10* and IJN subchaser *Ch 26*. *Fukkai Maru* was torpedoed *en route* by USS *Pogy* and sank within three minutes, with the loss of 52 IJA troops, five gunners and one crewman. The beleaguered convoy arrived at Hollandia on 19 December. *Kibi Maru* then left Hollandia for Palau with *Taiei Maru* escorted by *Ch 35* and *Cha 10* – arriving back in Palau on 5 January 1944.

At 0630 on 15 January 1944, a *Kibi Maru* departed Palau in an escorted convoy bound for Wewak, Papua New Guinea, before moving north to Moji in Japan. On 25 January 1944 at 1800, that *Kibi Maru* departed Moji in a large convoy with the auxiliary oiler *Sanko Maru* and a number of IJA transports escorted by the destroyer *Harukaze*, minesweeper

*W-17* and auxiliary subchaser *Tama Maru No. 7*. The convoy arrived at Palau on 5 February 1944.

With the approach of Task Force 58 having been detected in the immediate days before *Desecrate 1*, the convoy PATA-07 had been formed up to attempt to leave Palau in the face of the anticipated imminent US assault – and to escape to Takao, Formosa. The convoy had been due to leave on the evening of 29 March but was delayed and did not set off until first light at 0500 on the morning of 30 March.

As the first rays of sunlight filtered over the horizon from the east, the convoy started to leave the main anchorages of the Western Lagoon and move north up the west side of the main Palau island of Babelthuap in the main shipping channel north towards Toachel Mlengui Pass – the West Passage. In the approach to West Passage, the shipping channel is narrow and flanked on either side by dangerous reef flats only a few metres deep. There is little room for a large ship to manoeuvre – but the West Passage is the only convenient exit through the fringing reef to the west that is big enough for substantial ships from the Western Lagoon anchorages to navigate.

The first ships of the convoy started to move off northwards in line astern, the convoy being led by picket boats, *Patrol Boat 31 (PB-31)*, the destroyer *Wakatake* and auxiliary subchaser *Cha26*, whilst at the far southernmost end of the convoy several other freighters were congregating, waiting to join. The convoy included *Kibi Maru* (1941), the fleet oiler *Akebono Maru*, the auxiliary transport *Goshu Maru*, the IJN-requisitioned 2,838grt Standard Type 1C steamers *Raizan Maru* and *Ryuko Maru*, and the IJA transports *Teshio Maru* and *Hokutai Maru*.

Inbound *Lexington*, *Bunker Hill* and *Monterey* aircraft all quickly spotted the convoy, and *Bunker Hill* Avenger torpedo-bombers attacked the lead ships as *Lexington* Hellcats strafed. Meantime *Lexington* Grumman TBF Avengers were dropping aerial magnetic moored mines in the shipping channel and in West Passage to block it. Elsewhere around Palau's scattered anchorages other US mining groups were sowing air-dropped minefields to block strategically important shipping channels and passes.

As the attacks by TF58 aircraft went in on convoy PATA-07, despite the tight manoeuvring space and dangerous coral reefs surrounding them the ships in the convoy began to take evasive manoeuvres and return AA fire where possible. No doubt after seeing the mines being air-dropped, the convoy gave up any attempt to leave the lagoon and dissolved – the ships scattering. During the contact, *Kibi Maru* (1941), whilst still heading north, ran aground on reefs on the western side of the channel whilst *Teshio Maru* grounded on the eastern side. The *Hokutai Maru* successfully came about and headed back to Malakal Harbor.

Stranded on the reef, *Kibi Maru* was an easy target and was attacked by a number of different strike air groups from different carriers throughout the day. *Yorktown* dive-bombers scored a hit on her with a 1,000lb bomb whilst *Princeton*, *Enterprise* and *Lexington* aircraft all variously attacked her, scoring hits and near misses with bombs whilst all the time Hellcats repeatedly strafed her. She was set on fire fore and aft, but despite all the damage she still managed to return light AA fire. Five of her crew were killed in the action.

The stricken ship was left stranded on the reef as the last US aircraft returned to their carriers, speeding away from the Palaus. Her hull was badly holed and she had filled with water. At some point, years after the war had ended and perhaps driven off by a storm, she came off the reef and, rolling over, slid down the reef side into deeper water. She came to rest

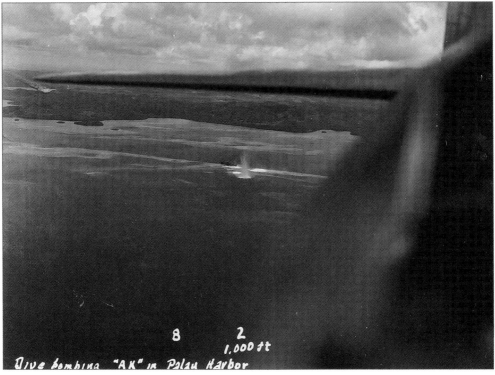

8     2
1,000 ft

Dive bombing "AK" in Palau Harbor

*Kibi Maru* under attack as she lies stranded on the reef on the west side of the main narrow shipping
channel that runs left to right in this image. (National Archives)

at the foot of the reef wall upside down and almost parallel to the side of the channel with
her bow to the north – the direction of her journey in 1944.

All the merchant ships of PATA-07 would be sunk over the two days of the *Desecrate 1*
raids – as would *Patrol Boat 31* and the escort destroyer *Wakatake*, which was sunk west of
Babelthuap in Karamadoo Bay near the West Passage.

## THE WRECK TODAY

Today the wreck of *Kibi Maru* (1941) lies upside down on a clean white sandy bottom
in about 34 metres of water on the west side of the main north–south shipping channel
that leads from Kosabang Harbor (west of Malakal Harbor), north to West Passage. The
wreck lies some 2–3 miles south of West Passage, parallel to the west reef wall of the
channel with her bows still pointing forlornly north towards her intended 1944 escape
route. The upturned hull is in good condition with little damage, and its welded plates
are easily visible. The top of the hull – the keel – is sagging downwards now by about
2 metres in the middle of the ship.

The times we have dived it we have entered the water immediately beside the west reef
wall some distance to the north of the wreck and done a free descent, not down a shot line,
as a gentle current swept us south towards the wreck. The upturned bows of the ship rising
up some 10 metres soon appear in the distance in a magnificent seascape, with the steep west

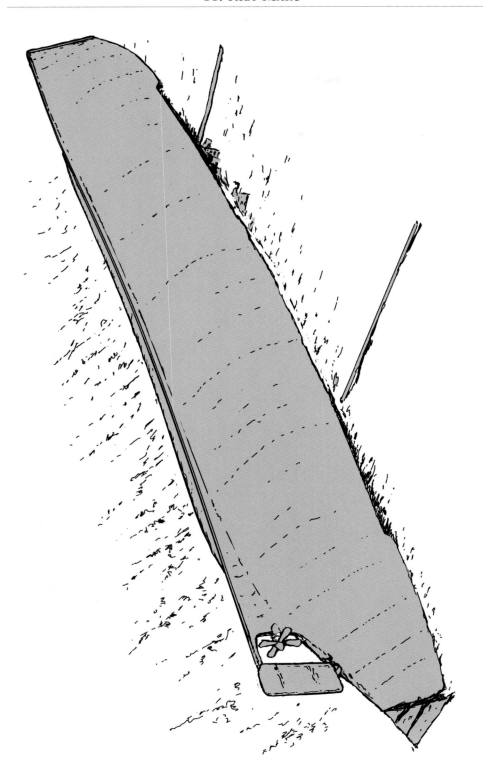

*Kibi Maru* rolled off the reef after the war – today she rests almost completely upside down at the foot of the reef in 28 metres of water.

reef wall to your right. At the bow the seabed is slightly shallower at 28 metres, whilst the seabed at the stern is at 34 metres. The top of the hull is well covered in corals.

The upturned fo'c'sle deck lies flush on the sand and there is no way to get under the ship here to see much. The port side seabed is slightly deeper whilst on the starboard side there is a space of just a few metres where sand has piled up against the side of the ship, before the wall of the reef rises up quite sharply. The port anchor is still held in its hawse.

Moving aft on the port side, at the point where the fo'c'sle deck would have dropped down to the well deck when she was afloat, the gunwale rises about a metre off the seabed allowing views under the ship to the foredeck holds – and possible entry for the more adventurous. A small section of foremast lies out flat on the seabed and runs off, disappearing into the seabed.

Aft of the foremast, the well deck gunwale continues aft a metre or two off the seabed with easier access below deck here. The well deck ends as the midships superstructure begins, and this is firmly embedded deep in the seabed.

As you pass aft of the superstructure, the gunwale sweeps up again a few metres above the seabed in the vicinity of the aft well deck, where a derrick boom sprung from the wreck sticks up at an awkward angle. Like the foremast, a section of main mast runs out at right angles to the wreck before disappearing into the seabed. It is noticeable that the mast

LEFT: Cut-off economy stern similar to *Kibi Maru*.
BELOW: The cut-off economy stern of *Kibi Maru*. (Author's collection)

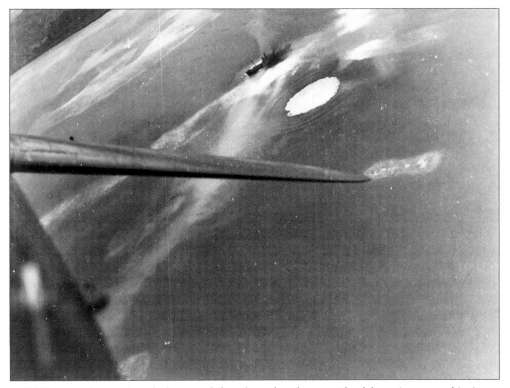

*Kibi Maru* under attack as she lies stranded on the reef on the west side of the main narrow shipping channel that runs left to right in this image. (National Archives)

obviously hit the seabed first as it was cleanly severed by the gunwale of the ship as its full weight came to rest on it.

As the well deck ends, the sterncastle deckhouse starts, again, well embedded into the seabed. The hull sweeps together to a narrow cut-off flat stern – very characteristic of quick-build economy-style standard ship hulls – and it is possible to glimpse the steering gear through some sprung plates. It is noticeable that there are none of the usual portholes along the hull at the sterncastle to allow light and air into the spaces and compartments here – perhaps another economy build consideration.

The rudder is still *in situ*, in the dead ahead position – and interestingly the propeller is still on the wreck. The propeller is the easiest and most valuable piece of ship for a salvor to remove – so the fact that this prop is still on this wreck makes me believe that the ship had rolled off the reef into deeper water before Fujita Salvage arrived in the 1950s. They surely did not know about its existence, and it is indeed not listed as one of the ships they proposed to work. Had Fujita been aware of its existence when they arrived in the 1950s, with the upturned prop being in such shallow water they would surely have salved it.

As you move forward from the stern up the slightly higher starboard side of the sterncastle, the seabed of the reef wall plunges away beneath the ship leaving a gap between gunwale and seabed several metres high and affording easier access underneath the hull to the sterncastle compartments and the aft well deck cargo hold hatches, which have high coamings. The two aft deck holds are one common space. A hatch cover beam sticks out at right angles flat on the sand, and a large cargo winch can be spotted.

The accessible aft well deck ends where the superstructure amidships disappears into the seabed, with aft-facing doorways offering tantalising access opportunities for the properly trained.

*Kibi Maru* is a lovely dive in fine conditions – don't be put off by her being almost totally upside down; there is lots to see. A few miles further north, on top of the reef flat in just a couple of metres of water sits the wreck of an American Chance Vought F4U Corsair fighter-bomber, which is fairly well preserved despite its exposed location. The Corsairs were the most capable carrier-launched fighter-bombers of World War II and would be operational until the 1960s. After your dive on *Kibi Maru* it may be possible to visit this aircraft wreck for a simple snorkel – a unique photo opportunity.

## SHIPWRECK – THE ESSENTIALS

| | |
|---|---|
| Type: | Type C standard cargo freighter |
| Built: | 1941 |
| Tonnage: | 2,759 grt |
| Dimensions: | Length 320 feet; beam 45 feet; draught 21 feet |
| Propulsion: | Coal-fired reciprocating engine – single shaft |
| Date of loss: | 30 March 1944. Slid off reef years later. |
| Cause of loss: | Bombed by Task Force 58 aircraft |
| Depth to seabed: | 28 metres – bow |
| | 34 metres – stern |
| Least depth: | 20 metres |
| Location: | West of Babelthuap – on approach to Toachel Mlengui (West Passage) |

# 12. Nagisan Maru

## WESTERN LAGOON

The 4,391grt auxiliary transport ship *Nagisan Maru* was laid down in Tama by Mitsui Bussan KK for Mitsui Bussan Kaisha Ltd (Mitsui Line) on 14 August 1930. She was launched and named on 5 March 1931, at which time her registered tonnage with Lloyd's was recorded as 4,300grt. After her fitting out afloat was completed, on 25 April 1931 she was registered in Kobe. She was 360 feet long with a beam of 50 feet and a draught of 29 feet. An eight-cylinder diesel engine built by Mitsui Bussan Kaisha Ltd powered a single screw that gave her a cruising speed of 12 knots and a maximum speed of 14 knots, and she was able to carry 960 tons of fuel oil. She was

Top: The 4,391grt auxiliary transport ship *Nagisan Maru*. With her engines aft construction she was misidentified as a tanker by US aviators during the raid.
Bottom: *Nagisan Maru.*

a modern, efficient design of ship that wouldn't look out of place in ports around the world today

She was built to an engines-aft design not dissimilar to a tanker, and indeed during *Desecrate 1* US pilots mistakenly identified her as a tanker as they attacked. She was built with a raised fo'c'sle and a raked stem, and after her subsequent requisition for war purposes a bow gun was fitted on the fo'c'sle deck. There were two foredeck holds with a masthouse in between, with goalpost kingposts and a topmast rising from it and cargo winches. The deck hold hatches were designed particularly large, to accommodate wood cargo.

A slender three-level superstructure forward of amidships held the navigating bridge and radio room at its top levels with officers' accommodation on the lower levels.

Abaft the bridge superstructure were three large holds, with Hold Nos 3 and 4 being separated by a section of deck with a masthouse from which rose a goalpost-kingpost pair. The aftmost hold, No. 5, had its own goalpost kingposts abaft, at the forward leading edge of the sterncastle.

The engine room and machinery were housed at the very stern, and being a diesel motor ship she had a relatively short and squat smokestack in comparison to the tall, slender stacks of coal-burning steamships. Covered walkways ringed around the sterncastle with doors leading to cabins off it, each with its own porthole and used as crew quarters, flanking the fireproof engine casing.

During 1931, her first voyages were dedicated to carrying coal and timber, and in 1932 her gross registered tonnage at Lloyd's was increased to 4,391 grt. In the years that followed, she carried timber, coal and other such cargoes to ports such as Karafuto (now Sakhalin) and Formosa (now Taiwan).

Prior to and during the Pacific War, the Imperial Japanese Navy requisitioned many merchant fleet cargo ships, passenger–cargo vessels and liners, and converted them to military use – they became known as *tokusetsu unsosen zatsuyosen* – or converted auxiliary transports – and were used to carry troops and military equipment such as tanks, weapons, munitions, crated aircraft, parts and stores. Between 1937 and 1945 more than 200 *zatsuyosen* were used by the Imperial Japanese Navy, and during the war 65 other ships were re-rated as *zatsuyosen*; some were requisitioned by the Imperial Japanese Navy but not enlisted.

*Nagisan Maru* was requisitioned by the Imperial Japanese Navy on 31 July 1941 to serve as a general requisitioned transport (*ippan choyosen*). These transport vessels were operated by the Imperial Japanese Navy but carried a civilian crew, and the captain was often a navy reserve officer.

On 20 December 1941, just days after the Pearl Harbor attack, *Nagisan Maru* arrived at the Kawasaki Heavy Industries KK shipyard for conversion to military duty. Her conversion works were completed on 3 January 1942 when she was assigned to the Combined Fleet as an auxiliary transport attached to the Maizuru Naval District, with Maizuru as her homeport. In the months that followed she served on voyages to Bali, Timor Island, Kupang, Celebes (now Sulawesi), Mindanao and Formosa before returning to Osaka on 26 June 1942 for a refit.

Once refitted, she carried cargoes to Saipan, Rabaul and Kobe before returning to Yokkaichi, Japan, on 29 September, when she was assigned to the Combined Fleet, 11th Air Fleet, to undertake troop and supply voyages in convoy from Japan to the south-east area, the Marshall Islands, Taroa, Saipan, Tinian and Kwajalein.

On 6 February 1943 she departed Saipan and later in the voyage, whilst unloading off Tinian, she was hit by a torpedo from the American submarine USS *Flying Fish*. She was set on fire and started to flood – and was forced to beach to prevent herself sinking. Two of her crew had been killed during the attack. The damage to her hull was repaired, and she was refloated and was able to return to Saipan on 15 February 1943.

From Saipan, on 10 May 1943, she set off back to Japan, arriving at Yokosuka on 19 May, where she underwent extensive permanent repairs at the Asano Shipyard KK until November 1943. At this time she was fitted with a Type 3 hydrophone; she was re-rated as an auxiliary transport on 1 October.

With her repairs complete, she worked around Japan for a few weeks before departing Yokosuka on 28 November 1943 for Truk in a convoy of auxiliary transports escorted by the *kaibōkan Fukue*.

The following day, about 15 miles north-west of the Izu Islands, off Tokyo Bay, the convoy was intercepted by the American submarine USS *Snapper*. *Kenryu Maru* was hit by a torpedo and set afire, and as she settled by the bows, burning fiercely, her crew abandoned ship. She sank the following day. The remaining ships of the convoy arrived at Truk on 12 December 1943.

Six days later, *Nagisan Maru* departed Truk in a convoy bound for Rabaul. On 22 December the convoy was attacked just after 1000 by USAAF bombers. One bomb narrowly missed *Nagisan Maru*, but she was able to escape unscathed. Later that same day, at about 2200, the convoy was attacked once again – and four bombs fell close to *Nagisan Maru* causing some minor flooding.

The convoy finally arrived at Rabaul on 23 December and after pausing there for a period *Nagisan Maru* departed Rabaul for Palau in a convoy of IJA transports escorted by the subchasers *Ch 17* and *Ch 18*. The convoy arrived at Palau on 15 January 1944. On 26 January she left Palau in a convoy bound for Balikpapan in Borneo – and from there she moved to Surabaya before returning to Balikpapan. With its rich petroleum resources, Balikpapan was an important source of an assured supply of fuel for Japan.

At 0730 on 15 March 1944, she left Balikpapan for Palau in a convoy of 21 ships including the fleet oiler IJN *Iro*, the auxiliary oiler *Hishi Maru No. 2*, the fleet oiler *Tsurumi*, the auxiliary oiler *Kyoei Maru*, the IJN-requisitioned cargo ship *Raizan Maru* and the IJA transport *Hokutai Maru*, escorted by the destroyers *Harusame* and *Shiratsuyu*, the minesweeper *W-36*, the subchaser *Ch 6* and the auxiliary subchaser *Cha 52*. The following day the destroyer *Michishio* joined the convoy as some of the Balikpapan escort vessels departed. Other escorts would arrive to take over their duties a few days later.

Early in the dark hours of 22 March, the American submarine USS *Tunny* picked up the convoy on its radar and began to close. By daybreak the US submarine had manoeuvred into a firing position on the surface, using rain squalls and poor visibility to cloak its approach. *Tunny* fired a full bow spread of six torpedoes at two cargo ships – successfully hitting both ships.

*Tunny* then turned its attention to the destroyer *Michishio*, which was moving at high speed across its stern – firing four stern torpedoes before crash-diving as depth charges from an auxiliary subchaser exploded on its port quarter. *Tunny* was able to successfully evade the counter-measures and leave the scene despite almost 90 depth charges being dropped by Japanese surface vessels. During the engagement the fleet oiler *Iro* was hit in the bow from the starboard side, blasting a hole 5–10 metres across at the foot of her stem forward of her collision bulkhead.

The convoy, including the stricken *Iro* (now Palau's most famous wreck), arrived at Palau on 23 March 1944 – just as, unknowingly, Task Force 58 vessels were gathering together to prepare their move westwards for the strike against Palau. One week after *Nagisan Maru*'s arrival in Palau, Operation *Desecrate 1* exploded across the skies of the tropical paradise.

On 30 March, the first day of the operation, seven *Bunker Hill* Helldivers of Strike 1B attacked her early in the morning whilst she was anchored with her port anchor in a cove in the central part of the Western Lagoon about 300 yards off the shore. Two 1,000lb bombs hit amidships, causing a large explosion that killed two of her crew and started a fire. Damaged, she started to leak oil or gasoline, and a large slick started to form.

After a further dive-bomber strike which resulted in several near misses, her crew abandoned ship. A single Grumman Avenger torpedo-bomber from *Bunker Hill* made a further attack in the afternoon, scoring a hit amidships. But *Nagisan Maru* remained afloat.

The following day, 31 March, the fires were largely out, but she was still smoking when the first US aircraft overflew the lagoon. A torpedo-bomber made a masthead attack on her, scoring a hit on the starboard side amidships beside her bridge superstructure, which started another fire. When she was photographed by US photo-reconnaissance aircraft she was seen

*Nagisan Maru* is ablaze from stem to stern and listing to starboard in this attack photograph. Her decks were super-heated by the intense heat, melting and sagging. (National Archives)

to be listing badly and burning fiercely with a large column of smoke rising from her – her cargo of fuel oil in 55-gallon drums had caught fire.

She burned for two days uninterrupted; the heat from the fires was so intense that steel decking and cargo booms melted and sagged like wet cardboard. She finally succumbed and sank to the bottom to rest upright on her keel.

## THE WRECK TODAY

The wreck of *Nagisan Maru* was located in 1978 by author Dan Bailey – who searched for it using the original US combat photos from March 1944 as his guide.

The wreck of this large vessel rests on an even keel in 31 metres of water in a relatively small cove where visibility in the shallows is excellent – but depending on the state of tide you dive at, the deeper areas of the wreck near the seabed can be very cloudy with stirred-up sediment. The shallower fo'c'sle and bow area in 18 metres can be bathed in sunlight with crystal clear water, whereas the further aft you go the siltier the wreck becomes, and by the time you arrive at the stern, visibility can be down to just 3–5 metres. That notwithstanding, this is a large, interesting wreck and the seasoned wreck diver should have no difficulty handling the visibility and navigating about it. But if you're looking for good vis, fish life and coral – try somewhere else!

Combat photos show the vessel aflame from stem to stern – and even after the attack, this ship burned fiercely for several days. Of all the wrecks I have dived internationally, this wreck shows most clearly the effects of a fierce, sustained fire, which super-heated metal

The wreck of *Nagisan Maru* lies in 31 metres of water in a sheltered area. Her main deck melted and sagged during the fires, and her cargo hatches and mast houses are now well below the level of her gunwales. A minesweeping paravane has been dropped onto her and is now embedded upright on the starboard side of her fo'c'sle deck near the bow.

decks and deckhouses causing them to melt and sag. The forward well deck looks as though it has melted like soggy paper. The fires have burnt away every trace of wood on the vessel.

At the bow, the port anchor is run out and hangs vertically from its hawse to the seabed where it then runs out at right angles to the wreck. The starboard anchor is still held snug in its hawse.

The two anchor chains lead from their hawse pipes on the fo'c'sle deck to the double-anchor windlass, which sits at a depth of about 18 metres. Aft of the windlass stands the skeletal remains of her semi-circular bow gun platform – its central support rising up from the well deck hard up against the aft bulkhead of the fo'c'sle. The gun itself is missing. The remains of guardrails dot the edges of this flush fo'c'sle deck.

The gun platform tilts downwards at its aft end due to the effects of heat and melting from the intense fire, which caused the fo'c'sle structures to sag. Fixed stairs lead up to the fo'c'sle deck from the main well deck on either side. Inboard, on either side of the bulkhead, entrance doors open into the fo'c'sle spaces. The port door is blocked by sagging metal work; however it is possible to enter the fo'c'sle spaces through the starboard door and the lamp room can be found here. When the wreck was first found the navigation lanterns were all still present – and today one has been taken out and placed on top of the fo'c'sle deck on the starboard side. What looks like a large minesweeping paravane appears to have been dropped down to the wreck and embedded itself nose first into the fo'c'sle deck near the bow on the starboard side. There is no gunwale to the fo'c'sle – just the collapsed remnants of guardrails.

The forward well deck accommodated two large cargo holds and is ringed by a high gunwale. The deck itself clearly shows the effects of severe fire over a sustained period and sags by several metres down towards the large rectangular cargo hatches – with the result that the top of the masthouse between the hatches is actually lower than the gunwales at either side. The forward holds have a deep layer of sediment at 28 metres but contain mangled debris, pipes and 55-gallon fuel drums.

The forward goalpost kingposts that rose from the masthouse in between Hold Nos 1 and 2 have fallen aft into Hold No. 2. Derrick cargo booms run forward and aft from the base of each kingpost leg. The forward booms have melted and weakened and now curve over the coaming for Hold No. 1 before disappearing into the hold. The two aft derrick booms do the same over the hatch for Hold No. 2. The separating bulkhead between the holds is buckled due to bomb damage.

The bridge superstructure was situated just forward of amidships and fixed steps at either side of the well deck lead up its forward bulkhead to promenade walkways down either side. Perhaps weakened by fire and perhaps by the bomb hit forward of amidships, the deckhouse has sagged and collapsed downwards on the starboard side. The outside starboard side of the hull and deckhouse here has then collapsed inwards so that the starboard side of the deckhouse with its rows of portholes is almost horizontal in places.

Only the bottom two deck levels of the bridge now remain recognisable – still studded by rows of forward-facing portholes. The uppermost deck level, which held the wooden navigating bridge or pilot house, has been completely burnt away by the fires. An AA gun and mount has fallen from the top of the bridge superstructure to lie half-buried in silt on the port side well deck in front of the bridge.

Aft of the bridge front, the roof and inner spaces of the superstructure have all sagged and collapsed downwards, perhaps weakened by fire, to leave open spaces with lots to explore.

Top: Minesweeping paravane embedded near the bow in the fo'c'sle deck. (Author's collection)

Bottom: Fixed steps lead up from the starboard side well deck to the fo'c'sle deck. An open doorway allows access inside the fo'c'sle to the lamp room. (Author's collection)

Aft of the collapsing bridge superstructure is the wide expanse of deck between the bridge and sterncastle that held Hold Nos 3, 4 and 5. The deck here, as with the foredeck, is collapsing downwards – again probably due to the effects of fire heating the metal red hot – so that the hatches are below the deck level by several metres.

In between the hatches for Hold Nos 3 and 4, the heavy-duty large goalpost kingposts still stand *in situ*, rising out of the mast house with cargo booms still goosenecked to them, running forward down into Hold No. 3. The aft derricks booms are also still attached to the kingposts, their ends angled inwards and downwards into the sagging Hold No. 4.

Hold Nos 4 and 5 contain more 55-gallon barrels and cables, and the hull shows heavy deformation from the intense fires.

The skeletal remains of a circular aft gun platform which stood between Hold Nos 4 and 5 with a fixed ladder access leading up to it from the deck, can be found partially collapsed aft; as at the bow, the gun itself is gone.

Immediately aft of the aftmost hold, No. 5, the wide goalpost kingposts at the forward bulkhead of the sterncastle still stand, complete with derricks and rigging. The sterncastle is in fairly good shape on the starboard side, with the walls of the deckhouse still in place and dotted with portholes. This deckhouse held the engine casing and machinery, with cabins ringing around it.

Doors on the forward bulkhead allowed access inside – and on top of the sterncastle, on the boat deck, lifeboats were held in their davits either side of the smokestack amid a forest of forced-draught ventilators. Bombing and the fires that followed heavily damaged this aft area, and the smokestack has collapsed to port. The forced-draught ventilators that were studded around the deckhouse have fallen through to the bottom of the hull.

As with the bridge superstructure, the intense heat of the fires that consumed her have weakened the sterncastle, burnt away any wood and caused the roof to sag downwards. The promenade deck walkways that ran alongside the superstructure have had the wooden decking of their roofs burnt away to leave the corridors below open, exposing doors leading off to cabins and machinery spaces.

The engine room is difficult to understand due to the structural damage from the bombing attack – catwalks have been blown into awkward angles, and it is tight and confusing. The diesel engine is still in the wreck but is difficult to access due to collapsed structures.

The stern shows much bomb and fire damage with shell and deck plates torn and bent – the main destruction is on the port side. Just aft of the goalpost kingposts, on the port side the shell plating is blown out, curving in a dramatic sweeping section. At the very stern, in 25 metres, at the auxiliary steering position the T-piece at the top of the rudderstock, to which chains could be shackled for direct emergency steering of the rudder below, still stands in place. The rudder is still in place, too – although the propeller, if still present on the wreck, is well buried in the silty bottom; the ship seems to have taken a very close near miss here, which blew away the fantail, leaving the auxiliary steering apparatus just a few feet away from the edge of what remains.

Although the wreck of the *Nagisan Maru* clearly bears the scars of the terrible story of the bombing attack, she appears to have largely escaped the attentions of the post-war salvors. She is not listed by Fujita Salvage as being worked.

The wreck is not visited often but is an interesting dive, albeit in an area of cloudy reduced visibility.

At the very stern of *Nagisan Maru*, the auxiliary steering gear T-piece to which chains would have been shackled for emergency steering of the rudder directly below. (Author's collection)

## SHIPWRECK – THE ESSENTIALS

| | |
|---|---|
| Type: | Passenger–cargo vessel (1931) |
| | IJN general requisitioned transport (31 July 1941) |
| | IJN auxiliary transport (1 October 1943) |
| Built: | 1930/31 |
| Tonnage: | 4,391 grt |
| Dimensions: | Length 360 feet; beam 50 feet; draught 29 feet |
| Propulsion: | Diesel engines – single shaft |
| Date of loss: | Post 31 March 1944 |
| Cause of loss: | Bombed by Task Force 58 aircraft |
| Depth to seabed: | 31 metres |
| Least depth: | 18 metres – fo'c'sle |
| Location: | Western Lagoon anchorage |

# 13. IJN Nissho Maru No. 5 (the Helmet Wreck?)

CONVERTED AUXILIARY TRANSPORT

## NORTH-EAST MALAKAL HARBOR

The 783grt cargo vessel Nissho Maru No. 5 was laid down in Osaka at the Ohara Zosen Tekkosho KK shipyard for Marusho Kaiun KK on 1 October 1934. She was launched and named on 25 January 1935 and completed on 1 March 1935. She was registered in Osaka but in 1937 her port of registry was changed to Ura.

The 783grt cargo vessel and auxiliary net layer *Nissho Maru No. 5*. The writer believes that this is the Helmet wreck.

*Nissho Maru No. 5* was 180.4 feet long with a beam of 31.2 feet and a draught of 15. 6 feet. She was powered by a single vertical triple-expansion reciprocating steam engine and a single shaft. A single-deck steamship, she was built with a raised fo'c'sle with no gunwale, that was ringed by guardrails. She had two foredeck holds forward of her bridge, with her foremast set on the portion of well deck in between their hatches. A single derrick boom led forward over Hold No. 1 and a single derrick boom projected aft over Hold No. 2 to rest in a cradle at the foot of the bridge when not in use.

Steps led up either side of her well deck to the shelter deck of her composite bridge superstructure, which held the officers' accommodation on its lower levels, the radio room above and then the navigating bridge and chart room at its highest level. Abaft the bridge stood her tall coal-burner's smokestack with forced-draught ventilators dotted around its base and lifeboats swung in davits either side here on the boat deck. Her boiler room was located immediately beneath.

Abaft her boiler room was her engine room – her vertical triple-expansion engine most likely gave her a service speed of about 11 knots.

Her aft well deck had a single large hold worked from her main mast, which rose up through the main deck hard up against the forward bulkhead of the sterncastle. Her delicate single-storey sterncastle held her steering gear and auxiliary steering position. She had a delicate schooner stern, below which she was fitted with a square-topped rudder.

After six years of civilian duties *Nissho Maru No. 5* was requisitioned by the Imperial Japanese Navy on 26 August 1941 in the immediate run-up to Japan's Pacific War, which would open on 8 December 1941. She was registered in the Imperial Japanese Navy as an auxiliary netlayer attached to the Kure Naval District; on 15 October 1941 her conversion to military duty at Osaka was completed at Namura Zosensho KK shipyard, and the same day she was assigned to the Kii Defence Corps.

The standard armament for netlayers was one 80mm deck gun, one depth charge launcher, two depth charge racks, 24 depth charges, two catching nets and one K-type hydrophone.

On the opening day of the war, 8 December 1941, she was assigned to sea defence forces under the Osaka Guard District, and was soon engaged in minelaying duties and ferry duties, working out of Yura through the early part of 1942. She was dry docked at Namura Zosensho KK's shipyard in Osaka for maintenance and repairs on 15 April 1942.

She was undocked on 26 April, and recommenced patrols from Yura for the rest of the year and until 28 September 1943, when she was scheduled to be converted to an auxiliary transport attached to the Kure Naval District. She was reclassified as such on 1 October 1943.

On 1 January 1944 she was assigned to the Combined Fleet as an auxiliary transport, and was soon involved in carrying troops to New Guinea.

On 21 February she departed Yokohama as command ship of a fishing boat fleet that was being repositioned south to Saipan, each of the fishing boats carrying a small amount of ammunition for the garrison there. The convoy arrived at Saipan on 7 March and from there *Nissho Maru No. 5* moved south to Palau – arriving there on 24 March as unknowingly, US naval forces gathered far to the east for their strike against Palau.

On 31 March 1944 she was bombed and sunk 'at Palau Harbor' by TF58 aircraft – taking hits to her bridge area and to her hull. She sank quickly, and was removed from the Navy List on 10 May 1944.

The wreck of *Nissho Maru No. 5* has never been formally identified in Palau Harbor. I believe that there is a strong possibility that the *Nissho Maru No. 5* is the 'Helmet Wreck', an unidentified but popular shipwreck in Palau Harbor. Although nothing definite has ever been found on the Helmet Wreck to identify it since its intact wreck was found in about 1989, the shape, approximate tonnage, measurements, design and fitments, cargo and layout all coincide with that vessel, which was previously believed to have possibly been salvaged by Fujita Salvage in the 1950s. A preliminary survey document prepared by Fujita lists *Nissho Maru No. 5* as a *possible* for salvage lying in 28 metres of water in the Palau Harbor area – a depth that coincides with the deeper bow section of this wreck. There is no mention of her, however, in the list of wrecks actually salved by that company.

The beam of *Nissho Maru No. 5* is listed at Lloyd's as 31.2 feet. On my last dive trip to Palau, Gary Petrie and I measured the beam of the Helmet Wreck and got it as 30 feet 7 inches

Combat photo of Malakal Harbor. *Nissho Maru No. 5* is one of the two vessels top centre. (National Archives)

across the foredeck immediately in front of the bridge. Dan Bailey also measured the beam and notes it in his book *WWII Wrecks of Palau* as being 31 feet 4 inches. Both measurements are pretty close, ours just being a rudimentary measurement with a tape measure. *Nissho Maru No. 5* was carrying 24 depth charges at the time of her loss. The Helmet Wreck still holds a number of depth charges in her aft hold, giving her an early nickname of the Depth Charge Wreck. For all the other reasons why *Nissho Maru No. 5* might be the Helmet Wreck – and for possible diving information on *Nissho Maru No. 5* – see Chapter 8, 'The Helmet Wreck'.

# 14. USS Perry

DD-340/DMS-17, Clemson-class destroyer (1921)

## ANGAUR ISLAND

The *Clemson*-class destroyer USS *Perry* was laid down on 15 September 1920 at the Mare Island Navy Yard at Vallejo, California. She was launched on 29 October 1921 and was the third vessel to carry that name.

The 1,190-ton *Clemson*-class destroyer USS *Perry*. (National Archives)

Displacing 1,190 tons, she was 314 feet 5 inches long with a beam of 30 feet 8 inches and a draught of 13 feet 6 inches. Her twin screws could push her to 35 knots and she had a range of 4,900 nautical miles at 15 knots. She was powerfully armed, with four 4-inch main guns set one at the bow, one either side of the superstructure abaft the bridge and one astern. She also carried four triple 21-inch torpedo tubes.

USS *Perry* was named after the United States Navy Commodore Oliver Hazard Perry (1785–1819), who served in the West Indies during the war with France as well as in the Mediterranean during the Barbary Wars and in the Caribbean, fighting piracy. During the 1812 Anglo-American war, he was pivotal in the creation of an American naval fleet at Erie, Pennsylvania, and earned the title 'Hero of Lake Erie' for leading US forces to a decisive naval victory against the British Royal Navy at the Battle of Lake Erie. This fleet victory was a turning point in the 1812 war, as it opened up Canada to possible invasion whilst protecting the Ohio Valley. It was the first time that an entire British naval squadron had surrendered.

USS *Perry* was commissioned on 7 August 1922 and operated with the Pacific Fleet out of San Diego on the west coast of America until 17 January 1923 when she was decommissioned. She remained in

USS *Perry* under construction alongside USS *Decatur* at Mare Island Navy Yard, California, in 1921. (National Archives)

reserve until April 1930 when she was recommissioned, and thereafter she began operating off California and took members of the US Senate on an inspection trip cruise to Alaska. Throughout the 1930s she operated in the eastern Pacific, the Caribbean and the west Atlantic.

In the early part of 1940, as part of the US response to Japanese expansionism, the US Pacific Fleet was instructed to take up an advanced position at Pearl Harbor in Hawaii. On 2 April 1940, *Perry* departed her San Diego base for her new homeport at Pearl, escorting the battleship USS *Arizona* – which would so tragically blow up during the Japanese air attack on 7 December 1941.

Once she had taken her battleship charge safely to Pearl, she went on to patrol Hawaiian waters for the next five months before entering the naval shipyard at Pearl for conversion to a high-speed minesweeper. At this time her aft smokestack was removed and her torpedo tubes were replaced by mining and minesweeping gear installed aft, two depth charge tracks, depth charge projectors and a sweeping winch with torpedo-like paravanes and towed cables. Minesweepers would slowly sweep an area to be cleared, dragging long tails of magnetic cable behind them, streaming paravanes to port and starboard and emitting loud sounds from a trip-hammer mechanism mounted under the bow. In this fashion, magnetic, contact and acoustic mines could all be dealt with. She was redesignated *DMS-17* on 19 November 1940.

On 7 December 1941 she was moored in Pearl Harbor as the Japanese carrier aircraft swept over Hawaii for their surprise attack. She immediately got under way and opened fire with her machine guns at the Japanese planes within range as General Quarters was sounded. Four planes were shot down within range of her and at least one of these was claimed by the *Perry*. Sometime after the raid started, officers on her deckhouse saw a submarine partially surfaced and heading towards US naval vessels. Fire was commenced with Number Four 4-inch gun, and it was believed that a hit was scored on the submarine's conning tower. The *Perry* then took up patrol and minesweeping duties in the approaches to the harbour entrance.

She continued combat patrols offshore from Hawaii until May 1942 when, after some alterations in California, she was tasked to perform minesweeping and rescue missions and act as convoy escort in the north Pacific until Kiska, in the Aleutian Islands of Alaska, was retaken on 15 August 1943.

She returned to Pearl Harbor on 27 November 1943, and joined the 5th Fleet then staging for the Marshall Islands campaign. On 31 January 1944 she arrived at Kwajalein and started performing ASW duties, escorting troop ships and carrying out minesweeping in the Solomons. She was then moved to New Guinea waters where she remained until 6 May 1944, when she headed east to rejoin the US 5th Fleet in the Solomons for the invasion of the Marianas.

USS *Perry* participated in Operation Forager, arriving off Saipan and commencing forward minesweeping operations on 13 June 1944 under cover of the big guns and AA screen of the Task Force 58 battleships. She then undertook screening duties in the forward area for transports moving towards the assault beaches during the amphibious landings that began on 15 June.

She was subsequently moved to Eniwetok and then to Guam where from 14th to 20th July she screened the major warships of the Operation Forager fleet as they pounded Japanese shore defences with a pre-invasion softening-up bombardment. As amphibious troops made their assault on 21 July she joined the screen of fire support units.

After joining in the shelling of Rota five days later, she returned to Guam before moving to Eniwetok in a transport screen. She was then assigned to the invasion of Palau scheduled for September 1944.

On 6 September 1944 Mining Squadron 2 (MinRon 2) sortied from the Florida Islands, now known as the Nggela Islands, a small group in the central area of the Solomon Islands immediately north of the more famous island of Guadalcanal. On 12 September, MinRon 2 reached Peleliu Island and *Perry* started sweeping operations.

USS Perry rolls to port as she goes down by the head – this is the last known photo of her afloat. (National Archives)

At 0811 a mine explosion destroyed *Perry*'s port sweep gear. It was soon replaced and she continued operations until the afternoon. That night she carried out anti-submarine patrols and early the next morning resumed her minesweeping duties.

On 13 September 1944 USS *Perry* was operating less than a mile – just some 1,000 yards – off the south-east coast of Angaur Island, at 06° 52' 23" N, 134° 08' 41" E. She was so close that Japanese troops ashore were firing at her with artillery and small arms rifles. At 1418 (ship's time) she scraped a Japanese mine – the resulting violent explosion on her starboard side amidships in her engine room area shook the entire ship. As seawater poured into her hull and entered the boiler room, a boiler exploded, killing several of her crew. All steam to her main engines was lost, and the forward fire rooms were damaged and flooded.

*Perry* quickly took on a 30-degree list to port which increased rapidly, and she began to settle quickly by the bow. Within minutes, at 1420, there was no alternative but to give the order to abandon ship, leaving only a skeleton crew of essential personnel. The *Clemson*-class destroyer USS *Preble* approached the stricken *Perry* in an attempt to save the ship – but the attempt was in vain and had to be abandoned at 1515, at which time all remaining personnel were ordered off.

At 1605, the elderly destroyer capsized, breaking into two sections that remained connected at the keel. She then sank into 75 metres of water. The position for her sinking was recorded in her log as 06°52' 45" N, 134°08' 40" E, but despite several searches for her over the years her wreck was not rediscovered until the year 2000.

## THE WRECK TODAY

The wreck of USS *Perry* was located by one of Palau's main dive centres, Fish 'n Fins, in 2000 after contact from one of the surviving crewmen, Larry Tunks, who returned to Palau and helped locate the wreck by following his instincts and his memories of the fateful day in 1944. A seabed anomaly was detected in 75 metres of water, and Fish 'n Fins owner Navot Bornovski and dive instructor Jeff Wonnenberg dived – and when they surfaced they were able to confirm to a delighted Larry Tunks that the long-lost destroyer had indeed been found.

The long, slender ship rests on her port side in two sections at a relative angle of some 70 degrees – with both halves still connected at the keel.

The wreck of USS *Perry* lies in 75 metres of water off the southernmost island of Angaur.

The shorter bow section still carries the 4-inch bow gun *in situ*. Near the bow on the keel can be found the electronics sonar pod used for acoustic ASW.

Up on deck on the main section of the wreck, coils of heavy-duty sweeping cables used for ASW can be found. Her uppermost starboard side 4-inch gun abaft the bridge can be seen, and her aftmost 4-inch gun is also still in place. Both large propellers are still on the wreck, flanking the rudder just astern. The uppermost starboard side section of free prop shaft runs out some distance from the prop tunnel to its supporting bracket.

The stern remains intact, with minesweeping gear lying nearby on the seabed. A large, round Japanese contact mine lies half-buried in the seabed just off the wreck – perhaps its tether became snagged as the ship sunk and it was carried down. The aft quarterdeck still carries the minelaying tracks and ASW apparatus.

The underwater visibility in this area outside the lagoon is excellent. With visibility of several hundred feet, the whole ship can be often be seen on the descent.

Nevertheless, to dive the USS *Perry* requires a considerable degree of planning. Lying in 75 metres with a least depth of about 65 metres she is firmly in the realm of the suitably trained technical diver using helium gas mixes. The tides in this area are strong and unpredictable, and as she is outside the protection of the lagoon, sea conditions have to be right.

The wreck lies on the south-east side of Angaur Island – more than 40 miles south of Koror where most of the land-based dive centres are located. It is possible to dive the wreck using the local fast day boats used for general diving around Malakal – but conditions have to be just right for a run each way of two or three hours. It is often possible to break the journey by overnighting on Peleliu Island before a shorter run the next day to the wreck site. She can also be dived from a liveaboard dive boat by a group chartering the boat for that purpose.

Diving the USS *Perry* requires a lot of careful planning and a degree of luck, as much can go wrong; the weather can turn, and even if you get to the site the unpredictable strong currents can make diving impossible.

In 2005 the wreck was the subject of a Deep Sea Detectives episode, when a memorial plaque was laid at the site.

## SHIPWRECK – THE ESSENTIALS

| | |
|---|---|
| Type: | *Clemson*-class destroyer *DD-340* (1921) |
| | *DMS-17* (1940) |
| Built: | 1920/21 |
| Displacement: | 1,190 tons |
| Dimensions: | Length 314ft in.; beam 31ft 8in.; draught 13ft 6in. |
| Propulsion: | Diesel engines – twin screw |
| Date of loss: | 13 September 1944 |
| Cause of loss: | Mined |
| Depth to seabed: | 75 metres |
| Location: | South-east of Angaur Island, the southernmost island of the Palau archipelago |

# 15. Raizan Maru

STANDARD TYPE C CARGO STEAMSHIP (1942)  IJN-REQUISITIONED CARGO SHIP (1943)

## LLEBUCHEL, KOSABANG HARBOR

The 2,838grt steamship *Raizan Maru* was a Standard Type C cargo vessel built at the Namihaya Dockyard in Osaka during the 1st War Standard Building Programme. She was launched in July 1942 and after fitting out afloat was completed later that year in December 1942 for her owners, Tsurumaru Kisen KK. The Imperial Japanese Navy requisitioned her as a cargo ship in 1943.

Type C cargo steamship similar to *Raizan Maru*.

Whilst most Japanese merchant fleet vessels built pre-war were known to the Allies, such was the secrecy surrounding Japan's mass shipbuilding programme that the *Raizan Maru* is not included in the 1944 restricted US Intelligence *Japanese Merchant Ships Recognition Manual* ONI 208-J (now declassified). Nor is she listed in the American Division of Naval Intelligence *Standard Classes of Japanese Merchant Ships*.

The Type C *Raizan Maru* was 321 feet long with a beam of some 45 feet and a draught of 21 feet, and was one of approximately 30 Type C engines-amidship freighters constructed by Japan between 1941 and 1944. The composite superstructure was slightly aft of amidships, with two holds in the forward well deck and two in the aft well deck. The foremast rose from a mast house in between Hold Nos 1 and 2 and the main mast between the aft holds, Nos 3 and 4.

The tall smokestack, characteristic of a coal-burning steamer, was set immediately aft of the bridge with the engine casing below in the composite superstructure. The ship was powered by a vertical triple-expansion engine that drove her single screw to provide a service speed of 11 knots and a top speed of 13 knots.

Variations of the Standard Type C freighter appeared – some with goalpost kingposts in place of masts. Several Type C merchant ships were sunk in Palau during Operation *Desecrate 1*, including both *Kibi Maru*s, *Shinsei Maru No. 18*, *Ryuko Maru* and *Raizan Maru*.

After her 1943 IJN requisition, she is recorded as departing the southern Japanese port of Moji on 15 August 1943 in an escorted convoy and arriving at the port of Mako in the Pescadores Islands (between Formosa and China) on 20 August 1943. By 17 September, she was back in Moji, departing in an escorted convoy to Takao in Formosa: arriving there on 25 September.

On 3 December 1943 she departed Miike, (no doubt with a cargo of coal, as Miike was Japan's largest coal mine) in a large escorted convoy, which arrived at Takao on 8 December. On 17 December 1943, *Raizan Maru* was on the move again, departing Takao for Manila and Luzon in the Philippines in a convoy of 12 ships escorted by the destroyer *Fuyo*, subchaser *Ch 46* and auxiliary minesweeper *Wa-7*.

On 25 January 1944 she departed Halmahera, Indonesia, escorted by IJN minesweepers *W-4* and *W-5* on a short passage to Ambon – arriving there on 27 January. She quickly moved off on a further transport run before making her way back towards Ambon. On 4 February she was met by IJN minelayer *Itsukushima* 30 miles off Ambon and escorted to port. After several other voyages, by the middle of March she was in Japan's important oiling port of Balikpapan in Borneo.

At 0730 on 15 March 1944, *Raizan Maru* departed the Borneo seaport of Balikpapan, which held an important Japanese oil refinery, in a large convoy of oilers and tankers. The convoy was heading north-east for Palau in three echelons and comprised the large *Shiretoko*-class fleet oilers *Iro* and *Tsurumi*, the small coastal tankers *Hishi Maru No. 2*, and *Kyoei Maru*, and the cargo ships *Nagisan Maru* and *Hokutai Maru*. Such was the importance of this major fuel convoy that it was escorted by the destroyers *Harusame* and *Shiratsuyu*, the minesweeper *W-36*, the subchaser *Ch 6* and the auxiliary subchaser *Cha 52*. The destroyer *Michishio* joined the convoy *en route* on 16 March.

On 22 March the large convoy was picked up on radar well to the west of Palau by the American submarine USS *Tunny*, which began to close on the surface using rain squalls and poor visibility to cloak its approach. A Japanese escort destroyer spotted *Tunny*, but in the poor visibility the submarine was able to evade the destroyer and continue to close on the convoy. Once in a firing position, *Tunny* fired a full bow spread of six torpedoes at two Japanese cargo ships – with hits on both vessels. In the poor visibility, *Tunny* herself was almost run down by one of the coastal tankers that suddenly appeared out of the haze.

Lookouts on the conning tower of *Tunny* spotted the Japanese escort destroyer *Michishio* moving at high speed across her stern. *Tunny* fired a spread of four torpedoes before crash-diving as the first of almost 90 depth charges were dropped. In the following four-hour-long contact, the large fleet oiler IJN *Iro* was hit by a torpedo at the very bottom of her bow on the starboard side. Perhaps a less important target for USS *Tunny*, *Raizan Maru* escaped unscathed, and the convoy, including the beleaguered oiler *Iro*, arrived at Palau the following day, 23 March 1944 at 1800 – just a week before *Desecrate 1*.

With the approach of Task Force 58 having been detected around 25 March, preparations began for a convoy, PATA-07, to be formed up to attempt to leave Palau in the face of a possibly imminent US assault. The convoy would head for a safe refuge at the Japanese-held port of Takao (the present-day Kaohsiung City) in south-west Formosa (now Taiwan). *Raizan Maru* was one of the convoy ships selected to make the escape bid; in her holds she carried a cargo of valuable nickel ore. Convoy PATA-07 was scheduled to leave Palau's anchorages within the Western Lagoon on the evening of 29 March, but the departure had to be delayed.

At first light the following morning the convoy ships started to leave the main Western Lagoon anchorages at 0500 and move up north. As you move north from the open expanses of Kosabang Harbor to the west of Koror, shipping starts to funnel towards the main navigation channel that leads north up the west side of the main Palau island of Babelthuap to Toachel Mlengui – the West Passage through the fringing reef.

The main channel in the immediate approach to West Passage is narrow and is flanked on either side by steep reef walls rising sharply from the depths to form large expansive coral flats only a few metres deep on either side; there is little room for large ships to manoeuvre.

In addition to *Raizan Maru*, convoy PATA-07 included *Kibi Maru* (1941), the fleet oiler *Akebono Maru*, the auxiliary transports *Goshu Maru* and *Ryuko Maru*, and the IJA transports *Teshio Maru* and *Hokutai Maru*. Escorting the convoy was *Patrol Boat 31*, the destroyer *Wakatake* and auxiliary subchaser *Cha 26*. The convoy was led by picket boats and the *Wakatake*, whilst at the far southern end of the convoy several other freighters were congregating, waiting to join.

At 0300, just two hours before the first ships of PATA-07 moved off, the various task groups of Task Force 58 were reaching their assigned holding positions some 70–110 miles south of Palau after their approach at speed following detection by Japanese aircraft on 25 March. On arrival, TF58 immediately assumed launching formation, and the first F6F Hellcat fighters of the initial fighter sweep started to launch just an hour and a half later, at about 0430. As the first convoy ships moved up north along the west side of Palau, flights of Hellcats were already airborne and inbound towards Palau for the initial fighter sweep. Grumman Avenger torpedo-bombers were also inbound, tasked to bomb Peleliu Airfield and carry out aerial mining operations in the important shipping channels of the lagoon.

The convoy of seven large ships and their escorts was quickly spotted by incoming American aircraft from *Lexington*, *Bunker Hill* and *Monterey*, and some 50 minutes after the convoy ships had started to depart Kosabang Harbor, the convoy was attacked by F6F Hellcats, Douglas SBD Dauntless dive-bombers, Grumman TBF Avenger torpedo-bombers and SB2C Helldiver aircraft.

*Bunker Hill* Avenger torpedo-bombers attacked the lead ships as *Lexington* Hellcats strafed. Land-based AA batteries and the AA guns of the ships and their naval escorts opened up on the American attackers. Meantime, mines were being air-dropped in the northbound channel and the West Passage to block these to shipping.

No doubt, after seeing their escape route through West Passage blocked by mines, and in the face of this powerful US attack, the ships in the convoy began to take evasive manoeuvres – the convoy was dissolved and the ships scattered. During the contact, *Kibi Maru* ran aground on the west side of the narrow channel whilst *Teshio Maru* grounded on the eastern side. *Hokutai Maru* was able to come about, and headed back south towards Kosabang Harbor.

Stranded on the reef, and with limited AA defences, the unfortunate *Kibi Maru* was an easy target for the US aircraft and was attacked by a number of different strike air groups from different carriers throughout the day. She was set on fire fore and aft, but nonetheless still managed to return light AA fire.

*Raizan Maru*, near the end of the line of seven ships in the convoy, was attacked by dive-bombers just after 0600 local time as she was in Komebail Lagoon to the west of Ngerekebesang Island, where the Japanese had their Arakabesan seaplane base. One bomb hit her on the port side astern causing an explosion. She remained afloat for some considerable time but eventually sank by the stern in the middle of a bay formed by the northern claw of Malakal Harbor, Ngerchaol, and the reefs that link it to Ngerekebesang Island to the north. All the other ships of the convoy were also sunk over the two days of *Desecrate 1*.

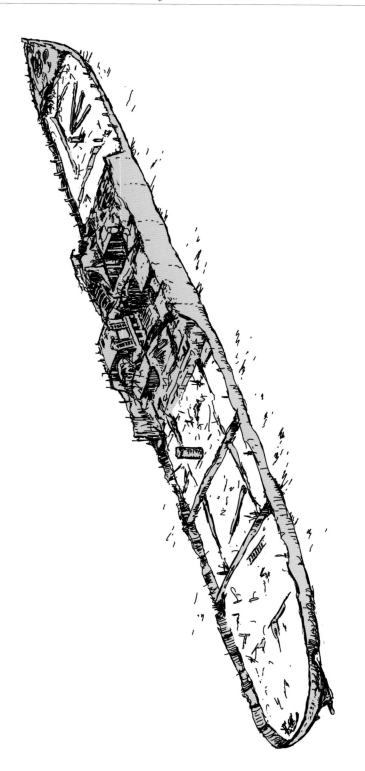

The cut-down remains of *Raizan Maru* lie in 35 metres of water with her bows pointing forlornly to shore.

Fujita Salvage Company records reveal that it worked the wreck of *Raizan Maru*, which is located less than 1 nautical mile from shore to the south-west of the present -day Palau Pacific Resort in 33 metres of water – they give a rather inaccurate position of 7° 20' 50" N, 134° 26' 12" E. Fujita recovered her cargo of 2,500 tons of valuable nickel ore, along with a significant amount of scrap iron from the wreck. The propeller was removed, and the superstructure and upper hull shell plating was cut away with acetylene torches. Subsequent salvage works on the wreck using explosives to free up her steel caused much damage to her.

## THE WRECK TODAY

The wreck of *Raizan Maru* sits on an even keel in a pleasant bay almost directly to the south-west of the Palau Pacific Resort on Ngerekebesang Island (Arakabesan). She rests with her bows pointing forlornly to shore –no doubt after she was hit she was attempting to run to the sandy shores adjacent to the Palau Pacific Resort to beach, in an attempt to save herself and her cargo.

The wreck rests in a general depth of about 35 metres. The water in this bay is clear in the shallows, but deeper down on the wreck has a slightly milky feel to it – but once you become adjusted to it the average visibility would be in the region of 10–20 metres. This wreck is home to a lot of fish life, with schools of barracuda spotted regularly.

The forward section of the ship ahead of the composite bridge superstructure area has been cut right down, and the hull shell plating has been removed to some 4–5 metres above the seabed – basically to about the old waterline level. The hull frames and lower shell plating are still present – bent outwards in places, particularly on the starboard side where explosives have been used to free up sections of metal for lifting to the surface. Here, in places the shell plating has been blown completely off the hull frames – which are bent heavily outboard. On the port side her hull is cut away in places to just 3 metres above the seabed, whilst on the starboard side forward she is cut down to almost level with the seabed.

At the very tip of the cut-down bow, piles of loosely coiled cables are found – no doubt dumped there by the salvors when they finished their job. The starboard anchor chain is run out more than 50 metres along the seabed, which slopes away gently to about 38 metres.

The foredeck innards of the cut-down ship have become infilled with sand, and the whole foredeck, which once held two holds, is now one common space with hatch cover beams strewn about, 55-gallon oil drums, sections of derricks and a section of coaming from the leading edge of Hatch No. 2 still present.

The ship resumes something of its shape as you approach the composite superstructure, with the bulkhead to the boiler room still present. But moving past this bulkhead there is a scene of devastation caused by the superstructure being largely cut away down, and heavy use of explosives to free up the valuable engine room fitments. The lower innards of the ship are recognisable, the engine casing having kept much of its shape. The engine room is accessible from above through the large rectangular hatch where large engine fitments would be lowered in during construction. It is now an open area with catwalk gratings and walkways, pipes and spars, all unworthy of salvage, having been knocked around to lie at strange angles. At the bottom of this area, the prop shaft can be located disappearing into the prop tunnel aft. There are two generators side by side on the starboard side of the engine room, the same style as on the wreck of *Bichu Maru*. A further generator is located on the port side.

Top: The cut-down stem of *Raizan Maru*. Photo © Richard Barnden, Unique Dive Expeditions.
Bottom: Engine room fitments on *Raizan Maru*. Photo © Richard Barnden, Unique Dive Expeditions.

As the composite superstructure ends there is a drop down to the aft section of the ship. This resembles the forward section in that the hull has been cut down on either side and become infilled with sand. In a general depth of 29 metres here, there are many scattered spars, hatch cover beams and torn sections of ship strewn around. There is little trace of both aft holds – as with the foredeck area, this aft area is one open section with the base socket for the main mast still *in situ* and giving a clue to the original layout of this area.

The entire sterncastle has been cut away down to the same level as the aft holds area – some 4–5 metres above the seabed. The stern still retains its shape lower down, although the fantail has been removed almost directly at the top of the rudderstock. The rudder itself has been cleanly cut away at its top and bottom mounts, and the propeller has been unbolted and removed, leaving a section of free shaft projecting outwards with its thrust bearings visible.

## SHIPWRECK – THE ESSENTIALS

| | |
|---|---|
| Type: | Standard Type C cargo vessel |
| Built: | 1941/2 |
| Tonnage: | 2,838 grt |
| Dimensions: | Length 321 feet; beam 45 feet; draught 21 feet |
| Propulsion: | Triple-expansion steam engine – single shaft |
| Date of loss: | 30 March 1944 |
| Cause of loss: | Bombed by Task Force 58 aircraft |
| Depth to seabed: | 35 metres |
| Least depth: | 25 metres |
| Location: | Kosabang Harbor, 1 nm south-west of Palau Pacific Resort |

# 16. Ryuko Maru

STANDARD TYPE C CARGO VESSEL (1941)        IJN AUXILIARY TRANSPORT (1944)
IJN GENERAL REQUISITIONED TRANSPORT (1943)

## LLEBUCHEL, KOSABANG HARBOR

The 2,764grt peacetime Standard
Type C cargo vessel *Ryuko Maru*
was laid down in Asano on 10
March 1941 at the Nippon Kokan
KK shipyard, and was launched
and named on 18 December 1941.
She was a similar ship to the other
Palau Type C casualties such as the
*Shinsei Maru No. 18*, and *Raizan
Maru*, and many such Type Cs were

TOP: The 2,764grt standard Type C cargo vessel *Ryuko Maru*.

completed between April 1940 and December 1942 for various shipping companies. Most
were requisitioned by the Imperial Japanese Navy and converted to specific military uses
such as auxiliary water tankers, auxiliary transports and auxiliary minesweeper tenders,
and were fitted with at least two 120mm deck guns.

She was 321 feet long with a beam of 45 feet and a draught of 21 feet. A three-
island steamer, she had a raised fo'c'sle at her raked bow, a well deck holding her two
forward holds with the foremast set in between, a composite superstructure holding
her bridge forward and her engine casing abaft, with her smokestack hard behind the
bridge.

Her aft well deck had two further holds with the main mast in between, and a sterncastle
held her steering gear and auxiliary steering position above her cruiser stern. She carried
318 tons of coal for her boilers, and her vertical triple-expansion steam engine gave her a
service speed of about 11 knots and a maximum speed of 13 knots. She had an operating
radius of about 5,800 miles.

After fitting out afloat, she was completed and registered to her new owners, Taiyo
Kogyo KK, in Kobe on 16 March 1942 and – at this point still a civilian vessel – she was set
to work on voyages to ports such as Moji, Japan, and Nanking in China. The following year,
1943, her registry port was changed to Tokyo.

Throughout the early part of 1943 she was engaged in convoy work, carrying cargoes
around Japanese ports such as Tokyo, Yokosuka, Aioi, Osaka and Mutsure, as well as
making longer passages to Shanghai, and Takao in Formosa (Taiwan).

On 15 July 1943, after arriving at Kirun (now Keelung) in Formosa, she was requisitioned
by the Imperial Japanese Navy as a general requisitioned transport and attached to the

Sasebo Naval District, with Sasebo as her home port. For the next couple of months she made voyages around Japanese ports such as Kirun, Osaka, Tokuyama and Sasebo before arriving at Takao, Formosa, on 19 August 1943.

On 22 August she departed Takao in a large convoy bound initially for Hainan Island, China, and then further south to Saigon in Indo-China (now Ho Chi Minh City, Vietnam). After discharging the remainder of her cargo there, she departed Saigon, again in an escorted convoy, northbound to Takao before returning to Osaka via Moji.

After a few more months of local work around Japanese home ports, on 6 November 1943 she departed Saeki, Japan, in a large escorted convoy southbound for Palau. The convoy arrived safely in Palau on 17 November – despite the attentions of a reported five American submarines *en route*.

Two days later, on 19 November, she left Palau in an escorted convoy bound for Rabaul, New Britain. With the Allies on the offensive and growing stronger by the day, the convoy was plagued by American submarine attacks – the *Kenzan Maru* was torpedoed and sunk by the American submarine USS *Albacore* with the loss of seven crew.

The convoy arrived in Rabaul on 28 November and after a brief pause *Ryuko Maru* departed Rabaul on 5 December in a small escorted convoy bound for Palau. The convoy arrived in Palau on 12 December and on 21 December she departed Palau in another small escorted convoy for the return passage to Japan. She arrived safely at Niihama, Shikoku, on 31 December 1943.

On 1 January 1944 she was registered by the Imperial Japanese Navy as an auxiliary transport, attached to the Sasebo Naval District and assigned to the South East Area; she made several short passages between Wakamatsu, Kure, Kobe, Yokosuka and Yokohama.

On 4 February 1944 the long-range US photographic reconnaissance of Truk Lagoon took place, and the Imperial Japanese Fleet was photographed in strength down below in the lagoon, along with scores of merchant ships offloading their cargoes. The Allies determined to strike immediately, and preparations for Task Force 58 began forthwith.

That same day, no doubt unaware of the long-range US reconnaissance overflight of Truk and what it would trigger, *Ryuko Maru*, heavy with a cargo of ammunition, formed up in a convoy bound for Truk that was transporting troops of IJA 52nd Infantry Division. The modern *Yugumo*-class destroyer *Fujinami* would escort the convoy, along with the minelayer *Natsushima*, the powerful modern *kaibōkan* escort vessel *Amakusa* and the subchaser *Ch 31*.

After calling *en route* at Hachijo Jima on 9 February 1944, in the early hours of 17 February, the convoy was 185 miles north-west of Truk. Unknown to the Japanese, the nine aircraft carriers of Task Force 58, carrying more than 500 combat aircraft, had taken up station in their holding position 90 miles east of the lagoon the night before. Unseen in the darkness, just over 250 miles away, Task Force 58 crew were preparing their aircraft on the carrier flight decks for the dawn initial fighter sweep of Truk Lagoon.

The powerful Japanese convoy was detected by the patrolling US submarine USS *Tang* – and just after 0200, *Tang* fired four torpedoes. Two hits were scored on the large 6,854grt IJN transport *Gyoten Maru*, which was carrying IJA 52nd Division infantry. *Gyoten Maru* split in two and sank a few minutes later, with the loss of eight crewmen and an unknown number of soldiers. The convoy escorts attacked the submarine with depth charges. *Tang* was able to survive the depth charge attack – but as she was driven deep and broke off her attack, the convoy was able to slip away.

Meanwhile in Truk Lagoon, within an hour or two of the dawn initial fighter sweep by 72 F6F Hellcats, Japanese airpower had been almost completely degraded and American air superiority achieved. Throughout the day, successive strike groups of Grumman Avenger torpedo-bombers and Douglass Dauntless dive-bombers escorted by Hellcats were able to range over the lagoon, attacking and sinking the vulnerable merchant vessels below.

At about 1400 that day, 17 February 1944, as the strike groups pummelled the beleaguered shipping below, Task Force 58 aircraft attacked the large convoy still inbound for Truk.

At 1415 the 2,812grt IJN transport *Zuikai Maru* was hit by bombs and sank with great loss of life. Five minutes later the large 5,784grt IJA transport *Tatsuha Maru*, loaded with 16 Type 95 Ha-Go light battle tanks, 1,050 infantry of the 52nd Division and field hospital troops, and packed with ammunition, was hit. She exploded and sank with the loss of more than 500 crew and troops. Once night had fallen and brought some relief, the destroyer *Fujinami* and the *kaibōkan Amakusa* returned to the site of the sinking and in the darkness were able to pluck many survivors from the water.

*Ryuko Maru*, battle-scarred and now carrying survivors from the IJA transport *Tatsuha Maru*, continued to Truk with the remnants of the stricken convoy. They arrived there the following day, 18 February – Day 2 of Operation *Hailstone*. Despite further intensive air strikes throughout the morning and into the afternoon, *Ryuko Maru* survived the US operation.

On 8 March *Ryuko Maru* left Truk for Woleai in the central Carolines, from where, on 16 March, she set off for Palau – arriving there on 19 March.

On 25 March the approach of the massive Task Force 58 was detected, and on 29 March convoy PATA-07 was, in the face of the imminent US assault, formed up to attempt to leave Palau for Takao in Formosa. *Ryuko Maru* joined the convoy – which also consisted of the IJN transports *Raizan Maru* and *Kibi Maru* (1941), the fleet oiler *Akebono Maru*, the auxiliary transport *Goshu Maru*, and the IJA transports *Teshio Maru* and *Hokutai Maru*. The convoy was escorted by *Patrol Boat 31*, the destroyer *Wakatake* and auxiliary subchaser *Cha 26*.

Although the convoy had been due to leave on the evening of 29 March, it was delayed and set off at first light at 0500 the following morning. As the convoy started to leave the main anchorages of the Western Lagoon and move north up the west side of Palau towards Toachel Mlengui – the West Passage through the fringing reef – the task groups of Task Force 58 were already in their holding positions 65–110 miles to the south, with the 72-strong flight of Hellcats and torpedo-bombers, some laden with aerial mines, already inbound.

Fifty minutes after the convoy had started to depart Kosabang Harbor, the TF58 Hellcats swept over the skies above Palau. Strike groups from the carriers *Lexington*, *Bunker Hill* and *Monterey* soon spotted the convoy and immediately attacked.

The ships in the convoy began to take evasive manoeuvres as the convoy was dissolved, and the ships scattered. During the contact, *Kibi Maru* ran aground on the western side of the channel whilst *Teshio Maru* grounded on the eastern side. *Hokutai Maru* was able to come about, and headed back to Malakal Harbor.

*Ryuko Maru* moved relatively close into shore and anchored with her starboard anchor parallel with the north shore cliffs of the northern claw of Malakal Harbor, Ngerchaol. No doubt she was seeking protection from US aircraft by using the high headlands to her south. But she was attacked later in the day by *Lexington* Helldivers, and three bomb hits were reported. A short-delay-fuzed bomb appears to have exploded just after impact near the third hold of *Ryuko Maru*, blowing a hole in the side of the ship from the bilge keel near the hull bottom to about 10 feet below the bulwark. She started to smoke and took on a list to port but remained afloat.

The following day she was attacked by *Yorktown* Grumman Avenger aircraft. The damage was too much for her, and she sank by the stern just to the north of and parallel with Ngerchaol. Her bow remained visible for some time before she disappeared completely – not that far from *Raizan Maru* in the bay between the Ngerchaol and the reefs that link it to Ngerekebesang Island.

All the ships of the convoy were eventually sunk during the two days of *Desecrate 1*.

## THE WRECK TODAY

Today the wreck of the 2,764grt IJN auxiliary transport *Ryuko Maru* sits upright on a sandy bottom in 33 metres of water just on the north side of Ngerchaol, the north claw of Malakal Harbor, within direct sight of Palau Pacific Resort to the north. She lies in an area of generally good visibility, with her starboard side parallel to the nearby cliffs of Ngerchaol and her bows pointing into the bay. She has least depths of about 15 metres to the top of her bridge superstructure, 19 metres down to her fo'c'sle and 24 metres to her well deck. The ship is substantially intact but does show damage to her amidships area from a combination of US wartime bombs and subsequent post-war salvage works in the engine room area.

The bow is raked with a modern soft nose, and the fo'c'sle appears largely undamaged. There are reinforcing spirket plates either side of the bow. Two independent anchor windlasses sit side by side on the fo'c'sle deck, with the chain for the starboard anchor rising from its chain locker through its spurling pipe, then running to the windlass and from there out through the hawse pipe and straight down to the bottom, where it is piled up, indicating she sank straight down, without drifting. The port anchor and chain are missing.

The fo'c'sle is still ringed by heavily encrusted guardrails, and cable reels are still *in situ* at the aft rail. The fo'c'sle spaces can be entered via a forward-facing door in the fo'c'sle bulkhead at well deck level.

The foremast rose from a mast house situated on the well deck in between the long rectangular hatches for Hold Nos 1 and 2. The foremast itself appears to have been completely removed – not cut away. Short kingposts flanked it with derrick booms fastened to them by goosenecks. Both forward derrick booms leading from the masthouse kingposts rest on the forward port coaming of Hold No. 1 – immediately beside fixed steps which lead up from the well deck to the fo'c'sle deck. Both foredeck holds are empty, and there are no tween decks to the holds – a design that varies amongst Type C ships.

Two derrick booms lead aft from the masthouse over Hold No. 2; the derrick head for the port derrick rests on the well deck beside the port gunwale, whilst the derrick head for the starboard derrick is also swung slightly to port over the middle of Hold No. 2. This pattern is repeated with the aft deck derricks, so the combination of piled-up anchor chain and all derricks swung to port confirm action reports that she took on a list to port as she sank at anchor – before landing upright on the seabed.

The composite superstructure amidships rises up for three decks and has promenade deck walkways running along either side at shelter deck level, accessed from the well deck forward by fixed steps either side of her beam. Just inboard of each set of steps, half-open

The virtually intact wreck of the Type C cargo vessel *Ryuko Maru* lies in 33 metres of water.

doorways allow access into the lower deck spaces, which have a row of portholes dotted along the hull.

Rows of portholes stud the two lower deck level forward bulkheads – the uppermost navigation bridge had large rectangular windows for all-round visibility. It appears that an intense fire swept the bridge, as all trace of wooden structures and decking is gone. The rooms below the navigating bridge held the radio room and crew quarters.

The bridge, at just over 15 metres, can be entered through doorways to either side. The wooden decking that formed its roof has been burnt away to leave only the grid-like skeletal frames of its structure and allowing much ambient light to penetrate. Lateral athwartships beams are braced by a thick herringbone beam that runs fore and aft. Encrusted heavy-duty electric cabling hangs down from the roof.

The floor of the bridge is strewn with large 2-inch-thick concrete slabs – most shattered. These slabs were layered on top of the bridge roof and were a cheap way to armour the top of the bridge against plunging machine gun fire from aircraft – they are a common sight on World War II wrecks. As the roofing of the bridge burned away and weakened, these simply fell through from above. A companionway staircase leads up into the aft of the bridge from the deck levels below.

Inside the bridge, at the front to starboard, a single AA machine gun, still on its large pedestal, lies on its side amidst the debris. It would have been mounted on top of the superstructure, and would also have fallen through the bridge roof as it weakened. A

Looking forward towards rectangular windows inside the bridge of *Ryuko Maru*. An AA gun still on its mount lies where it has fallen through the roof from above. The fractured 2-inch slabs once layered the roof of the bridge – a cheap and effective form of armour plating against strafing. (Author's collection)

corresponding port AA gun also can be found lying on its side on the strong deckhouse beams above. Radio gear can still be found in the radio room below.

Abaft the topmost navigating bridge deck, the superstructure steps down one level where, immediately behind the bridge, is a rectangular loading chute for coal for her boilers. Behind that there are four short kingposts, dotted one at each corner of a rectangular hatch, down to the boiler and engine rooms below. The pitched roof and skylights of the boiler room here has been ripped off and dumped on deck on the port side, and there are twisted and bent engine room gratings and catwalks strewn around on top of this deckhouse. A coaling kingpost or derrick boom juts out at right angles to port here amidst the jumble of bent and torn sections of ship. Some of the plating around the engine room area is convex – being blown out by the force of salvage explosives or a boiler room explosion.

The smokestack has collapsed down into the boiler room, and behind it there is a large rectangular hole about 5 metres long down into the engine room, which from the evident damage in this area, appears to have been used by post-war salvors to remove the triple-expansion engine, condenser and other valuable machinery fitments. It also appears that there was a boiler explosion as ship sank, and cold water contacted her hot boilers – a common occurrence on many wrecks – as there is a large hole blasted outwards through the side of the ship. On the port side, the shell plating under the bridge has been blown inwards from a near-miss bomb.

As the superstructure ends, mirroring the forward arrangement, steps lead down from the promenade decks to the well deck, where doors allow entry to the machinery spaces. Both forward derrick booms run from short kingposts either side of the socket for the main mast on the large masthouse situated between the aft holds. The booms have swung to port – the derrick heads coming to rest together beside the steps to the promenade deck on the port well deck as the ship heeled to port and sank.

The mainmast has collapsed to port; it now rests partly on the port gunwale, and runs down until its top rests on the seabed. Fixed ladder rungs run up the mast, and a jumbo derrick is still attached to it.

A derrick boom runs aft over Hold No. 4 from the starboard kingpost; its derrick head has swung slightly to port to rest on the aft coaming of the hatch – almost inside the open starboard door into the stern castle. The port derrick boom is missing. Interestingly, if you swim up the port side of the main superstructure at promenade deck level, you will find a derrick boom sticking out of the vessel almost at right angles, in the vicinity of a substantial amount of damage to the superstructure abreast the engine room area caused by salvage blasting. As all the derrick booms are in place throughout the ship other than the port aft boom over Hold No. 4, can it be that this is the port boom, perhaps blown here as a result of an American bomb? The derrick boom seems to me to be on the small side for that boom, and was more likely a boom used for coaling the vessel.

The two aft holds and tween decks are empty, and there is now no dividing bulkhead between them below deck. The result is one large common space with the shaft tunnel running along the bottom, aft from the engine room. There is a large triangular hole blown inwards on the starboard side of the hull here – no doubt the fatal blow that sank her.

The sterncastle is in good condition and unusually, on the centreline, athwart steps run inwards and up from either side of the well deck to meet at a platform, and then one single set of steps leads up aft to the poop deck. The starboard doorway into the sterncastle is flung wide open, and the starboard derrick head projects almost inside the doorway – the door

The aft starboard derrick head rests on the coaming of Hold No. 4, its head projecting almost inside an open doorway into the sterncastle spaces. Angular steps lead up on the centre line to the poop deck. (Author's collection)

must have been open before the derrick head moved into this position because the derrick is essentially now jamming it open. The port side door is closed.

Guardrails encircle the sterncastle, and the poop deck is strewn with cables and ship's fittings. The lifeboat davits are in the swung-in position, indicating that these lifeboats did not launch.

The rudder is still *in situ*, rising out of the sandy seabed at 33 metres. The propeller however has been removed.

The *Ryuko Maru* is a popular dive – the wreck is in relatively good shape, holds lots of interest and has abundant sea life. With generally good visibility on this wreck and with her uppermost superstructure in relatively shallow water, she is a wreck suitable for less experienced divers, whilst seasoned wreck veterans will be able to delight in long explorations that allow the story of her demise to be pieced together.

## SHIPWRECK – THE ESSENTIALS

| | |
|---|---|
| Type: | Standard Type C cargo vessel (1941) |
| | IJN general requisitioned transport (1943) |
| | IJN auxiliary transport (1944) |
| Built: | 1941 |
| Tonnage: | 2,764 grt |
| Dimensions: | Length 321 feet; beam 45 feet; draught 21 feet |
| Propulsion: | Triple-expansion steam engine |
| Date of loss: | 31 March 1944 |
| Cause of loss: | Bombed by Task Force 58 aircraft |
| Depth to seabed: | 33 metres |
| Least depth: | 15 metres – bridge superstructure |
| | 19 metres – fo'c'sle deck |
| | 25 metres – main deck |
| Location: | North side of Ngerchaol, Kosabang Harbor |

# 17. IJN Sata

SHIRETOKO-CLASS FLEET OILER (1921)

## URUKTHAPEL ANCHORAGE, WESTERN LAGOON

The *Shiretoko*-class fleet oiler *Sata* was laid down on 7 March 1920 at the Yokohama Dock KK shipyard, which also built her sister *Shiretoko*-class oiler *Shiriya*, her hull being laid down a few months later, on 4 July 1921. *Sata* was 470 feet 8 inches long at the waterline with a beam of 58 feet and a draught of 26 feet 6 inches, and she displaced 15,450 tons. She was one of a class of ten such oilers built during 1920–1924,

The 15,450grt *Shiretoko*-class fleet oiler IJN *Sata* – sister ship to IJN *Iro*.

which included the *Shiretoko, Notoro, Erimo, Tsurumi, Ondo, Hayamoto, Naruto, Shiriya* and the famous Palau shipwreck *Iro*. Being military IJN fleet oilers and thus naval vessels, they did not carry the suffix '*Maru*' that requisitioned civilian vessels often carried.

*Sata* was launched on 28 October 1921 – whilst *Shiriya* was launched two months later, on 11 December 1921. After fitting out afloat, *Sata* was completed on 24 February 1922 when she was registered in the Sasebo Naval District. She was equipped to carry 8,000 tons of oil and powered by a vertical triple-expansion engine, her single screw giving her a service speed of 9 knots and a maximum speed of 14 knots.

*Sata* was built with a raised fo'c'sle and a foremast flanked by goalpost kingposts on her foredeck above her oil cargo tanks. A slender bridge superstructure forward of amidships rose up four deck levels, with an inner structural steel core of deckhouses flanked by extended bridge wings made largely of wood on a skeletal steel structure.

Abaft her superstructure, the hull space was given over to further oil cargo tanks, with another goalpost-kingpost pair in the middle. In hot weather, the oil cargo in a tanker expands and in cold weather it contracts; if the ship's tanks were completely sealed this expansion and contraction of the cargo would create a vacuum and dangerous internal pressures. So to let the cargo breathe, small pipes came from the top of each tank and ran up the ship's masts to flameproof venting outlets, safely high above the deck and away from any possible causes of ignition. At the bottom of the cargo tanks, a system of heating coils was installed through which steam was passed if the cargo was heavy grade oil which required heating to enable it to be pumped.

Each cargo tank could be filled and emptied independently of the others so that different types of oil could be loaded into separate tanks and discharged without being cross-contaminated.

Numerous valves linked each cargo tank to a system of pipelines inside the ship that led to the ship's pumps. Another set of pipelines led up from the pumps to where valves were conveniently located at the side of the deck for connecting to shore pipelines for loading and discharging. The ship's pumps were primarily used for pumping oil out of the ship to vessels being refuelled or to shore storage tanks and for pumping ballast water in or out of the ship. Shore pumps were used for pumping the cargo aboard from the land.

The deck was a continuous weather deck only penetrated by small raised cargo access hatches, one for each tank, which were fitted with watertight steel lids, which were kept dogged down and sealed when the ship was loaded. Larger holds for dry cargo were situated near the fo'c'sle and forward of the sterncastle

As with all oilers and tankers, the sterncastle held her machinery – the boiler room, engine room and steering gear. She was fitted with two 140mm (5.5-inch) low-angle guns – set one at the bow on a bandstand type platform on her fo'c'sle and the other on a similar platform at her stern. She also carried two 80mm (3-inch) high-angle AA guns.

In April 1925, IJN *Sata* departed Yokosuka in Japan, with the light cruiser IJN *Yūbari* for a flag-flying cruise of the western Pacific, including a call in Australia. *Sata* refuelled Yubari during the voyage and gad returned to Sasebo by June that year. In 1937, she was involved in operations in the war with China.

In October 1941, *Sata* was involved in the rescue of survivors from the submarine *I-61* that had sunk after a collision with the gunboat *Kiso Maru* off Iki Island, southern Japan. In December 1941, she was assigned to the Sasebo Naval District before being attached to the Navy Department on 11 February 1942. In the months that followed she was engaged in transporting aviation fuel from Sasebo to Kure, Kanokawa, in the western Inland Sea, and to St Jacques and Saigon in Indo-China.

On 28 May 1942 *Sata* joined the supply group oilers IJN *Tsurumi*, IJN *Genyo Maru* and IJN *Kenyo Maru* and the repair ship *Akashi* as part of the IJN 2nd Fleet's Midway Invasion Force – an operation that would go disastrously wrong for the Japanese despite numerical superiority in vessels and aircraft. An American dive-bombing attack on the superior Japanese naval forces at Midway on 4 June 1942 was one of the most effective of the war, with three Japanese carriers, *Akagi*, *Kaga* and *Sōryū*, being heavily hit and sunk – a fourth carrier, *Hiryū*, was sunk later in the afternoon. For the Japanese Navy, the loss of the Battle of Midway marked the end of any real strategic offensive capability. As the Battle of Midway was beginning on 4 June 1942, *Sata* was arriving at Truk Lagoon.

After further voyages, between Yokosuka, Kure, Ominato, Yokkaichi, Truk and Singapore, *Sata* arrived at Yokohama in early October 1942 where she was briefly dry docked before setting off on oil transport duties in home waters.

In February 1943 she was operating between Japan and Singapore, Palembang (in Sumatra) and Balikpapan and Tarakan (both in Borneo) before arriving in Manila on 3 July 1943; she then returned to Japan. By October 1943 she was back in Singapore and then on 4 November 1943 she departed

The 15,450grt fleet oiler IJN *Sata*.

Balikpapan in a convoy consisting of the auxiliary oilers *Seian Maru* and *Kyoei Maru*, escorted by the destroyer *Sanae* and auxiliary subchaser *Cha 37*. The convoy arrived in Palau on 14 November 1943. On 17 November, she then left Palau in a heavily escorted convoy bound for Truk – arriving there safely on 24 November with a cargo of fuel oil. On 1 December she was attached directly to the Combined Fleet, and set off from Truk for Singapore via Balikpapan in an escorted convoy.

On 28 January 1944 *Sata* arrived at Palau carrying 8,000 tons of fuel oil in her tanks. After a few days in Palau, on 31 January she set off for Truk – arriving there on 7 February, where she transferred 1,150 tons of fuel oil to the passenger–cargo vessel *Asaka Maru* on 8 February 1944.

On 10 February, as a direct result of the long-range US reconnaissance overflight of Truk Lagoon on 4 February, Admiral Koga had started scattering the valuable naval units present at Truk. On 12 February, *Sata* departed Truk in a convoy consisting of the oiler *Hishi Maru No. 2*, the ammunition ship *Nichiro Maru* and the cargo ships *Kamikaze Maru* and *Kitagami Maru*. The convoy was escorted by the destroyer *Hamanami*, subchaser *Ch 30* and the auxiliary subchasers *Takunan Maru No. 2* and *Shonan Maru No. 5*.

At about 2200 on the moonlit night of 17 February, as darkness had brought the first day's air strikes of Operation *Hailstone* to a close at Truk, about 150 miles north-east of Palau, the American submarine USS *Sargo* intercepted the convoy and fired eight torpedoes at the valuable tanker *Sata* in a surface attack. One of the torpedoes struck and disabled her. Several minutes later USS *Sargo* fired two more torpedoes at the ammunition ship *Nichiro Maru*, one of which set off a secondary explosion that caused her to sink immediately with great loss of life.

On 19 February the ammunition ship *Aratama Maru*, which was not part of the convoy, arrived *en scene* and took the beleaguered *Sata* under tow for Palau. *Aratama Maru* and *Sata* safely reached Palau the following day, carefully entering the Western Lagoon through the narrow West Passage before turning to head south down towards the sheltered anchorages of Kosabang Harbor. With her potentially dangerous cargo of oil, she was moored well away from other ships in the bay south of the southern claw of Malakal Harbor – Ngeruktabel.

On 29 February 1944 repairs were started on *Sata*, and on 23 March the crew on *Sata* were able to watch as their sister *Shiretoko*-class fleet oiler, *Iro*, limped into the same bay and anchored half a mile away. *Iro* had been hit in the bow by a torpedo from USS *Tunny* on 22 March. The two large fleet oilers at anchor dominated the bay with their very size, and both *Sata* and *Iro* were still under repair on 30 March as the first strikes of Operation *Desecrate 1* began. They were anchored with their bows pointing eastwards into the bay towards shore – presenting their port sides to the open expanse of sea to the west, from where any torpedo attack run would be made.

Just after 0500 on 30 March, for the first bombing strike of the day – Strike 1A – 38 aircraft lifted off from TBG 58.2 carrier *Hornet* and sped towards the lagoon following on after the initial fighter sweep. Strike 1A was made up of Helldiver dive-bombers and Grumman Avenger torpedo-bombers, with 12 Hellcats as escort. By 0630, two Strike 1A Grumman Avenger torpedo-bombers were targeting *Sata* from the west. She was hit by an aerial torpedo on the port side just forward of her stern that blasted a large 10-metre-wide hole directly into her cavernous engine room, which immediately started to flood. Later that day she took several hits or near-miss 500lb bombs from USS *Enterprise* Avengers.

In this combat photograph a Hellcat fighter swings in for another attack (left). IJN *Iro* is already ablaze and billowing clouds of black smoke from her stern at the bottom of shot and has just taken a near miss on her starboard beam. IJN *Sata* is already down by the stern and taking near misses in the centre of shot. To the top of the shot inside the claws of Malakal Harbor, IJN *Amatsu Maru* is ablaze at the stern, whilst *Chuyo Maru* is obscured by clouds to her right. (National Archives).

The combat photo (above) shows *Sata* smoking and down by the stern in the middle of the bay, whilst at the bottom *Iro* is on fire with a plume of black smoke coming from her stern. *Sata*'s stern is probably resting on the seabed at this point. To the left of the picture, a Grumman F6F Hellcat swings in for another attack. Despite her predicament, with her built-in strength and internal subdivisions *Sata* stubbornly remained afloat, refusing to succumb to her wounds.

The following day, at about 0700, *Sata* was bombed at mast level by Avengers and Dauntless dive bombers from TG 58.3 carrier USS *Lexington* in Strike 3A-2, and took two or three further hits. One bomb was a near miss between the torpedo damage and her rudder, whilst another bomb – a large 2,000lb bomb with a delayed fuze – was dropped from 150 feet and was a near miss forward of the bridge superstructure along the waterline on the port side. Coming into the water at an angle, the bomb travelled directly under her keel before exploding and blasting a large hole some 10 metres across directly up into one of her cavernous oil cargo tanks.

By this time *Sata* was already down by the stern and her foredeck was awash. The loss of much of her remaining buoyancy in her forward tanks was too much – she succumbed, rolled over to port, then capsized and completely submerged.

The wreck appears not to have been worked by post-war salvors, as the large valuable propeller – normally the first thing most easily removed from a wreck – is still present. Given that the ship is upside down and the prop not embedded in the seabed, this would have been a relatively easy salvage job. In addition, the valuable engine room fitments are still present on the wreck. There is no mention of the *Sata* in Fujita Salvage's records so it is likely it was simply unaware of her existence or location during its works in the 1950s.

## THE WRECK TODAY

Today the wreck of IJN *Sata* lies upside down in 35 metres of water just over half a mile north-north-east of her sister *Shiretoko*-class fleet oiler IJN *Iro*, to the west of Urukthapel Island and to the south of the southern claw of Malakal Harbor, Ngeruktabel. The two ships were almost identical sister ships of the same class, and for many years there was much doubt about which wreck was which vessel. Discovery of the *Sata* bell subsequently confirmed the position. Both huge wrecks lie just a short boat ride from the dive shops of Koror. Other than the localised bomb and torpedo damage that sank her she is in structurally good condition – her welded shell plating still strong and intact.

As a result of *Sata*'s orientation to the local tidal stream, diving her is somewhat tide-dependent. If the current is favourable, the vis will be crisp and clear. Dive her at the wrong time and her massive hull, broadside to the tidal flow, may have produced an impenetrable haze of disturbed sand at the bottom.

The least depth to her upturned keel at the bow is 24 metres. Despite being upside down she is a fascinating dive, with lots to see and impressive penetration possible with care into her cavernous engine room where the large triple-expansion engine, con rods and crankshaft are all easy to locate.

At the bow, the straight stem plunges down from about 24 metres to the seabed at 35 metres. Both anchors are run out – with the starboard chain first running around the stem on the seabed to where it becomes entangled with the port anchor chain before continuing. This result suggests to me that she rolled to port as she capsized. A row of portholes dots the fo'c'sle near the seabed. Where the fo'c'sle ends, the gunwale rises 1–2 metres off the seabed at the forward well deck area.

Up on top of the upturned hull, as you move aft from the stem, the narrow keel broadens out quickly to its full size. It is noticeable just how flat her hull bottom is, and her hull sides appear flat as well – she resembles something of a long rectangular box with only her bilge keels breaking her form at either side of the keel; the bilge keels are thin strips of steel that run along the edge of either side of her keel and are designed to give her flat keel a cutting edge for manoeuvring. On the port side there is a small concave section of plating from a near-miss 500lb bomb.

About 50 metres back from the bow, there is a large hole some 10 metres across, caused by the 2,000lb delayed-fuze bomb going off directly under her keel. The effects of such a large bomb are clearly evident, with large sections of plating deformed and blown downwards (originally upwards) into the wreck. There appears to be no double bottom to the keel, and the keel keeps its shape at the aft part of the hole where a strong transverse frame has withstood the blast. It is only the 1-inch steel plating of her bottom that has been almost effortlessly blown in in between this transverse frame and the one forward – the frames being well separated and spaced. There is plenty of room to drop down into the forward oil tank, where the heating coils can be spotted. A fixed steel ladder runs up the tank wall. The sides of the tank have all taken the blast and escaped relatively unscathed – the power of the explosion seemingly spent by this point.

Continuing aft outside the wreck again and back down at seabed level, the forward well deck gives way to the bridge superstructure forward of amidships. Another row of portholes line the hull here – these are the officers' accommodation cabins. The higher decks

The massive 15,450grt fleet oiler IJN *Sata* lies upside down in 35 metres of water just half a mile from her sister ship IJN *Iro*. The 5-10 metres wide gash of a torpedo hit is evident in her port side aft, whilst near her bow a large US bomb has detonated under her keel and blown in a large section of plating into one of her oil cargo tanks.

A large section of plating is blown into her forward oil cargo tank towards the bow. (Author's collection)

levels of this delicate bridge superstructure were all crushed and buried in the sandy floor of the lagoon as the ship came to rest on the bottom, leaving only the lower deck level, integral to the hull, visible above the sand. An open doorway on the port side allows entry to experienced wreck divers – here cabins, galley, officers' mess, lounge, and heads with WCs and baths can be found.

Abaft the bridge superstructure, the hull is largely intact with a little gap between gunwale and the sand at the well deck. The vessel is resting on its sterncastle, which is well embedded in the sand.

The unmistakable hole blown in her by a torpedo can be found just 10–20 metres forward of the stern on the port side. The wound is about 10 metres across and opens directly into the huge engine room. Immediately on entering through this gash you can find the large upside-down vertical triple-expansion engine hanging down from above. It is possible, with care, to move past it further forward and locate the large boilers. Forward of the boilers there is coal piled up on the bottom from her coalbunker. Outside the wreck the smokestack can be spotted flat on the seabed and crushed – but still bearing its markings. Its orientation is again evidence of a port roll as she capsized.

There is a vertical rip or tear in the hull immediately aft of the torpedo damage – big enough to accommodate a diver at the lower level where it again enters into the engine room. Hull shell plating has been sprung off its frames here, just as the hull starts to rapidly widen from the rudderstock at the stern to accommodate the engine room. On the corresponding starboard side of the hull there is also a vertical ripple in the shell plating. This mirror-image damage to both sides of the hull has been caused by compression of

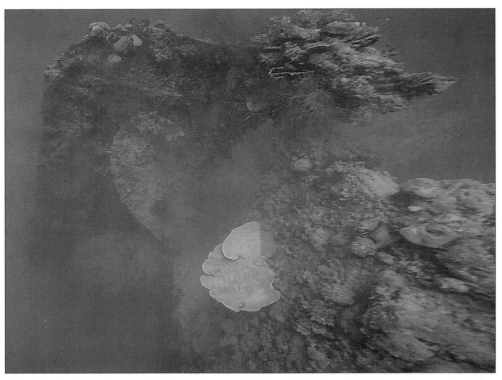

*Sata*'s keel strip was bent and broken as her stern hit the seabed. Her rudder is jammed to port hard up against her massive prop. (Author's collection)

the hull when the colossal waterlogged weight of the stern grounded. Immediately aft of this ripple in the hull there is a section of concave shell plating from a near-miss bomb.

The delicate stern sits with its upturned poop deck flush on the seabed at about 32 metres here – slightly shallower than the bow. The massive rudder is jammed hard over at 90 degrees to port, against the propeller blades. On top of the wreck at about 25 metres, the thin keel strip that runs out aft from the hull and tapers towards the rudderstock is noticeably bent and buckled by the weight of the ship bearing down on it as the stern hit the seabed; at one point, the keel strip has been severed and sprung off the keel just forward of the strong rudder stock, and the massive rudder itself has been moved forward to jam itself against the prop blades by the impact of her hitting the ground.

## SHIPWRECK – THE ESSENTIALS

| | |
|---|---|
| Type: | *Shiretoko*-class fleet oiler |
| Built: | 1920/22 |
| Displacement: | 15,450 tons |
| Dimensions: | Length (waterline) 470ft 8in.; beam 58 feet; draught 26ft 6in. |
| Propulsion: | Vertical triple-expansion steam engine |

| | |
|---|---|
| Date of loss: | 31 March 1944 |
| Cause of loss: | Bombed/torpedoed by Task Force 58 aircraft |
| Depth to seabed: | 32 metres – stern |
| | 35 metres – bow |
| Least depth: | 25 metres – to upturned keel |
| Location: | Urukthapel anchorage, Western Lagoon |

# 18. Teshio Maru

IJA STANDARD TYPE 1C CARGO VESSEL    (1942/43)

## KOMEBAIL LAGOON

The 2,840grt army cargo ship *Teshio Maru* was built for Ohi Sempaku as a Standard Type 1C cargo steamer. Such was the wartime secrecy surrounding the Japanese mass shipbuilding programme that she is not listed in the wartime classified US briefing document *Japanese Merchant Ships Recognition Manual.*

Standard Type 1C freighter similar to *Teshio Maru*.

Built during 1942 and the early part of 1943, her name first starts to flag up in convoy shipping records in the later part of 1943. She was 321 feet long with a beam of 45 feet and a draught of 21 feet.

The Standard Type 1C freighters were built with a raised fo'c'sle, large foredeck holds and a composite superstructure slightly aft of amidships holding the bridge forward, and engine and boiler rooms immediately abaft – her smokestack being set close behind the bridge. The aft section of the ship accommodated two further large holds and she had a sterncastle that held her steering gear. A coal-fired triple-expansion steam engine gave her a radius of 5,500 miles at her service speed of about 11 knots. She had a maximum speed of about 13 knots. Masts were centred in the fore and aft well decks. She had a raked bow and a cruiser stern.

A large number of similar vessels were produced before the war, and approximately 30 were believed by US Intelligence to have been constructed between 1941 and 1944. She is very similar in design to her Type C standard sister ships sunk at Palau, such as *Ryuko Maru* and *Raizan Maru*.

Although *Teshio Maru* was sunk at Palau during Operation *Desecrate 1* in March 1944, another *Teshio Maru* was operating in November 1944 around Penang on the west coast of Malaysia. That *Teshio Maru* was sunk on 26 March 1945 whilst in a Japanese convoy, bound for Port Blair, east of Khota Andaman, that was attacked and annihilated by a British destroyer squadron.

By the autumn of 1943, the *Teshio Maru* sunk at Palau was part of the Japanese maritime transport system. On 20 October 1943 she departed Saeki in a convoy of eight *Maru*s and one auxiliary oiler, escorted by a torpedo-boat and three auxiliary minesweepers – the convoy arriving at Palau on 29 October.

Just a few days later, on 2 November 1943, she departed Palau in a convoy of six *Maru*s bound for Rabaul, escorted by subchasers *Ch 22*, *Ch 24* and *Ch 39*. The convoy was attacked on 4 November, and two torpedoes from a US submarine narrowly missed *Kogyo Maru*. The convoy escorts counter-attacked, allowing the convoy to continue. On 9 November, a US B-25 bomber attacked the convoy without causing damage. The convoy arrived at Rabaul on 10 November.

*Teshio Maru* then returned to Palau and on 30 November she departed Palau for Saeki, Japan in an escorted convoy. *En route*, high seas forced her to detach for Manila. From there she was subsequently able to return to Japan where, on 7 February 1944, she set off from her home port of Moji bound for Takao in Formosa in a large escorted convoy of 14 merchant ships. The following day, the American submarine USS *Snook* attacked the troop transport *Lima Maru*, scoring two torpedo hits that caused her to explode and sink with the loss of almost 3,000 troops and crew. The beleaguered convoy arrived at Takao on 15 February 1944. By the end of March 1944 *Teshio Maru* was back in Palau. She would never leave.

With the approach of the massive Task Force 58 having been detected several days earlier, convoy PATA-07 was formed up on 29 March 1944, to attempt to leave Palau in the face of the imminent US assault. If the convoy could slip away it would head for Takao in Formosa. The convoy consisted of IJN transports *Raizan Maru*, *Kibi Maru* (1941) and *Ryuko Maru*, the fleet oiler *Akebono Maru*, the auxiliary transport *Goshu Maru*, and the IJA transports *Teshio Maru* and *Hokutai Maru*, and was escorted by *PB-31*, the destroyer *Wakatake* and auxiliary subchaser *Cha 26*.

The convoy had been due to leave on the evening of 29 March but was delayed and was only able to set off at 0500 the following morning. The convoy started to leave the main anchorages of the Western Lagoon and move north up the west side of the main Palau island of Babelthuap into the main narrow channel leading north towards Toachel Mlengui – the West Passage through the fringing reef. The channel is quite deep with general depths of 50–60 metres, but it is constricted in width, with large reef flats only a couple of metres deep rising on both sides in places. A strong current of up to 2.25 knots flows through this channel.

Unknown to those in convoy PATA-07, the three task groups of Task Force 58 were already in their holding positions some 70 –110 miles to the south. The 72-strong flight of Hellcats for the initial fighter sweep, along with Grumman TBF Avengers of the mining operation, were already airborne and inbound towards Palau.

Several picket boats and the second-class destroyer *Wakatake* led the convoy – whilst at the far southern end of the convoy other vessels waited their turn to join. It would be a dangerous voyage, as Japanese ASW technology was poor; their sonar was rudimentary, and a lack of depth charge forward-throwing ability hampered their subchasers – and with American submarines prowling the seas in strength, there was huge attrition of Japanese shipping.

The Japanese vessels were also inadequately protected, with too few and too poor AA guns. Even their most advanced AA guns were inaccurate and largely ineffective against the new, fast American aircraft. The 25mm Type 96 autocannon was one of Japan's most effective AA guns, with a rate of fire of between 200 and 260 rounds per minute. But it was most effective only at close ranges of less than 1,000 metres, with fire at aircraft at more than a range of 2,000 metres being completely ineffective.

The Japanese 25mm Type 96 was in fact a mediocre weapon hampered by slow training and slow elevation speeds, excessive vibration and muzzle flash. The sights were found to be ineffective against high-speed targets such as the new American aircraft. Worse, ammunition was fed from a 15-round fixed magazine, so that the gun had to cease firing every time the magazine had to be changed. The Type 96 was vastly inferior to the 40mm Bofors used by US vessels which could put out a sustained rate of fire with a constant-fire top-fed ammunition clip design. Many of the Japanese ships had larger 3-inch to 5.5-inch bow and stern guns – but these were often almost antiques, salvaged from old decommissioned military vessels from the early part of the 20th century. These guns were useful against submarines on the surface but of little use against fast, modern aircraft. It was going to be a tough fight for PATA-07 whichever way things went.

Fifty minutes after the convoy had started to move north through Kosabang Harbor and Komebail Lagoon, the initial fighter sweep F6F Hellcats swept over the skies above Palau. Group strikes by Douglas SBD Dauntless dive-bombers, Grumman TBF Avenger torpedo-bombers and SB2C Helldiver aircraft would follow. The strike groups from the carriers *Lexington*, *Bunker Hill* and *Monterey* immediately spotted the large convoy – it was a very valuable target and was immediately attacked.

*Bunker Hill* Avenger torpedo-bombers attacked the lead ships as *Lexington* Hellcats strafed. Meantime, Avenger torpedo-bombers were air-dropping mines in the West Passage and other vital shipping channels in the lagoon to block them to shipping.

The ships in the convoy immediately began to take evasive manoeuvres, no doubt having seen the mines being air-dropped and their escape blocked; the convoy was dissolved and the ships started to scatter in an attempt to return to the apparent safety of the main anchorage, where protection could be sought from land-based AA batteries.

During the chaos of the contact, *Kibi Maru* ran aground on the western side of the channel. Stranded on the reef, she was an easy target and was attacked by a number of different strike air groups from different carriers throughout the day. She was soon ablaze. *Hokutai Maru* was able to come about, and headed back to Malakal Harbor.

Dive-bombers attacked *Raizan Maru* in Komebail Lagoon just after 0600 local time. One bomb hit her on the port side astern, causing an explosion. She remained afloat initially but would eventually succumb.

*Teshio Maru* came about and started to head south back down the main channel through Komebail Lagoon heading towards Koror. As she did so she was strafed, torpedoed and bombed by aircraft from the US carriers *Bunker Hill* and *Belleau Wood*. She took a bomb hit on her starboard side into Hold No. 1, and she was crippled at her stern by a bomb that went right through the poop deck of her sterncastle before exploding inside and damaging her steering gear. Unnavigable, she drifted with the current in the main channel until she beached on the Rael Edeng Reef in the western part of Komebail Lagoon.

*Ryuko Maru* was attacked later in the day by *Lexington* Helldivers, and three bomb hits were reported. She started to smoke and took on a list. The following day, whilst seeking shelter close into the jungle-clad high cliffs of the north shore of northern claw of Malakal Harbor, Ngerchaol, she was attacked by *Yorktown* Avenger aircraft and she sank by the stern.

All the ships of the convoy were eventually sunk during the two days of *Desecrate 1*. The escort destroyer *Wakatake* was sunk west of Babelthuap in Karamadoo Bay near the West Passage, and the ex-*Momi*-class destroyer *Patrol Boat 31* was sunk offshore outside the lagoon.

After the war, whilst still on the reef, *Teshio Maru* was partially salvaged, with the propeller and much non-ferrous material being removed. After a number of years on the reef, she slipped off and sank parallel to the underwater coral slope, coming to rest on her starboard side with her bows pointing south. It would appear, given the nature of the damage apparent on the wreck, that salvage of her engine, condensers and so on took place after she had slid down the reef to her current resting place. The uppermost port side of the hull has been blown and the engine lifted out. The lower starboard side of the hull is intact.

It would also seem that she slid off well before Fujita Salvage arrived in Palau in the 1950s, as its records make no mention of her at all and they did not work her. If she had still been on the reef, then she would have been dismantled.

## THE WRECK TODAY

Today the wreck of *Teshio Maru* lies well north of Malakal Harbor in Komebail Lagoon to the west of Palau, just to the west side of the main shipping channel, in 24 metres of water. Lying in an area swept clear of the silt that is commonly found within Malakal Harbor and many of the bays, she lies in area of crystal clear visibility and abundant coral and fish life. She is one of the most beautiful and interesting wrecks in Palau, with lots to see.

*Teshio Maru* lies on her starboard side on a sandy bottom in gin-clear water with her bows facing south-west – she was heading back south towards Malakal Harbor when she was attacked and disabled.

With a greatest depth of 24 metres to the seabed and a least depth to her uppermost port side gunwale of just 8 metres, and with abundant fish and beautiful corals, she is an ideal

Finning away from the bow of *Teshio Maru* reveals her soft nose, her port anchor still in its hawse and her bow gun platform – a must for photographers. (Author's collection)

The wreck of *Teshio Maru* lies on her starboard side in the main shipping channel up the west side of Babelthuap in an area renowned for its 100-metre underwater visibility.

dive for the less experienced – whilst more experienced divers will love exploring this wreck in a depth that allows for long bottom times with minimal deco. Her dramatic bow, bow gun, fo'c'sle and anchors are a must for photographers – her cruiser stern is iconic of the era.

The ship has a markedly raked bow and a raised fo'c'sle still ringed by guardrails. The stem is a soft nose of almost rounded plating and, as she was under way when she was attacked, her two anchors are still held snug in their hawses. Swim away from the bow for some distance to get a good overview of the whole bow area in 50+ metres vis.

Two bulkhead doors from the forward well deck allow access forward into the fo'c'sle spaces. Outboard of the access doors, fixed steps lead up from the well deck to the fo'c'sle deck, which has a number of forced-draught ventilators, cable reels and twin mooring bollards dotted around. A large twin-anchor windlass dominates the centre line of this deck, with chains running out to both hawse pipes.

At the very bow there is a small gun platform, its circular top exactly level with the top of the stem. The gun appears to be a 3-inch manually operated short gun dating from the early 20th century. It is swung about 110 degrees to starboard, and now points down towards the seabed; this tells us that the US aircraft were attacking *Teshio Maru* on her starboard beam from seaward as she headed south back down the shipping channel towards Malakal Harbor. It is interesting to note that there is a large bomb hole in the starboard hull at the aft end of Hold No. 1, aft of the fo'c'sle. Is the gun locked in time in the position it was in as it fired at the incoming aircraft that did this damage? The whole dramatic raked bow with its fo'c'sle, anchors and gun platform is a particularly photogenic 'must do' for photographers.

The two interconnecting foredeck holds, Nos 1 and 2, are long and rectangular with high coaming. They are both largely empty and intact, but here and there in Hold No. 1 can be found shells for the bow gun. There is blown-in hull shell plating on the lower starboard side of this hold – the plating curved back effortlessly from the effects of an American bomb to now expose the seabed beneath.

The foremast rises from a mast house on the well deck between the hatches for the foredeck holds, and has four winches for cargo handling set in the deck one at each corner of the masthouse. Underneath the masthouse in the holds there is a mass of electric cables running up from below for operating the steam-driven winches, running lights and communications along with a fixed ladder that led up from the bottom of the holds into the mast house. A few hatch cover beams are scattered about on the seabed around these holds and the aft holds.

The foremast has snapped a few metres from its base and now angles down to rest its starboard crosstree on the seabed (as does the main mast). The topmast above the crosstree extends further, running out along the seabed. The foremast is flanked either side on the masthouse by two short kingposts, each still goosenecked with two derrick booms that ran aft over Hold No. 2 and forward over Hold No. 1. All the derrick booms are now angled down to starboard so that their derrick heads rest on the seabed. The jumbo derrick used for unusually heavy lifts runs out from near the starboard side of the masthouse to its fixing to the topmast well above the crosstree. Rigging still hangs from the foremast here and there.

The composite superstructure amidships contains the bridge forward, with radio room and accommodation in the levels below, and the engine room and boiler rooms aft. The smokestack was located close behind the bridge.

Looking forward on the fo'c'sle deck of *Teshio Maru* towards the bow gun – still swung to starboard as it was during the fateful attack.

The two lower superstructure deck levels are dotted with rows of portholes and, either side of the well deck, forward-facing doors opened into the accommodation spaces within. Just outboard of the doorways, either side of the well deck, fixed stairs led up to the promenade deck walkway that ran down either side of the superstructure at shelter deck level and had cabins leading off it.

The highest navigating bridge deck had large rectangular windows for all-round visibility, and bridge wings that project out to each side for docking and close manoeuvres. All wood decking and roofing of the bridge has been burnt away, to leave the structural latticework of beams and girders exposed with guardrails running along the top.

Immediately abaft the slender bridge, the deckhouse drops down one level to the boat deck, where a rectangular athwartships coaling hatch for bunker coal is located, along with short kingposts to work it.

The large smokestack has broken off a few feet from its base, and fallen to lie crumpled on the seabed below – still with its markings visible. Where the smokestack entered the hull there is now just a large opening that is flanked by forced-draught ventilators and access hatches.

At the aft end of the superstructure, guardrails ring around the deck and forced-draught ventilators rise up from the aft well deck. Salvors have used explosives – a lot of explosives – to blast the engine room open, to access the valuable non-ferrous fitments. The hull, just at the aftmost end of the superstructure, is torn apart all the way down to the keel strip, leaving wide-open spaces directly into the engine room and catwalks bent and twisted.

Although the port side of the hull here has been opened up, the boat deck was left untouched – the ship was lying on its starboard side, so there was no need to touch it. The square superimposed box of the engine room roof is still present and untouched – other than the small, pitched roof itself and its skylights being missing. Four forced-draught ventilators are dotted, one at each corner.

As you move aft of the superstructure, the ship steps down to the aft well deck which held Hold Nos 3 and 4. With the salvage blasting that has taken place, the uppermost port side of the ship aft of the split has been weakened and has collapsed down into Hold No. 3, leaving the higher port side of the hatch coaming exposed and projecting free in open water

The two large aft holds are separated by a small section of well deck from which the main mast still rises from its masthouse. The mast now runs out horizontally from the wreck, to rest with its starboard crosstree on the seabed. Fixed ladder rungs run up its aft length. Either side of the main mast are short kingposts which still have derricks goosenecked on them, with both derrick booms forward and both derrick booms aft dropping downwards so that their derrick heads rest on the seabed.

The hatch for the aftmost Hold No. 4 is in still present, but the hold is empty. The uppermost port side of the hull here has collapsed downwards, leaving the hatch partly standing in free water. At the foot of the holds the prop shaft tunnel runs aft along the centre line of the vessel.

The now horizontal sterncastle is still largely intact with open forward doorways and steps either side, partially falling towards the seabed. The uppermost port gunwale is sagging downwards in places, its strength gone. The sterncastle displays a very pronounced tapering

Another view of the bow gun of *Teshio Maru*. (Author's collection)

of the hull towards the stern – a straight economy-style narrowing of the hull towards what is almost a point, characteristic of the mass-produced, cheap, fast-build standard ships of the war.

The poop deck is dotted with mooring bollards, ventilators and large winches to port and starboard. It also displays a deep puncture wound just forward of the fantail, where a US aerial bomb came in from slightly astern and punched right through the deck plating before exploding inside the ship and no doubt wrecking the ship's ability to manoeuvre. A further tear in the deck can be seen just forward, and what appears to be another bomb entry wound on the starboard side; this ship took a lot of punishment in this area.

Her pronounced cruiser stern sits hard up against a coral rise and following its curve around (originally underneath the hull) leads to the rudder lying flat on the seabed and partly covered by the encroaching sand and coral. The propeller itself has been neatly removed – apparently whilst she was still on the reef.

## SHIPWRECK – THE ESSENTIALS

| | |
|---|---|
| Type: | Standard Type 1C IJA cargo vessel |
| Built: | 1942–43 |
| Tonnage: | 2,840 grt |
| Dimensions: | Length 321 feet; beam 45 feet; draught 21 feet |
| Propulsion: | Triple-expansion engine – single screw |
| Date of loss: | 30/31 March 1944 |
| Cause of loss: | Bombed/strafed and torpedoed by Task Force 58 aircraft |
| Depth to seabed: | 24 metres |
| Least depth: | 8 metres |
| Location: | Komebail Lagoon |

# 19. IJN T.1

## NORTH SHORE OF NGERCHAOL

The 1,500-ton fast transport *T.1* with *Koryu* midget submarines and landing craft on her aft deck.

The wreck of the fast transport *T.1* stands apart from the other major Japanese shipwrecks of Palau – in that she is not a legacy of Operation *Desecrate 1*, but is a casualty of Operation *Snapshot*, the US photo-reconnaissance mission of the Palaus undertaken in July 1944 in preparation for the amphibious assault of the Palaus in September.

The background to the presence of this interesting and unusual type of vessel in Palau today goes back to the Guadalcanal and Solomon campaigns of 1942 and 1943. These operations revealed that in the face of American air superiority, the large, slow Japanese transport *Maru*s and the destroyers that had been converted for use as high-speed transports were simply unable to carry and land the large quantities of troops and supplies required for extended combat operations. The slow *Maru*s were too vulnerable to air attack – and American air superiority was overwhelming by this stage of the war.

But the problem for the Japanese convoys just didn't come from the air, as the number, quality and operational ability of Japanese convoy protection ASW vessels was poor and inadequate. The *Maru*s were thus relatively easy prey for marauding US submarines on the high sea – and whilst offloading their cargoes in lagoon anchorages, they were sitting ducks for air attack. The *Maru*s suffered appalling losses, and had an unacceptably high rate of attrition.

In April 1943 the IJN began working on designs for a new fast and powerfully armed assault transport that could be used for amphibious operations by launching and recovering amphibious tanks and landing craft as well as transporting up to 500 assault troops. The design finally arrived at then evolved to become the new *T.1*-class fast naval transport. These were vessels which could be mass produced quickly by using pre-fabricated sections which could be welded together, in much the same fashion as the American Liberty ship construction process was conceived for the Battle of the Atlantic.

The construction process was simplified and standardised as much as possible, with a welded flush-decked hull without sheer or 'tumblehome', which is the narrowing of the beam of a ship higher above the waterline, the beam at the main deck being less than the beam at the waterline. The sections were assembled at Kure, and construction of this class of vessel took just three to six months.

The 1,500-ton *T.1*-class vessels were based on the *Matsu*-class destroyer hulls. This class of destroyer had evolved at a time in 1942 when the Japanese realised that they could not construct sufficient new large destroyers quickly enough to make up for those lost in action. The *Matsu*-class therefore would be suitable for quick mass production and was able to be built in six months as opposed to the previous build time of one year for earlier units. For the *T.1*-class the basic *Matsu* design was altered by the removal of one set of engines to create space to carry large numbers of troops or cargo. This reduced the *Matsu*-class speed from 28 knots to 22 knots. The *T.1*-class units were 315 feet in length with a beam of 33 feet 6 inches and a draught of just less than 12 feet.

The *T.1* class incorporated a unique stern, with the aft main deck sloping down to and then submerging beneath the waterline to where it was squared off. The aft deck was fitted out with two sets of twin tracks and rollers to allow a speedy roll-off into water and easy recovery of landing craft and tanks. The *T.1*-class transports were capable of very rapidly launching their four Daihatsu landing craft, which could be packed with troops. One 13-ton and four 5-ton derricks were fitted for cargo handling.

In the years that followed, the design was changed to allow the *T.1*-class vessels to carry two 46-ton Type A or 59-ton Type D *Koryu* midget submarines with general cargo. Alternative loads were seven Type 2 amphibious tanks, or six *Kaiten* human torpedoes or *Shinyo* explosive motorboats.

*T.1* under construction seen from astern. Note the twin roll on/off sets of tracks for rapid deployment of landing craft.

The *T.1*-class vessels were equipped with twin Type 89 127mm (5-inch) 40-cal AA guns on an elevated platform on the foredeck in front of the bridge superstructure. The Type 89 had a fast rate of fire and excellent elevation and training speeds, but its main shortcoming was a relatively low muzzle velocity and thus a short range and low AA ceiling. The first of the *T.1*-class were fitted with 15 25mm autocannons, but by May 1944 this had been increased to 26 Type 96 25mm AA autocannons in triple, twin and single mounts and five Type 93 13mm machine guns, in addition to 42 depth charges and sonar. Radar was added in 1945. Heavily armed, they were also used as minelayers and escorts.

In October 1943, just six months after the Imperial Japanese Navy had ordered the technical department to come up with the design, 46 *T.1*-class units were ordered. Initially, 15 were built at Kure Naval Arsenal and six at Mitsubishi Heavy Industries – the orders for the remaining vessels were cancelled in April 1945. Most of Kure's vessels were completed within 80 days of the laying down of their keels. Propelled by a geared turbine and two boilers, their single screw could make 22 knots, and they had an operating radius of 3,700 nautical miles at a service speed of 18 knots.

*T.1* was laid down at Kure Naval Arsenal on 5 November 1943. She was launched on 8 February 1944 and her fitting out afloat was completed by 10 May 1944, two months after the *Desecrate 1* Fast Carrier strikes against Palau of 30/31 March 1944. Her sea career would be short-lived.

At dawn on 29 May 1944, just two weeks after her completion, she departed Tokyo as one of five naval escorts for a convoy of nine merchant ships carrying troops of the IJA 43rd Infantry Division and the 115th Airfield Battalion bound for Saipan, along with cargoes of trucks, provisions, timber and fuel. At this time American submarines roamed the seas waging a terrible war of attrition against Japanese shipping. The Japanese ASW sonar was basic in comparison to Allied capabilities; as a result this convoy, like many others, would be heavily engaged by US submarines

As the convoy moved south, *T.1* and the other escorts conducted ASW sweeps. Despite this, on 4 June at about 1530, the American submarine USS *Shark* was able to approach the convoy, and torpedo and sink the transport *Katsukawa Maru*, which was carrying almost 3,000 IJA troops of the 43rd Infantry Division; almost one half of the troops being carried were lost in the attack. USS *Shark* continued to shadow the convoy during the night as it moved south, hiding on the surface in the darkness.

Despite further anti-submarine sweeps, the following day, USS *Shark* attacked again – successfully torpedoing and sinking the transport *Takaoka Maru* in the late afternoon. Immediately afterwards USS *Shark* torpedoed the *Tamahime Maru*.

On 6 June, about 200 nautical miles north-west of Saipan, the American submarine USS *Pintado* sank the transport *Kasimasan Maru*, which was carrying a cargo of gasoline and landing craft. *Pintado* then fired three torpedoes at the transport *Havre Maru*, sending her to the bottom with the loss of troops and a large number of her crew. The survivors were picked up and landed at Saipan later that same day.

*T.1* arrived at Saipan on 11 June 1944 – five of the nine transports had been sunk during the voyage. The following day, the American Operation *Forager* – the invasion of Saipan – began with an amphibious assault by Task Force 52 marines.

On 13 June 1944, south-west of the Marianas Islands and Guam, several hundred miles north-east of Palau, Grumman F6F Hellcats from Task Force 58, which had been supporting the Saipan operation, attacked a convoy that was being escorted by *T.1*.Accurate strafing from the Hellcats severely damaged *T.1* – she lost power and became unnavigable. She was taken in tow by the 1,900grt Standard Type 1D cargo steamer *Akishima Maru* and towed to Palau for repair.

On 18 July 1944 *T.1* was anchored close into and parallel to the rock face of the northwest corner of the north claw of Malakal Harbor, Ngerchaol. Protected by the steep sides of Ngerchaol, she had been moored there as a powerful floating AA battery. Her starboard side faced Ngerchaol and was only a matter of metres away from the sheer cliff face, whilst her port side faced out across the open waters of the lagoon. In an attempt to make her invisible to American aircraft above, she had been camouflaged with netting, branches and leaves to make her blend in and become part of the nearby coastline.

On 26 July 1944 Operation *Snapshot* began – the US photo-reconnaissance mission in preparation for the forthcoming amphibious assault on the Palaus. When the reconnaissance film was returned and studied, it was found that there were a number of Japanese ships hugging the coastline and camouflaged with netting, branches and leaves – some of them moored so close to Ngerchaol as to be virtually indistinguishable from the island itself. US analysts studying the images, however, spotted the giveaway straight unnatural lines of the camouflaged ships, and ordered air strikes.

Six Curtiss SB2C Helldiver dive-bombers from USS *Lexington* attacked and bombed *T.1*, their pilots claiming one hit and five near misses. Bombs hit the sheer stone cliffs just behind the starboard side of *T.1*, causing a large section of the limestone cliff to collapse downwards.

The following day, 27 July, Curtiss SB2C dive-bombers and Grumman TBF Avenger torpedo-bombers from *Lexington* and dive- and torpedo-bombers from USS *Bunker Hill* again attacked the beleaguered *T.1*, scoring several hits or near misses with 1,000lb and 2,000lb bombs. Such devastatingly large bomb hits on a small, lightly protected vessel mortally wounded her; *T.1* was hit forward of her superstructure –such was the impact that she almost split in two.

She rolled over onto her port side and disappeared beneath the waves, her two sections, still connected by twisted steel, each attempting to roll down the steep underwater slope of Ngerchaol in different ways; each playing on the other. She eventually came to rest broadside on to the slope in about 31 metres of water with her bow section flat on its starboard side. The largest section of ship from amidships to the stern ended up completely upside down.

After the war, *T.1* received attention from commercial salvors who removed the propeller and heavily blasted the midships engine and boiler rooms area to get at the valuable non-ferrous fitments. At some time later, sections of the weakened cliff nearby gave way and large boulders, one the size of a small house, tumbled down the slope to come to rest upon her upturned stern section.

## THE WRECK TODAY

Today the wreck of this fast transport is a fascinating glimpse of a unique type of Japanese World War II vessel. The wreck site lies just 10 minutes' boat ride from the Koror dive centres on the north side of the northmost claw of Malakal Harbor.

The wreck of *T.1* lies in an area of good visibility, perhaps 40–50 metres on average. It is interesting to see a vessel that was almost split in two by bombing and then, almost separated but still snagged and connected, clearly tumbled, much like a Slinky, broadside

The wreck of the fast transport *T.1* tumbled down the underwater slope before coming to rest, her sections twisted, in 31 metres of water on the north side of Ngerchaol.

A section of the steep rocky cliffs immediately behind *T.1* was brought down during the attack and now marks her resting place directly beneath. (Author's collection)

down the steep shelving underwater slope of the island until her two sections came to rest seemingly in one straight shiplike form – but in fact at completely different orientations to the seabed.

Topside, her location is marked by a significant collapse of the limestone cliff wall behind her due to impact or weakening from near-miss American bombing. The large … really large … chunks of rock you see lying around the wreck on the seabed are all pieces of the weakened cliff that have detached and tumbled down the slope in the years after the sinking.

After the dive, on the way back round to Malakal Harbor you can get close to a water's-edge cave with a large Japanese coastal defence 5.5-inch gun projecting from it. This gun is now only accessible from the sea; however during wartime the Japanese had constructed an access cave to service it from high above. It is believed that the Americans blew up and collapsed the cave after taking the island to deny its future use.

The forward bow section of the ship rests on the bottom with its starboard side flat on the plunging seabed at an angle of about 45 degrees. Over the years since she sank, soft sand has been tumbling down the slope and accumulating against her flat foredeck, which consequently is now half-buried by the encroaching seabed.

The ship has a modern raked bow but a soft-nosed almost rounded stem. Her very prow is squared off, and projects outwards as though it was designed to push against other ships or docks; this may have been a quick and efficient way for her to embark her 480 marines from larger troop transports at sea before an assault, or to quickly disembark them to piers and docks, as opposed to coming alongside – much like modern-day offshore crew transfers in the oil industry.

The squared-off, soft-nosed stem of *T.1* lies on its starboard side, slowly being engulfed by the encroaching seabed. (Author's collection)

She was at anchor when she was attacked, and it appears that she rolled over completely as she tumbled broadside down the slope – as the port anchor chain is run out up and over the foredeck to disappear to starboard into the sloping seabed.

The front 25 metres of the ship, the bow section, is completely intact, lying hard on its starboard side on the sloping seabed. Twin mooring bollards, cleats and fairleads dot its clean foredeck; she was flush-decked, there is no fo'c'sle and the guardrails are long gone. A large circular steam-driven capstan sits aft on the foredeck, immediately before the start of the separation damage.

The two sections of the wreck still abut each other, and you can move from one section to the other almost unknowingly. Aft of the separation damage, however, the orientation of the wreck changes. Although still lying on its starboard side, the wreck has collapsed and buckled downwards so that the port bulwark rail is now just a few metres off the sand and the main deck returns backwards under the shell plating.

As you move along the higher port side of the wreck, the main deck soon is lying at the same orientation as the shelving seabed with a gap of just a few metres to the port bulwark. In the chaos of the area where the break has taken place, the barbette for the main twin Type 89 127mm (5-inch) AA guns situated on the foredeck can be found, with an open doorway allowing views to the lightly armoured barbette and the base of the gun mount.

When you look under the overhanging port bulwark immediately aft of the large steam capstan, the double barrels of the Type 89 127mm guns can be found lying on the sand and facing aft. Immediately aft of the main twin Type 89 guns, a windlass sits on the port side main deck immediately before the start of the bridge superstructure, but the encroaching seabed has now largely buried the bridge superstructure itself.

The triple 25mm autocannon AA platform, which was stationed on a platform high up abaft the bridge, lies crushed almost flat on the seabed with the triple 25mm muzzles projecting outwards from underneath it. The muzzles are trained out to port – no doubt they remain exactly as they were during the attack when, protected by the high cliffs to her starboard side, the guns would have been firing at incoming US aircraft from the skies above the open water on her port side.

Abaft the 25mm platform there is a deck hatch on the port side of the deck that it is possible to swim down and through before emerging into open space where the hull has seen the attentions of salvors and is collapsing.

The narrow bridge superstructure returned inboard after the forward high section of the bridge to allow space for lifeboats or landing craft to be stowed alongside. At either side there are tracks with roll on/off runners and a large deck-mounted steam-driven winch for hauling up the three Daihatsu landing craft that could be secured along either side of the low machinery deckhouses.

As you move aft from the bridge towards the boiler and engine rooms, the hull loses its shape almost completely due to the attentions of salvors. The middle section of the wreck here in the vicinity of the boiler and engine rooms is completely devastated – having been blasted wide open to free up valuable non-ferrous engine fitments for salvage. The ship has lost its shape essentially for the full length of the bilge keels, and is now an open debris field

Triple 25mm autocannon barrels project out from underneath the gun platform abaft the bridge.
(Author's collection)

with scattered sections of ship and mangled pipes, plates and spars lying around along with a section of her mast. Large sections of ship lie on the seabed to either side where they have been blasted or pulled off the wreck by salvors. Surprisingly, in the midst of this chaos what looks like a Kampon boiler stands as if ready to be lifted to the surface.

Once aft of the boiler and engine room areas, the ship largely regains its structure and it is immediately apparent that this stern section is completely upside down. Sections of the narrow bilge keels remain, running down either side of the keel to give the flat bottom a cutting edge for manoeuvring. Although the ship regains its form here, there is a narrower furrow-like gouge right up the middle of the keel aft for some distance. The edges of the hull plating around this large gouge are all blown outwards from the hull and are clearly the results of salvage work, presumably intended to free the valuable prop shaft from the wreck. This gouge ends at the end of the bilge keels, where the lower hull starts to narrow towards the flat keel strip, which runs out from the hull towards the rudder.

The robust keel strip comes to an end and angles sharply down (originally up) towards where the unusually long free section of propeller shaft exits the hull and runs aft. A long section of free shaft like this would make a ship very vulnerable to near-miss bombs, which could damage or buckle this section of shaft; so although it was necessary for the design requirements of the vessel, it was something of an Achilles' heel. The propeller itself is missing – removed by salvors. On the deeper starboard side of the hull there is a small hull deformation from a near-miss bomb immediately abeam the prop.

From the point where the free section of shaft emerges from the prop tunnel aft, the hull bottom to the stern is noticeably very flat, with a large rudder projecting up from it. During

The prop shaft projects out from right of shot towards the upright rudder. (Author's collection)

her sea career, the section of aft deck used for launch and recovery of tanks and landing craft dropped away beneath the surface, to end just a few feet above and aft of the top of the rudder.

The very stern is markedly squared off, and the transom is a rectangular bar about a foot high. With the transom sitting almost level with the top of the rudder stock, it would have been deep in the water. Two sets of twin tracks, with heavy-duty rollers on them, sit one pair at either side of the upturned quarterdeck here – designed for launching and retrieving landing craft, amphibious tanks or midget submarines and other heavy equipment over the stern. The upturned main deck slopes away smoothly under the upturned deck down towards the seabed where the wreck now rests on the section of deck that would have been above the water, topside.

Uphill, on the higher port side, there is a massive rock the size of a bus, and a number of other unusually large rocks which have tumbled down to rest on or against the hull – obviously having come down after the ship had sunk. A number of other smaller rocks have also tumbled onto the flat upturned hull here – so it looks as though a section of the cliff must have been weakened during the attack and given way subsequently and collapsed.

## SHIPWRECK – THE ESSENTIALS

| | |
|---|---|
| Type: | *T.1*-class fast transport |
| Built: | 1943/44 |
| Displacement: | 1,500 tons |
| Dimensions: | Length 315 feet; beam 33ft 6in.; draught 11ft 9in. |
| Propulsion: | 1 x Kampon geared turbine, 2 x Kampon water tube boilers – single screw |
| Date of loss: | 27 July 1944 |
| Cause of loss: | Bombed by aircraft during Operation *Snapshot* |
| Depth to seabed: | 31 metres |
| Least depth: | 20 metres – bow |
| Location: | North shore of Ngerchaol |

# 20. Type F Standard refrigerated cargo ship – unidentified

MALAKAL HARBOR

Artist's impression of a Type F standard cargo ship.

Under the Japanese war programme of standard shipbuilding, many small vessels of under 1,000 gross tons were built to serve as ore carriers and general cargo ships –standard ship Types E and F.

The Type E standard ship had a gross tonnage of about 830–880 tons and was 210 feet in length with a beam of 36 feet. Some 200 ships of the Type E class were built. The Type F was very similar in design to the Type E. US Intelligence believed that some 18–20 of the Type F standard ships were built at Hong Kong. It is believed that the unidentified refrigerated cargo ship sitting in the southern part of Malakal Harbor is a Type F, modified to carry refrigerated cargo.

The Type E and F standard ships were small coastal freighters with the superstructure and engine machinery set at the very stern. The remainder of the hull in front of the aft superstructure was given over to interconnecting cargo holds, with a single mast rising from the well deck in between hatches. The Standard Type F had two cargo hatches, whereas the wreck in Malakal Harbor is the modified refrigerated version with three small hatches just a few metres across in place. A small fo'c'sle at the bow held the chain locker.

Combat photo showing Ngeruktabel, the southern claw of Malakal Harbor. The unidentified Type F cargo vessel is the small freighter backed into a small bay in centre left of shot. (National Archives)

At the time of *Desecrate 1*, this small aft-engine refrigerated cargo ship was spotted and photographed by US aircraft anchored with its stern backed close inshore in a small bay on the southern claw of Malakal Harbor, Ngeruktabel – no doubt seeking protection from the nearby high jungle-covered hills against air attack. There is a combat photo of it with another small vessel anchored a few hundred metres away to the east. The circumstances of its sinking are not recorded in any detail or known to me.

## THE WRECK TODAY

The wreck of this small coastal freighter lies about 70 metres offshore in a small bay about three quarters of a mile north-west along Ngeruktabel from the site of the *Akashi*.

Sitting in shallow water of about 13 metres in Malakal Harbor, this vessel was an easy target for salvors, with the only parts of any great value being the engine, the condensers and the non-ferrous engine room fitments in the machinery spaces at the stern of the ship – and the propeller. Salvors used explosives to blast the engine areas open, and this has resulted in the aft ship being almost severed from the rest of the vessel by a powerful explosion which has destroyed the stern superstructure and bridge, bent the keel and blown hull plating outward. There is now only a mass of scrap where the aft section of the ship used to be. The remnants of the bridge can be seen lying on the seabed alongside forced-draught ventilators and refrigeration pipes.

The remainder of the ship rests on her port beam with the fore and midships sections in fairly good condition. The bow is largely intact and has a raked stem, and the starboard anchor is run out – the chain crossing the bow but severed before it reaches the seabed. The lower port anchor hangs from its hawse. The fo'c'sle deck plating and planking has disappeared leaving only the skeletal framing visible. Inside the fo'c'sle on the starboard side is the electrical control room with heavy switches, some hanging

Close-up showing the unidentified Type F freighter backed into a small bay just to the right of the words 1,000 ft. Akashi can be seen moored between small islands at top of shot whilst *Gozan Maru* can be seen bottom centre. (National Archives).

down on their cables. The chain locker, with the port chain piled up in it, is visible.

The main well deck has three small hatches set in it – each only a few metres long and wide but with high coaming. The holds have numerous cooling coils, and traces of the original insulation for the walls and deck, made of cork covered with plywood. Set in the bottom of the hold, square-shaped hatches to access the double bottoms can be seen still bolted down.

Around the aft part of Hold No. 2 there is much damage, and the deck bulges up in this area – from a combination of wartime bombing and the venting of the blast from salvors blowing the aft part of the ship away.

The identity of this vessel is not known, even though some 25 years have passed since Klaus Lindemann and Francis Toribiong first located it in 1989 after an aerial survey. With the bridge superstructure destroyed and the remainder of the ship holding little of interest, this wreck is now seldom dived.

## SHIPWRECK – THE ESSENTIALS

| | |
|---|---|
| Type: | Type F standard refrigerated cargo vessel |
| Built: | Unknown |
| Tonnage: | Approx. 800 tons |
| Dimensions: | Length approx. 210 feet; beam approx. 35 feet |
| Propulsion: | Diesel engine – single shaft |
| Date of loss: | 30/31 March 1944 |
| Cause of loss: | Bombed by Task Force 58 aircraft |
| Depth to seabed: | 13 metres |
| Location: | Malakal Harbor – north shore of Ngeruktabel |

# 21. IJN Urakami Maru

IJN Urakami Maru-class Auxiliary Salvage and Repair Ship (1941)

## MALAKAL HARBOR

The 4,317grt auxiliary salvage and repair ship *Urakami Maru* was laid down as a Standard Type B three-island cargo ship at Mitsubishi Shipbuilding's yard at Kobe on 5 November 1940, for Fukuyo Kisen KK of Kobe. She was 387 feet long with a beam of 51 feet and a draught of 24 feet. She was fitted with one geared turbine steam engine that gave her a service speed of 11 knots and a top speed of 13 knots

The 4,317grt auxiliary salvage and repair ship IJN *Urakami Maru*.

with her single screw. She was launched and named on 27 June 1941.

*Urakami Maru* was built with a raised fo'c'sle, two foredeck holds in the well deck split by the foremast and mast house, and a further hold in the extended section of superstructure in front of the high composite superstructure, which held the navigating bridge at its top deck level. The tall funnel was situated immediately abaft the bridge, surrounded by forced-draught ventilators and with lifeboats swung in derricks at either side. The engine and boiler rooms were located below.

Two after-deck holds were split by the main mast before the poop deckhouse at the stern, which held the steering gear and auxiliary steering position.

*Urakami Maru* was requisitioned by the Imperial Japanese Navy from her civilian owners on 12 November 1941 and registered to the Sasebo Naval District on 1 December. Work began to convert her to a salvage and repair ship on 10 January 1942, and she was fitted with two 4.7-inch guns on platforms at bow and at stern, and a number of AA guns. She also received powerful pumps and hoses for use in preventing a damaged ship from sinking. Repair ships such as *Urakami Maru* and *Akashi* carried large amounts of spare parts, from spare pistons and sheet metal to steam pipes of different diameters; in most of them a smithy and metal workshops were fitted out in the hold forward of the bridge.

Her conversion work was completed by 25 January 1942, and she was assigned directly to the Combined Fleet and then reassigned to the 6th Fleet at Truk, providing repairs for ships at Kwajalein in the Marshall Islands and Ponape in the Caroline Islands.

Later that year, in September, the submarine *I-33* was moored alongside her in Truk Lagoon, with *I-33*'s stern secured to the wharf on Dublon Island. Three engineers from *Urakami Maru* began repairs on *I-33*, on her lowermost port torpedo tube. During the repairs, to try and counteract a difficult swell an attempt was made to alter her buoyancy to raise her bow. Things went badly wrong, however, when the drain cock on her aft main tanks was opened and she partially flooded. With her buoyancy fatally compromised, the hawsers securing the stern to the wharf snapped, and she sank in about two minutes into 120 feet of water with the loss of 33 crew. A rescue operation from *Urakami Maru* was immediately launched, and although divers initially reported that some crew members were still alive inside the flooded hull on the seabed, all rescue attempts subsequently failed.

As Operation *Hailstone* exploded over Truk Lagoon on the morning of 17 Feb 1944, *Urakami Maru* was at anchor in the lagoon. Unlike most other vessels present, *Urakami Maru* survived the operation relatively unscathed and claimed to have shot down two US aircraft and damaged others. She left Truk Lagoon after the raid on 20 February before returning later to assist with repairs.

On 6 March 1944 *Urakami Maru* departed Truk Lagoon bound for Saipan in an escorted convoy that arrived at Saipan on 10 March. From there she left in an escorted convoy but on 21 March the American submarine USS *Bashaw* fired six torpedoes by radar at a large ship south-east of Palau, scoring one hit – it was *Urakami Maru*, and she was immobilised by the strike.

The destroyer *Minazuki* took *Urakami Maru* in tow to Palau, screened by the destroyer *Yuzuki*, and once there she was anchored in the middle of Malakal Harbor, not far from the repair ship *Akashi*.

In the first strikes of 30 March, as Operation *Desecrate 1* began, a Curtiss SB2C Helldiver from *Hornet* attacked the anchored *Urakami Maru*. The dive-bomber dropped a 1,000lb bomb, but the air crew could not be certain of the result.

In a later group strike, the large target of *Urakami Maru* was again attacked – this time by two Grumman TBF Avenger torpedo-bombers with large 2,000lb bombs. One bomb was reported to have hit the fantail and the other was a near miss – the ship caught fire.

Wounded in her aft section, *Urakami Maru* began to settle by the stern and to list to starboard. She would sink later that day, leaving only an oil slick to betray her presence below to US photo-reconnaissance aircraft the following day.

In the 1950s *Urakami Maru* was partially dismantled by Fujita Salvage Co. for scrap, with the removal of the prop and the blasting open of her uppermost port side hull to get at the valuable non-ferrous engine room fitments. Subsequent, more minor, salvage work was carried out by another local salvage company, which used smaller explosive charges to blast free the uppermost structures. Some 1,300 tons of metal were reported to have been recovered before operations ceased. The poop deckhouse was left untouched perhaps due to safety fears about the shells for the main defensive stern gun.

## THE WRECK TODAY

Today the large wreck of *Urakami Maru* lies on her starboard side in the middle of Malakal Harbor, just 10 minutes' boat ride away from most of the dive centres. She rests in 38 metres of water and has a least depth down to her upturned port side of 22 metres. Despite her being in the middle of Malakal Harbor, the visibility is surprisingly good with crisp, clear 30+ metres vis on the higher parts and slightly murky vis of 5–10 metres lower down near the seabed. She is a wreck that has clearly seen a lot of attention from salvors but nevertheless she is full of interest and makes a fine dive with a lot of sea life – the times I've dived her, there has been an occasional encounter with a shark to keep you on your toes.

The wreck of the auxiliary salvage & repair ship *Urakami Maru* lies on her starboard side in 38 metres of water in Malakal Harbor. Her bow was blown off during *Desecrate 1* and she was part-salvaged after the war.

The first time you dive this wreck, if you stay up high on the uppermost port side of the ship, she can be quite difficult to understand. Here, salvors have used acetylene torches to neatly cut away the uppermost shell plating of the port hull right down to the bilge keels for most of the length of the upper port hull. In the middle of the ship's length, a lot of damage has been caused by salvage blasting in the composite superstructure amidships to get at the valuable non-ferrous engine and boiler room fitments. There is little left recognisable of the superstructure. To quickly get a grasp of this wreck you need to hit the bottom.

The lower starboard section of the ship's length has been left largely untouched by salvors – there was no need, and no commercial value in removing the hull plating here. In contrast to the confusion high up, a dive along the lower section of the ship makes the wreck far easier to understand.

Whilst the sterncastle has been left completely untouched by salvors, the whole bow has been completely blown off the ship and the bow gun now lies upside down on the seabed, detached from the wreck, with boxes of 4.7-inch shells lying around.

Wartime combat reports speak of a hit on the fantail – however the whole stern and sterncastle are completely intact. If a 2,000lb bomb had hit here, this would have been a scene of devastation. With the bow, however, almost blown off it seems likely that the 2,000lb bomb hit there, and I suspect that the US aviators in the heat of battle, from a great height and with targets obscured by smoke and plumes of spray – perhaps also due to the prevailing cloud cover on the day obscuring their view – simply made an understandable error in reporting.

The stern area has no doubt been left alone by salvors due to the large number of loose ready-use 4.7-inch shells lying around for the stern gun and the full boxes of 4.7-inch shells that also lie on the seabed here. If salvors stayed away from working the stern due to fears over the 4.7-inch shells there, they would probably have stayed away from the bow for the same reason so the blast damage here is likely from the war and not from salvage work.

On deck at the very stern, directly above the rudderpost, the non-ferrous auxiliary steering helm pedestal can be found still securely bolted to the deck. The rounded flat top held the rudder direction indicator – it is well covered with corals but no doubt will still have its pointer and manufacturer's details on it if exposed. The helm axle and the hub with its locating slots for the spokes of the wheel are still present on the aft side of the pedestal, but all trace of any wood has gone – no doubt burnt away in the fires that consumed the ship.

Immediately in front of the auxiliary helm, a deck hatch allows entry down to the steering gear and quadrant. Two small generators are located nearby, and the wall has a number of gauges still mounted on it. On the uppermost port side of the intact stern hull, ladder rungs are welded up the outside of the ship to allow access to and from tender vessels like Daihatsu landing craft. Following the stern around, her cruiser stern is very distinct.

As a protection against magnetic mines this vessel was fitted with degaussing cables around her hull. Magnetic mines detect the increase in magnetic field when the steel of a passing ship concentrates the Earth's magnetic field above it – and German magnetic mines had caused major shipping losses for Britain during the early days of World War II. To counter this, British Admiralty scientists developed systems that induced a small 'N-pole up' magnetic field in ships – so that the net magnetic field was the same as the background. The Germans used the gauss as the unit of the strength of the magnetic field in their mine-trigger mechanism, and hence the Admiralty scientists started to call the magnetic mine

The auxiliary helm and rudder direction indicator is still securely bolted to the deck at the very stern.
(Author's collection)

countermeasure process 'degaussing'. The Japanese had adopted the process, and distinctive degaussing cables can be seen running round the outside of the hull here.

The propeller has been neatly removed by salvors unbolting the retaining nuts

The large 4.7-inch stern gun and splinter shield is still *in situ* on its skeletal circular platform – its barrel pointing upwards to port. The large breech is open, and training handwheels are easily visible below the squared-off rear edge of the splinter shield. Immediately underneath the gun, boxes of 4.7-inch shells and a number of spent 25mm AA cartridges lie on the seabed. The sterncastle forward bulkhead to the well deck has two open doors allowing access, and fixed steps leading up to the poop deck from the well deck are situated at either side. Twin mooring bollards are dotted around the well deck and poop deck.

Forward of the sterncastle, the two aft deck holds can be located with a section of well deck in between. The uppermost port side of the hull here was cut away by salvors down to just a few metres above the bilge keel. This has opened up the holds down to their lowest level and has exposed her keel framing and the lower starboard sections of her tween deck and main deck hatches.

As a contrast to the higher, confused port side of the ship, the lower and deeper starboard side of the ship is much more intact and the coaming of her aft holds can be made out, along with sections of intact well deck and gunwale with scuppers. Here and there, cargo booms, unworthy of salvage, lie dumped alongside the wreck on the seabed. The large tubular steel main mast has collapsed to now lie on the seabed.

The remains of the composite amidships superstructure dominate the centre part of the ship. As you approach from aft over the aft deck holds down at the seabed level, the gunwale rises up to shelter deck level with the fixed steps still in place that allowed access to the promenade deck walkway that ran along the side of the superstructure to the foredeck.

Higher up on the port side on the wreck, the ship here has almost been completely removed by salvors to access the engine and boiler rooms. The forward and aft bulkheads of the engine casing, the fireproof steel wall that wrapped around the engine and boiler rooms, now project out horizontally from the bottom of the ship. Unworthy of salvage, the two casing bulkheads delineate the machinery spaces and the transition to the former bridge and radio room spaces. The spaces aft of the engine casing would have held the galley.

Salvors have blown and cut away the whole upper ship to open up these engine and boiler rooms to lift out her engine, condensers and other valuable non-ferrous pieces of machinery. The engine room is virtually a large empty space, open from above. Much of the superstructure that would have been above and in front of these spaces has collapsed or been dumped – the transverse beams and girders of its structure lying around in a confused mess. Lying flat on the seabed, however, is the intact starboard side of the superstructure, which is still dotted with rows of portholes.

The smokestack has collapsed in three sections to now lie flat on the seabed in the midst of this confusion. At the forward end of the superstructure the compass binnacle can be found lying on the seabed, and the radio room, originally underneath the navigating bridge, is largely intact.

There were three foredeck holds: Hold No. 3 higher up at shelter deck level on the extended section of superstructure in front of the bridge, and Hold Nos 1 and 2 in the well deck. Part of the higher port side of the superstructure, still dotted with portholes, and part of the higher port side of Hold No. 3, have lost their structural strength because of the salvage work. As a result, a large section of flat port hull has collapsed downwards onto the lower part of the ship – such that the uppermost port gunwale is now just a few metres above the seabed.

As you move forward from Hold No. 3, the shelter deck now drops away horizontally to the well deck Hold No. 2. Here, the shell plating on the port side of the hull has been removed, exposing the portside hull frames. As with Hold No. 3, the port hull frames have collapsed downwards onto the starboard side of the ship now almost touch the seabed. A workshop, smithy and spares can be found in Hold No. 2.

In between the two well deck holds the foremast can be found, collapsed to the seabed.

The starboard gunwale of Hold No. 1 is initially still intact with a section of deck inboard and the hatch visible. There is a lot of mangled steelwork around here – and as you move forward the distress to the vessel becomes noticeably apparent with bent and twisted frames and decking and shell plating everywhere. Then, abruptly, the wreck suddenly comes to a violent end where the bow has been sheared off, completely severed from the rest of the ship. This catastrophic damage could possibly be from salvage blasting; however, it is more likely to have been a 2,000lb wartime bomb that blew her bow off. I cannot see salvors using this amount of explosive in an area of little commercial value for them. Add to this the fact that Hold No. 1 held the 4.7-inch shells for the bow gun, and it would simply make it too dangerous for salvors to use this quantity of explosive to blow off a relatively worthless bow.

The fo'c'sle is simply gone – and as a result of the explosion, the bow gun and its platform are now lying upside down on the seabed about 10–20 metres forward in 38 metres of water with boxes of 4.7-inch shells lying around on the seabed, as at the stern. The large 4.7-inch gun and splinter shield dates from the beginning of the 20th century, as was common on Japanese ships and was no doubt cannibalised from an older vessel during refit.

## SHIPWRECK – THE ESSENTIALS

| | |
|---|---|
| Type: | Standard Type B cargo steamer (1941) |
| | IJN *Urakami Maru*-class auxiliary salvage and repair ship (1941) |
| Built: | 1940/41 |
| Tonnage: | 4,317 grt |
| Dimensions: | Length 387 feet; beam 51 feet; draught 24 feet |
| Propulsion: | Geared turbine steam engine – single screw |
| Date of loss: | 30 March 1944 |
| Cause of loss: | Bombed by Task Force 58 aircraft |
| Depth to seabed: | 38 metres |
| Least depth: | 22 metres – port side bilge keel |
| Location: | Malakal Harbor |

# 22. IJN Wakatake

SECOND-CLASS DESTROYER (1922)

## KARAMADOO BAY, BABELTHUAP

The second-class destroyer *Wakatake* was laid down as Destroyer No. 2 on 13 December 1921 in Kobe at the Kawasaki Heavy Industries Yard. At that time she had the tentative name assigned to her of *Kikyo*. She was being built under the 1921 construction programme – and was one of 12 second-class destroyers designed as

IJN *Wakatake* 2nd-class destroyer

improved versions of the *Momi*-class units of the 1919 construction programme – these would be the last second-class destroyers built.

The second-class destroyers were slightly smaller and more lightly armed versions of the IJN first-class destroyers. Originally thirteen units had been planned, but the class was reduced to nine units, and then *No. 14* was cancelled in 1922. Initially the units were given simple numbers, but from 1 August 1928, the remaining units were given names once more.

*Momi*-class vessels had inherited a number of features from the larger *Minekaze* class – based on influences from German destroyers handed over to Japan at the end of World War I as war reparations. They boasted three heavy 4.7-inch guns, two 7.7mm machine guns and minesweeping gear – as well as being the first destroyers to be fitted with four 21-inch torpedo tubes fitted in a well deck in front of the bridge. The new second-class destroyers displaced 1,100 tons fully loaded, and were 280 feet in length with a beam of 26 feet 6 inches – and with their draught of just 8 feet 3 inches, they proved excellent for use in the shallow waters along the coast of China to support amphibious landings during the Second Sino-Japanese War. They had a range of 3,000 nautical miles at 15 knots and carried a crew of 110.

The *Wakatake* was launched simply as *Destroyer No. 2* on 24 July 1922 and was completed on 30 September.

The *Momi*-class destroyers were hailed at the time as the fastest in the world. Brown-Curtis double turbines and three Kampon boilers drove twin shafts that gave a top speed of 35.5 knots. These were the last second-class destroyers to be built, and they were also rated as minelayers and minesweepers. All subsequent destroyers would have a larger displacement and be designated first-class destroyers. From August 1928, the second-class destroyers were given names once more, and Destroyer No.2 became *Wakatake*.

She may have been a fast ship at the time she was built (even now almost 100 years later, she would still be a fast ship) but by the eve of World War II the *Momi* class vessels were outdated old ships of little strategic value. To try and make her useful in the conflict that would surely follow, in 1938 *Wakatake* had her fore funnel capped and additional ballast added to improve stability. Her displacement rose to 1,113 tons and her speed was reduced to 31 knots. On 1 December 1938 *Wakatake* was put on the Reserve List as a fourth-class warship.

In 1939, in the immediate run-up to war, a number of the second-class destroyers underwent a refit that drastically reduced their speed to 18 knots by the removal of one of their three Kampon boilers. The outdated 21-inch torpedo tubes were removed as well as the minesweeping gear and one of the three 4.7-inch guns. The vessels were then refitted for escort duty with eight 25mm AA autocannons, 60 depth charges and some depth charge throwers being installed.

With the outbreak of war in December 1941, *Wakatake* was assigned to escort duties, and throughout 1942 she was escorting convoys operating between ports such as Takao in Formosa, Lingayen Gulf in the Philippines, Mako in the Pescadores, and Moji and Mutsure in Japan.

In 1942, further refit work was carried out – she now carried two quick firing (QF) 4.7-inch main guns, six 25mm AA autocannons and a number of 13mm AA machine guns, but had a reduced depth charge capability of 36–48 depth charges.

During 1943 she was carrying out escort duties between places like Singapore, St Jacques in Indo-China, Mako, Manila and Takao. Several of her tasks took her to Palau towards the end of the year, and she frequently called at Balikpapan to pick up convoys from this important petroleum-rich outpost.

On 21 January 1944 *Wakatake* departed Miri escorting a convoy of several tankers and transports bound for Manila. The following day, the American submarine USS *Tinosa* attacked the convoy just before sunset. The tanker *Koshin Maru* was struck and sunk, and the tanker *Seinan Maru* was also sunk. *Wakatake* attacked *Tinosa*, dropping 17 depth charges – but the American submarine was able to evade and escape.

The convoy arrived at Manila on 31 January and after a brief refuel and victual, *Wakatake* set off just two days later, escorting another convoy to Takao. From Takao she moved to Moji to pick up another convoy for a return to Takao. On 20 March she departed Takao with the minelayer *Maeshima*, escorting a convoy. On 26 March, in a violent rainsquall, the American submarine USS *Tullibee* attacked the convoy. The Japanese escorts counter-attacked the American submarine – without success – and then in the poor visibility swept the seas with machine gun fire.

To Japanese surprise, a large explosion was then heard. A search of the area located a single American survivor from *Tullibee*. He had been standing on the open bridge of the submarine as it fired a torpedo at the Japanese vessels. The torpedo, however, ran a circular course and came back to detonate against the American submarine and send it plunging to the bottom; the fortunate crewman had been thrown from the conning tower into the water.

On 27 March 1944 the convoy arrived at Palau amidst frantic preparations for an imminent assault – the approach of Task Force 58 had been detected just days earlier. Truk had been hit and neutralised six weeks earlier, and the Japanese on Palau now knew what they would soon be facing.

Convoy PATA-07 was formed up to make a dash to leave Palau before the American raid began. If the convoy got away it would head for Takao, Formosa. The convoy was scheduled to leave on the evening of 29 March but was delayed and was not able to set off until 0500 on the morning of 30 March.

At 0500, the ships of convoy PATA-07 started to leave the main anchorages of the Western Lagoon and move north through Komebail Lagoon before entering the narrow main channel north on the west side of the main Palauan island of Babelthuap that leads towards Toachel Mlengui – the West Passage through the fringing reef. The convoy included the 1941 *Kibi Maru* along with the fleet oiler *Akebono Maru*, the auxiliary transport *Goshu Maru*, the IJN-requisitioned Standard Type C steamers *Raizan Maru* and *Ryuko Maru* and the IJA transports *Teshio Maru* and *Hokutai Maru*. The large convoy would be escorted by the ex-*Momi*-class destroyer *Patrol Boat 31*, the *Wakatake* and the auxiliary subchaser *Cha 26*.

*Wakatake* was at the van of the convoy, and several slow picket boats ranged far ahead, looking to spot any trouble. Meantime, many miles to the south at the far southern end of the convoy, several other freighters were congregating, waiting to join.

At 0550, the first waves of American F6F Hellcats and Grumman Avengers swept over the lagoon's anchorages in the initial fighter sweep and mining operation; the large convoy was immediately spotted, with *Lexington*, *Bunker Hill* and *Monterey* aircraft all reporting the convoy. *Bunker Hill* Avenger torpedo-bombers immediately attacked the lead ships whilst *Lexington* Hellcats strafed. Meantime mines were being air-dropped in the channel ahead of the convoy to block it.

As the attacks by TF58 aircraft went in, the ships in the convoy began to take evasive manoeuvres – no doubt after seeing the mines being air-dropped and realising their escape was now blocked; the convoy was dissolved and the ships scattered. During the ensuing melée, *Kibi Maru* ran aground on the western side of the channel whilst *Teshio Maru* lost propulsion and drifted before grounding on the eastern side. *Hokutai Maru* came about and headed back to Malakal Harbor.

A destroyer was spotted by US aircraft some 20 miles off Palau that could have been *Wakatake* or *Patrol Boat 31*, as they both looked roughly the same from the air. This destroyer was attacked, strafed and bombed by *Enterprise* and *Yorktown* aircraft – and finally sunk five miles south-west of Kossol Passage in oceanic depths of water. It was *Patrol Boat 31*.

Meantime, *Lexington* Hellcats and Avengers attacked three Japanese naval vessels in the main channel north, up the west side of Babelthuap. *Wakatake* was strafed and as the convoy scattered she turned east into Karamadoo Bay along the west shore of Babelthuap opposite Toachel Mlengui. She hove to about 100 feet off the north shore, no doubt seeking protection from the land whilst she engaged the American marauders with her AA guns.

*Wakatake* was attacked by dive-bombers and took three bomb hits and several near misses. Such damage on a lightly protected destroyer was catastrophic – she began to smoke heavily – and then broke in two. A further attack went in – and by the end of the day as the area was overflown, she was reported as sunk, with only an oil slick betraying her presence below. One of the other naval vessels reported near *Wakatake* as the American aircraft attacked, is possibly the auxiliary subchaser *Showa Maru No. 5* (ex-*Galicia*).

Japanese destroyer under attack during *Desecrate 1*. This destroyer was initially believed by US aviators to be IJN *Wakatake*, but is now believed to be *Patrol Boat 31*. (National Archives)

The Japanese themselves may have carried out salvage work on *Wakatake* during the war, and she was certainly subjected to post-war salvage work involving the heavy use of explosives.

## THE WRECK TODAY

The wreck of the second-class destroyer *Wakatake* today rests in an area of consistently poor visibility where fresh run-off water from the land mixes with the seawater. The wreck is covered in silt, and visibility can vary from just a few feet to 15 feet. There are also reports of salt-water crocodiles being seen on the wreck. A crocodile appearing out of murky water is not what you want to see.

There is a gap of about 15 metres in between the two sections of ship. The 15-metre-long bow section rests in about 10 metres of water some 25 metres off the north shore of the bay.

The remaining larger section of the ship lies diagonally along the steep slope as it drops off into deeper water. Her top hamper and main decking are almost unrecognisable due to the damage from bombing and salvors.

A section of the aft part of the hull and superstructure is relatively intact, and in amongst torn and twisted metal and bits of ships some of her 25mm AA cannons can be made out, along with minesweeping paravanes, torpedo tubes and torpedoes.

The torn remains of the aft part of the ship drop down to about 30 metres in increasingly murky water where a prop shaft finally marks the end of the stern.

The combination of a heavily salvaged, smashed-up vessel, poor visibility and the potential for crocodiles means that this vessel is only very rarely dived and is one for the wreck-diving purist.

## SHIPWRECK – THE ESSENTIALS

| | |
|---|---|
| Type: | IJN second-class destroyer |
| Built: | 1922 |
| Displacement: | 1,100 tons fully loaded, 1,113 after 1942 refit |
| Dimensions: | Length 280 feet; beam 26ft 6in.; draught 8ft 3in. |
| Propulsion: | Brown-Curtis geared turbine – twin screw |
| Date of loss: | 30 March 1944 |
| Cause of loss: | Bombing and strafing by TF 58 aircraft |
| Depth to seabed: | 10–30 metres |
| Location: | Karamadoo Bay, Babelthuap |

# The Aircraft Wrecks of Palau

# Aichi E13A Imperial Japanese Navy Seaplane

ALLIED REPORTING NAME: JAKE

The Aichi E13A single-engine twin-float long-range reconnaissance monoplane seaplane was built with an all-metal construction with fabric-covered control surfaces. The aircraft was 37 feet in length with a wingspan of 47 feet 7inches. It carried a crew of three, seated in tandem in an enclosed,

The Aichi E13A single engine twin float long-range reconnaissance monoplane seaplane – Allied reporting name, Jake.

glazed cockpit. She was a slow-flying reconnaissance aircraft, her three-bladed propeller being powered by a Mitsubishi Kinsei 43, 14-cylinder air-cooled radial engine that had been specially developed for the Imperial Japanese Navy as long ago as 1934.

The initial need for the Aichi floatplane stemmed from the need to replace the ageing Kawanishi E7K2 series. Competitive tenders were sought from Aichi, Kawanishi and Nakajima aircraft firms, with the Aichi design being selected. A prototype was then produced and ordered into production after 1940. The Allied reporting name for the Aichi E13A during the Pacific War was Jake.

The Jake was fitted with one flexible rear-firing 7.7mm Type 92 machine gun and one flexible downward-firing 20mm Type 99 Model 1 cannon. It could carry an external load of one 250-kg (550lb) bomb or four smaller 60-kg bombs or depth charges.

A total of 1,418 Aichi E13As were built during the war, and the Japanese used them in a variety of roles for combat, transport and air sea rescue. They had a range of 1,128 nautical miles and became the most important such aircraft for the Japanese navy during World War II. It was the Aichi that reconnoitred the American navy base at Pearl Harbor, Hawaii, in preparation for the infamous attack on 7 December 1941.

The E13A aircraft also carried out carrier-based strikes against land targets, and general reconnaissance missions. They were regularly deployed with cruiser battle groups, being mounted on catapults on Japanese battleships. They would be launched to scout ahead of the naval squadron before returning to their mother vessel, coming alongside and being lifted from the water by crane and recovered back aboard. The Aichi E13A also operated in the war with China.

The Aichi E13A was used throughout the Pacific War for coastal patrols and strikes against Allied transports, and in the later days of the war was used for kamikaze missions. US forces frequently encountered the Jake in combat during the Battles of the Coral Sea and Midway.

The Aichi E13A served through to the end of the war, though its potential became increasingly limited as the later years of the war brought new generations of faster, more powerful US carrier-based aircraft that were far advanced compared to any Japanese aircraft in theatre at that time.

By way of example, the 1934-era Jake had a maximum speed of 234 mph at 2,180 metres, and had a service ceiling of 8,730 metres. Compare this to the American Grumman F6F Hellcat fighter, which had its combat debut in 1943; it had a speed of 380 mph and a service ceiling of more than 11,000 metres. It becomes clear just how vulnerable the Jakes were. Many Jakes were relegated to kamikaze attacks on American ships towards the end of the war.

## TODAY

a) There are a number of Jake seaplane wrecks in different states of condition around Palau, but the one most easily accessed and in the best condition can be found just a 10-minute ride north-west from the Koror dive centres.

   The main section of the aircraft, from engine to aft of the cockpit, rests upright in 15 metres at an angle of about 30 degrees, with its starboard wing resting on the seabed. The port wing stands higher, resting on its intact float and wing supports.

   The engine cowling and prop have broken off from the fuselage and lie nose downwards just in front of the cockpit. The Jake appears to have been sunk whilst she was taxying or stationary on the surface, as her propellers are straight and not bent back at the tips as they would have been had she crashed at speed. The tail section and the starboard pontoon broke away and can now be found 20 feet away covered in thick layers of coral.

   Underwater visibility here is excellent – but for best visibility, dive this Jake at high tide when the wreck can be seen from the surface. This is an easy and popular night dive.

b) Another largely complete Jake can be found submerged in shallow water in Pipiroi Inlet near the middle section of the Toagel Mid Passage between Koror and Babelthuap.

   A natural cave in the side of the heavily forested steep shoreline allowed the Japanese to conceal and protect two or more seaplanes, whilst others were moored close by. An aircraft engine with its propeller blade protruding above water lies just outside the entrance to the cave, although this aircraft has largely disintegrated.

   Nearby, to the south-west of the cave, another Jake had been backed up into a natural cut into the steep cliff face which is covered in overhanging undergrowth. This Jake is in far better condition, resting upright in just 3–4 metres of water, not far beneath the surface and clearly visible from above. The aircraft rests on its twin floats and is complete except for the tail, which has been blown apart, and some damage from strafing or bomb blast just aft of the three-seat cockpit. The engine has broken from its mounts and now lies canted downwards with part of fuselage still attached.

Top: This Jake soft-landed in the sea not far from Koror – her prop tips are not bent. She lies in 15 metres of water. (Author's collection)

Bottom: The Jake off Koror. (Author's collection)

# 2. The Mitsubishi A6M Reisen Zero fighters

ALLIED REPORTING NAME – ZEKE

The Mitsubishi A6M Reisen was a long-range fighter developed as a greatly improved successor to the Mitsubishi A5M fighter which had entered service in 1937. Based on its pilots' immediate combat experiences of the A5M in China, in May 1937 the Japanese navy sent out its requirements to Nakajima and Mitsubishi for a new carrier-based fighter with a speed of 370 mph and a climb to 9,840 feet

The Mitsubishi A6M Reisen long-range fighter – Allied reporting name Zeke or Zero.

in 3.5 minutes. The fighter was to have drop tanks to achieve 6–8 hours' flight at an economical cruising speed.

The first prototype of the improved A6M fighter was completed in March 1939. Fifteen were built, and before testing had been completed they were shipped to the war zone in China. They arrived in Manchuria in July 1940 and first saw combat in August. They proved to be almost untouchable by the Chinese fighters, the Polikarpov I-16s and I-153s that had been such a problem for the A5Ms. In one clash, 13 A6Ms shot down 27 I-16s and I-153s in under three minutes – for no loss.

Flushed with this success, the Japanese navy immediately ordered the A6M into production as the Type O Carrier Fighter. The A6M was usually referred to by its pilots as the 'Zero-sen', zero being the last digit of the imperial year 2600 (1940), when it entered service with the navy. The Allied reporting name during World War II for the A6M was Zeke, although Zero was commonly adopted by the Allies later in the war.

The Zero was almost 30 feet long with a wingspan of 39 feet. It was fitted with two 7.7mm Type 97 machine guns in the upper fuselage decking with 500 rounds per gun, and two wing-mounted 20mm Type 99-1 cannons with 60 rounds per gun. The Zero had a cruising speed of 230 mph and a top speed of 331 mph at 15,000 feet. She had a range of over 1,600 miles on her internal fuel tanks, and this increased to 1,929 with drop tanks.

This plane's exceptional manoeuvrability and extraordinary range made it become the backbone of Japanese air power, and it participated in the majority of naval actions – outmatching all Allied aircraft early in the Pacific War; it has become the iconic image of the Japanese World War II fighter.

In British-ruled Malaya, the RAF had set up a handful of new fighter squadrons, but with a shortage of British fighters due to the European war these were equipped with American-built Brewster F2A Buffalo fighter aircraft which had a top speed of 323 mph. These had been rejected for service in Britain because of fuel starvation issues above 15,000 feet but, desperate for fighters for the Pacific and Asia, Britain had ordered a number from America. The Buffalo would be shown to be no match for the Japanese Zero fighter in combat; the RAF in Malaya was almost wiped out during the first days of the Pacific War in December 1941.

After the delivery of only 65 A6M1 aircraft by November 1940, a variant was developed, the A6M2 Type O Model 21, which had folding wing tips to allow it to deploy to aircraft carriers. Carrier-based Zero fighters spearheaded the surprise attacks on Pearl Harbor and the Philippines on 7 December 1941, and were involved in the attacks on Wake Island, Darwin and Ceylon. The Zero was unstoppable during the first six months of the war, emerging victorious over all the Allied carrier- and land-based aircraft it encountered.

With the introduction from 1942 onwards of modern Allied fighters in the Pacific theatre such as the Chance Vought F4U Corsair, the Lockheed P-38 Lightning and the Supermarine Spitfire, the Zero, once king of the skies, was unable to match their speed, armament and protection, and began to take heavy losses in combat. It could still hold its own in low-altitude engagements, but it was outclassed at higher altitudes and was no match for the new Allied fighters.

Heavy losses of aircraft and carriers at the Battle of Midway in June 1942 stopped the Japanese offensive advances. Japan was pushed onto the back foot, and the Zero was forced to operate more in a defensive role for the rest of the war – where lack of armour and fuel tank protection made it very vulnerable; it was common for the Zero to catch fire when hit.

After further developments with the A6M3 and A6M4, in September 1943 the A6M5 was deployed – it was considered the most effective variant, and carried heavier-gauge skin, redesigned wings and thrust-augmentation exhaust stacks, although the same engine was retained. But the A6M5 fared poorly in combat with the Hellcat, which was more strongly built and better protected – and had a top speed of 380mph compared to the Zero variant's 331mph. The Hellcat had a service ceiling of 37,300 feet compared to 33,000 feet for the Zero. The Zero was not very good in dives, and had manoeuvrability limitations at speeds above 180 mph.

By March 1944, other Zero variants had been introduced, to improve on previous weaknesses, with improved armament, armoured glass for the cockpit and automatic fire extinguishers for fuel tanks. Even these later models were, however, outdated in comparison to the new American fighters, and they suffered heavy losses to US Navy Hellcats during the Marianas Turkey Shoot.

The need to have as many fighters as possible to stave off the inexorable Allied advance towards Japan kept the by now obsolete A6M in production. From October 1944, when the Philippines came under assault by US forces, many Zekes were fitted with bombs and used in kamikaze attacks against US ships.

## TODAY

There are several Zero wrecks around Palau, but best would be:

1. Ngaremedui Reef, south of Koror.

    This Zero lies some 5–6 miles south of Koror and about 15 minutes by boat from several dive centres. This Zero sits in water of just 3 metres on a shallow reef and is a popular snorkel, only accessible at high tide.

    It is believed that this plane was damaged during the dogfight, and ditched with its gear up and prop feathered. One propeller blade sticks vertically up with the other two buried, indicating that it was not rotating when it water-landed. The canopy enclosing the cockpit is missing, and all the controls and gauges have been stripped out.
    Depth: 2–3 metres

2. Ngel Channel, south-east of Koror.

    This Zero lies upside down in 18 metres of water near Short Drop Off. The aircraft remains in good condition with its nose buried in the sand and both wing tips resting on the bottom. The wheels are retracted into the underbelly of the aircraft as during flight – the wheel covers are still present and the tyres are visible. The engine still remains, and one straight prop blade is visible with other two buried. It appears that the pilot of the Zeke feathered the props and with the landing gear up made a successful water landing. Bomb or fuel tank racks are visible on the undersides of the wings, and further back is the arrestor hook for carrier landing. The wing-mounted 20mm cannons are present.
    Depth: 18 metres

# 3. Vought F4U Corsair

The Chance Vought F4U Corsair was a single-seat American fighter introduced in 1942 that was designed as a carrier-based aircraft. Its difficult carrier landing performance, however, rendered the Corsair unsuitable for navy use until the British Fleet Air Arm later overcame the issues. Thus, with the Grumman F6F Hellcat a resoundingly successful carrier-based aircraft, the navy initially released the Corsair to the US Marine Corps. With no requirement for carrier landings, the Marine Corps deployed the Corsair to heavy and devastating success from land bases supporting US Marine Corps operations.

After the carrier landing issues had been tackled, in late 1944 it quickly became the most capable carrier-based fighter-bomber of World War II and would go on to

The Chance Vought F4U Corsair single-seat American fighter bomber. (National Archives)

serve throughout the subsequent Korean War in the 1950s. The Corsair was in service by several air forces until the 1960s.

The F4U was 33 feet 4 inches long with a wingspan of 41 feet; 150 lbs of armour-plate was fitted to the cockpit and a bullet-resistant glass screen was fitted behind the curved windscreen. The F4U incorporated the largest aircraft engine available at the time, the 2,000hp Pratt & Whitney R-2800, coupled with a large three-bladed propeller. This gave the first variants a maximum speed of 417 mph, faster than the 380 mph of the Grumman F6F Hellcat and much faster than the 331 mph of the Japanese Zero. Later variants could make 453 mph. The Corsair had a range of over 1,000 miles.

The Corsair was armed with six 0.50-inch Browning machine guns, three in each of the outer wing panels, with 400 rounds per gun. She also could carry four high-velocity rockets and/or 2,000 lbs of bombs.

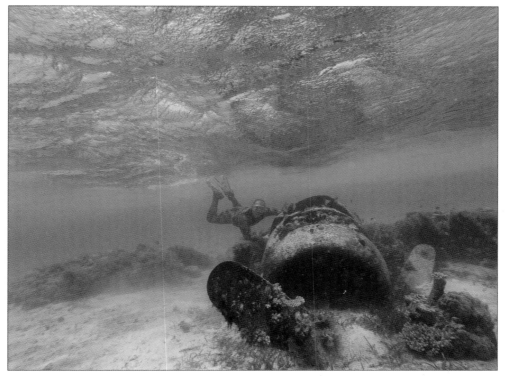

The wreck of a Corsair lies in shallow water north of Toachel Mlengui – West Passage.
(Author's collection)

## TODAY

The wreck of a Corsair lies several miles north of Toachel Mlengui – West Passage – on reef flats well to the west of Babelthuap. To get to the wreck involves motoring over the reef flats only a few metres deep for some distance before the dark blurred outline of the aircraft finally disrupts the green and brown colours of the sandy bottom and corals.

Nothing definite is known about the circumstances that brought the pilot to ditch this aircraft in the reef shallows of just 2–3 metres. The aircraft obviously hit the water at a speed sufficient for its still-turning propeller to be ripped out of the engine cowling – it now lies a little forward, upside down and angled to the port wing. Both wings are still attached – now covered in corals – but aft of the cockpit the aircraft is missing.

Corsairs were not involved in the Task Force 58 Operation *Desecrate 1* raid against Palau in March 1944 – Corsairs only began to deploy from carriers in late 1944. It is thus likely that this aircraft was shot down here in late 1944 either flying from land bases nearby or from a carrier.

# Operation Desecrate 1
# US Task Force 58
# Strike Aircraft

# 1. Curtiss SB2C Helldiver

The Curtiss SB2C Helldiver was a US Navy carrier-launched two-person dive-bomber; it replaced the much slower Douglas SBD Dauntless. Initial development and production of the SB2C Helldiver was plagued by delays, and it was finally deployed only in November 1943 from USS *Bunker Hill* in an attack on the Japanese -held port of Rabaul on the island of New Britain, north of New Guinea.

Curtis SB2C Helldivers. (National Archives)

Early opinions of the Helldiver in combat were very negative – due to its size, weight, electrical problems, poor stability, lack of power and reduced range compared to the Douglass Dauntless. In the Battle of the Philippine Sea, 45 Helldivers were lost due to running out of fuel as they returned to their carriers. The lack of power was finally corrected in 1944 with a change of engine.

The Helldiver was a much larger aircraft than the Douglas Dauntless it replaced, able to operate from the latest aircraft carriers and carry a considerable array of firepower in addition to an internal bomb bay that reduced drag.

The aircraft had folding wings for storage, and carried a crew of two, the pilot and radio operator/gunner. It had a top speed of 295 mph and a range of 1,165 miles, with a 1,000lb bomb load and a service ceiling of 29,100 feet. The SB2C carried two 20mm wing-mounted cannon, and two 7.62mm Browning machine guns in the rear cockpit. It could carry 2,000 lbs of bombs or one aerial torpedo in its internal bomb bay – in addition to 500 lbs of bombs on each wing.

The aircraft was flown during the last two years of the Pacific War, participating in battles over the Marianas, the Philippines (where it was partly responsible for sinking the Japanese battleship *Musashi*), Taiwan, Iwo Jima and Okinawa. Helldivers were used in 1945 against the Ryuko Islands and the Japanese home island of Honshu in tactical attacks on airfields, communications and shipping as well as combat patrols at the time of the nuclear bombs being dropped. The advent of air-to-ground rockets ensured that the SB2C was the last purpose-built dive-bomber produced; rockets allowed precision attacks against surface naval and land targets whilst avoiding the airframe stresses and aircraft vulnerability of near-vertical dives close to the target.

# 2. Douglas SBD Dauntless

LEFT: Douglas SBD Dauntless dive-bomber over the carrier USS *Enterprise*. (National Archives)
RIGHT: A Douglas SBD Dauntless dive-bomber in action. Note the air brakes on the wings.
(National Archives)

The Douglas SBD Dauntless was the US Navy's main carrier-borne scout plane and dive-bomber from 1940 to mid-1944. The SBD was well respected as an excellent naval scout plane and dive-bomber that possessed long range, good handling characteristics, a potent bomb load, good diving characteristics, defensive armament and toughness. It was the Douglas SBD Dauntless that sank the cream of the Japanese aircraft carriers at Midway, as other US aircraft, such as the Grumman Avengers and Devastators, were shot down in numbers. Fifty SBDs dived on the *Akagi*, *Kaga* and *Sōrū*, leaving them as blazing hulks.

The SBD carried a crew of two – the pilot and a radio operator/gunner. It had a maximum speed of 255 mph – slow compared to the top speed of its 1944 successor, the Helldiver at 295 mph. The SBD had a range of 1,115 miles and a service ceiling of 25,530 feet. It was more lightly armed than the SB2C Helldiver successor, carrying two 12.7mm (0.50-inch) forward-firing synchronized fixed Browning M2 machine guns in the engine cowling and twin 7.62mm (0.30-inch) flexible Browning machine guns mounted in the rear of the cockpit. It lacked the powerful 20mm wing-mounted cannons of the SB2C Helldiver. It could carry 2,250 lbs of bombs.

# 3. Grumman TBF Avenger

The Grumman TBF Avenger was a US Navy torpedo-bomber that entered service in 1942 and first saw action during the Battle of Midway. It was the successor to the Douglas TBD Devastator which had been the Navy's main torpedo-bomber since 1935 but which by 1939 had become obsolete.

The Avenger was the heaviest single-engined aircraft of World War II and took a crew of three: (i) a pilot, (ii)a rear-turret gunner, and (iii) a radio operator/ventral gunner/bombardier.

One 0.30-inch (7.62mm) machine gun was mounted in the nose, a 0.50-inch (12.7mm) gun in a rear-facing electrically powered turret, and a 0.30-inch hand-fired machine gun mounted under the tail, used to defend against fighters attacking from below and to the rear. Later models

A Grumman TBF Avenger torpedo-bomber. (National Archives)

dispensed with the nose-mounted gun in favour of a 0.50-inch machine gun in each wing for better strafing ability.

The Avenger had a large bomb bay that could carry a Mark 13 aerial torpedo or a single 2,000lb bomb – or up to four 500lb bombs. This was a rugged and stable aircraft, well equipped, with good handling and a long range. It had a top speed of 275 mph, a ceiling of 30,000 feet and a fully loaded range of 1,000 miles. The same folding wings as with the Hellcat were fitted.

The Avenger's traditional role was to torpedo surface ships – and Avengers played an important role in several naval battles, such as in the Solomon Islands in August 1942 where they sank a Japanese light carrier – and at Guadalcanal in November 1942, when they helped sink the crippled battleship *Hiei*.

In addition to surface shipping kills, Avengers claimed about 30 submarine kills and were the most effective submarine killers in the Pacific theatre.

In June 1943, future US President George H.W. Bush became the youngest naval aviator of the time, being shot down in his Avenger on 2 September 1944 over the Pacific island of Chichi Jima. Both his crewmates were killed, but he managed to release his payload and hit the target before having to bail out. He received the Distinguished Flying Cross. The famous Hollywood actor Paul Newman flew as a rear gunner in an Avenger. The post-war disappearance of a flight of Avengers, known as Flight 19, added to the mystery of the Bermuda triangle.

# 4. Grumman F6F Hellcat

The Grumman F6F Hellcat was a carrier-based fighter aircraft conceived to replace the earlier Grumman F4F Wildcat in the United States Navy. Although the F6F resembled the Wildcat, it was a completely new design, powered by a 2,000hp Pratt & Whitney engine. The F6F was best known for its role as a rugged, well-designed carrier fighter, which, after its combat debut in early 1943, was able to counter the Mitsubishi Zero and help secure air superiority over the Pacific.

The F6F was designed to take damage and get the pilot safely back home. A bullet-resistant windshield and 212 lbs of cockpit armour was fitted, along with armour around the oil tank and oil cooler; a self-sealing 250-gallon fuel tank was fitted in the fuselage. (A 150-gallon drop tank could be carried under the fuselage.) This heavy armour and protection is in stark contrast to the almost complete lack of pilot and fuel protection in most Japanese combat aircraft; just a few rounds (even small arms fire), striking a Japanese aircraft could be enough to set it on fire. The lack of pilot and fuel protection was a crucial flaw in Japanese strategic thinking and led to the early loss of most of their experienced front-line pilots.

A Grumman F6F Hellcat is prepared for a carrier launch in 1944.

The Hellcat could be used in a variety of combat roles – as a fighter, night fighter, fighter-bomber and rocket platform. In all, more than 12,000 Hellcats were produced in two major variants.

Six 0.50-inch M2 Browning air-cooled machine guns with 400 rounds per gun were fitted. Later variations were equipped to carry bombs or high-velocity aircraft rockets under the wings. The wings could be hydraulically or manually folded, with a folded stowage position parallel to the fuselage, the leading edges pointing down. Further bombs or a torpedo could be carried under the fuselage on a centreline rack.

The Hellcat was 34 feet long with a wingspan of 43 feet. It had a top speed of 380 mph compared to the Zero's 331 mph, and had a service ceiling of 37,300 feet compared to 33,000 feet for the Zero.

F6F Hellcats were credited with destroying 5,223 aircraft while in service with the US Navy, US Marine Corps and the British Royal Navy – more than shot down by all the other combat aircraft combined.

They are the iconic US Navy fighter of the Pacific War.

# Bibliography

Alden, John D.: *U.S. Submarine Attacks during WWII*. Naval Institute Press (1989)

Bailey, Dan: *WWII Wrecks of the Kwajalein and Truk Lagoons*. North River Publications (1989)

Bailey, Dan: *World War II Wrecks of the Truk Lagoon*. North River Diver Publications (2000)

Bailey, Dan: *WWII Wrecks of Palau*. North River Diver Publications (1991)

Blair, Clay Jr: *Silent Victory – the U.S. Submarine War against Japan*. J.B. Lippincott Company (1975)

Boyd, Carl and Yoshida, Akihiko: *The Japanese Submarine Force and World War II*. Blue Jacket Books, Naval Institute Press (1995)

Broadwater, John D.: *Kwajalein – Lagoon of Found Ships*. Three States Printing Company (1971)

Churchill, Winston: *The Second World War*. Houghton Mifflin Company (1948–54)

Cressman, Robert J.: *Official Chronology of the U.S. Navy in World War II*. U.S. Naval Institute Press (1999)

Crowl, Phillip A. and Edmond F. Love: *The United States Army in World War II – The War in the Pacific – Seizure of the Gilberts and Marshalls*. U.S. Government Printing Office (1955)

Evans, David C. and Mark R. Peattie: *KAIGUN. Strategy, Tactics and Technology in the Imperial Japanese Navy 1887–1941*. Naval Institute Press (1997)

Francillon, R.J.: *Japanese Aircraft of the Pacific War*. Funk & Wagnalls (1970)

Falk, Stanley: *Bloodiest Victory – Palaus*. Ballantine Books (1974)

Fukui, Shizuo: *Japanese Naval Vessels at the end of World War II*. Naval Institute Press (1987)

Grover, David H.: *U.S. Army Ships and Watercraft of World War II*. Naval Institute Press (1987)

Hayashi, Hiroshi: *Senji Nippon Senmeiroku 1937–1950*. Senzen Senpaku Kenkyukai (2006)

Hocking, C.: *Dictionary of Disasters at Sea during the Age of Steam*. Lloyd's Register of Shipping (1969)

Hough, Major Frank O., USMCR: *The Assault on Peleliu*. Historical Division HQ U.S. Marine Corps (1950)

Ito, Masanori: *The End of the Japanese Navy*. Norton Publishers (1962)

Jane, Fred T.: *Jane's Fighting Ships 1944–45*. David & Charles Ltd (1971)

Jensen, Lt. Oliver USNR: *Carrier War*. Pocket Books Inc. (1945)

Jentschura, Hansgeorg: *Warships of the Imperial Japanese Navy 1869–1945*. Naval Institute Press (1976)

Koenig, William: *Epic Sea Battles*. Octopus Books Ltd (1975)

Lester, Robert E.: *U.S. Navy Action and Operational Reports from World War II. Part 3. Fifth Fleet and Fifth Fleet Carrier Task Forces*. University Publications of America. (1990)

Lindemann, Klaus: *Desecrate 1*. Pacific Press Publications (1988)

Lindemann, Klaus: *Hailstorm over Truk Lagoon*. Pacific Press Publications (1989)

Lloyd's of London: *Lloyd's Register of Shipping*. London

Macdonald, Rod: *Force Z Shipwrecks of the South China Sea – HMS Prince of Wales and HMS Repulse*. Whittles Publishing (2013)

Macdonald, Rod: *Dive Truk Lagoon*. Whittles Publishing (2014)

Middlebrook, Martin: *The Sinking of the Prince of Wales & Repulse*. Allen Lane (1977)

Mitscher, Vice Admiral Marc A., USN: Desecrate One Operation, Action Report of. (12 April 1944)

Morison, Samuel E., *History of U.S. Naval Operations in World War II*. Little Brown & Co. (1975)

Odgers, George: *Air War against Japan 1943–1945*. Advertiser Printing Co. (1957)

Office of the Chief of Naval Operations: *Basic War Plan-Rainbow No. 5(WPL-46)*, 26 May 1941

Office of the Chief of Naval Operations – Division of Naval Intelligence: *Japanese Merchant Ships Recognition Manual ONI 208-J – Restricted*. U.S. Government Printing Office (1944)

Office of the Chief of Naval Operations – Division of Naval Intelligence: *Standard Classes of Japanese Merchant Ships* ONI 208-J (Revised) Supplement 3. U.S. Government Printing Office (1945)

Office of the Chief of Naval Operations – Division of Naval Intelligence: *Far Eastern Small Craft* ONI 208-J Supplement 2. U.S. Government Printing Office (1945)

Office of the Chief of Naval Operations – Division of Naval Intelligence: *The Japanese Navy* ONI 222-J. U.S. Government Printing Office (1945)

Office of the Chief of Naval Operations – Division of Naval Intelligence: *Aerial Views of Japanese Naval Vessels* ONI 41–42. U.S. Government Printing Office (1945)

Peattie, Mark R.: *Nanyo – The Rise and Fall of the Japanese in Micronesia 1885–1945*. University of Hawaii Press (1988)

Prados, John: *Combined Fleet Decoded*. Random House (1995)

Rosenberg, Phillip Alan: *Shipwrecks of Truk*. Philip Alan Rosenberg (1981)

Smallpage, Roy: *Truk: The Ultimate Wreck Site*. Underwater Publications (1994)

Stewart, William H.: *Ghost Fleet of the Truk Lagoon*. Pictorial Histories Publishing Co. (1986)

Stille, Mark: Imperial *Japanese Navy Destroyers 1919–45 (1)*. Osprey Publishing (2013)

Stille, Mark: *Imperial Japanese Navy Destroyers 1919–45 (2)*. Osprey Publishing (2013)

Tillman, Barrett: *Hellcats over Truk*. U.S. Naval Institute Proceedings (1977)

U.S. Joint Army–Navy Assessment Committee: *Japanese Naval and Merchant Shipping Losses during World War II by All Causes*. U.S. Government Printing Office (1947)

USS *Perry, Action Report of Japanese Air Raid on Pearl Harbor* (7 December 1941)

Warren, Alan: *Singapore 1942*. Talisman Publishing (2002)

Watts, A.J.: *Japanese Warships of World War II*. Doubleday & Co. Inc. (1966)

## WEBSITES REFERRED TO

www.combinedfleet.com Nihon Kaigun

www.fischer-tropsch.org Japanese minesweeping gear & equipment

# Index